Latin America and the United States:
The Changing Political Realities

Contributors

Heraclio Bonilla

Julio Cotler

Luigi R. Einaudi

Richard R. Fagen

Jorge Graciarena

Octavio Ianni

Marcos Kaplan

Abraham F. Lowenthal

Carlos Estevam Martins

Luciano Martins

Ernest R. May

Christopher Mitchell

Theodore H. Moran

Guillermo O'Donnell

Olga Pellicer de Brody

Aníbal Pinto

Aníbal Quijano Obregón

John Saxe-Fernández

Philippe C. Schmitter

Alfred Stepan

Osvaldo Sunkel

Maria Conceição Tavares

Edelberto Torres Rivas

Latin America
and the United States:
The Changing
Political Realities

Edited by Julio Cotler & Richard R. Fagen

Stanford University Press, Stanford, California

A Spanish-language edition of this work was published simul-
taneously with the English-language edition under the title
Relaciones Políticas entre América Latina y Estados Unidos,
by Amorrortu Editores, Luca 2223, Buenos Aires, Argentina.
All rights other than those in the Spanish language are held by
Stanford University Press.

Stanford University Press, Stanford, California
© 1974 by the Board of Trustees of the
Leland Stanford Junior University
All rights reserved
Printed in the United States of America
Cloth ISBN 0-8047-0860-6
Paper ISBN 0-8047-0861-4
Original edition 1974
Last figure below indicates year of this printing:
84 83 82 81 80 79 78 77 76 75

*To all the Chileans and other citizens of the
Americas who have suffered and continue to suffer
the consequences of the brutal military coup
that overthrew the Popular Unity government in Chile*

Acknowledgments

We are indebted to the Joint Committee on Latin American Studies of the Social Science Research Council and the American Council of Learned Societies (composed of scholars from the United States and Latin America) for providing the financing for this project. Both the Lima conference, for which the papers and comments in this book were written, and the preparation and publication of the final manuscript, in English and Spanish, were supported by the Joint Committee under a program designed to encourage research on subjects considered of prime importance to the further development of Latin American studies. Among other projects that have been funded are one on economic history (jointly sponsored by CLACSO, the Consejo Latinoamericano de Ciencias Sociales) and another on the license and patent system as it relates to Latin American technological dependency and development.

Before, during, and after the conference, the Institute of Peruvian Studies in Lima provided logistical and administrative aid, playing host in a most gracious manner to two dozen participants during the gathering itself. The staff of the Ford Foundation office in Santiago, Chile, also aided in bringing the English and Spanish versions of the manuscript to completion.

Finally, we wish to express our gratitude to the dedicated group of Americans from both hemispheres who aided in the preparation of various translations. There are eight who will see this book in print: Judy Brister, Heather Dashner, Luis Domínguez, David Hathaway, Leslie Krebs, Mishy Lesser, Connie Sue McDuffee, and Fernanda Navarro. The ninth, Charles Horman, was killed by the Chilean military in the National Stadium on September 18, 1973. His death is an ironic and tragic comment on the changing political realities in Latin America and the United States.

J.C.
R.R.F.

Contents

Latin America and the United States:
The Changing Political Realities

Introduction: Political Relations Between Latin America and the United States

JULIO COTLER AND RICHARD R. FAGEN

Almost all the papers and commentaries included in this volume were originally prepared for a conference held in November 1972 at the Institute of Peruvian Studies in Lima. This gathering had a history, a rationale, and a set of goals, and it subsequently developed a dynamic— and polemic—of its own. This is not to say that we knew from the outset exactly what would or ought to take place, but there was a plan, undergirded by a set of assumptions and purposes, and our readers are entitled to share in this information. Thus, before discussing some of the main themes that run through the written work and the polemic that ensued, it is necessary to specify what the conference itself was intended to be, do, and achieve.

The Conference: Origins, Purposes, and Organization

To many people, it has become increasingly obvious that much of the manner in which we think about politics in the hemisphere, especially political relations between the United States and Latin America, is irrelevant, anachronistic, or simply wrongheaded. Whether it is the statements that issue from the White House and the State Department concerning the "inter-American community" (minus Cuba, of course), or the effusions of polemicists who see the dark hand of the CIA in every contact across the Rio Bravo, or the postulations of scholars who continue to insist that politics involves only governments (while ITT works to overthrow Allende in Chile), the nonsense diminishes slowly, if at all. It is not, however, just the quantity of such material emanating from foreign ministries, publicists, and academics—North and South—that is disturbing. Rather, what most concerns us—and, we hope, many others— is the absence of a strong countercurrent of serious professional work on hemispheric relations. Such a countercurrent is, in our view, the *sine qua non* of the gradual improvement of the conceptual, informational, and moral bases on which foreign policies are erected.

Julio Cotler is with the Institute of Peruvian Studies, Lima; Richard R. Fagen is Professor of Political Science at Stanford University, Stanford, California. Throughout the essays, mentions of Chile refer to late 1972 and early 1973, when the Allende Government was still in power; no attempt has been made to update or change these references.

If such a view seems overly optimistic or arrogant—academics playing philosopher king—the history of the Alliance for Progress provides sobering evidence to the contrary. If nothing else, the Alliance represented the "best" of early 1960s liberal scholarly thought—both Latin American and North American—transmuted into programmatic action.[1] In retrospect, as repeatedly pointed out in this book, the conceptual edifice on which the policy was erected was flawed to its very foundations. But its flaws were certainly not so apparent when the design was drawn, and no viable contenders for attention and implementation existed. In short, our concern with the lack of a contemporary body of relevant scholarship, equal to the task of guiding public debate and ultimately informing policy, established the setting in which the conference was conceived.

But the argument has two sides: on the one hand, the continued encouragement of serious critical work seems particularly necessary in the United States because of its immense power and the historic misuse of that power; on the other hand, such work is necessary in Latin America precisely because of a series of mutually reinforcing weaknesses. General analyses—often with a clear ideological content—are not in short supply, and their importance should not be underestimated. But if well-phrased denunciations of imperialism and dependency were alone sufficient to understand the changes taking place in the hemisphere and to identify ways of capitalizing on opportunities, Latin America would today be well on the way to becoming one of the most fully liberated areas in the world. But such is not the case, and persons of widely differing political persuasions thus concede the necessity of creating an indigenous capacity to generate and utilize knowledge about politics in the hemisphere. Yet it is also widely acknowledged that most if not all Latin American nations are abysmally lacking in this capacity for knowledge-making and knowledge-using. Neither in the universities, nor the research institutes, nor the government bureaucracies of Latin America does one normally find centers for the study of "international relations," much less institutional groups engaged in work on the United States or on U.S.-Latin American relations. And it can almost be said that precisely those nations that are most disadvantaged in power politics are also those with the weakest and most underdeveloped infrastructure for making and using relevant knowledge.

No conference, of course, can hope to make more than the merest dent in such a situation. Moreover, the possibility of having even marginal

---

[1] In a number of places in this Introduction and in the rest of the book, the phrase "North American" is used as if it were synonymous with "United States." This practice is so common in the hemisphere—even among the Mexicans and Central Americans most tarred by its imprecision—that we have not always attempted to substitute more awkward, although more accurate, nouns and adjectives.

influence diminishes unless specific focus is given to the subject. Thus, from the outset, we tried to limit our attention. Briefly, we were concerned with *political relations* between the United States and Latin America in a hemisphere and a world that are changing rapidly. Without trying to give precise definition to the notion of political relations, we at least suggested a set of concerns by commissioning papers on subjects such as the politics of the multinational corporation, the mass media as political actors,[2] and military elites and military thinking. In short, we sought to add our voices to those who insist that one must often look outside of government-as-actor for the sources and much of the substance of international politics.

At the same time, as attested to by the case studies commissioned on the United States, Mexico, and Brazil,[3] we must acknowledge that nation-states in some larger sense remain the primary units into which the hemisphere is divided. Whatever the private motives and interests at play, it is after all the Dominican Republic that was invaded by the United States in 1965, and it is Allende, acting in the name of the nation, who recognized Cuba and undertook the reorientation of Chilean foreign policy. Thus, in planning for the conference, we tried to strike some balance between the need to emphasize the role of non-national or transnational actors, and the need to reemphasize and reorient an understanding of the role of government-as-actor.

Another major concern was with the analysis of *changing* political relations in a *changing* context. One reason for the banality of much dialogue about politics in the hemisphere is that the discussion is frequently a decade or more behind the times. Not only have great-power inter-relations shifted significantly at the world level, but Western and Eastern Europe as well as Japan all have a growing Latin American presence. As one sign of the times, the relative dollar importance of Latin America to the North American economy diminished during the 1960s, as is well documented in Aníbal Pinto's essay. Furthermore, as suggested by Luciano Martins, the easy cooperation between American state power and the multinational corporations is giving way to significant tensions at the same time that the corporations expand and diversify. Latin American regional cooperation is growing—if haltingly—while Cubans, Chileans, Peruvians, Mexicans, Brazilians, and others make their voices heard in the search for a new definition of the Latin American community.

Does any of this mean that "the American empire" is coming unrav-

---

[2] For diverse reasons, a few of the papers that were originally commissioned do not appear in this volume.

[3] In planning the seminar, studies on Cuba and Chile were contemplated. It was not possible, however, to secure Cuban participation. The Chilean paper was actually begun, but its authors had to set it aside in favor of other responsibilities.

eled, or that domination and dependency have decreased? Answers depend in part on what one means by the American empire and how one conceptualizes domination and dependency. But the very posing of the question in these terms also suggests how entrapped most of us are in theoretical frameworks, perspectives, and data that may rapidly be losing their validity—if they have not already done so. In this vein, we commissioned papers on the changing context and content of U.S.-Latin American relations, and on possible trends in U.S. foreign policy. Furthermore, we encouraged several authors to examine the utility, limitations, and possibilities of various explanations of past or contemporary political relations. In this case, our aim was to subject the theoretical frameworks and models of explanation in use to the closest possible scrutiny. As the discussion in the latter part of this Introduction will suggest, no unanimity was achieved, but the interaction of theory, cases, data, and changes in the real world was constantly on the agenda.

Finally, running through all our thinking was the conviction that the sheer *diversity* of U.S.-Latin American political relations receives too little attention. The weak and dependent status of Latin America as a whole tends to obscure the variety of conditions and situations that prevail at the national level. From the socialist experience of Cuba, to the experiments now under way in Peru and Chile, to the special kind of expansionism and dependence evidenced by Brazil, increasing differentiation seems the order of the day. At the empirical level, it is impossible to talk about "inter-American rélations" as a whole except in the most general terms. Different local and national conditions and histories define different "degrees of freedom" for different governments and societies. And the recognition of this diversity in turn underlines the paucity of relevant knowledge that is at once produced close to home, tied to national needs, and specific enough to orient action. We labored under no illusions that the conference itself would actually generate such knowledge, but we did agree explicitly that our ultimate objectives ran in that direction.

The themes of politics, change, and national diversity just elaborated were basic to establishing a list of paper topics. But we honored other criteria also in considering the style of the papers, the need for comments, the persons to be invited, and the actual organization of the conference itself. With respect to papers, we made it clear to participants that for the Lima meeting the presentation of research results was considered secondary to the critical examination of hemispheric political relations within the terms of reference mentioned. Thus, we urged authors to float hypotheses, examine changes, and speculate about trends, while nevertheless using data where appropriate and citing sources where possible. The sum total, needless to say, is a hybrid. Some essays are quite close to "conventional" scholarly analyses, while others are more polemical and speculative. Along a related dimension, some are quite closely anchored to data, while others drift easily without much empirical ballast. With hindsight, we can see that our rather open charge to authors bore with it some unanticipated advantages and disadvantages—some of which will be taken up in the following section. But we were also aware, well in advance of the conference itself, that with any collection of authors as diverse as those likely to be gathered in Lima, attempts to impose greater stylistic and substantive uniformity were sure to be subverted, resented, or simply ignored.

From the outset, we selected commentators for all but two of the commissioned papers. Authors were asked to circulate their draft papers to all participants in advance of the conference, and commentators were asked to arrive in Lima with written critiques. Our intention was twofold. First, we considered all the assigned papers to be controversial and assumed controversy to be conducive to the larger, long-term aims of the conference. To formalize this assumption, we structured the debate in Lima such that commentary would be offered in written form. Second, since a wider audience could share in the Lima debates only through study of a published volume, we sought a way to convey to that audience some of the pulling and hauling that we were sure would take place and some of the bases for divergent ideas and viewpoints. In some cases, these comments rivaled the essays themselves in both length and interest; because of limitations of space, we have had to restrain the tendency to length in the published versions.

Invitations to authors and commentators were issued with a number of criteria in mind. Given blatant imbalances between the United States and Latin America in opportunities and facilities for the study of hemispheric political relations, we opted—somewhat arbitrarily—for a ratio of two Latin American participants for every North American. Within the Latin American group, we also attempted to represent a variety of countries, disciplines, and points of view. Wishing to avoid the problems that always ensue with conferences that depend on simultaneous translation, we established Spanish as the language of discussion, thus limiting the pool of North Americans on which we could draw. Needless to say, not all of these criteria could be fully met in a gathering of two dozen persons, but refusals and withdrawals were minimal.

Finally, in order to make even a dent in the larger problems identified above, we decided to make a special effort to prepare and publish Spanish and English versions of the revised papers and comments as quickly as possible. All too often, multinational academic efforts involving North

Americans end up published only in English, thus further contributing to the imbalances in knowledge and opportunities that we have already deplored. Thus, a high priority was given to translating and editing these materials for both Spanish and English publication.

Like many such gatherings, the four days of discussion and debate in Lima assumed an immediacy and a life of their own, somewhat independent of the papers and comments around which they were ostensibly organized. A number of months later, however, in reflecting on the conference and in editing the written materials, the distinctions between the two had faded. Instead, we were struck by the manner in which both the discussions and the written materials clustered around similar themes, returned to similar problems, and emphasized recurring tensions. Thus, in what follows we have not necessarily attempted to identify the original source of the theme, problem, or tension we treat. Rather, we assume that any serious attempt to analyze political relations between the United States and Latin America would find itself touching upon these or similar points, encountering similar problems, and raising issues of these sorts. Such, at least, was our experience.

Models of Politics: Class, Institutions, Government

By placing heavy emphasis on studies of foreign policy, we ensured that a number of quite traditional questions of political analysis would be addressed: How do decisions get made? Why these decisions rather than others? What are the consequences of these decisions? What is the relationship between domestic and international factors in policy formation? What social and economic forces enter into the equation? Who benefits? Who pays? What new coalitions or configurations of domestic and international forces are in the making? Is the complex of explanations that aids in understanding Nation X also useful in understanding Nation Y? This list—its questions overlapping, amorphous, unfocused, or ambiguous, as such questions always are—could be extended.

What is notable, however, is not the smorgasbord of questions that can be generated *post facto* out of the papers and discussion, but rather the way answers to these questions tend to cluster. In other words, although the questions can be multiplied almost endlessly, the explanatory models tend to converge. Actually, these explanatory models do not provide "answers" to the questions in any strict sense. Rather, they imply approaches, emphases, and different weights attached to different clusters of variables. As such, they also derive from different theoretical positions and imply, at least, different methodologies.

Explanations of political relations, of course, are only one element within much larger models of how the world works. In Lima, two such macro-models or paradigms were almost constantly present, in competition with each other, and—consequently—influential in shaping both the presentations and the ensuing debate. On the one hand was a "dependency" paradigm, emphasizing the structural relationships of imperialist domination within which all other inter-American relationships must be located and understood. As a corollary of this paradigm, changes not directly affecting these structural relationships were seen as relatively secondary, expected fluctuations and necessary adjustments in a continuing pattern of domination. On the other hand was a "liberal" paradigm, emphasizing asymmetries in power and resources, mechanisms for the redress of those asymmetries, and the multiplicity of influences on policy. As a corollary of this paradigm, enlightened policy, goodwill, and the proper combinations of human resources and information were seen as sufficient to effect critical changes in inter-American relations. Like all dichotomies, this one necessarily involves a simplification of complex perspectives and arguments, but it serves to set the stage for an understanding of the explanatory postures taken by various authors.

The three concepts that enter most repeatedly into the papers—as elements of description and explanation—are class, institutions, and government. While we will here make no attempt to arrive at definitions of each, it is clear that in their everyday meanings they are useful points of departure for sorting out the way in which various contributors approach the subject of political relations. It would deny the subtleness with which most authors treat their subjects simply to label their approaches as being class-based (social-structural), institutional, or governmental (bureaucratic). Nevertheless, the emphases and explanatory importance that various contributors give to these factors reflect very profound differences in the manner in which they understand political processes and inter-American relations.

In the essays by Ianni and Quijano, for example, class (defined in the Marxist sense as the social-structural expression of the relations of production) is elevated to a first-order element in the descriptions and explanations offered. In so doing, the authors do not argue that other institutions or the state apparatus are unimportant. Quite the contrary: the state apparatus is viewed as the organized and legitimated representative of the dominant class, classes, or fractions of classes in society. It is thus an essential indicator of the social and economic forces at work as well as the key dispenser and implementer of public policies. But it is in no sense an autonomous institution, not itself the source of the policies it promulgates. In other words, for persons who share this perspective, the analysis of political power and public policy must begin with the analysis of class, for it is the latter that in one way or another shapes the former.

The complexity of the argument is naturally intensified when the analysis of classes is extended across national boundaries—as must be the case when hemispheric relations are under examination. Class struggle is generalized, reflected both in national and international politics. The linkages between the bourgeoisies in the countries of the center and those of the periphery are conceptualized as key elements in the maintenance of economic and political domination in the hemisphere. The relationships of dominated classes across national boundaries are also seen as important in the explanation and prediction of hemispheric politics.

Elements of institutional analysis and explanation can be found in the interior of almost all the papers and comments, but they are more central to some than to others. The common thread in these diverse arguments is an insistence on the autonomous political capacity of the institution in question. Luciano Martins's characterization of the multinational corporation as increasingly capable of formulating and implementing its own foreign policy is one example of this thread. Another surfaces in Saxe-Fernández's treatment of the military (reinforced in this instance by Stepan's comment) as a group having values, connections, and ambitions that render it an independent force to be reckoned with in hemispheric politics.

Note that there is no fundamental analytical incompatibility between this kind of institutional analysis and a class perspective. What is in question is the *relative* decisional and operative autonomy of institutions such as corporations and military elites from the class interests they ultimately serve. As Heraclio Bonilla points out, "no es posible inferir una identidad absoluta entre *clase* y *poder,* puesto que entre ambos existen mediaciones institucionalizadas." It is the detailed study of these "mediaciones institucionalizadas"—and even more so the attempt to relate such detailed study to class interests—that gives rise to debate. C. E. Martins's analysis of the sources of Brazilian foreign policy, and Tavares's comment, illustrate the level of complexity that such attempts and debates can assume. Analyses of class, class fractions, linkages between domestic and foreign groups, multinational corporations, and different tendencies and ideologies within the state apparatus all entered into the various explanations of Brazilian foreign policy that were presented.

The other approach vying for attention and legitimacy as a way of describing and explaining politics is the analysis of government, or—more accurately—the analysis of intragovernmental or bureaucratic relations. Especially in the contributions of May, Mitchell, and Lowenthal, foreign policy (in this case, of the U.S.) is viewed as the product of a complex intragovernmental clash of bureaucratic interests, values, personalities, and points of view. More than just a refinement of institutional approaches to the study of government and foreign policy, this perspective elevates *intra*-institutional factors to first-order explanatory importance. As is almost inevitable when any bureaucracy or large organization is examined in such detail, sources of tension, difference, and conflict are clearly identified. Both the making and the implementing of policy are seen as bedeviled by these schisms. The picture that emerges is mixed: poor coordination, opportunities missed, and conflict on the one hand, pluralism of purpose and values on the other. The telescope of high-powered analysis reveals all the cragginess and diversity of a foreign policy landscape that to the casual glance appears integrated and organic.

The comments of O'Donnell and Graciarena, on the May and Mitchell papers respectively, take issue with this perspective, and there is no need to rehearse their arguments here. It should be pointed out, however, that the debate over the usefulness of intragovernmental analysis in the understanding of hemispheric politics came early to the gathering and stayed late. More precisely than any other difference that emerged, it represented in microcosm the larger paradigmatic competition between *dependencia* and liberal perspectives on inter-American relations. As suggested above, the competition derives, in the first instance, from epistemological differences. It involves conflicting perspectives on the meaning of knowledge, understanding, and explanation in the social sciences, and it leads organically to different evaluations of the meaning of change in concrete policies. These differences were not resolved in Lima, nor can they be here. All we can do is remind the reader that the differing explanations and emphases presented in the essays, though important in and of themselves, are also the manifestations of a set of concerns as old and fundamental as the systematic study of society itself.

Theory and Cases, Wholes and Parts, Continuity and Change

The conventional wisdom of the social sciences pays homage to the unbreakable bond between theory and research. Without constant testing against reality, theory stagnates and eventually turns to dogma. Without the guidance of theory, research founders, ultimately degenerating into a mindless empiricism that confuses data with reality. In Lima, there were no basic disagreements on generalizations of this sort. What did emerge, however, was a number of tensions involving the proper *relationship* between research and theory—more specifically, the relationship between, on the one hand, concrete studies of events, institutions, and issues, and, on the other, an understanding of the larger whole of which each forms a part.

This tension between the analysis of parts and the understanding of wholes is most clearly illustrated by the controversy that embroiled the emphasis given to the study of intragovernmental relations in the essays by May, Mitchell, and Lowenthal. As mentioned previously, this "bureaucratic politics" perspective was sharply criticized by a number of other participants. But the criticisms were not made on empirical grounds; no one said: "No, it didn't happen that way," or "No, group X really believed otherwise." What *was* said, in effect, was "Yes, this is all in one sense true, the conflicts and the differences do exist, but it all takes place within a structure that lends unity and coherence to disparate behavior." To which others replied, "There is some possibility that such unity and coherence exist in the most general sense, but if this is so, the way to an understanding of the system leads inevitably through an understanding of its many elements." Stated in this fashion, the controversy would seem negotiable. Both the detailed study of the parts of the system and the continuing analysis of the system as a whole are needed. But although consensus might be reached at this level, the investigation of actual case materials unearths related problems that spoil the appearance of agreement.

One such problem has to do with the multitude of purposes to which a single case can be lent. This is nowhere more dramatically illustrated than in the various ways in which the Alliance for Progress is beaten, chopped, flavored, cooked, and served up in different essays and comments. In the pages that follow, the Alliance is used to "demonstrate" (a) that the U.S. Government was committed to the economic *development* of Latin America; (b) that the United States was committed to the economic *subjugation* of Latin America; (c) that either "a" or "b" might be the case, but it really doesn't matter since the North American political-bureaucratic apparatus was so confused and inconsistent as to be incapable of achieving much of anything; (d) that whatever the motives of the founders of the Alliance, they so misunderstood the political-economic situation in Latin America that the Alliance was essentially an exercise in illusion and misplaced emphases; (e) that the dominant classes in the United States never really wanted to do "a," but were clever enough to see that they had to pretend to do "a" both in order to achieve some of "b" and also to prevent the Latin Americans from taking charge of their own development; or (f) that the Alliance for Progress can be put to any or all of uses (g) through (z).

At one time or another, scarcity of information and scarcity of space lure all analysts into arguing by example. If this were all that is illustrated by the above list, its implications would not be too serious. But more is at stake, for in addition to being a case in a larger series of foreign policy actions (which is to say, an element in a whole), the Alliance is also a complex system in its own right, with constituent parts, stages, and elements:

there is the Alliance of the first years and the Alliance of the later years; there is the Congressional-Executive element, the AID overseas-bureaucracy element, the Latin American elite element. And all of these and other elements in interaction constituted a system that was not the simple sum of its parts. Different fragments, when viewed at close hand, do give aid and comfort (in the form of data and example) to multiple interpretations. There is, in other words, an objective basis—rooted in complexity—for various interpretations of the Alliance.

However, an even stronger statement can be made: investigators approaching the Alliance from different theoretical perspectives will *necessarily* use it in different ways to discover different "truths." Even were the elements under investigation held constant, diversity of interpretation would not necessarily diminish. The meanings of the Alliance, which is to say its reality as reconstructed, are not and cannot be independent of the theoretical perspectives brought to bear on it, whether the latter are consciously or unconsciously held.[4] In short, the differences that are found, the interpretations that are in conflict, do not derive solely from the complexity of the case itself; they are the empirical and interpretive manifestations of different theoretical perspectives. More research—further information about the Alliance, no matter how detailed or exhaustive—will not adjudicate or reconcile all the differences. As was suggested in the discussion of different explanations of politics, the battles will have to be fought on other terrain. Recognizing this is a necessary first step in using research and the detailed study of cases to achieve a more profound understanding of the hemisphere.

Related to these issues is another that bedevils almost all work in the social sciences, but which we precipitated quite directly by insisting that *change* form a central theme of the conference. Again and again we saw cases used by some participants to argue change, fastened upon and refashioned by others to argue continuity. The Alliance is once more a case in point: Was it a significant break with the Eisenhower-Dulles foreign policy of the 1950s or was it simply the Kennedy version of a long-standing imperialist policy, cut and tailored to the 1960s? Does the current political-economic situation involving Peru and the United States (and other countries) signal a structural shift in center-periphery relationships, or is it simply the old dependency in new guise? If, as Luciano Martins claims, multinational corporations find it increasingly difficult to turn to the North American government in troubled times and thus are developing their own political capacity, should this be seen as a break

---

[4]We have not chosen to explore the epistemological assumptions undergirding this statement. Our purpose here is the more limited one of pointing out that (1) research is always a reconstruction of reality, and (2) theory is a principal arbitrator of the validity of the reconstruction.

with the past or simply an adjustment to new realities? Just because the Marines have not landed since 1965, does this mean that the more aggressive ramifications of imperialism have declined? Such questions simply cannot be answered in the abstract. They begin to make sense—and therefore to have answers—only when embedded in a larger theoretical framework that establishes at least minimal guideposts to the debate. In this sense, dilemmas in the analysis of continuity and change are a special case of the tension between the understandings of wholes and parts, and both reflect the paradigmatic differences mentioned earlier.

The discussion of continuity and change is also related to the dialectic between theory and cases. On the one hand, the study of concrete cases leads us to recognizing and confronting change. The multinational corporation is demonstrably different today from what it was a decade ago; and three decades ago there would have been no such corporation to study. Castro's Cuba is sufficiently changed from Batista's to have generated at least a Spanish long ton of books and articles—not to mention the Bay of Pigs invasion and the missile crisis. Henry Kissinger's notions of a sane foreign policy are not John Foster Dulles's. Almost inevitably, comparisons and the subsequent identification of differences emerge from the detailed study, through time, of events, institutions, and issues.

On the other hand, the conventional demands and requisites of theory construction often lead us in different if not opposite directions—toward the general, the timeless, the inclusive. Although there may be no logical incompatibility between the two enterprises, in practice—as illustrated by the essays in this volume—the tensions and empiricist temptations that are generated if one takes the study of change seriously are not easy to manage or resist.

Social Science, Social Policy, Social Action

The frequency with which the discussion in Lima turned to what is wrong in the Americas suggests more than just shared indignation in the face of exploitation and inequality. It reflects also a continuing concern with the relationship of social science to policy and action. Never too far below the surface lurked the expectation that social science will make a difference, that ideas and information will eventually filter through the subsoil of the policy-making process and contribute in some way to the amelioration of injustice in the hemisphere. One need not have a well-articulated model of the relationship of words to events in order to have faith in their interconnectedness. In fact, to doubt this relationship and the possibilities for influence that are implied is to call too much into question.

In truth, however, neither the essays nor the discussion produced specific proposals for making research on inter-American relations—as the expression goes—"more relevant." On the other hand, concerns did eventually cluster around several continuing issues in the nexus between social science, social policy, and social action. These have to do with *who* does research, on *what* topics, for *what* purposes, and in *what* institutional settings.

Most obvious are the social-science ramifications of hemispheric asymmetries in social, economic, and political power. The maldistribution of scholarly resources, infrastructure, and productivity is dramatic. There are probably several hundred North Americans studying Latin America for every Latin American who is studying the United States (although, ironically, there are thousands of Latin Americans studying *in* the United States). Only in Mexico, in all of Latin America, is there an academic research center that devotes itself at least part-time to the systematic study of the United States. Even where language and access would seem to favor Latin Americans, scholarship has in many instances been dominated by foreigners, usually North Americans. The bibliographies on politics and change in modern Mexico and revolutionary Cuba—containing as they do works written in most cases by non-Mexicans and non-Cubans—are only two of the more striking examples.

The main outlines of the causes of these asymmetries in the production of knowledge are fairly clear, but the consequences are just now beginning to come into focus. Quite apart from the indignity of having the bulk of knowledge about matters of vital concern generated by outsiders, there are more serious consequences. Most obviously, whole sets of problems are untouched, *tierra incógnita,* because the outsiders either do not care or do not dare to explore the terrain. Other problems are studied in great detail, the fragments assembled, packaged, and sent out of the country to be used or misused.

More subtly, the usefulness of many studies that do get done is sharply skewed by the non-national structures and frameworks within which they are produced. This emphasis on structural skew is important, for it relocates the issue in differing national conditions and needs, not in the motives or capacities of the investigators. Quite simply, what a Peruvian investigator "needs to know" about North American foreign policy in the 1960s is not necessarily what a Yankee professor needs to know, even though they may have similar training and values. The massive bibliography on the formulation of North American foreign policy is barren of Latin American contributions. And when and if such contributions begin to appear, they will almost assuredly be cast in a different framework and reveal a different reality than the studies done to date. The view from below is necessarily different from the view from within, and the view from Chile is different from the view from Guatemala; from each vantage point, different questions will be asked and different answers will be found. And even in those relatively rare instances when the questions and answers might turn out not to be so very different, the process of creating the knowledge at home, instead of importing it, is in itself significant in terms of potential audiences and impact. In short, the question of relevance cannot be separated from considerations of *where, by whom,* and *for whom* the knowledge is produced.[5]

Other issues touch upon the question of relevance from a different angle. If many participants were concerned with the manner in which imbalances in knowledge-producing capacity reflect larger imbalances in power, they were also concerned with *what kind* of knowledge is getting produced in different places. At several points during the conference, the Latin American tradition of historical and macro-sociological studies was set against the North American tradition of more sharply focused, detailed, empirical studies of events and institutions. Without wishing to draw the lines strictly on a geographical basis, we would acknowledge that an analysis of the literature on hemispheric relations produced to date by Latin Americans and North Americans would undoubtedly support these generalizations.

This distinction assumes a special meaning in the context of the search for policy-relevant knowledge. Since it is extremely difficult to assess the long-term influence of a body of social theory, discussions of relevance often get transformed into examinations (and celebrations) of the decisional utility of more limited and concrete investigations.[6] With a special twist, this is well exemplified by Saxe-Fernández's concern with the dangers that inhere in much North American empirical research on Latin America. He is not worried that the theoretical magnificence of these studies will dazzle the beholder, creating false images—to the contrary, he generally holds them in low regard as lasting contributions to social science. Rather, precisely because of their detail and specificity they are seen as potential *materia prima* for intelligence agencies: their

---

[5] In this sense, there can be no "international community of scholars" and no fully supranational body of social-science knowledge, however necessary and useful increased cross-national communication and cooperation may be. The actual denationalization of scholarship has, in some cases, gone very far. Again, the literature on the Cuban revolution provides a dramatic example: for a variety of reasons, even a series of events so critical in hemispheric history as the Cuban revolution has received minimal scholarly attention *in Latin America,* having been expropriated more than a decade ago by Western Europeans and North Americans.

[6] This is not to say that relevance necessarily *should* be defined in this way. The long-term significance of a tradition of social thought or the clarification or extension of a theoretical perspective may be much greater than the aggregate utility of a series of concrete studies. What is here emphasized is that many decision-making processes "need" a certain kind of social science and thus define the latter as relevant whatever history's long-term verdict may be.

empiricism makes them useful; imbalances in power and malevolence of purpose make them dangerous.

It is not necessary to reduce the notion of relevance to the lowest common denominator of the informational needs of intelligence agencies to appreciate the force of this argument. The general point is that the closer one gets to operative problems of decision-making, the more the balance gets tipped in favor of the utility of a social science that concentrates on the study of cases and parts. The more specific point is that the North American research tradition in social science is more likely than the Latin American to produce a steady stream of those cases and parts *even when* the researchers themselves are not in the service of the official apparatus. Furthermore, North American bureaucracies, both public and private, are much better equipped than their Latin American counterparts to consume social-science knowledge wherever it is produced. Thus, already existing imbalances in power and productivity are joined and reinforced by a bureaucratic culture that encourages, seeks, and incorporates special sorts of social-science inputs.

The dilemmas that result are cruel, involving both the kind of knowledge that is or should be produced and the role of the social scientist. Even partial resolutions will be long in coming. For example, the search for a critical, anti-status-quo social science was so much the dominant tone in Lima that no one suggested that the problems of linking social science to policy and action could be solved simply by "joining the team." In the first place, this usually implies the production of a certain kind of social science—not necessarily what the investigator sees as most needed or useful. Second, since the state apparatus is so frequently seen as a primary obstacle to desired changes—rather than their instrumentality—minimal consistency dictates that direct associations with it cannot be put forth as a once-and-for-all solution in all countries at all times. Even were these arguments not so strong, in Latin America at least, structured opportunities to work and produce in settings with demonstrable links to the policy-making process are minimal. Where are the specialized academic centers, policy institutes, and research bureaus (of whatever political coloration)? In the United States, other problems exist. The hegemonic machine is a voracious consumer of the *materia prima* produced by the social science community, and it is also a tremendous subverter of talent and independence. How does one continue to practice the craft in ways that diminish or harness the power of that machine rather than contributing to it?

Not even the surface of these problems was scratched in Lima. In any event, only very partial answers will be found around the conference table. It is in the struggle to do work that illuminates critical problems, to create the institutions that make such work possible, to defend those institutions from both threats and temptations, and to link them more directly to social action that more substantial progress will be made. At a minimum there can be agreement that the search for a social science appropriate to the conditions in which we live—and in which others suffer—is certainly worth our best efforts. To date, those efforts have not been good enough.

Some Challenges

In the planning stages of the conference, it was hoped that one of the outcomes of the gathering would be "suggestions for future work." To a great extent, this task got lost in a welter of other problems, and no formal proposals were made. Nevertheless, a number of common concerns were expressed, and although not all participants would agree on them, there was sufficient implied consensus to warrant their presentation here.

Although the conference was called "political relations . . . ," the predominant posture taken by paper writers and commentators—especially the Latin Americans—was what might be called a political-economic view of hemispheric relations. To a great extent this is a perfectly predictable outcome of a gathering in which a majority subscribe to a *dependencia* paradigm in one of its many variations. It is also an outcome reflecting objective conditions, a hemispheric reality so dramatic that one often wonders why the relation of economics to politics is not immediately apparent to all. Whether as manifested by the immense maldistribution of wealth and power (or its correlates, the patently political role of multinational corporations, or the staffing, rationale, and behavior of aid and fiscal agencies), hemispheric realities would seem to be capable of giving birth directly—without the need for social-science midwives—to the fundamental insight that politics and economics are inextricably linked.

It is one thing, however, to recognize and pay homage to the essential relationship of economics to politics, and quite another to manage that relationship creatively while analyzing hemispheric relations. One must cut into the complexity at some point, emphasize certain sequences and factors, and downplay or ignore others—usually in ten thousand words or less. Thus, it is not surprising that in the papers presented in this volume a number of different approaches to the linkages between politics and economics have been used.

In some instances—most notably in Luciano Martins's paper on the multinational corporation—a nominally economic institution is studied in its various political roles. Emphasis is placed on the multiplicity of parts played by the actor, appearing at one moment on the stage as a profit maximizer and at the next moment as a subverter of governments.

In other instances—as in much of the foreign-policy analysis included in these essays—politics is purposefully set against the backdrop of economic analysis. For convenience or out of conviction, the examination often begins with the specific acts of a foreign-policy apparatus and then works "backward" to a consideration of the economic forces in play. In other instances, the sequences are reversed, as in the essay by Pinto and the comment by Sunkel. Without ever mentioning politics, Pinto sketches macro-changes in hemispheric economic relations. Sunkel then speculates on the political consequences of these changes.

Abbreviated characterizations of this sort cannot do justice to the seriousness with which most authors and discussants took up the challenge of attempting to join economic and political analysis. But even when the written work has been wrung dry of insights and all appropriate allowances for "limitations of space" have been made, one is still struck by how partial and fragmented most attempts are. Even those most committed to classical Marxist models would admit that they offer only the most general guidance to the study of specific foreign policies or the emergence and changing behavior of transnational actors. At the same time, those most experienced in the detailed investigation of specific instances of the interplay of economics and politics are quick to confess that their findings to date usually have limited transfer value. The revealed "truths" about Guatemala are not necessarily the "truths" about Argentina, and yesterday's relationships are not necessarily today's or tomorrow's.[7]

As emphasized previously, other questions have to do with the relative importance and autonomy of political processes and nominally political structures. All would agree that there are political dynamics in Mexico and Brazil that are not only different from each other but also from those in Cuba or Chile. And it is equally well accepted that the governments that speak in the name of these nations (and which reflect in some manner these political dynamics) interact in different ways with a hemispheric landscape that is by no means of their own making. In all of this, politics is seen as critical to determining specific outcomes, however fundamental economic factors may be in setting limits on what is possible or probable.

But when the moment arrives to reach beyond confessions and generalizations of this sort, agreements fragment, disciplinary chauvinisms erupt, sacred texts are quoted, and ideological, professional, and national

---

[7]There is no reason, *in theory,* why such should be the case. Sound studies of national realities should always illuminate more general truths. What is here being emphasized is how infrequently *in practice* concrete studies are embedded in the kind of political-economic theoretical matrix that would extend their meanings in time and space.

differences become paramount. Perhaps at this time we can do no better, for our increasing sensitivity to the interrelatedness of politics and economics has not to date been accompanied by equal advances in either the theory or the methodology needed to study them. And, as has been demonstrated on numerous occasions, among the consequences of inadequate theory and methodology are almost inevitably fractured dialogue and undue emphasis given to issues of secondary importance. In short, one of the lessons that emerged most clearly from the papers and the discussions is how difficult it is to create a body of thought about political economy that would be more adequate to ordering and explaining these mutually interdependent aspects of hemispheric relations.

It is one more index of the political and economic imbalances of the hemisphere that the majority of attention in Lima and in the papers and comments was focused on the United States, on North American-based institutions and actors, and on the causes and consequences of their behavior. Admittedly, the conference was structured to encourage such a focus, but the level of concentration was even higher than expected. Even when the foreign policy of a country as important in its own right as Mexico or Brazil was under consideration, the questions raised most often had to do with the influence (direct and indirect) of the United States on that policy. Countries that have been as innovative as Chile and Cuba in developmental and foreign relations entered into the discussion primarily because they represent challenges to Yankee hegemony and thus test the limits of U.S. power. At times, it was almost as if Latin America did not exist except as defined by U.S. interests and actions.

At the risk of overgeneralizing, let us suggest that the following proposition would be accepted by most contributors to this volume: The central intellectual problem in the study of inter-American relations is to understand the structure and functioning of the system of North American domination—imperfect, halting, and contradictory though that system might be.[8] To generations of scholars and students raised on—or reacting against—interpretations of inter-American relations that denied the very existence of such a system, the urgency and attractiveness of organizing one's work around such a central conception of the task at hand are undeniable. "Harmony of interests" and "all states are equal" approaches to inter-American relations are rejected. By concentrating on American power and its maintenance and extension, purpose is given to scholarship, previously disparate concerns are knit together, and a loose,

---

[8] None of the authors represented here can be said to hold a dogmatic or mechanistic view of American hegemony. All recognize the contradictions of imperialism and the limitations of power. Some might even be accused of erring in the opposite direction, of seeing the actual exercise of power as overly fragmented, uncoordinated, and purposeless.

open-ended structural model of how the hemisphere works is made available for testing and modification.

But despite the heuristic value of this model, the questions that it poses do not exhaust the subject matter of hemispheric relations, and at times they actually distort, by making it difficult to recognize that Latin America is important for reasons not directly related to its subordinate status. Is the Chilean case important only because it represents a challenge to Yankee hegemony and thus tests the limits of U.S. power? Or, in fact, is it also of interest because it illuminates a host of developmental difficulties and possible solutions that involve the United States only marginally, if at all? Does Cuban foreign policy not deserve to be conceptualized in terms of political forces and beliefs reflecting more than simple reactions to past and present pressures from the United States? In fact, is it not true that over the past 14 years Cuba has exerted considerable influence *over* the United States, not simply vice versa? Are not the new and changing faces of Latin American nationalism too complex and too deeply rooted in distinct national situations to be understood wholly in terms of North American attempts to dominate? If the tired old OAS does not dance to the tune of the Yankee piper as mechanically as it did in the 1960s, is the piper simply blowing some wrong notes, or must explanations be sought elsewhere? And what must be said about the Andean Common Market and other attempts at integration?

Questions posed in this fashion suggest their own answers: Yes, the Chilean case is of intrinsic interest. Cuba certainly has influenced domestic groups and foreign policy in the United States. And Latin American nationalisms are clearly more than just a reaction against North American attempts to dominate. Yet what became increasingly clear in our discussions was how difficult it sometimes is to come to grips with these and other questions when the basic model in use is one of the structure and functioning of U.S. imperialism. The other questions are relegated to secondary status, or ignored completely. And, ironically, a primary consequence is to downplay—even to denigrate—the importance and capacity of Latin America itself. The periphery becomes of interest only *because* it is weak, dependent, and the object of aggression. It is celebrated as the living proof that imperialism exists.

Having seen elements of this dynamic in action, we are thus suggesting that conscious effort ought to be made to pay more attention—and attention of a different kind—to Latin America on its own terms, to national differences, degrees of freedom, class struggle, new forms of collective action, and future possibilities. Shared concern with the creation and strengthening of counterimperialist strategies argues that "know thyself" should be given equal billing with "know thine enemy." In no way does this imply that studying the United States and mechanisms of domination and control is unimportant. To the contrary, we have already suggested that much more detailed study of the United States by Latin Americans is a first-order priority—implying as it does, different purposes and perspectives and the satisfaction of different requirements for knowledge. But this should not be allowed to obscure the fact that the realities of Latin America are changing more rapidly than knowledge about these realities. If scholarship on inter-American relations is not to be cast into the dustbin of history—along with outmoded forms of social and economic organization—then it must face squarely the challenge of a Latin America that can no longer be understood as merely the shadow cast by the Colossus of the North.

Part One
Some Latin American Perspectives

Imperialism and Diplomacy in Inter-American Relations

OCTAVIO IANNI

After World War II, the United States Government was primarily concerned with how to continue the war in modified form. England, Belgium, Holland, France, Italy, Japan, and other allied and enemy nations had all lost or were in the process of losing their colonies and spheres of influence. The destruction of these empires and colonial systems marked the beginning of North American expansion; and at the same time, the Soviet Union was emerging as a second world superpower. The creation of socialist governments in Central European countries and the victory of socialism in China in 1949 strengthened the position of the Soviet Union with respect to the U.S.-led capitalist countries. Politically, at least, the socialist world was no longer a weaker and less dynamic system; and it gradually became strong militarily under the leadership of the Soviet Union.

This was the world situation at the onset of the cold war. In the sense that World War II was an international civil war as well as a war between national states, the cold war was actually a continuation of the same war in disguise. The cold war defined the limits of the world superpowers' zones of influence. During the tensest moments of the cold war, the world was sharply divided: from the points of view of both the North American and the Soviet governments, the division was a political, economic, military, and cultural bipolarization. John Foster Dulles, Secretary of State during General Dwight D. Eisenhower's administration (1952–60), was probably the most explicit spokesman for the cold war.

It was Foster Dulles who said that neutralism was immoral in a cold war. Thanks to a system of military alliances, he was able to group the poor nations of the world under the North American cudgel. Those alliances forced costly, useless armaments

---

Octavio Ianni is a member of the Brazilian Center of Analysis and Planning (CEBRAP), São Paulo, Brazil.

on the poor countries; and led the United States to catastrophic interventions, ending a decade later in disaster in the jungles and rice paddies of Vietnam.[1]

Virtually none of the agreements, treaties, resolutions, conferences, interventions, repressive acts, coups, or other developments since World War II can be interpreted correctly without examining U.S. cold-war policies in Latin America.

Hemispheric Security

We must bear in mind that the gradual alignment of Latin American countries on the side of the "allied powers" and against the "axis powers" from 1939 to 1945 was an important step in reformulating and strengthening inter-American relations. For Latin America, war against Nazi fascism meant breaking off trade with European and Asiatic nations that had been partners in commercial and other interchanges since before 1939. At the same time, the economic, political, and military presence of the United States in those countries increased. Argentina barely managed to retain her neutrality during World War II, maintaining her economic, political, military, and cultural relations with European countries, especially England. In general, it was during World War II that most governments of Latin American countries adopted the doctrine of hemispheric security. The doctrine was supposedly drawn up to protect Latin American solidarity from penetration by foreign interests in the hemisphere—but it was ultimately designed to protect North American interests. Until the war, the main fear involved "European colonialism"; but after the war, when the United States and the Soviet Union confronted each other as the two world superpowers, North Americans became concerned chiefly with "international communism." In both cases, the U.S. Government presented the problem as one of safeguarding the solidarity of the American Republics against "foreign aggression," as President Theodore Roosevelt said in 1904. In both cases, a basic tenet of the Monroe Doctrine emerged over and over again.

The Monroe Doctrine, stipulating the exclusion of European political institutions and territorial acquisitions from the Western Hemisphere and thereby allowing the preponderance of the United States free play, is the most comprehensive unilateral proclamation of a sphere of influence of modern times.[2]

Thus, after World War II, the political, economic, military, and cultural relations of dependency in Latin America unfolded according to the exi-

[1] John Kenneth Galbraith, "Os E.U.A. Despertam de um Sonho Imperial," *Jornal do Brasil* (Rio de Janeiro), July 23, 1972, Cuaderno Especial, pp. 2–3.
[2] Hans J. Morgenthau, "Historical Justice and the Cold War," *The New York Review of Books,* July 10, 1969, pp. 10–17, quotation p. 13.

gencies of the cold war and the new international expansion of North American capitalism.

Meanwhile, just as the U.S. Government worked to develop and safeguard its interests, so nearly all Latin American governments tried to consolidate their positions and secure benefits. The dominant bourgeoisie in the majority of Latin American countries continued to consolidate its position as an associated class. New alliances and associations were established between bourgeoisies on an inter-American scale. Thus, the internationalization of social classes was accelerated, and contradictions between classes became more intense.

The doctrine of hemispheric security consolidated economic, political, and military interdependence. In other words, U.S. supremacy in Latin America plus Latin American governmental interests led to the doctrine of mutual security, and permitted the political, economic, and military development of dependent relations. Soon the harmony-of-interests doctrine was drawn up between all countries of the Americas with the help of government officials, businessmen, experts, politicians, ambassadors, and social scientists.[3] The doctrine was supposed to protect the values of hemispheric societies from foreign as well as domestic subversion, in the name of the security and stability of existing institutions. This proved to be indispensable for the operation and prosperity of private business in the form of the multinational corporation.

In this context, counterinsurgency doctrine was also adopted, and spread rapidly. It was a new and coherent development in U.S. hegemony over Latin American countries. In alliance with the majority of Latin American governments, the North American government initiated a systematic program to militarize political power. Obviously these governments had only rarely been independent of military support or influence in the past. Civilian and military oligarchies often alternated or united for control of the state apparatus. The presence of the military in Latin American politics is, then, nothing new. In the majority of cases, what took place in the decades following World War II was a new kind of militarization of political power in the name of hemispheric security, counterinsurgency, and interdependency. For the governments involved, the common enemy was international communism and its manifestations as internal subversion. Now, more than ever before, the military dedicates itself to *internal security,* not simply to *national defense.* As class contradictions sharpen, the armed forces increasingly enter into the struggles that spring from these contradictions. A new kind of militarization of

[3] James Petras, "La 'armonía de intereses': Ideología de las naciones dominantes," *Desarrollo Económico* (Buenos Aires), vol. 6, nos. 22–23, July-December 1966, pp. 443–67.

political power becomes the nucleus of the capitalist state. In the end, the state apparatus is the most important link in the hemispheric security system, the base of North American supremacy.

The U.S. political objective is to counteract any trend on the part of Latin America to drift toward the Communist or neutralist camps. Obviously, it is of great importance to the U.S. to have Latin America's UN vote (one-fifth of the total UN vote) on its side and to get Latin America's firm support for U.S. policies inside the Organization of American States. It is apparent, also, that U.S. political interests in Latin America are intimately related to the military and economic interests, for the development of an anti-United States stance in any Latin American country would jeopardize U.S. military and economic assistance programs and U.S. trade and private investment as well. [4]

Under the counterinsurgency doctrine, the United States Government exported experts (advisers, etc.) and know-how to Latin American countries in order to strengthen capitalism in the hemisphere. It is clear that the repressive apparatus in the broadest sense had and still has priority in these "modernization" programs.

Where order is in jeopardy, men fear one another, the ordinary business of government and of private life cannot proceed, any future plans are overshadowed by the uncertainty of incipient violence, and the stakes of participating in politics rise sharply. Awareness of the importance of public order has been one of America's motivations for seeking to promote "stability" in many areas of the world.

Foreign assistance can encourage public order by improving police mobility and techniques. The police and military establishments are the principal instruments of "public order." The implicit intimidation that comes from the presence of effective police and/or military forces will prevent many disorders and challenges to a regime that otherwise might be faced with serious rebellions. [5]

But more than just the repressive apparatus was modernized as new class relations developed on the continent. Other sectors of the state received and continue to receive techno-scientific, material, organizational, and human resources. [6] The political power of the bourgeoisie acquired new modalities of action over the years. In different ways, U.S. and Latin American governments were able to "capitalize" on their experience with the ephemeral Arbenz government in Guatemala, the victorious socialistic revolution in Cuba, the Bay of Pigs invasion failure in Cuba, the successful armed intervention in the Dominican Republic, and others.

---

[4] Edwin Lieuwen, *The United States and the Challenge to Security in Latin America* (Columbus, Ohio: 1966), p. 22.

[5] Howard Wriggins, "Foreign Assistance and Political Development," in *Development of the Emerging Countries: An Agenda for Research,* The Brookings Institution (Washington: 1962), pp. 181–214, quotation p. 186.

[6] Albert Waterston, *Development Planning: Lessons of Experience,* The Economic Development Institute, International Bank for Reconstruction and Development (Baltimore: 1969).

Nevertheless, Latin American social, political, and economic forces for change have not given up the search for new ways in which to escape from imperialistic domination. The Velasco Alvarado government in Peru and the Salvador Allende government in Chile are proof that these forces are seeking other ways in which to develop themselves, even within the institutional framework of a capitalist state.

The existence of these governments is another reason why North American governments and some of their Latin American allies continue to emphasize the importance of the fight against social, political, and economic forces that could alter the structures of political domination and economic appropriation. The United States is constantly forced to perfect its methods in the struggle against so-called "subversive threats to security and internal order," characterizing their mission as "fulfilling Latin American governments' legitimate interest in modern security forces." That "legitimate interest" in turn is determined by the requirements of U.S. hegemony.

Our objective, in the first instance, is to support our *interests* over the long run with a sound foreign policy. The more that policy is based on a realistic assessment of our and others' interests, the more our role in the world can be. We are not involved in the world because we have commitments; we have commitments because we are involved. Our interests must shape our commitments, rather than the other way around.[7]

Partnership Between Unequals

Organized in 1961 to carry out the program of the *Punta del Este Charter,* the Alliance for Progress was a counter-revolutionary operation. Beneath the language of reformism, the Charter and the Alliance constituted the regrouping of reactionary and conservative forces in the hemisphere. This was the first continental effort to show that U.S. and Latin American governments were actively organizing and learning from the success of the Cuban revolution. President John F. Kennedy's New Frontier diplomacy was a curious and ingenious combination of reformist jargon and counter-reformist politics. It was this same diplomacy that created the Peace Corps and intensified the national and continental programs against "internal subversion." For the second time in the century, North American hegemony in Latin America was to take on the tones of "Good Neighbor imperialism." Franklin D. Roosevelt's administration (1932–44) was the first, and John F. Kennedy's (1960–63) the second, to "speak softly and carry a big stick," in handling the ambiguities, controversies, and contradictions characteristic of U.S. relations with Latin America.

[7]President Richard M. Nixon, *United States Foreign Policy for the 1970's: A New Strategy for Peace* (special chapter on "The Western Hemisphere," pp. 17–21). A Report to the Congress, Washington, February 18, 1970, italics added.

The Charter and the Alliance were two chapters more in the history of the cold war in Latin America. As elements of a counter-revolutionary operation against any social, political, or economic reform that challenged the existing power structure, they were successful. Confronted with forces that preached reform or revolution, their main objective was to maintain the status quo; and indeed, through them, many governments were able to broaden state control and perfect their repressive apparatuses.

The reformist language of the Charter and the Alliance would scarcely have mattered in a period of such immense social and political upheaval. The policies put into practice were different, however, given the perspectives of those struggling against structures of domination (political) and appropriation (economic). Note that President Kennedy announced the Alliance in March 1961; and in April, scarcely a month later, came the Bay of Pigs invasion, authorized by the North American government. At the same time, programs of militarization of political power in Latin America were being carried out under the pretext of attending to the legitimate needs of modernizing the security forces. These and other facts force us to conclude that reformist language and antireformist practice were the terms of the paradox of Alliance for Progress diplomacy— or the terms of the New Frontier for further U.S. capitalist expansion in Latin America. Let us examine what President Kennedy said, and what he did.

I have called on all people of the hemisphere to join in a new Alliance for Progress— *Alianza para el Progreso*—a vast cooperative effort, unparalleled in magnitude and nobility of purpose, to satisfy the basic needs of the American people for homes, work and land, health and schools—*techo, trabajo y tierra, salud y escuela.*[8]

The concern of the President and his top assistants was reflected in efforts to train United States as well as the Latin American armed forces for counterinsurgency operations. Additions of the new courses, or material, were made to the curriculums of the country's major military training institutions.
In 1961, the President asked Congress for funds to support an increase in army personnel strength to permit expansion of guerrilla, warfare units . . . .
On June 10, 1962, the State Department announced that in cooperation with other agencies of the Government, it was inaugurating a series of seminar courses called the "National Interdepartmental Seminar on Problems of Development and Internal Defense." For administrative purposes the seminar was organized under the jurisdiction of the State Department's Foreign Service Institute. The official announcement declared that, "The Seminar demonstrates the United States' determination to assist the less developed countries of the free world in developing balanced

---

[8] President John F. Kennedy's White House speech in honor of the Latin American Diplomatic Corps, March 13, 1961, as quoted by Arthur M. Schlesinger, Jr., *A Thousand Days* (New York: 1967), p. 193.

capabilities for the total defense of their societies against internal as well as external threat."[9]

The diplomacies of the dollar and the big stick were again dynamically combined with a certain degree of success in a modern version—this time to combat sharpening class distinctions in Latin America. The most visible proofs of polarization were the reformist politics of the Arbenz government (1951–54), the popular demonstrations against Vice-President Nixon in Latin America (April and May, 1958), and the revolutionary policies of the Fidel Castro government (since 1959). Confronted with these realities, most governments entered into agreements to control or repress the political programs and ambitions of social classes fighting for reforms or changes that could affect the existing power structure. In this sense, the Alliance was just one more vehicle for U.S. intervention in the internal affairs of Latin American countries.

In the wider sense, intervention is inherent in United States power. Whatever policy the United States pursues in Latin America will be intervention in some form; the question is how the objectives in furtherance of which she seeks to influence her weaker neighbors are regarded by the latter. The Bay of Pigs affair was one kind of intervention; the Alliance for Progress, another. The promotion of the inter-American system and the support she gives it represent—as this study has tried to show—an attempt by the United States to shape the international relations of Latin America in her own interests.[10]

The Alliance for Progress was obviously not the only agency through which the U.S. Government structured and intensified its control over internal Latin American affairs. Inter-American and world organizations, among others, became efficient instruments for intervention in the economic, political, military, and cultural affairs in the countries of the hemisphere. These organizations generally facilitated the "depoliticization" of the ambiguities, controversies, and contradictions inherent in imperialistic relations. Member countries could choose either to maintain the illusion of participation in decision-making or to submit openly to bilateral negotiations with the United States. Latin American governments, as well as the United States, used multilateralism to depoliticize the problems of imperialistic domination. Thus multilateral organizations developed side by side with the doctrine of "mature partnership" between unequals. It was not pure coincidence that these elements of world diplomacy were combined in the Pearson and Rockefeller Reports (1969) and the Peterson Report (1970).[11] In an October 1969 speech

[9] Willard F. Barber and G. Neale Ronning, *Internal Security and Military Power: Counterinsurgency and Civic Action in Latin America* (Columbus, Ohio: 1966), pp. 142–43.
[10] Gordon Connell-Smith, *The Inter-American System* (Oxford: 1966), p. 311.
[11] Nelson A. Rockefeller, *The Rockefeller Report on the Americas,* The Official Report of a

to the Inter-American Press Association on foreign policy in the hemisphere, President Nixon emphasized that multilateralism is an important facet of a mature partnership between an imperialist nation and dependent nations in the hemisphere:

Our partnership should be one in which the United States lectures less and listens more, and in which clear, consistent procedures are established to ensure that the shaping of Latin America's future reflects the will of the Latin American nations.

I propose that a multilateral Interamerican agency be given an increasing share of responsibility for development assistance decisions. CIAP—the Interamerican Committee for the Alliance for Progress—could be given this function. Or an entirely new agency could be created. Whatever the form, the objective would be to evolve an effective multilateral framework for bilateral assistance, to provide the agency with an expert international staff, and, over time, to give it major operational and decision-making responsibilities.

The Latin American nations themselves would thus jointly assume a primary role in setting priorities within the Hemisphere in developing realistic programs, and in keeping their own performance under critical review.[12]

These, then, are some of the terms of the "mature partnership" designed to carry on the principal campaign (1) against foreign and domestic "subversion" in the name of peace and tranquility, and law and order; and (2) in favor of "private business," which once "properly motivated . . . has a vital role to play in social as well as economic development."[13]

Many multilateral organizations serve just these goals. They cooperate by depoliticizing the ambiguities, controversies, and contradictions characteristic of U.S. domination on the continent. Furthermore, they help to facilitate, systematize, and promote the multinational interests of North American corporations. Both the Latin American Free Trade Association (LAFTA) and the Central American Common Market (CACM), are examples of such tendencies. They are multinational organizations created in the spirit of mature partnership diplomacy. In many instances, they serve mainly the multinational interests of North American business. This is clear in the handling of intergovernmental negotiations of duties and import taxes in LAFTA countries.

According to the negotiations, agreements, and execution of so-called complementary pacts in LAFTA, the governments of two or more countries concede tariff cuts—

United States Presidential Mission for the Western Hemisphere (Chicago: 1969); Lester Pearson, *Partners in Development* (New York: 1969); Rudolph A. Peterson, *U.S. Foreign Assistance in the 1970's: A New Approach,* Report to the President from the Task Force on International Development, Washington, March 4, 1970.

[12]President Richard M. Nixon, speech in Washington, October 31, 1969, to the Inter-American Press Association.

[13]*Ibid.*

reduced duties or import taxes—that have been solicited by companies that themselves participate in a sectorial meeting and draw up an agreement (to be accepted or signed by the respective governments). But the companies do not propose reduction of customs duties in order to compete with each other. That is out of style. Each produces one or more tax-free products in a given country. Thus, behind the tariff agreement that governments sign believing that it will create a larger competitive market, the companies have made private agreements according to which each specializes in one line of products in each country. The consequences are obvious: neither the government nor the public of the countries involved realize how it is that they become increasingly dependent on foreign deals for products that may be strategically important for the smooth functioning of their national economy.[14]

As we can see, the "supranationality" inherent in the creation and functioning of multilateral organizations is just one more technique for preserving and strengthening U.S. hegemony over Latin America. In the partnership between unequals, the inequality tends to maintain itself or grow rather than diminish. Inequality does not disappear through partnership, especially when one country tends to perfect its domination, control, and decision-making techniques. Nevertheless this kind of partnership can produce and aggravate some controversies and contradictions. For example, the government and ruling class of the dependent country may initiate efforts to change the political and economic conditions that determine the form and amount of exportation of economic surplus. On another level, the refinement of relations and structures of dependency develops and sharpens internal contradictions, especially between governments and the salaried classes. As long as the economic surplus derives from the profits produced by the proletariat, the working class tends to join the struggle to destroy or reformulate those relations and structures of dependency.

All U.S. Government documents, decisions, and acts with respect to Latin American economic, political, and military affairs reveal controversies and contradictions in imperialistic domination. Furthermore, these same sources suggest the frequencies and particular ways in which politics and economics are combined in the diplomacies of the dollar and the big stick, just as state interests and private business interests are combined on an international scale. Such are the characteristics of the Good Neighbor policy and "mature partnership"; and they appear in the analyses and recommendations of the Rockefeller Report, prepared in 1969 by a U.S. Presidential Mission headed by Nelson A. Rockefeller. A North American government document on problems and solutions for Latin America, the Rockefeller Report is itself clearly an act of intervention in the internal affairs of the countries in the hemisphere.

[14]Constantino Ianni, *Descolonização em Marcha: Economia e Relações Internacionais,* Civilização Brasileira (Rio de Janeiro: 1972), p. 269.

Nearly all the recommendations of the Rockefeller Report were inspired by North American cold-war doctrine in its Latin American version. Thus the report talks about communist subversion, hemispheric unity, interdependence of nations on the continent, and the harmony of U.S. interests with those of Latin American countries. In the name of these principles—guaranteeing U.S. hegemony on the continent—the report presents an analysis of and recommendations on economic, social, military, labor, urban, demographic, educational, scientific, and other problems. Every section of the report, moreover, sets down rules for Latin American governments on how to analyze situations, make decisions, and take actions. The report is especially oriented toward establishing guidelines for the control and suppression of increasing antagonisms: (1) between Latin American countries and the United States; and (2) between classes within each country. In either case, North American hegemony is threatened. This is why the report opens by discussing changes that might occur in the near future to upset U.S. hegemony in the hemisphere:

While it is not possible to predict with any precision the precise course of change, the hemisphere is likely to exhibit the following characteristics in the next few years:
    1. Rising frustration with the pace of development, intensified by industrialization, urbanization, and population growth;
    2. Political and social instability;
    3. An increased tendency to turn to authoritarian or radical solutions;
    4. Continuation of the trend of the military to take power for the purpose of guiding social and economic progress; and
    5. Growing nationalism, across the spectrum of political groupings, which will often find expression in terms of independence from U.S. domination and influence.[15]

As we can see, in spite of the development of North American diplomacy in Latin America, U.S. leaders were forced to admit that their hegemony over the region was troubled and had no clear prospects. In 1971, as in 1961, and much more often than in previous decades, North American diplomacy confronted unexpected difficulties. The September 1970 electoral victory of socialist candidate Salvador Allende in Chile was not the only problem. Already in 1968, following the overthrow of President Belaúnde Terry in Peru, the government of Velasco Alvarado had begun to cause problems for the United States. Simultaneously, unexpected political situations developed in Mexico, Argentina, Brazil, and other countries. In response, North American diplomacy began to look around for new policies to meet a situation by now rather unfavorable to the continuity of U.S. economic, political, and military hegemony. On top of everything else, conditions for military interventions had be-

[15] Rockefeller, *Rockefeller Report,* pp. 35–36.

come increasingly difficult, even in the small Caribbean and Central American countries. The search for new information, doctrines, and diplomatic guidelines began—often under difficult conditions. In 1969, when the Presidential Mission headed by Nelson A. Rockefeller was sounding out Latin American governments, an American magazine made the following comments:

He has visited ten countries so far, been confronted with anti-U.S. demonstrations of one sort or another in five, cut short his stay in one because of threats of rioting and been disinvited by three . . . Rocky's troubled receptions have probably done more to dramatize the sorry state of U.S.-Latin American relations than anything since Richard Nixon's own tumultuous tour of the southern continent in 1958. Last week, conceding that there is "some discontent" among Latin Americans over their relations with the U.S., Secretary of State William P. Rogers declared that "there is no part of the world more important for us" and that the Administration does not want relations to deteriorate further.[16]

It is possible that recent surprises in political and social events in the hemisphere are a consequence of the mature-partnership diplomacy announced by President Nixon. For this policy determines the importance of each country according to the economic, political, and military interests of the United States.

Most countries to the south of us are not of vital importance to the U.S. national interests. Some are important. Some are more important than others. United States interests vary from country to country. The United States response must be carefully geared to support the importance [of] our real interests in each place. Anarchy in Uruguay may be different from anarchy in Mexico. Rapid development in Colombia may be of higher priority than development in Paraguay. A war between Brazil and Argentina would raise different problems from a war between Haiti and the Dominican Republic. Serious policy discussions cannot be held unless we are prepared to talk realistically.[17]

The partnership between the United States and Latin American countries is thus an unequal partnership between unequals. Moreover, Latin American countries themselves are unequal. This is a basic reason why North American governments have played the diplomatic game of "most favored ally" with Mexico, Brazil, and Argentina. Mature-partnership diplomacy has been primarily directed toward these countries. Under a mature partnership, the most favored allies are delegated political, military, and even economic responsibilities.

[16]*Time* (New York), June 13, 1969, p. 37.
[17]David Bronheim, "Inter-American Relations in the 1970's," in *Issues for the 1970's,* Conference on the Western Hemisphere held at the Center for Inter-American Relations, April 29–May 2, 1971, New York, pp. 107–21, quotation p. 112. For more on mature partnership, benign neglect, and low profile, see "Liberated Documents; New Imperial Strategy for Latin America," *NACLA's Latin America and Empire Report* (New York), vol. 5, no. 7, November 1971.

Socialism and Inter-American Relations

The victory of the Cuban socialist revolution in 1959 converted North American cold-war diplomacy into a day-to-day element in U.S.-Latin American relations, and in relations between Latin American countries themselves:

It was the Caribbean that made the cold war a reality in Latin America. Events in two small nations—Guatemala and Cuba—altered the terms of battle in the hemisphere. In both, a non-communist revolution was taken over by the communists or, as Cuban Marxists would argue, was driven by the "objective conditions" (i.e., the contradiction between imperialism and national freedom and social justice) into socialism. In both nations, the United States sought to overthrow the resultant regime. In Guatemala the effort was a success; in Cuba it was a resounding failure.[18]

Since then, the existence of a socialist state in Cuba has been amply discussed and manipulated by North American and Latin American governments. Since the Cuban revolution, more than was previously the case, these governments have sought to play down their controversies and strengthen their internal positions. As far as possible, they have tried to capitalize on the threat of "international communism" as an element with which to unify their interests at a hemispheric level. It could be said that Latin American political, economic, and military problems began to develop as continental issues much more widely and rapidly after 1959. Multilateral inter-American organizations for analysis and decision-making regarding political, economic, military, business, religious, cultural, scientific, labor, and other problems have proliferated since that date. To a large extent, these organizations are a condition and a consequence of the unification and systematization of the continental ruling classes' interests—within the requirements of North American hegemony. The creation of a socialist state in Latin America revealed the following aspects of Latin American reality to the governments and people of the hemisphere:

In the first place, it demonstrated that socialism, as a political strategy of economic, social, and cultural development, is not foreign to Latin American reality. It became clear, in other words, that Latin America is a part of "Western civilization." In the final analysis, socialism as theory and practice was a product of the internal contradictions in capitalism.

[18]Raymond Carr, "The Cold War in Latin America," in John Plank, ed., *Cuba and the United States,* The Brookings Institution (Washington: 1967), pp. 158–77, quote p. 163. See also Robert N. Burr, ed., *Latin America's Nationalistic Revolutions,* special number of *The Annals of the American Academy of Political and Social Science* (Philadelphia), vol. 334, 1961; Adolf A. Berle, *Latin America—Diplomacy and Reality* (New York: 1962); Herbert L. Matthews, ed., *The United States and Latin America,* The American Assembly (New York: 1959).

Meanwhile, the North American government campaign to represent the Cuban revolution as something restricted to the exotic, adventuresome Caribbean, was a failure. After 1959, then, socialism became a real factor in inter-American relations, something that actually happened and might happen again.

Second, it became clear to both governments and peoples that class contradictions in certain Latin American countries had significantly increased. Both social reforms and political repression were influenced to greater or lesser degree by this increasing level of class struggle. The Punta del Este Conference in August 1961, the Charter, and the Alliance that was subsequently created were all continental responses to the first socialist experience in Latin America and to the growing class antagonisms in the hemisphere. At Punta del Este, the Cuban delegate made the following observations:

Cuba believes that this is a political conference; Cuba does not accept the separation of economy and politics. They constantly go hand in hand. That is why there is no such thing as an expert who just talks technology, when a people's destiny is in question. I will explain why this is a political conference: It is a political conference because it has been conceived against Cuba, against the example that Cuba represents for the entire American continent.[19]

The interests of the ruling classes naturally intensified and united across the continent; and the conferences, pacts, treaties, and multilateral organizations spread. In the same way, many coups in Latin America since 1959 have been justified as a response to the threat of the "foreign enemy" allied with the "internal enemy."

Third, the circumstances and development of the socialist revolution in Cuba reveal the decisive role that imperialism can play both in its containment and in its intensification. Note the curious pendulum movement of North American imperialism in Latin America. In 1954, the U.S. intervenes in Guatemala, taking a decisive part in the overthrow of President Arbenz. In 1959, confused by the developing Cuban revolution, the U.S. relies on the local subordinate bourgeoisie. In 1965, fearing a repetition of the Cuban experience, it intervenes in the Dominican Republic. In 1970, the U.S. is confused again by policies of the socialist government in Chile, relies on local allies, on the intrinsically capitalist character of the existing representative democracy, and on its own ca-

---

[19] Ernesto Guevara, speech at the Meeting of the Inter-American Economic and Social Council in Punta del Este, Uruguay, unabridged transcription in *Ciencias Políticas y Sociales* (Mexico City), vol. 7, no. 25, 1961, pp. 445–77; quotation p. 446. The political significance of the Alliance for Progress, with respect to Cuba, socialism, and class contradictions in Latin America, are analyzed by Schlesinger, *A Thousand Days,* esp. chaps. 7 and 8; J. Warren Nystrom and Nathan A. Haverstock, *The Alliance for Progress* (Princeton, N.J.: 1966); Lincoln Gordon, *A New Deal for Latin America—The Alliance for Progress* (Cambridge, Mass.: 1963).

pacity to exert pressures from outside. The ambiguity implicit in this pendulum movement is expressed in a two-point summary of the analysis of Chile by ITT (International Telephone and Telegraph Company) in November 1970:

1. The view by Chilean conservatives, now trying to make deals with Allende, that U.S. economic and political reprisals will force Allende farther to the left is a correct assessment. It ignores a fact, however, that whether or not he likes it, Allende will be forced far to the left eventually regardless of what policy Washington adopts.
2. The view among [those of] another sector that U.S. reprisals will force Allende into the left-wing extremist camp and that this will trigger a popular and military reaction against his government has little merit. The military has shown no disposition to act in the clutch. There is little reason to believe their mood has changed. It is even questionable that they have the capacity to handle the kind of massive nationwide reaction the far left can mount: general strikes, urban guerrilla warfare. Time is swiftly eroding the military capacity to move against the Allende coalition, even in defense of the Constitution, if such a moral issue arises.[20]

This ambiguity seems to be inherent to imperialism. To the extent that domination is not and cannot be monolithic, the national and international ruling class splits into antagonistic factions; and as a result, imperialism frequently loses its perspective on how its interests are best served, or misinterprets the meaning of events. In concentrating all its attention and resources on the menace of "international communism," it is unable to understand the real character of increasing class antagonisms in the hemisphere. Imperialism takes ideology for the reality of things.

The U.S. attitude to Latin America has therefore normally been based on the belief that without the intervention of global factors, U.S. power is virtually absolute, and Latin American forces alone are feeble to the point of being negligible. Yet a more careful analysis of hemispheric relations, and occasional bitter experience, suggest the opposite. U.S. power is limited, and any attempt to exceed those limits leads to defeat or failure. To be more accurate, while the power of the U.S. economy is overwhelming and remains decisive, its political (and military) power is not. Moreover, even the immense force of U.S. capital is to some extent at the mercy of political forces which Washington cannot override.[21]

[20] *Documentos Secretos de la ITT,* photocopies of the originals in English and their translations in Spanish, Empresa Editora Nacional Quimantú Ltd. (Santiago: 1972), p. 85.

[21] E. J. Hobsbawm, "Latin America as the U.S. Empire Cracks," *The New York Review of Books* (New York), vol. 16, no. 5, March 25, 1971, pp. 3–9, quotation p. 4. Some aspects of imperialism's active role in the formation of Cuban socialism were examined by William Appleman Williams, *The United States, Cuba and Castro* (New York: 1962); J. P. Morray, *The Second Revolution in Cuba* (New York: 1962). For an analysis of the central concerns and policies of North American governments with respect to leftist movements and political parties in Latin America before 1959, see Robert J. Alexander, *Communism in Latin America* (New Brunswick, N.J.: 1957); Matthews, *United States and Latin America;* Ronald M. Schneider, *Communism in Guatemala (1944–1954)* (New York: 1958).

As we have seen, the September 1970 victory of the socialist candidate in the Chilean elections is another indication of the ambiguities and failures of imperialism in Latin America. The event was a new factor, an exception to the rule in U.S.-Latin American relations and relations between Latin American countries themselves.

The political, social, economic, and cultural program of the Allende government is the expression of an emerging new power structure in Chile. In addition to carrying out land reform and initiating a new policy of income redistribution, the Allende government nationalized foreign companies, from the mines to the banks. Under the Popular Unity Government program, Chile's foreign policy is that of an incipient socialist state. (The Popular Unity is a coalition of predominantly leftist parties that form the political base of the government.) The following are some of the basic goals of the socialist diplomacy inaugurated by the Allende government in 1970:

The international policy of the popular government will be directed toward affirming the complete political and economic autonomy of Chile.

There will be diplomatic relations with all the countries of the world, irrespective of their ideological and political position, on the basis of respect for self-determination and the interests of the people of Chile . . . .

The position of active defense of Chilean independence implies denouncing the OAS as an instrument and agency of North American imperialism and to struggle against all forms of Pan-Americanism implicit in this organization. The popular government will opt for the creation of an organism that is truly representative of Latin American countries.

It is considered indispensable to revise, denounce, and ignore, according to individual cases, the treaties or agreements that mean compromises, that limit our sovereignty, and concretely the treaties of reciprocal assistance, the mutual assistance pacts, and other pacts that Chile has signed with the United States.[22]

According to the Allende government, a foreign policy must contribute to the construction of socialism in Chile; it is necessary to evaluate the positions of nonaligned nations and to practice active solidarity with the struggles of Asian and African peoples against all forms of dependency. Meanwhile, such a foreign policy establishes guidelines for the emancipation of Latin America from the tutelage of North American diplomacy.

We would like the Organization of American States, as part of the United Nations system, to act as a complementary regional organization for facilitating dialogue between the United States and Latin America. We believe that the future of the OAS depends on its ability to go beyond the original tenets of the organization; it must not base its actions on more or less tacit assumptions that hide and falsify reality.

[22] "UP Program of Government," in *New Chile*, prepared and edited by North American Congress on Latin America (NACLA) (New York: 1972), pp. 130–43, quotation pp. 141f.

In the first place, it is an illusion that 23 states meet here as equals.
In the second place, it is an illusion that these states have homogeneous interests, objectives, and ideals.
There is an enormous difference in power between the United States and each of our Latin American countries. It is impossible to work efficiently, truthfully, constructively, if we assume that we are all equal.
Northern and southern interests are so obviously in conflict in various aspects of political and economic life that it becomes impossible to build anything solid and lasting if we insist on distorting reality.[23]

Chilean foreign policy has clearly taken an unusual route under the Allende government. In addition to clarifying the concrete objectives of the socialist government, Chilean foreign policy has tried to discard assumptions or practices that contradict the interests of the wage-earning classes. Foreign policy adopts the viewpoint of these classes, not the bourgeoisie's. That is why setting goals for Chilean diplomacy implies critical tasks, avoids the conventional, and enters into polemical areas. This was particularly clear in President Salvador Allende's speech at the inauguration of the United Nations Conference on Trade and Development, UNCTAD III, which took place in Santiago during April and May 1972.

If the analyses and conclusions of UNCTAD III are to be realistic and revealing, we must confront the world as it is, defend ourselves from illusions and mystifications, while at the same time seeking imaginative, creative solutions to our old problems.
First, it is clear that our community is not homogeneous, that it is fragmented into rich and poor nations. We must realize, moreover, that even among poor countries—unfortunately—some are poorer than others, and conditions in many are insufferable. Foreign powers dominate their economy; foreigners occupy part or all of their territory; they still live under the colonial yoke—and in some cases the majority of their population is subjugated to the violence of racism and apartheid. In many of our societies there are profound social differences which crush the masses while benefiting small privileged groups.
Second, it is clear that we poor countries are subsidizing the rich countries with our resources and our labor. It is not our intention to enumerate injustices here, but rather to prove that the present structure of international trade has become an instrument for exploiting, for bleeding the less developed countries.[24]

Under the Allende government, then, an independent foreign policy is based on the program of a burgeoning socialist state; and at the same time it becomes a necessary condition of this program. The nonviolent route to socialism requires great structural changes in foreign as well as

---

[23] Clodomiro Almeyda, Chilean Minister of Foreign Relations, in a speech at the General Assembly of the Organization of American States (OAS), April 15, 1971. Cf. transcription in *Estudios Internacionales* (Santiago), year 4, no. 16, pp. 189–98, quotation p. 194.
[24] Salvador Allende, "El deber de los pueblos es superar el régimen capitalista y avanzar por un nuevo camino," transcribed by *Desarrollo Indoamericano* (Barranquilla, Colombia), year 6, no. 18, 1972, pp. 11–16, quotation p. 12.

in domestic affairs. Note that an independent foreign policy in a capitalist state is merely the reformulation of dependency within the framework of world capitalism. On the other hand, diplomacy for the Allende government becomes an essential element for destroying the relations of dependency characteristic of capitalist economies. At the same time, diplomacy becomes a basic tool in the creation of a socialist state as a national, hegemonic entity.

Once again Latin American governments are forced to recognize that imperialism cannot always successfully combat the development of class struggle. With the victory of the socialist government in Chile, it also became clear that "representative democracy" does not necessarily prevent the working class from taking power. Once again, Latin American governments saw that the so-called national bourgeoisie is incapable of confronting the salaried classes, particularly the politically organized proletariat. So long as it accepts its subordinate role with respect to imperialism, the bourgeoisie will confuse its contradictions with the proletariat and with imperialism, and it will end by defeating its own purposes.

In conclusion, then, socialism is no longer foreign to political, economic, military, and intellectual reality in Latin America. Two socialist governments were established in Latin America in a period of eleven years, from 1959 to 1970. Cuba, in the Caribbean, had previously been totally integrated into the imperialist system. There, the socialist state was created by means of a revolution against the repressive capitalist state co-governed by dictator Fulgencio Batista and U.S. imperialism. On the continent, Chile was already reformulating relations with imperialism when the Allende government took power. There, construction of the socialist state began as a consequence of an electoral process characteristic of "representative democracy"—in other words, within the framework of a democratic capitalist state. The socialist governments of Cuba and Chile are examples, then, of two political strategies for profound structural change: the revolutionary and the nonviolent. The two processes, each in its own manner, affect U.S. hegemony over the continent, and each alters diplomatic relations between Latin American countries.

Ideological Monolithism

Latin American political and economic forces, whose interests have been constrained by populist governments and damaged by socialist governments, are in general organized both nationally and continentally. The consolidation of forces accelerated after 1959 in reaction against the Cuban socialist revolution. Thus the Cuban experience, which was viewed as an example of the possible outcome of class struggle all over Latin America, had to be eliminated or contained. These same forces mobilized further after the 1965 popular insurrection in the Dominican Republic and the victory of socialist candidate Salvador Allende in the September 1970 presidential elections in Chile.

On the continental level, these forces continue to draw support from the Inter-American Treaty of Reciprocal Assistance (Rio Pact), approved at the 1947 Inter-American Conference (August–September, Rio de Janeiro); and from the OAS Charter, approved at the Ninth Conference of American States (March–May 1948, Bogotá). These documents were revised and complemented with other pacts and treaties in later years. In crisis situations the doctrine of hemispheric interdependence and security established therein has been reinterpreted and fortified to conform to the ruling classes' interests.

This was the case, for example, during the 1965 insurrection in the Dominican Republic. Directed by the U.S. Government, certain Latin American states decided to organize an Interamerican Peace Force, intervene in the country, crush the rebellion, and set up a government which fit better with the doctrine of hemispheric interdependence and security. Thus, on May 6, 1965, thirteen Latin American governments approved the creation of a joint military force to "restore peace and democracy in the Dominican Republic."[25] All of this took place *after* President Lyndon B. Johnson's April 28th decision authorizing the U.S. Marine landing in Santo Domingo "to restore public order in that country."[26] The U.S. Government and its Dominican allies had lost control of the masses; the popular movement had to be crushed. Accordingly, the U.S. Government decided that military intervention, with verbal support or troops from some Latin American governments, was the best way to prevent "international communism" from destroying the "hopes of Dominican democracy."[27]

Note that the majority of Latin American countries had—for several decades—been demanding that North American diplomacy be based on the principle of nonintervention. In 1933, at the Montevideo Conference of American States, the U.S. Government first accepted the principle of nonintervention in the internal affairs of the hemisphere. President Franklin D. Roosevelt was inaugurating his Good Neighbor diplomacy;

[25] James R. Jose, *An Inter-American Peace Force Within the Framework of the Organization of American States: Advantages, Impediments, Implications* (Metuchen, N.J.: 1970), esp. pp. 106–7.
[26] Abraham F. Lowenthal, *The Dominican Intervention* (Cambridge, Mass.: 1972), p. 104.
[27] Lowenthal, *Dominican Intervention;* Tad Szulc, *Revolución en Santo Domingo,* Ediciones Cid (Madrid: 1966); Gregorio Ortega, *Santo Domingo 1965,* Ediciones Venceremos (La Habana: 1965); Theodore Draper, "The Dominican Crisis," *Commentary* (New York), December 1965; Larman C. Wilson, "Estados Unidos y la guerra civil dominicana," *Foro Internacional,* no. 30, El Colegio de México, 1967.

but that did not prevent U.S. governments from interfering in internal
Latin American affairs. The circumstances and justifications varied:

In 1933 we agreed not to intervene in the political affairs of Latin American states.
Now we are intervening. Why? Because since 1959 the American family has been
faced with a reality that it could not have foreseen in 1933. Fidel Castro himself
stated that his revolution is not Cuban and that the regime established in his country is not unique to that country. It is a Marxist-Leninist regime. The Soviet Union
and Communist China, atomic powers, intervened in America through their Cuban
satellite. It is an extracontinental, military intervention. My government believes it
important to stress that international communism is the most serious threat in Latin
America today.[28]

For North America and several Latin American governments, intervention is justifiable, necessary, and urgent, as long as class antagonisms
challenge the power of the ruling class or the capitalist state. Even the
existence of some nationalist, popular-based governments preoccupies
certain other Latin American governments. The preoccupations become
real worries when a government turns populist. When the Chilean socialist government was inaugurated in 1970, certain countries in the hemisphere took all kinds of measures to protect themselves from the threat
to "the security of the Western Hemisphere."

Some Latin American governments have clearly been ambiguous in
supporting and condemning intervention—even military intervention—at
one and the same time. They favor nonintervention in controversies between factions of the ruling class, on either the national or the international level. Meanwhile, when class contradictions begin to challenge the
power structure, they try to link themselves with the ruling classes of
the United States and of other Latin American countries, so as to "restore public order." Frequently, if not always, the U.S. Government has
the best information and is best prepared to analyze the "seriousness of
the situation," and to propose solutions and put them into action.

This ideological monolithism is based on the same economic, political, military, and cultural bipolarism that U.S. governments have disseminated throughout the hemisphere during the period of cold war diplomacy. But it is not pure coincidence that some Latin American governments continue to base their diplomacy on bipolarism—a position basic
to the sharpest phase of the cold war—despite U.S. efforts to change to
a diplomacy of peaceful coexistence.

In the first place, ideological monolithism corresponds perfectly to
the combined interests of most Latin American ruling classes. They use
it to broaden and consolidate their political power over other classes.

[28] Ambassador Averell Harriman, "O Surpreendente Diálogo Frei-Harriman no Chile," in *Política Externa Independente* (Rio de Janeiro), no. 2, August 1965, pp. 262–64.

Also, ideological monolithism tends to develop even further as class contradictions sharpen internally and externally. The followers of this ideology are forced to condemn even "representative democracy," especially
for tolerating political forces that stand for structural change, i.e. for
radical modifications in the structures of power. Thus a Brazilian editorial of 1970:

The first act of foreign policy under the new Chilean government was the renewal
of diplomatic relations with Cuba. There is nothing surprising about this, since the
socialist solidarity forged by the Communist International is a reality. Moreover, in
addition to measures taken later in order that Latin America become the principal
front of the cold war, what Salvador Allende acclaimed as an "independent, self-
determined, and revolutionary act" had really been prepared by the "Christian Democrat" government of Eduardo Frei . . . .

Castro's defiance of traditional Latin American values, up until now Quijotesque,
becomes a real danger today . . . . The Havana-Santiago axis, which appears to be
extending to Lima and La Paz, is a direct threat to the rest of Latin America, a serious challenge to the "status quo," continental politics, and the *traditional* cultural
and political values of Brazil.[29]

This is the ruling classes' position in a period of sharpening class contradictions on national and international levels. From this basically monolithic viewpoint, the Subregional Andean Integration Agreement signed
in 1969 by Bolivia, Chile, Colombia, Ecuador, and Peru has been met
with reservation and even hostility. It disturbs governments that favor
the integration of the Latin American economy according to the requirements of private multinational corporations, especially those based in
the United States. To the extent that Chile forms part of the Andean
bloc, and because the Allende government has chosen a socialist strategy
for economic, social, political, and cultural development, the proponents
of ideological monolithism reacted by taking the offensive. They believe that renewal of diplomatic relations between Santiago and Havana
threatens "to subvert all inter-American values and institutions." They
demand that governments of the hemisphere intensify the struggle for
continental interdependence and security. Again, a Brazilian editorial:

The Andean Pact was originally planned as a subregional common market; but, under
the influence of revolutionary warfare, it will eventually acquire political and ideological content—a content that is combative and expansionist and which runs counter
to four centuries of Latin American cultural and historical identity . . . . Chile is

[29] "Desafiados o Brasil e o Continente," editorial in *O Estado de São Paulo,* November 14,
1970, p. 3. Some geopolitical elements of this style of thought are summed up by General Golbery do Couto e Silva, *Geopolítica do Brasil,* Livraria José Olympio Editôra (Rio de Janeiro:
1967); Oliveiros S. Ferreira, "O Brasil e a Crise Continental," *O Estado de São Paulo,* November
15, 1970, p. 6; Ferreira, "O Cêrco, a Fé e as Obras," *O Estado de São Paulo,* March 21, 1971,
p. 6.

attempting to take over continental leadership in order to subvert all inter-American values and institutions, whose principal guardian is now Brazil. . . .

What makes the situation worse in Latin America is the power vacuum in the hemisphere created by the U.S. "low profile" policy. For various reasons, discussed many times in our columns, the U.S. has been surprisingly unresponsive to attacks from and the partial successes of its principal adversary, the Soviet Union. Meanwhile, there are some undeniable advantages for Brazil in this situation. Brazil offers a complementary and alternative argument that regional powers now finally have a chance to claim and exercise what have always been their rights based on their power, geography, numbers, and economic and technological progress.[30]

In other words, the emphasis on "foreign subversion" as the instigator of "internal subversion" is politically, ideologically, and practically the best way to transform (internal) class antagonisms into (international) diplomatic antagonisms. By thinking and acting this way, those skilled in this type of diplomacy reveal—in their own special language—the international character of class contradictions. When they identify external subversion with internal, and the external enemy with the internal, they identify and affirm the generality of their own interests. This is an inevitable consequence of the continentalization of Latin American power structures, polarized—in turn—around the doctrine of hemispheric interdependence and security.

In the second place, ideological monolithism rather successfully safeguards the interests of the U.S. Government and U.S.-based multinational companies operating in Latin America. Monolithic diplomacy clearly seems anachronistic when President Richard Nixon is promoting the diplomacy of peaceful coexistence. We should remember, however, that U.S. global diplomacy has been forced to confront unfamiliar, unexpected, unpleasant situations, even in the Western Hemisphere. Since 1968 it has had to deal with an unusual economic nationalism in Peru. And since 1970 it has had to confront the foreign and domestic policy of the Chilean socialist government. Faced with these and other problems, North American governments have tried to maintain cold-war diplomacy on the continent, while promoting peaceful coexistence in other areas. It was not just by chance that U.S. Government interests coincided with ITT's with respect to the foreign and domestic economic measures adopted by the Allende government. In the section on North American policy in Latin America in his February 1972 Message on the State of the World, President Nixon protested the nationalization and "unsatisfactory" indemnification of U.S. copper companies. He deplored the fact that economic nationalism was obstructing "mutually beneficial relations between states." In other words, he was speaking simultaneously for the Government and for ITT.

---

[30] "O Brasil Passa a Ofensiva," editorial in *O Estado de São Paulo,* November 29, 1970, p. 3.

We and other public and private sources of development investment will take account of whether or not the Chilean Government meets its international obligations.[31]

To the extent that the terms of this statement conceal a thinly veiled threat, we can say that in February 1972 President Nixon made official the governmental policy proposed by ITT in October 1970 following Allende's victory in the Chilean elections. One of the conglomerate's proposals was for systematization of U.S. pressures against Chile.

Without informing President Allende, all U.S. aid funds already committed to Chile should be placed in the "under review" status in order that entry of money into Chile is temporarily stopped with a view to a permanent cutoff if necessary. This includes "funds in the pipeline," "letters of credit," or any such.[32]

In 1972 the Allende government, by now hurt by the international economic boycott, made a public accusation on July 24. It was also forced to take measures to reduce the effects of the embargoes ordered by the U.S. Government under the pretext of unsatisfactory indemnification to nationalized U.S. copper companies. According to a statement by Vice-President Jorge Arrate of the Copper Corporation (CODELCO), Chile transferred her banking accounts from the United States to Europe in order to avoid new embargoes. He added:

We are taking emergency measures because we fear further embargoes of national property in the United States in the near future. We have not seen the end of the reprisals of the North American companies against the special Chilean court ruling.[33]

As we can see, ideological monolithism is not abstract. It takes the form of concrete decisions and acts that interfere directly in the foreign and domestic affairs of any nation that seeks to solve its problems outside the framework of imperialism.

The North American Most-Favored-Ally Policy

Economic, political, military, scientific, religious, academic, and labor relations between the United States and the rest of the hemisphere are generally strengthened, weakened, or reoriented according to new or unexpected problems that arise on the continent. Thus, "hemispheric security," "inter-American solidarity," "mature partnership," and similar

[31] Richard M. Nixon, *U.S. Foreign Policy for the 1970's: The Emerging Structure of Peace.* A Report to the Congress, Washington, February 1972.

[32] *Documentos Secretos de la ITT,* quotation p. 81. *Time* stated that "[ITT President Harold] Geneen has built ITT into the eighth largest U.S.-based industrial concern and the biggest of all multinational conglomerates." From "The Clubby World of ITT," *Time* (New York), March 27, 1972, p. 40.

[33] From the transcription "Frei Considera Grave a Atual Situação do Chile," *O Estado de São Paulo,* August 15, 1972, p. 5. See also, "Allende Denuncia o Cêrco Econômico," *O Estado de São Paulo,* July 25, 1972, p. 8.

slogans have been used to affirm and reaffirm U.S. hegemony in Latin America. On another level, the U.S. governments have employed bilateralism and multilateralism in order to safeguard their interests and take advantage of the animosities and ambitions of Latin American governments. Let us take a look now at the concept of the most favored ally—another move in the diplomatic game of U.S. relations with Latin America.

First, it is important to review some of the main problems of inter-American relations, for they are at the root of most-favored-ally diplomacy. Then we will be able to understand what the real rules of the game are, and how the U.S. governments utilize the leadership ambitions of various Latin American countries.

There are perhaps three countries in the area south of us, Mexico, Argentina, and Brazil, that may be serious powers in the near future. . . .

We must be prepared publicly to discover that some places in the hemisphere are more important to us than others. Some, in fact, may not even be of great importance to us. We might even understand, not merely that Mexico, Brazil, and Argentina are more important than Barbados, Nicaragua, and Paraguay, but also that our relations with the three bigger countries shape our image far more than do our relations with others in the hemisphere.[34]

The United States was clearly confronted with new, unexpected problems in its relations with Latin American countries. Particularly important are events that reveal the emergence of new political strategies for the organization of economic, political, social, and cultural development—strategies constituting an escape from North American hegemony. Some of the events in question were mentioned earlier in this essay, but we shall reexamine them here in a different light.

In the first place, from a historical point of view, we must remember that several Latin American countries are taking their first steps toward economic emancipation. The sporadic economic nationalism and independent foreign policy of Argentina, Brazil, Mexico, and Peru are examples of government efforts toward political emancipation by way of economic emancipation. Populist governments have tried to strengthen national autonomy in economic decisions, and to promote national capitalism by increasing state activity. Political regimes whose diplomacy is based on economic nationalism and independent foreign policy have been called populist, Bonapartist, militarist, Nasserist, and third-world governments. The political and economic nationalism typical of such regimes is a central topic of the analyses and recommendations of the Rockefeller Report:

[34] Bronheim, "Inter-American Relations," pp. 116–21.

This national sensitivity has been fed by the fact that, in the other American republics, U.S. management, capital, and highly advertised products have played a disproportionately visible role. A high percentage of overseas investment has come from the United States, principally to seek raw materials or to preserve markets.

The forces of nationalism are creating increasing pressures against foreign private investment. The impetus for independence from the United States is leading toward rising pressures for nationalization of U.S. industry, local control, or participation with U.S. firms. Most economists and businessmen in the other American republics recognize the clear need for U.S. capital and technology, but they want them on terms consistent with their desire for self-determination.[35]

In the second place, U.S. hegemony has been confronted with anti-imperialist blocs. From 1945 to 1955, the Perón government tried to lead a "justicialista" bloc of the "little countries" (Bolivia, Chile, Paraguay, and Uruguay) bordering on Argentina. The bloc was anti-imperialist, intended to lessen dependency on the United States; but at the same time it was designed to affirm Argentina's hegemony with respect to Brazil. These two equally important goals still reappear frequently in Argentine diplomacy, a diplomacy particularly sensitive to Brazilian initiatives toward countries of the Rio de la Plata Basin.[36]

Since 1969, the countries of the Subregional Andean Integration Agreement, or the Andean Pact, have also tried to construct an anti-imperialist bloc. The conditions here were obviously not the same as in the Peronist era, and so the bloc came to defend the Bolivian, Chilean, Colombian, Ecuadorian, and Peruvian national economies from uncontrolled penetration by foreign capital and technology. Together, the countries of the Andean Pact have taken steps, first, to confront imperialism, and second, to protect themselves from the national and international companies located in Argentina, Brazil, and Mexico. Companies in those countries, particularly U.S.-based multinational companies, enjoy special privileges and have obtained the best negotiating positions in the Latin American Free Trade Association. This explains the nationalism, the two-pronged anti-imperialism, of the Andean countries' agreements: the Bogotá Declaration (1966), the Cartagena Agreement (1969), and Decision No. 24 (1970). But the documents are doubly anti-imperialist, because they are designed to protect the economy of the Andean countries against the

[35] Rockefeller, *Rockefeller Report,* p. 29. See also the analysis of political power and the military, pp. 32–33.
[36] Connell-Smith, *Inter-American System,* pp. 28–29; Oscar H. Camilión, "As Relações entre o Brasil e a Argentina no Mundo Atual," *Revista Brasileira de Política Internacional* (Rio de Janeiro), year 12, no. 45/46, 1969, pp. 26–43 (in the same number see other articles on the Rio de la Plata Basin); Alberto Tamer, "Trigo e Rios Impedem Entendimento no Prata," *O Estado de São Paulo,* August 19, 1971, p. 100; "Bolívia Apoia Tese do Brasil no Prata," *O Estado de São Paulo,* February 2, 1972, p. 9; "Prata Discute sua Integração," *O Estado de São Paulo,* August 15, 1972, p. 1.

privileged conditions enjoyed by (1) U.S.-based multinational corporations and investors *and* (2) those in Argentina, Brazil, and Mexico. Confronted with the dominant position of these companies and investors, the
"little countries" of the Andean Pact joined forces and created decision-
making structures in order to defend their national economies, and the
political and economic future of their development and autonomy.

We believe that private foreign capital can considerably benefit Latin American economic development, so long as it stimulates the capital growth of the country where
it is based; and so long as it allows for ample participation of national capital in development, and does not create obstacles to regional integration.[37]

Foreign capital and technology can play an important part in subregional development and complement national effort to the extent that they make an effective contribution toward integration and fulfillment of national developmental plans.[38]

In the third place, U.S. dominance in Latin America often conflicts
with the "big countries'" interests, as the latter attempt to rule their
neighbors or control decision-making in inter-American affairs. As we
have seen, the anti-imperialist, "justicialista" bloc headed by the Perón
government in Argentina included a plan for controlling the "little countries" bordering on Argentina. Other Argentine governments, before and
after Perón, have adopted this kind of diplomacy. On various occasions,
they have tried to upset the equilibrium of, or anticipate, Brazilian diplomacy, which in turn historically reflects the leadership ambitions of
several governments. This is one of the basic reasons for the diplomacy
of "ideological pluralism" adopted by the government of General Alejan-
dro Lanusse. Confronted with the "ideological monolithism" practiced
by the U.S. in Latin America, supported by several Latin American governments, and facing nearby populist, nationalist, and socialist experience, the government of Argentina chose to practice ideological pluralism
in its relations with South American countries.

Some students of inter-American relations interpret certain moves of
Brazilian diplomacy as an attempt to expand Brazilian supremacy in
South America. Of these, some use geopolitical arguments, contending
that Brazilian hegemony is implicit in Brazil's common borders with

---

[37] *Declaración de Bogotá,* August 16, 1966, from the unabridged transcription in the *Acuerdo
de Integración Subregional Andina* (Lima: 1969), ed. Banco Industrial del Perú, pp. 56–67, quotation p. 66.
[38] *Decision No. 24,* in which the Andean Pact countries establish uniform regulations for foreign capital in the form of trademarks, patents, royalties, and preferences. For an analysis of political and economic problems of Andean Pact countries, see also: Miguel S. Wionczek, *Inversión
y tecnología extranjera en América Latina,* Joaquín Mortiz (Mexico City: 1971), esp. chaps. 3
and 4; Claudio Veliz, "Cambio y continuidad: El Pacto Andino en la historia contemporánea,"
Estudios Internacionales (Santiago), year 4, no. 16, pp. 62–92.

many "little countries." These countries need economic resources and technical aid in order to solve economic and social problems which in turn cause internal political instability. The arguments for this thesis are reinforced by the "encirclement doctrine," which asserts that Brazilian security and economic growth cannot risk instability and subversion in the smaller South American countries. And finally, they remind us that Brazil must fill the "power vacuum" left by the United States on the continent. Despite differences in language, this thesis on Brazilian diplomacy is based on arguments similar to those frequently used by North American governments—hemispheric security, interdependence, common historical traditions, the threat of international communism, defense of Christian, Western civilization (in the Latin American version), and other semantic variations. A second thesis is that Brazilian hegemony in South America is directly related to the country's economy. Its supporters contend that the new phase in Brazilian economic development can succeed only through exportation of merchandise, capital, business experience, and ideas about the solidarity and interdependence of Latin American economic subsystems, etc., to countries that are deficient in these resources. But it is clear that these interpretations are really two sides of the same basic conception of Brazilian hegemony in South America. It is often impossible to separate geopolitical and economic explanations, as we can see from the following:

The expansion and modernization of our industry, together with increased exports of manufactured goods, will definitely help strengthen the country's political position on the continent. Experience the whole world over during the last fifty years had amply established the intimate correlation between industrial development, political power, and the capacity to defend national interests efficiently and energetically from possible foreign enemies. Brazil will soon be able to participate as an equal "in the assembly of the great nations" because the government and the private sector have created a dynamic industrial sector.[39]

[39] "Indústria e Posição Continental," editorial in *O Estado de São Paulo,* May 13, 1971, p. 3. See also do Couto e Silva, *Geopolítica;* Ferreira, works cited; "Duvidar do Brasil É Desunir as Américas," *O Estado de São Paulo,* February 1, 1971, p. 1; Gilberto Paim, "Imperialismo do Brasil Provoca Temor," *O Estado de São Paulo,* May 7, 1972, p. 75; *Revista Brasileira de Estudos Políticos* (Belo Horizonte, Brazil), special number on National Security, no. 21, 1966; *ibid.,* special number on Major International Political Problems Today, no. 32, 1971; J. A. de Araújo Castro, "Uma América Latina em Mudança num Mundo em Mudança," *Digesto Econômico* (São Paulo), no. 224, 1972; de Araújo Castro, "O Congelamento do Poder Mundial," *Revista Brasileira de Estudos Políticos* (Belo Horizonte, Brazil), no. 33, 1972; *Brasil 1969,* Center for Inter-American Relations (New York: 1969); Celso Lafer, "Política de Blocos, Segurança e Desenvolvimento: uma Perspectiva Brasileira," *Revista de Administração de Emprêsas* (São Paulo), vol. 12, no. 2, 1972; Oscar Camilión, "As Relações entre o Brasil e a Argentina no Mundo Atual"; José Goldenberg, "Brasil, Argentina e Energia Atômica," 1 and 2, *O Estado de São Paulo,* June 25 and 27, 1972; "Cuenca de Plata: Unión o División," *The Economist para América Latina* (London), May 15, 1968, pp. 22–24; Herval Faria, "Médici e Lanusse Podem Acertar o Passo,"

Fourth, and finally, North American supremacy on the continent is confronted with the existence of two socialist states—one already constituted in Cuba, and the other in the process of establishing itself in Chile. Thus U.S. supremacy faces new and difficult problems. The formation of socialist governments in the hemisphere shows that: (1) class contradictions and class struggle have advanced a great deal, sufficiently to make possible the replacement of a capitalist state by a socialist state; (2) socialism, as a political strategy of economic, social, and cultural development, is compatible with "Western civilization" in the hemisphere; and (3) the two governments are examples of two different models of transition to socialism—the revolutionary and the peaceful.

In sum, these are some of the most important diplomatic problems confronting the United States and the hemisphere. Historically, North American governments have reacted in different ways when confronted with such challenges. From the dollar to the big stick, through civic action, low profile, and mature partnership, the models for diplomacy have been numerous and flexible. One now stands out among the rest: the diplomacy of the most favored ally. Let us see what it consists of.

As we understand it, most-favored-ally diplomacy has come to be an inherent part of U.S. hegemony over countries with different levels of economic, industrial, military, political, cultural, and demographic development. It is not a recent invention, but rather part of the bilateral orientation that has always been an important element in North American diplomacy. This diplomacy has always manipulated the animosities and ambitions of Latin American governments in their relations with each other as well as with the United States.

In addition, the most-favored-ally policy plays off countries in different states of dependency. For example, in order to build the confidence of foreign capital and investors in the national economy, governments compete to establish law and order and maintain the safest, most stable conditions. This kind of competition improves conditions for North American investors. At the same time, it consolidates and may even improve the position of local governments with respect to the social classes that are not represented in the state apparatus. In other words, the most-favored-ally policy both strengthens the national bourgeoisie's domestic position while assuring its international subordination.[40]

O Estado de São Paulo, March 2, 1972, p. 15; José Carlos de Andrade, "O Modelo Brasileiro É Aplicado em La Paz," *O Estado de São Paulo,* March 30, 1972, p. 7; Rodolfo Schmidt, "Brasil Tem 'Status' de Potência Militar na América Latina," *O Estado de São Paulo,* February 24, 1972, p. 14.

[40] Tools for sociological and political analysis of the national bourgeoisies can be found in Pablo González Casanova, *Sociología de la explotación,* México Siglo XXI (Mexico City: 1969); Octavio Ianni, *Imperialismo y cultura de la violencia en América Latina,* México Siglo XXI (Me-

These are some of the implications of the mature partnership policy, the partnership between unequals. On this level, the most-favored-ally policy is an efficient and flexible technique conducive to safeguarding U.S. supremacy in relations with "the three greats" in Latin America— Argentina, Brazil, and Mexico. As we saw earlier, the diplomatic history of these countries shows that on several occasions their governments have opted to form blocs as a means of establishing their own hegemony.

In addition, most-favored-ally diplomacy permits United States governments to delegate duties and responsibilities. It is a politically convenient way of practicing so-called "benign neglect" and "low profile" diplomacy in relations with dependent countries in general, and especially with the "little countries." Moreover, it conveniently diminishes direct, visible U.S. presence. As an important part of North American foreign policy, especially at the doctrinal or ideological level, one or more countries had to present themselves as candidates to fill the "power vacuum" left by the United States in Latin America. This is one of the implications of the Nixon doctrine, the "low profile"—i.e. the invisible presence. After all, United States governments and their allies on the continent understand perfectly well the significance of the increased discussions and activities in the struggle against imperialism. It is thus very important to "depoliticize" North American domination. The new form of interdependence between countries in the hemisphere becomes mature partnership, preferably within the context of multilateral organizations in which all participate formally in decision-making.[41]

It would be wrong to present most-favored-ally diplomacy as a simple imperialistic game in which the United States has free reign. United States governments use it in their relations with "the three greats"—one by one, and one against the other. And they try to control or intervene in these countries' relations with the "little countries" wherever they can. But that is not the end of it.

The truth is that imperialism is forced to confront the contradictions inherent in domination. Imperialism creates unfavorable as well as favorable conditions for domination. For example, at one level, production and appropriation of the national *economic surplus* are in question on a

---

xico City: 1970); André Gunder Frank, *Lumpenburguesía: Lumpendesarrollo,* Editorial Nueva Izquierda (Caracas: 1970); special number on "Imperialism and Dependency in Latin America," *Sociedad y Desarrollo* (Santiago), no. 1, 1972; *Foreign Investments in Latin America,* United Nations (New York: 1955); *Foreign Financing in Latin America,* United Nations (New York: 1964); *Estudio Económico de América Latina* (Santiago: CEPAL), vol. 2, 1970; *Estudios Especiales* (Santiago: CEPAL), mimeographed edition, 1971; Fernando Fajnzylber, "Estratégia Industrial e Emprêsas Internacionais: Posição Relativa da América Latina e do Brasil" (Rio de Janeiro), IPEA/INPES edition (relative position of Latin America and Brazil), 1971.
[41] Nixon (see notes 7, 12, 31).

world scale. Combinations or partnerships between ruling-class groups or factions thus tend to develop in national and international circles. The result is an alliance between the "national" bourgeoisie and the hegemonic bourgeoisie, strengthening imperialist domination. At the same time, however, antagonisms and struggles between groups or factions of the same ruling classes emerge to alter or weaken imperialist actions. On another level, it is production and appropriation of *profit* that is in question. In this case, contradictions and struggles develop between social classes, particularly between the proletariat on the one hand and the "national" and international bourgeoisies on the other. Here imperialist domination can be altered, weakened, and even eliminated.

Moreover, the imperialism of the United States Government and/or that of international conglomerates inevitably threatens the sovereignty of national states. Imperialist relations and structures can control the state apparatus as well as the local bourgeoisie. This becomes yet another arena of combinations and antagonisms.

As we have seen, most-favored-ally diplomacy is thus not simply a discreet maneuver, not simply a game. It emerges as a political product of the inherent contradictions of imperialist domination itself.[42]

[42] "A Hegemonia Brasileira É Obvia, Diz Lincoln Gordon," *O Estado de São Paulo*, July 12, 1972, p. 9; Joseph Novitski, "Brasil Desponta como Novo Líder Continental," *O Estado de São Paulo*, March 25, 1971, p. 6; "O Brasil Ocupa Vácuo na América Latina," *O Estado de São Paulo*, June 25, 1971, p. 42; "Brasil ou México: a Opção em Debate," *O Estado de São Paulo*, June 21, 1972, p. 14; "México Pede Conferência," *O Estado de São Paulo*, June 17, 1972, p. 6; Jeremiah O'Leary, "Nixon Tenta Dourar Pílula Brasileira para os Mexicanos," *O Estado de São Paulo*, June 16, 1972, p. 2; John Gunther, *Inside South America* (New York: 1968); "Henry Kearns Exalta o Dinamismo Brasileiro," Statement of Eximbank President Henry Kearns at the American Chamber of Commerce in São Paulo, transcribed in *O Estado de São Paulo*, September 1, 1972, p. 3.

Commentary on Ianni

MARCOS KAPLAN

This and other recent works by Octavio Ianni constitute an important effort to develop what is called "dependence theory." Given my essential agreement with Ianni's thesis, I shall concentrate on a critical examination of some limitations of the theory as it has been elaborated by a variety of individuals and groups.

Reflections on Dependence Theory

In recent years the external dependence of Latin American countries has been legitimately and correctly emphasized. The inquiry centers around development problems in the region and influences any comparison of diagnoses, solutions, and strategies; it is also a corrective to the currently inadequate focus on the international relations involved in dependence. The theory effectively questions the atomistic-mechanistic and legalistic conceptualization of international relations, and attempts to reduce the analytic dissociation between the domestic affairs of the nation-state and the workings of the international system. Thus, we may think of the internal and external workings as quantitatively but not qualitatively different, in order to reestablish the continuity, interrelationships, and interaction between them (later, I shall caution against possible distortion in the other direction).

Although the virtues of dependence theory are well known, most of its embodiments have limitations that can seriously distort the orientation and results of work already done or in progress. Preoccupation with the theory has contributed to the emergence of analytical schemes and proposals that distort the perception of reality: the theory tends to exaggerate the role of external factors and to minimize that of domestic factors; it attributes exclusive explanatory power to the external factors; and it shifts responsibility for the subordination, backwardness, and recurrent crises of the Latin American countries onto "others."

Marcos Kaplan is with the Bariloche Foundation, Buenos Aires.

Thus in one sense it is legitimate to affirm that the global interdependence system that emerged in the nineteenth and especially the twentieth centuries presents—with differences of structure and hierarchical level—an asymmetrical profile of developed-central-hegemonic countries on the one hand and underdeveloped-peripheral-subordinated countries on the other. The evolution of this worldwide system and the action of capitalist metropolises and international groups operating within it have implied the imposition of special kinds of ties on Latin American countries, their incorporation into the dynamics of developed centers and into a world market largely controlled by those centers, and the shaping and modification of internal socioeconomic, cultural, and political structures as functions of external interests, necessities, and demands. The general laws of the structure and process of the capitalist system are imposed in determinate fashion on the national societies of Latin America. The level and character of the dependence that results is influenced by the phases through which capitalist development passes in the metropolises and in the world, and by the predominance of one or another of the great powers during any given period.

But external action, though a necessary factor in the development of dependence, is not a sufficient factor; nor is it executed unilaterally, directly, mechanically, or along a single direction or dimension. It constitutes a multidimensional and multifaceted process. Dependence is therefore a relationship that presupposes two kinds of forces, one of forms and one of dynamics, in permanent interaction. Most important, this complex and variable association—especially in Latin America within the third world—gives rise to societies and nation-states that have an existence apart from the establishment or modification of dependency, that have their own sociohistorical dynamics and roots, their own productive structures, social stratifications, cultural and political forms, and particular relationships among these various factors. These domestic factors articulate and interact not only among themselves but also with external factors, over which they can in fact exert considerable influence. This internal dynamism reflects and incorporates, to be sure, the action of the metropolises and the impact of the international system, but it poses its own sociohistorical particularisms, its own peculiarities, its own special and random events; and at the same time it integrates and modifies the composition, orientation, and functioning of external actors, forces, and processes.

The internal and external actors, forces, and parameters do not always evolve with equal or convergent directions, meanings, or intensities; divergencies, tensions, and conflicts are possible. And for their part, the powers having hegemony over the dependent country also establish relations of accord, dissidence, or confrontation with other dominated national groups by means of processes that are in turn influenced by dependence.

The internal and external overlap and dialectic, then, with all their implications and consequences, influence the forms taken by socioeconomic and cultural-ideological forces and structures, the power structure, the political-institutional apparatus, and the decision-making mechanisms and processes, all of which in turn affect the relationships and dynamics of dependence.

While acknowledging the importance of external relations—in a world that tends more and more toward globalization—we must also acknowledge that they are not wholly determinant. They accelerate or brake, modify or block for a time the processes of development and change in national societies, but they never act entirely alone. The specificity of national societies arises as much from their own histories as from their relationships to foreign societies and the international system.

This perhaps helps to explain how and why certain international situations, sometimes independently of the will of the metropolis and international groups, can create opportunities and offer options that are taken advantage of in different ways by Latin American groups in order to assert greater autonomy and to significantly alter internal and external policies. Similarly, one of the factors determining the drift toward state interventionism derives from the necessity that the state act as arbitrator between internal and external groups, between the national society and the metropolis, between dependency and autonomy. Since this phenomenon is incompatible with a purely or predominantly externalist interpretation, it requires the explicating of internal dynamics and the underlining of their international impact.

External Dynamics

Ianni's analysis needs most particularly to be completed in the area of *external* dynamics, especially with respect to the new international context wherein relations between the United States and Latin America are continuously being defined and redefined. It seems to me essential that we dedicate more attention to, and analyze in detail, the implications of the cold war period, as well as the transition to a breakdown of bipolarity and the movement toward multipolarity.

In the period of bipolarization and the cold war—the first phase of postwar geopolitical change, which extended approximately from 1945 to 1962—it was essential that the United States and the Soviet Union reach détente. They perceived each other as multifaceted and permanent threats, and they confronted each other at all levels and on an international scale, by mobilizing the entire range of resources available to them and to the countries making up their spheres of influence. Through all these years, the dominant tone of the world situation was established by the tension between the two power blocs organized around and under the hegemony of the two superpowers. Each sought to prevail, to consolidate its interests, and to extend its clientele. The tension was, however, increasingly constrained, in order that direct armed confrontation could be avoided. Increasingly, the two superpowers sought new understandings, and the drive to détente came to dominate the international order. This underlying tendency appears in the Yalta Agreement; it extended through and even beyond the cold war—with different tactics but with the same objectives—as a policy destined to maintain the limits and the structure of the world system as a whole. The iron curtain (military, political, economic, ideological) was in fact established by mutual interest to avoid socialist revolution in the West and capitalist restoration (or autonomous national socialisms) in the Soviet bloc. The implications of this situation for Latin America arose simultaneously at the center of both blocs, and they tended to converge voluntarily and involuntarily toward a common outcome.

Concerning the United States and the capitalist bloc, some observations are in order. In the first place, the interests of monopoly capital, the state, and American foreign policy were not wholly coordinated. Giant corporations with assets greater than those of many countries came to operate on a global scale and tended to be transnational. The state, for its part, continued to operate as a relatively autonomous entity, with particular interests and its own logic and dynamics—and with an awareness of the necessities and demands of the global system. The essential unity between the state and the multinational corporations, expressed in extreme form in the military-industrial complex, failed, in the end, to bridge the gap that lay between them in the areas of ideology, political behavior, and concrete strategies—a gap manifested in diverse conflicts and clashes. Only in this manner can some gross errors of evaluation and certain blatant failures be explained.

In the second place, with respect to other developed capitalistic nations that were being bled or weakened, the United States achieved and consolidated, on an unprecedented scale, its hegemony over Latin America, and rapidly extended its influence to Europe, noncommunist Asia, and Africa. The United States perceived Western Europe as at once a constellation of rival interests, a region to colonize, and an ally against the USSR, Eastern Europe, and the colonial revolution. Thus, American policy toward Europe was necessarily contradictory. It was a question of penetrating and at the same time (but not utterly) dominating Europe, of restoring and consolidating it, increasing its economic, political, and military power to a certain extent, and establishing with its dominant classes and political elites an alliance expressing the community of interest and the shared need to oppose noncapitalistic national and international powers and currents. A similar process was pursued with respect to Japan. The chief implication of all this for Latin America was the decline of Western Europe and a consequent reduction in the maneuvering capacity of Latin American national bourgeoisies and governments. This, in turn, was reinforced by the logic of mutual security and the struggle against communism and subversion that prohibited every independent, direct relation with nations of the other bloc.

There were also various implications with regard to the Soviet Union and its bloc. On the one hand, since Yalta, the Soviet Union has in fact accepted the subordination of Latin American countries to American hegemony; the USSR pretended not to notice the forces and processes of change and liberation, or actually contributed to their derailment through the action of communist parties that acted as spokesmen for internal agencies of Soviet politics and diplomacy. On the other hand, the USSR imposed and maintained its hegemony over the satellite countries of Eastern Europe, and, in lesser degree, over new revolutionary regimes in Asia. The Warsaw Pact and COMECON made possible Eastern Europe's military, political, and economic integration into the hegemonic system centered around the USSR. Thus the USSR could dominate, exploit, and distort the remaining Eastern European economies, societies, and states, and encourage—through multiple pressures and even direct military intervention against heterodox experiments—a process of power concentration that was detrimental to the other members of the bloc. The images of internal Stalinism and an imperialistic foreign policy introduced confusion, disillusion, and despondency into the forces of change operating in Latin American countries, who in turn consequently saw themselves as deprived of a prestigious, successful model to oppose the one offered by the United States and defended by their own governments and national bourgeoisies.

A third component of the first phase of postwar international relations was the emergence of the "third world" as a result of the colonial revolution in Asia and Africa and the processes of change in Latin America. This generic, ambiguous term grouped together the periphery of underdeveloped and semideveloped countries, principally those that had been dominated in semicolonial fashion by the corporations and governments of the capitalist powers; of lesser importance were several countries drawn into the Soviet bloc.

Thus, the third-world countries appeared on the international scene with evident disruptive capacity, but also in a situation where they had little power and a decreasing share of world income and riches. Their domestic and international policies were predominantly determined by exogenous factors, adjusted in the final instance to the interests of the superpower to whose sphere they belonged. Thus, they interacted more with the great powers than with their equals, each pursuing its own objectives and interpreting international politics in its own way. Some states placed themselves openly in one camp; others played an ambiguous negotiating game that allowed them to accept aid from both camps while preserving a certain margin of independence and maneuverability. But their adroitness failed to spare them being treated as the objects of manipulation and the spoils of competition between the two major blocs.

Consequently, solidarity among third world countries as such was limited in this period. The forum supplied by the United Nations and the coexistence/competition between the United States and the Soviet Union did allow the third-world countries a certain capacity to influence decisions linked to anticolonial revolutions, modifications of the world political map, and the settling of certain conflicts (Korea, Vietnam 1954). But underdevelopment and dependence forced those who governed the third world to give priority to domestic conditions; and these conditions generated or reinforced divergent interests, tensions, and conflicts among the countries in this camp, thus limiting their capacity for political, diplomatic, and military initiative.

From 1962 until the present, the second postwar phase unfolded. This phase was characterized by *the rupture of the duopoly and a tendency toward multilaterality.* The forces, circumstances, and tendencies of the first phase were to some degree extended, without reaching–up to the present moment–a new, definitive, durable equilibrium. The original structures of both blocs persist, but they are tending to come undone; and no new combination of alliances is replacing the old. Zones of influence and similar arrangements have blurred; they intermix, interpenetrate, and overlap. Thus it has become problematic or impossible to align forces in coherent military and political-ideological coalitions. The term *multipolarity* has been used in an attempt to describe this confusing situation.

Movement to the second postwar phase was expressed and formed by a series of processes and circumstances related to modified relations between the two superpowers, symmetrical crises within both blocs, and the particular vicissitudes of the third world.

Through sheer mass, the two superpowers maintained an enormous capacity to influence the world, but their effective influence was beginning to erode. The 1962 Cuban crisis verified, on the one hand, that the strategy of mutual deterrence was still operative, but it revealed also the constraints of a détente between two superpowers that cannot use the absolute weapon, cannot risk attacking each other. Thus stalemated, they were not completely free to direct their forces toward other countries. The threat of atomic weapons became less credible. Both superpowers tended to consolidate their nuclear privileges, but they became incapable of totally determining the conduct of the smaller nations in their respective blocs or of defining situations elsewhere. No longer could they control incipient or developing local crises; they were able only to regulate such crises indirectly and to impede their degeneration into wider conflicts of the sort that led to direct participation and confrontation (Middle East, Vietnam).

Nuclear strength not only neutralized itself in the central arena but also diversified and spread (France, Great Britain, China), changing the rules of geopolitics by introducing new indeterminacies into the calculations of probability and risk. All of this encouraged and affirmed the emergence of centrifugal forces in the three worlds, forces that could make themselves felt in spite of the wishes and interests of the two superpowers.

There were also symmetrical crises within the two blocs. In the capitalist camp, the recovery of Japan and Western Europe, at first promoted by the United States, was beginning to escape the promoter's control. It had acquired an autonomous dynamic, and the apprentice threatened to turn against the sorcerer, causing the United States to lose its absolute hegemony of 1945, though retaining relative predominance. The economic growth of Western Europe and Japan prompted them to expand and extend their own political power in order to defend their investments and markets against U.S. control and interference. The configuration of economic forces now tends to favor only a relative degree of American domination; U.S. political-military predominance is not justified. Japan and Western Europe—which are in some ways advancing toward a community of their own—are seeking a more balanced relationship with the United States. And the alliance-protection component of that relationship is tending to be replaced by one in which responsibility is shared while rivalry over markets and zones of influence grows.

In the Soviet bloc also, centrifugal forces were at work. There were frontal confrontations with Yugoslavia, China, and Albania. And Vietnam, North Korea, and Rumania were demanding their autonomy. There were convulsions in Poland and Czechoslovakia, where Soviet repression won doubtful victories. As for Cuba, we are beginning to know more about the complex autonomy-subordination relationship that has governed its ties to the USSR. And in reaction to this process—and to justify and ensure its hegemony—the USSR found itself obliged to allow the re-maining "popular democracies" to have slightly more liberal political regimes and certain economic advantages within the COMECON framework.

At any rate, the unity of the Soviet bloc (and of the international communist movement) was being intensely and profoundly affected. Soviet hegemony was maintained through direct military, political, and economic pressure, but in unstable, fragile conditions that generated unpredictable outbursts. Up to the present, the most serious contradiction in this respect has been the People's Republic of China. According to certain indicators, China is close to becoming a superpower, and—following upon the giant convulsions of the Cultural Revolution—is now questioning and redefining its role and behavior in world politics. Whatever the result, China will have an expanding international role in the coming years and decades.

The third world, for its part, remains in a critical phase of definition. It has failed—as a whole and in its major regions—to achieve economic, political, or military unity. It is profoundly divided within itself and in its behavior toward the great powers. Within the third world as a whole, conflicts expressing a protracted crisis of hegemony multiply. There has been division and confrontation between divergent or antagonistic tendencies (conservative, reformist, revolutionary). From an international point of view, the neutrality of the third world was being exhausted. Merely denouncing colonialism and underdevelopment was not sufficient for the task of articulating demands, strategies, or tactics; nor did it give rise to the kind of dramatic, complex political situations obtaining in the Middle East and Indochina. On the contrary, the capacity for manipulation on the part of the neocolonial powers and the Soviet Union continued. The attempts to create a common front with respect to the great powers (UNCTAD, the Tricontinental) were unable to penetrate the resistance of the developed countries, which maintained their positions and their imperial stance.

A new fact meriting particular attention is that the political-ideological center of gravity of the third-world rebellion is being displaced from Asia and Africa toward Latin America, where the outlines of new and heterodox development models are emerging, models that must still be submitted to the acid test of historical verification (Cuba, Peru, Chile).

On the basis of this summary analysis, I must point out now some of the most obvious implications for Latin American relationships in this new international context. The most important seems to be the possibility of *a relative reduction of the hegemonic role of the United States* in Latin America and *a relative increase in the influence of other powers:* the European Community, Japan, the USSR, the People's Republic of China.

The sooner a dozen Western European countries form a *community* with a unified international strategy, the more rapidly will their possibilities as an active, influential presence in Latin America increase.

Numerous economic, political, and diplomatic conditions also favor an expansion of relations between Japan and Latin America. This may take place within the framework of a bilateral relation, through multilateral relations with Latin American blocs or subgroups, or even through a multilateral relation between Latin America, on the one hand, and Japan, Australia, and Asia, on the other.

Since approximately 1971, the Soviet Union has been outlining an economic-diplomatic offensive in Latin America. The USSR's behavior is now characterized by a no-nonsense pragmatism that leads it to avoid any new burden like Cuba, or any isolated commitment in one direction or with one nation. Principled ideological and political considerations have been set aside, and possibilities and operations are evaluated in strictly economic and diplomatic terms.

Finally, the People's Republic of China has spectacularly reentered the world. Possessing enormous resources and a strong will to develop, it is already one of the world's most important markets. As a member of the United Nations and the first underdeveloped atomic power in the Security Council and the Group of 77, it introduces a new and highly dynamic element into world politics. All of this, moreover, is reinforced by China's drive to replace the USSR as the Mecca of the socialist camp and the third world. Latin American countries are looking forward to commercial, financial, and diplomatic relations with China, and several are already establishing and intensifying these relations.

The aforementioned elements and processes indicate that *a new and extremely complex and flexible worldwide system of coexistence/competition is emerging.* It will eventually open vast possibilities for the national bourgeoisies on the one hand, and for the national-populist-socialist movements and regimes in Latin America and the third world on the other—possibilities to maneuver, seek advantage, and utilize confrontations and alliances.

Internal Dynamics

The preceding observations, which suggest ways of strengthening Ianni's analysis with respect to external dynamics, must be related also to internal dynamics.

Only as a first approximation do the international relations within the global system appear to be a network of relationships between states; they may also be conceived of as expressions and projections of the internal social relations of the several states. The internal social relations and the international relations are complex and dynamic in their composition, in distribution of forces, and in the manner in which they overlap. To the extent that the several states' wills are projected outward and integrated into international balances and processes, the individual government's initiative is limited, and the government acts with decreased autonomy and decision-making efficiency.

Internal socioeconomic, cultural-ideological, and political forces, structures, and processes influence the individual state's international relations through a gamut of mechanisms and exchanges, expressed through actors in the nation-state, some of whom operate simultaneously within both the national and international systems. For analytical purposes, we should distinguish at least the following:

1. Classes, components of classes, and groups; national organizations and institutions.

2. The nation-state as an actor in the domestic system, the international system, and international organizations.

3. Interstate and international (bilateral, regional, multilateral, worldwide) organizations.

4. Multinational, private, and public corporations.

5. International movements: religious, ideological, cultural, scientific, technical, political, youth, etc.

On this basis, we can formulate a series of observations designed to develop a theoretical framework, an analytical scheme, and a basic focus for the mass of empirical investigation that needs to be done. It seems particularly important that empirical studies be pursued, so that we might minimize the risk of stagnating in the purely abstract, overideologized language that characterizes most existing versions of dependence theory.

In order to analyze the international relations of Latin American countries, we must recognize the considerable importance of the social subsystem. Especially important in this subsystem are the hierarchical networks of class and group relationships; the processes by which they are created and modified; the control of property, resources, income, and decision-making; class and group interests, values, attitudes, and behavior; the means of exploitation and domination; and the dynamics of conflict, struggle, and social change.

We must also recognize the capacity of different classes, groups, and individuals to influence the decisions that define and constitute the foreign policy of Latin American states. This capacity arises from the existing social stratification, the power structure, and the cultural-ideological subsystem.

Ianni postulates the growth and systematic interaction of the propertied classes under the hegemony of the United States and according to its priorities, as well as the continentalization of these classes and their contradictions. On the basis of what has been said above, this argument seems questionable, *except as a hypothesis about tendencies.*

The hegemonic fraction of the ruling class in Latin America seems to be made up of the new oligarchic elite. This in turn is composed of the top sectors of the landholding, commercial, financial, industrial, political, and military groups, together with some subordinated co-participation from the new upper middle class, which is linked to commercial and financial activities, industrialization, the service sector, and the public and private techno-bureaucracy.

At the same time, this group as a whole interacts with the multinational corporations. As the most open and heterogeneous group of the traditional oligarchy, the new oligarchic elite exercises hegemony in a highly conflictive and dynamic national and international context, and establishes changing and complex relationships with national classes and with international centers and configurations of interests and power. Thus, its relations with the U.S. Government and North American corporations lead to a unity, but not identity, of interests and behavior. Unity, here, is with respect to dependence on foreign trade, investments, and forms of assistance, exploitation of resources, and common appropriation of the economic surplus that is generated. Also important to the relationship are the present or potential community of enemies and threats (dominated classes, and socialist and populist movements, parties, and governments). Complete identification does not and cannot result—as Ianni clearly indicates—because of the tension and conflicts issuing from the division of the economic surplus, and because the expansionist, hegemonic tendency of the U.S. Government and corporations can threaten the internal bases of domination and exploitation by the oligarchic elite (by creating or aggravating conflict between factions of the ruling class or between ruling and dominated classes). The minimum autonomy of the nation-state, and the very existence of the nation that the oligarchic elite exploits, governs, and administers is also threatened. The new oligarchic elite's capacity to resist, maneuver, and negotiate is, at the same time, limited by the basic interests it shares with the U.S. Government and the multinational corporations, and by its incapacity to mobilize in its own support the popular classes and national majorities.

At any rate, the intelligence-gathering capacity, political awareness, and influence over the definition and management of international relations seem to be strongly concentrated in the directors and representatives of the new oligarchic elite, who thus achieve a decisive role in the design and application of international policies. In this same category we should also place large landholders and businessmen—especially those who participate in international business—highly placed political, administrative, and military leaders, and a group of intellectuals, technicians, and international civil servants who are identified with those sectors.

The people who comprise the national majorities—much of the middle classes and the totality of urban and rural lower classes—are absorbed and enervated by the system of domination and exploitation, and by the oppressive and alienating conditions of work, daily life, the cultural-ideological climate, and the political system. They are isolated into their private lives and small groups, and experience little interchange with other individuals or groups. They are divided and set against each other. Individualism, egoism, social irresponsibility, competition, and conflict are stimulated among those who should naturally feel and act as allies. All of this deprives the national majorities of the time, energy, possibilities, and stimuli needed to widen and enrich their experience, knowledge, and social relationships, to interpret the complex world in which they live, and to identify the causes of their sufferings. Their comprehension, aspirations, initiative, and capacity—and their confidence in themselves and their class to control social mechanisms and to impose change on a seemingly permanent order—are thus limited.

If this situation is produced with respect to problems of national politics, it is understandably reproduced more forcefully with respect to international politics. Narrowness of experience blocks an awareness that there are direct relations between the problems of daily life and national and international politics. The international sphere in particular is viewed as both irrelevant and uncontrollable; its elements and alternatives are ignored; and the responsibility for dealing with it is handed over to those who also control social and political life at the national level—with the hope that at least foreign politics will not affect the common man harmfully or catastrophically. At the same time, acceptance of internal hegemony and domination makes people susceptible to passive acceptance of and participation in manipulatory movements and maneuvers—the mystifying machinations of different populist, *desarrollista,* and Bonapartist parties and regimes.

Finally we must consider the contrary role played by groups, movements, and parties whose interests and opinions clash with those of the hegemonic groups and dominant classes, groups capable in greater or lesser degree of specific or generalized criticism of the present system of international relations of Latin American countries and of the policies that express and reinforce them—and capable also of proposing alternative models. As Ianni clearly indicates, the coming to power of governments such as those in Cuba and Chile instantly produces a mutual conditioning of internal and external politics.

In any case, the decisive role of internal structures and dynamics in the configuration of international relations, whether to establish and maintain dependence or to diminish and destroy it, seems unquestionable.

We must also consider the problems attendant upon studying the actor par excellence of international relations, the nation-state. An examination of its nature, structure, and behavior is particularly important where Latin American countries are concerned. In Latin America's particular conditions of structural and hegemonic crisis, the state has been emerging and affirming itself as the actor that undertakes the following tasks and seeks the following goals:

1. To preserve the bases for, and encourage the requisite growth and relative modernization of, a dependent capitalism whose development is mixed and unequal.

2. To act as a supportive agent and to attend to problems created by new internal and external processes and imbalances, in seeking to satisfy old needs that have multiplied as well as new needs that are not adequately met by the behavior of the market, dominant groups, and national and foreign businesses.

3. To encourage policies that are compensatory, anticyclical, and growth-inducing.

4. To defend the dominant classes, to reinforce and consolidate their capital accumulation and power, and to legitimate the large firm as the fundamental unit of socioeconomic organization and action.

5. To create and maintain conditions favorable to continued social and political conciliation among the several components of the system of domination on the one hand, and aspirants and impediments to hegemony, on the other.

6. To regulate and arbitrate the ascent and limited incorporation of new groups into the "establishment"; correlatively, to exclude national majorities from real participation in decisions on income and power distribution.

7. To adjust internal processes to the new international conditions and to regulate harmony and conflicts of interests between dominant national and foreign groups.

The assumption of these tasks has made it necessary to refine governmental technique, to widen the repertoire of institutions, instruments, and norms, and to form new political-administrative and professional cadres. The state and its bureaucracy tend to be converted into a separate social conglomerate with its own interests and an appreciable degree of independence, a conglomerate that assumes a role as arbitrator among classes, factions, and groups. Its action is dual and ambiguous: on the one hand, it operates as an expression of the system and an instrument of the dominant classes, and its action corresponds, *in the final instance,* to their interests; on the other hand, there is no total identification between the state bureaucracy and a given class, nor is the former mechanically or instrumentally subordinated to the latter.

This summary characterization of the new interventionism of the state suggests the manner in which Latin American governments' international politics are shaped. For this, as for any other kind of politics, the key factors are the plurality, diversity, and complexity of interests, power bases, and decisions, and the strategies and modes of influence used. The result is that various rationalities proliferate: those of the *actors,* those of centers of interest, power, and decision-making (economic, social, cultural-ideological, political, military), and those of *both ends and means.* These multiple rationalities coexist and collide with one another; they seek to bend each other to their own purposes; and they operate sometimes as developed and dominating forces and other times as underdeveloped and dominated entities. Exchanges of information, tensions and conflicts, and negotiations and compromises are established between the different rationalities. None can be completely sacrificed to the others, nor can any be put into practice as if its concerns were unique.

Therefore, the plurality of centers, functions, ends, and means—principal and secondary, dominating and dominated—that emerges from and operates upon international relations must be articulated, integrated, and simultaneously optimized by the political arbitration of the state. In a given circumstance there can be only one decision; and it must be derived on the basis of a *preference function,* which in turn is determined by the rationality attending the coherence and stability of the total system.

The preference function applied to any decision in international politics is not a simple juxtaposition of rationalities. It represents the partial fusion of differences—which it does not exclude but rather reflects—into a complex whole that partakes of all the rationalities without identifying itself totally with any. It is a unity determined by the predominance of one or various rationalities over the others, for that circumstance. The latent capacity of the dominated rationalities for recourse against those that are dominant explains the evolutionary potential of a preference function in international politics.

The rationality of coherence and the preference function that expresses it and renders it concrete result from an integrative process that is always partial and incomplete. The optimum mix of participants and components is never known a priori; it is established in a gradual and uneven manner, under the pressure of events, through trial and error, under all sorts of dangers and uncertainties. The process produces a diversity of outcomes, from the removal of the larger inconsistencies to the implementation of rationalities that are increasingly appropriate.

In summary, the rationality of a state's international politics partakes of the rationality of the society and the state; it is conditioned by them, and is also one of the elements by which they are evaluated.

Imperialism and International Relations in Latin America

ANÍBAL QUIJANO OBREGÓN

The nature of the international relations of the Latin American nations, especially those with the United States, can be examined only in the context of the global system of imperialist domination, and only from the perspective of the class struggle. Strictly speaking, an investigation of the current status and trends of Latin American international relations would require an examination of the nature and tendencies of imperialist capitalism's present crisis, and the impact of this crisis on the class struggle in the world capitalist system—and, in particular, in the Latin American nations.

This paper, however, is restricted to presenting a series of preliminary propositions on changes in the mode of imperialist domination in Latin America, and to characterizing the effect of these changes on the region's sociopolitical struggles. I must stress also the provisionary nature of these notes, for they are in part the product of investigation and reflection in a field that remains largely a theoretical vacuum.

Two Stages of Imperialist Capitalism in Latin America

Since Lenin, it has generally been accepted that capitalism becomes imperialist when the monopolization of capital, under the control of finance capital, creates a need for international capital accumulation, as well as a need for the international realization of surplus value—a need that characterizes the earlier phase of capitalism's international economic relations. International capital accumulation has proceded in different ways, depending on the changes in the structure of capital and the specific conditions under which it must operate at any given moment in a given country or region within the international capitalist system. Such changes in the concrete modes of accumulation underlie changes in the power structure within the system, on both the dominant level and the

Aníbal Quijano Obregón is with the Peruvian Center for Social Studies and Research, Lima.

dependent level, as well as in relations between the two levels. We must consider, then, the way in which imperialist capitalist accumulation has evolved in the Latin American nations, and indicate its most significant political and social implications during each period.

In general terms, the history of imperialism in Latin America may be divided into two broad periods: (1) the period of semicolonial or primary export accumulation and (2) the period of urban-industrial-based accumulation.

The Period of Semicolonial Accumulation

This period lasted roughly until the 1950s. Its principal features are generally well known and can be summarized as follows:

1. The concentration of imperialist capitalist investment in the production of primary products.

2. The organization of this production in "enclaves," which are not organically connected among themselves in the dependent country's internal economy, but are individually connected to the metropolitan capitalist economy.

3. The combination of surplus value (generated in the "enclaves") and mercantile surplus (produced in the precapitalist sector) as a part of global capitalist profits.[1]

4. The realization and accumulation in the national-imperialist economy (that is, in the imperialist country in which the capital originates) of the greater part of the surplus value generated in the dominated country. In this sense, for the dominated country, the reproduction of capital represents only some fraction of the total.

On the one hand, these characteristics of the mode of capitalist accumulation are related to the level of development of the labor force and to the relations of production that imperialist capitalism encounters in Latin America, relations that during this earlier period were generally still mercantilist. On the other hand, they are related to the characteristics of capital itself, to the power structure of the imperialist bourgeoisie, and to the type of business organization: thus we have the predominance of finance capital, the division of the imperialist bourgeoisie into centers of national-imperialist interest, business organization along the lines of vertically integrated, preconglomerate corporations, national-imperialist states not yet operating according to a worldwide strategy of defending the system but primarily to a strategy of furthering national-imperialist ruling interests.

[1] See Aníbal Quijano Obregón, "Imperialismo, clases sociales y estado en el Perú, antes de 1930," paper presented at the Seminar on Social Classes and the Political Crisis in Latin America, Mexico City, June 1973.

The Latin American countries were not all integrated into this mode of imperialist domination in the same fashion. In one category was a small group of countries (Mexico, Brazil, Argentina, Uruguay, Chile) that by no accident belong to the Atlantic Seaboard or its immediate extension as respects mercantile traffic (Chile). In these countries, owing to diverse but convergent historical factors—the most decisive of which was probably close-knit integration into the nineteenth-century world market—centers of capitalist relations of production had already begun to develop, however incipiently, within the general feudal-mercantile matrix. Mercantilism was in full flower, expanding the domestic market with the creation of important urban centers; elements of the mercantile-capitalist bourgeoisie had managed to consolidate their hegemony over class and state; and an oligarchic national state was in the process of being consolidated.

In other countries, however, the mercantilism that had developed in the colonial period was stagnating, feudal and semi-feudal relations of production had become prevalent, the economy had become predominantly agricultural, the domestic market was small, and urban centers were on the decline even in those countries in which the colonial mercantile economy had brought a measure of strength. Under such conditions, the landowning class seemed unable to express itself politically. Its various mercantilist sectors were not sufficiently strong to impose their rule, and for this same reason the state's real social base was quite precarious and unstable. In fact, during almost the entire nineteenth century, the state could not really become a national state, and had thus to compete with the autonomous local power of the landowners.

Owing to these differing conditions in the two groups of countries, the penetration of imperialist capital and the domination of the imperialist bourgeoisie was in each case of differing scope and strength. The conditions under which interests of the imperialist bourgeoisie and those of the ruling classes in Latin America were associated varied along the continuum of domination-subordination; so also did the relations between national-imperialist states and the national-dependent Latin American states, as well as the relations between the latter and the imperialist bourgeoisies themselves.

If we compare, for example, the cases of Chile and Peru during the period in which imperialist domination begins and becomes consolidated, we encounter profoundly different situations. From the very beginning of the post-colonial period, the relations of the Chilean economy with the world market were close and uninterrupted, permitting the early integration of Chile's domestic market. Owing to this circumstance, and also owing to the marginal importance of the social relations of "internal colonialism" between Indians and non-Indians, a ruling class could emerge that was economically, socially, and politically integrated on a national level, and that had a mercantile-landowning base of power. This ruling class was able to construct a national state—oligarchic, to be sure, but firmly stabilized on the national level.

By the time the period of imperialist-capital penetration began, the landowning-mercantile, or mercantile-bourgeois, class was operating a consolidated national state and had firm control over the principal productive resources that formed the basis of its domination as a class. It was therefore economically and above all politically capable as a class of negotiating with the imperialist bourgeoisie the conditions under which the association of interests would take place. The imperialist bourgeoisie took over the mines—the country's principal productive resource in terms of its insertion in the world market—and as a result the imperialist bourgeoisie gained control of Chile's economic relations with this international market. However, the Chilean mercantile bourgeoisie, in retaining *all* the land, as well as the incipient industrial activity, was able to conserve its own internal power base, and thus to maintain firmly its domestic political power.

In Peru, by contrast, after the wars of independence, commercial relations with the world capitalist market declined almost to negligible proportions because the country was producing scarcely anything for that market. Once the colonial-mercantile network—in which the colonial-creole mercantile bourgeoisie was predominant—collapsed, mercantilism stagnated in Peru. The country's mining-mercantile centers abruptly declined, becoming little more than the residential centers of the landowners. The economy became almost entirely agrarian; and feudal, semifeudal, slave, and communal relations of production came to prevail.

Thus, the revitalization of mercantilism and world-trade relations in Peru during the guano and nitrate era was to take place under the direct control of the European capitalist bourgeoisie, and with minimal benefit for the Peruvian landowners and merchants, who participated only secondarily and subordinately in the guano boom. The precariousness and briefness of this boom prevented the mercantile bourgeoisie, politically organized at the time, from consolidating control over its own class and the state. Its efforts to do so were ultimately frustrated by war and subsequent defeat at the hands of Chile. When the penetration of imperialist capital began, the national state had thus not yet been built. On the contrary, the shaky political-administrative apparatus had collapsed, and nothing that in a strict sense could be called a mercantile bourgeoisie (effectively a national class, politically represented in the state) had appeared.

The imperialist bourgeoisie could, therefore, annex not just the mines,

as it had in Chile, but also the other productive resources formerly belonging to Peruvian landowners and merchants: land (turned to export
crops), oil, railroads, foreign trade, finance, and the incipient textile and
food industries. Moreover, the imperialist bourgeoisie came eventually to
administer directly the country's principal customs house, and approximately 80 percent of the budget of the nascent state came, before 1930,
to consist of loans, mainly from the United States.

Peruvian landowners were left only the land that was not of direct interest to imperialist capital. Peruvian merchants found themselves with
the leftovers of foreign trade and the small, disperse domestic market.
The incipient capitalist bourgeoisie, born in the shade of imperialist capital, was given the leftovers of exportable agrarian production, the small
mines, and that part of the manufacturing sector based upon cottage industry and the work of artisans.

The Chilean and Peruvian examples are good illustrations of the
breadth of differences and the degrees of penetration of imperialist capital in the control of the resources of production in Latin American countries during this period. But more important, they illustrate clearly the
relations established among classes under imperialist hegemony, and the
real social bases of the national-dependent states.

In some cases the dominant classes in Latin America managed, within
the general framework of their subordination to the imperialist bourgeoisie, to retain a national base of power and of state control. In other
cases, the imperialist bourgeoisie acquired control over virtually all the
resources necessary to capitalist production, leaving the nascent mercantile bourgeoisie and local capitalist sectors with no real operational base
of their own; as a result, the respective national states being formed
came to have extremely weak social bases.

The dominated classes and the emergent middle sectors in these countries during this period were incapable of vying for state power. Neither
were they able to make their influence felt in the determination of the
social bases of state control or in the establishment of the state's policy
with respect to imperialist domination. Nor did the intermittent peasant
uprisings—triggered by the increasing concentration of agrarian property
deriving from the penetration of imperialist capital and the revitalization
of mercantilism—affect the basic conditions determining the structure of
political power.

All of this helps make clear why it was possible that in Mexico, Brazil, Argentina, Uruguay, and Chile, the national-dependent bourgeoisies
were able not only to take advantage of the crisis of the 1930s by investing in domestic industries, enlarging their domestic markets, and diversifying their productive and social structures, but also, on this foundation,

occasionally to act as if they were pursuing autonomous national-capital-ist development and an independent foreign policy. To be sure, these pre-tensions were expressed mainly through the growing political influence of the middle sectors and salaried workers. These two social sectors seemed to be aligned, if precariously, with those sectors of the capitalist bourgeoisie that had important national interests.

In the other countries of Latin America, however, the political in-fluence of the middle and dominated sectors was always felt by the bour-geoisie to be a radical threat to its rule. Here, the bourgeoisie was weak and disperse, tied to the precapitalist and mercantilist landowners, and especially—through its feudalism—to the interests of the imperialist bour-geoisie. It was natural, in these conditions, that all attempts at autono-mous national-capitalist development, or at the democratization of the state's social bases and the mechanisms of domination, would be per-ceived by the bourgeoisie as a threat rather than as a desirable basis for a tactical alliance. This bourgeoisie had few national interests. Owing to its own lack of bases of economic and therefore political power, its con-crete interests depended on the expansion of imperialist capital in the economic sphere, and on its ties with the traditional landowners in the political sphere.[2]

It is thus not surprising that in all those countries that lacked a bour-geois class with national interests, the state was openly subjected to the dictates of imperialist firms, that this took place in a much more thorough manner than in other countries, and most important, that there was no long-term solution for this situation. It is also not surprising that the for-eign policies of these states invariably reflected the decisions of the hege-monic national-imperialist state(s). Moreover, to the extent that the for-eign policies of the principal national-imperialist states were not guided by a global strategy of defense of the system, but rather by the goal of expanding the domination of national-imperialism, these policies usually corresponded closely to the concrete concerns of the imperialist firms having interests in Latin America. Thus, the North American state oper-ated chiefly as a guarantor and as a "big stick" for the concrete interests of the imperialist firms, in opposition to the autonomist pretensions of some national bourgeoisies and their national states, and above all in op-position to possible political insurgencies on the part of the dominated classes and their allies in the middle sectors. This was not yet the stage at which the North American national-imperialist state would require, as it does now, the sacrifice of this or that concrete interest of this or that

[2]This situation is described well by Edelberto Torres Rivas, *Estructuras y procesos en una sociedad dependiente: El caso centroamericano* (Santiago: PLA, 1970); and Agustín Cueva, *El proceso de dominación política en Ecuador* (Quito: 1973).

imperialist firm in the interest of the global defense of the system, or in the interest of finding new allies in the middle sectors that it previously opposed. But for this very reason, in the countries with nationally based bourgeoisies, conflicts sometimes arose between the national interests of those bourgeoisies and the interests of certain imperialist firms, principally when the expanded political influence of the middle sectors and salaried workers accentuated the need for political democratization and the improvement of living conditions.

The Period of Urban-Industrial-Based Accumulation

Although in certain countries, notably Argentina, imperialist capital could be found operating in urban industrial sectors of the economy prior to 1930,[3] the bulk of this capital, taking Latin America as a whole, was concentrated in agro-extractive production for the foreign market, within the format of the semicolonial mode of accumulation. It was only following World War II that imperialist capital expanded massively and rapidly into all spheres of economic activity, shifting its center of gravity toward the urban-industrial sector.

For the countries in the first group, in which the capitalist relations of production were already in full expansion in the urban-industrial sector, but basically under the domination of nationally based competitive capital, this expansion of imperialist capital consisted above all in the denationalization of control over capital. National and foreign capital became integrated, thus associating the most important sectors of the national bourgeoisie with the capitalist-imperialist operation.

For the remaining majority of the nations, what generally took place was less a denationalization of capital already existent in the urban-industrial sector (which was still minimal) than an expansion and a diversification right from the start of the economic activity in that sector, under the direct control of imperialist capital. That this was so does not negate the fact that, in the course of this expansion, the most important sectors of the national capitalists were also integrating their capital with that of the imperialists and thus becoming junior partners in imperialist exploitation.

This expansion of imperialist capital in the urban-industrial sectors gave rise to a new model of imperialist accumulation, whose main features can be presented in the following manner:

1. Urban-industrial activity becomes the principal base of accumulation.

---

[3] See, for example, Javier Villanueva, "El origen de la industrialización argentina," *Desarrollo Económico* (Buenos Aires), vol. 12, no. 47, October-December 1972.

2. The dominated countries' "internal" markets are expanded and internationalized.

3. An increasing part of the surplus value generated is realized and accumulated locally, in order to broaden the global base of production and the reproduction of capital to be accumulated subsequently in the metropolitan economy.

4. In this sense, a tendency to modify the very structure of the accumulation of capital ensues. While, in the previous period, the surplus generated in the agro-extractive sectors under imperialist control was accumulated almost entirely within the national-imperialist economy in which the imperialist firm originated, an important part of this surplus value would now be accumulated locally, in the dominated country, but under the control of the same imperialist bourgeoisie.

5. Because of this trend, the Latin American nations whose urban-industrial capitalist development was more advanced become partially incorporated into the system of expanded reproduction. In other words, expanded reproduction, previously confined to the framework of national-imperialist economies, now becomes internationalized.

6. Because their productive bases are not sufficiently developed, the Latin American countries of recent urban-industrial development are not incorporated into this new international structure of expanded reproduction. In these countries, the bases of the generation of surplus value are expanded, and the bulk of the surplus value continues to be accumulated in the national-imperialist economies. However, the realization of surplus value of the urban-industrial sector now takes place predominantly in the internationalized "internal" market.

7. There is a disappearance of the "enclave" in this sector of the economy, and structural linkage ensues among the diverse sectors of the urban-industrial economy and between the urban-industrial economy and the metropolitan economy. In this respect the new phase is in contrast to the preceding phase, in which the "enclaves" were not linked to each other, but rather were connected separately to the metropolitan economy.

8. Within this new structure of the reproduction of capital, the enclaves themselves begin to be interconnected through the urban-industrial sector and therefore shed their enclave character. This process probably occurs differently in different countries, according to the development of the urban-industrial base of production. The "lesser countries" in particular are still likely to be caught in the previous stage of imperialist accumulation.[4]

[4]The phrase is from Edelberto Torres Rivas, "Notas sobre la crisis de la dominación burguesa en América Latina," paper presented at the Seminar on Social Classes and the Political Crisis in Latin America, Mexico City, June 1973.

9. In the "major" countries, and increasingly in the principal remaining countries, a tendency develops for the state to take on important functions of capital. Capital is increasingly concentrated by the state and by the national-imperialist and international corporations associated with the state through their interests and their mode of accumulation.

10. To the extent that the previous modes of imperialist accumulation have not been eliminated, they combine with the new modes in the overall structure of imperialist domination.

11. In this manner, the unevenly combined character of these countries' capitalist structures is accentuated and the following contradictions are deepened: (a) the contradiction between capitalism and the remaining precapitalism; and (b) the contradiction between the semicolonial mode of accumulation, with its purely national-imperialist base, and the new, internationally based mode of accumulation, especially in the sectors evolving toward an internationalization of expanded reproduction.

12. Finally, the foregoing would mean that in practice the Latin American nations entering into the world imperialist system are of at least three identifiable types: (a) countries in which the semicolonial mode of imperialist accumulation is still predominant; (b) countries in which this mode is combined with the new mode, but whose productive base does not yet permit their sectoral incorporation into the system of internationalized expanded reproduction; (c) countries in which these modes of accumulation are combined, but in which the newer mode includes sectors that have begun to be incorporated into the system of internationalized expanded reproduction. In general, (a) comprises the Central American and Caribbean countries (except Cuba) and Paraguay and Bolivia; (b) comprises Colombia, Chile, Uruguay, Peru, Venezuela, and to a lesser degree, Ecuador, a group that is elsewhere in this study referred to as "countries of the second group"; and (c) comprises Mexico, Brazil, and, to a lesser degree, Argentina, a group I refer to elsewhere as "countries of the first group."

These new conditions for the domination of imperialist capital in Latin America are related to profound changes in the very structure of capital and in the institutional structure it serves:

13. The previous differentiation of capital and the hegemony of finance capital give way to the integration of finance with productive capital.

14. The division of the imperialist bourgeoisie into centers of national-imperialist interests gives way to the growing integration of interests among those sectors, a process that is consolidated and reflected in the internationalization of the ownership of capital.

15. The old, monopolistic business organization of vertically inte-

grated corporations is replaced by the giant conglomerate firms that combine vertical and horizontal integration.

16. The principal national-imperialist states, despite their conflicts, operate basically according to a global strategy of defense of the system, and not just in defense of their separate interests of national-imperialist domination.

The New International Context: Changes in the Imperialist Network

One main observation is in order here: The changes in the structure of capital and in the structure of international ownership of capital, the international conflict of the world capitalist system with the emergent socialist camp, and the deepening of the class struggle within the capitalist system can be considered the fundamental reasons for the modifications in the imperialist network. So far as they concern the focus of this paper, two processes should be stressed, owing to their implications for international relations in Latin America: (1) the relative decline of both the hegemony of the North American national-imperialist bourgeoisie and the national-imperialist North American state, over the entire world capitalist system, and (2) the parallel, increased sharing of imperialist rule with lesser national-imperialist centers, principally Japan and West Germany. There is an increased autonomy of the principal conglomerate monopolies—both national-imperialist and those with more international bases—to operate outside the constraints of the foreign policies of the principal national-imperialist states, while at the same time continuing to use these states to further their expansion and domination.

The growth of the system of international expanded reproduction, to which some of the dependent capitalist countries are becoming partially and unevenly incorporated, gives rise to new, smaller centers of imperialist accumulation. The latter, however, are controlled by the principal national-imperialist bourgeoisies that were there previously, and by bourgeois sectors based on the international ownership of capital.

Thus, whereas in the previous period the international imperialist system was clearly divided into a very small group of dominant countries wherein monopoly capitalism centered its accumulation (countries that were also the producers of industrial goods and of technology) while all the other countries in the system were forced to serve as centers for the production of surplus value (basically through exporting raw materials), the imperialist system now takes another shape. That is, apart from the small group of central capitalist countries, several others have become new, less important centers of imperialist accumulation, under the control of the central-capitalist bourgeoisies, but associated and integrated with the bourgeoisies of the new subcenters. Moreover, the remaining countries are now divided into those that are almost exclusively producers of raw materials and others that are now beginning light and intermediate industrial production—under the control of the imperialist bourgeoisies and in association with local bourgeoisies. In other words, the international accumulation of capital grows on two levels: the level of expanded reproduction, and the level of partially expanded reproduction. At the same time, the international reproduction of surplus value in the countries producing raw materials multiplies, thus transcending precapitalist relations of production.

These processes signal profound changes in the organic and technical composition of imperialist capital. Technological advances in certain sectors of the economy, for example, may lead to problems of overaccumulation, especially in those sectors linked to the defense and space industries. Under such conditions, semicolonial reproduction in enclaves is no longer sufficient, nor is light or intermediate urban-industrial-based reproduction. What is necessary is the highest-level worldwide growth of the expanded system of reproduction of capital.

In Latin America, this development implies that countries are emerging from their previous histories of imperialist domination in quite diverse conditions, and therefore with quite unequal possibilities for being incorporated into the various levels of production and reproduction of capital resulting from the new needs of accumulation. Consequently, the readjustment of the system into a new imperialist network sharpens the contradictions of capitalism as a mode of production and as an international system of countries; it accentuates the unevenly combined development of capitalism; it aggravates social conflicts; and it undermines the social bases of states. This crisis seems to be neither merely cyclical, as it is in some cases, nor temporary, as it is in others, but rather to affect the very structure of the mode of production itself.

Three forms of imperialist domination thus appear, in combination with each other but also in competition for the field, thus deepening their contradictions. In Latin America especially, while countries like Mexico, Brazil, and Argentina have the productive bases required for sectoral incorporation into the system of expanded reproduction, others, such as Colombia, Venezuela, Peru, Chile, Uruguay, and perhaps Ecuador, are just beginning to consolidate small-scale expanded reproduction on the weak base of light and intermediate industry. The remaining Latin American countries (except Cuba) have not yet advanced significantly from their base of primary, semicolonial reproduction.

This does not complete the scenario, however. In each of these groups of countries, on very unequal scales, there are problems related to all the forms of imperialist domination. That is, in spite of the fact that the productive base of the countries in which capitalism is least advanced does not in any way permit these countries to become even partially incorporated into the system of expanded reproduction, the new forms of business operation brought by expanded reproduction are nevertheless being introduced, thus increasing the monopolization and concentration of capital. Furthermore, the need to broaden the base of the production of surplus value in these countries directly accommodates the global needs of the capital that is operating in the central countries or in the new subcenters. And in these subcenters, as a result of their partial incorporation into the system of expanded reproduction, both the production of surplus value (based on primary production) and the partially expanded reproduction of capital (based on industry) are growing through convulsive processes involving the readjustment of the relations of production—as in the characteristic case of Brazil.

New Agents of Imperialist Domination in Latin America

I shall take up now the new operational forms of the two fundamental agents of imperialist domination: the imperialist firm and the imperialist state.

The monopolistic conglomerates. Three elements can be considered the principal determinants of the change in structure and forms of the business operations of existing monopoly capital.

1. The tendency for firms that operate in different economic fields and sectors to form conglomerates. This tendency produces the combination of vertical and horizontal integration of economic activities within the field of operation of the same sector of capital. The tendency seems to be the extreme crystallization of the process of integration of different forms of capital (finance, industrial, commercial) in the different sectors of the economy.

2. The tendency of the principal monopolies to multinationalize their operations, a tendency that increasingly goes beyond the national-imperialist base of accumulation. Concretely, one group of monopolies, mainly North American in origin, carries out most of its operations (production, realization, and accumulation of capital) outside its central national base. For a firm to be considered multinational, at least 25 percent of its operations must be carried out overseas.[5]

3. The tendency for the ownership of capital in monopolies operating on a multinational scale to become internationalized. The currently

[5]On multinational corporations see, for example, J. Galloway, "Multinational Enterprises as Worldwide Interest Groups," paper presented at the Annual Meeting of the American Political Science Association, Los Angeles, September 1970; Charles Kindleberger, *American Business Abroad* (New Haven: 1969); Raymond Vernon, *Sovereignty at Bay* (New York: 1971).

available information in regard to this tendency does not allow us to determine if this internationalization of the ownership of capital also implies the internationalization of the control of capital. Such an implication would suggest the growth of an imperialist bourgeoisie with supernational interests.

The consequences flowing from these new forms of the concentration of capital, originating in changes in the organic and technical composition of capital, are twofold: first, the expansion of the bases of the production of surplus value, that is, the expansion of the capitalistic relations of production and the corresponding reduction in precapitalist relations in those countries or territories where those relations were or are still quite important; and second, the international expansion of the cycle of fully expanded reproduction of capital in those countries where the development of the productive forces already includes significant activity in the production of capital goods.

The principal consequence for international relations of these changes in the business structure and in the structure of capital, particularly in Latin America, is the tendency that now begins to be noted: the relative independence of these firms from the policy of the national-imperialist states, and the growth of the firms' capacity for realizing their own policies on a multinational scale. The capital concentrated in the hands of these firms, the extent of their operations, the complexity and flexibility of their structures, and their ability to macroprogram their operations not only converts them into powers stronger than most national-dependent states, but also allows them to adopt policies that are not always in keeping with the foreign policies of their own national-imperialist states. A recent illustration of this situation is the relationship that until recently existed between the State Department's policy toward the Peruvian military regime (regarding the International Petroleum Company problem) and the stance of the several financial firms that opted jointly to finance the Peruvian programs, despite the reservations of the State Department.

This tendency helps a certain type of political regime—such as the Peruvian, which is trying to readjust to the conditions of imperialist exploitation—to obtain a relatively important margin of maneuver for the development of a foreign policy that might be called independent (such a foreign policy reduces the country's immediate subjugation to the dictates of this or that national-imperialist state, especially the United States, without, however, permitting the country to withdraw from the sphere of domination of imperialist capital itself). The possibility of attaining this type of independence is furthered by the increasing international integration of capital, that is, the progressive internationalization of the ownership and the control of capital.

Nevertheless, when political regimes such as that of Chile openly seek not only to readjust the conditions of imperialist capital's operations in their countries, but also to break with the entire system of imperialist domination, the policy of the national-imperialist states—deriving from a strategy of global defense of the system—openly coincides with the policy of the multinational firms and conglomerates themselves, as is clearly seen in the behavior of ITT and Kennecott toward the Popular Unity regime in Chile. In other words, the multinational firms operating in Latin America must now adapt themselves to the political conditions resulting from the way in which internal class struggles have changed the concrete social bases of national-dependent states, in a manner different from that of previous periods.

Previously, imperialist firms were so constituted that a modification in the conditions of their operations in one country caused them severe problems. For this reason, these firms took the position of violent opposition to all change, however slight it might be. Now, however, they are able to readjust rapidly their forms of operation—and not simply because a totally negative attitude on their part would be impracticable in a given political situation and country, but mainly because these firms' modes of operation and their business structures are able not only to tolerate, but actually to derive future benefits from, certain adjustments.

Thus, for example, the political pressures exerted by reformist movements led by intellectual and technical middle sectors in the past (movements that sought to give to the state the principal responsibilities and functions of capital) were energetically resisted and repressed by imperialist firms before World War II. Now, however, the trends toward the construction of state capitalism in certain countries, trends that produce a readjustment of the conditions of imperialist exploitation in the sense of an association between state and international imperialist capital, are likely to be supported by international imperialist capital, since such trends would permit a policy of cooperation and a higher concentration of capital. It is here that finance capital clearly plays a key role.

This is what is currently taking place, not only with regard to individual countries, but also in relation to the process of subregional economic integration. The cases of the Andean Pact and the Cartagena Agreement (where the integration of the high and medium income markets of member countries permitted the extension of the scale of imperialist operations and a greater concentration of capital) are closely related to the recent forms of state capitalism that arise in greater or lesser degree in this group of countries and especially in Peru.

The national-imperialist state. As has been pointed out, under the conditions that predominated in the period prior to 1950, with regard both to capital and to the international order, the national-imperialist states acted on the dominated countries chiefly in response to the need to secure and to broaden the domination of the national-imperialist bourgeoisie's interests—meaning that the principal conflict was among national-imperialist interests. And given the prevalent business organization and the basic mode of capital accumulation, national-imperialist states supported the interests of each imperialist firm in each situation.

After 1945, and especially after the consolidation of the socialist revolution in China, the conflict pivoted around the global defense of the system in the face of the advance of the world socialist revolution. At this time, the world capitalist system reorganized, integrating itself under the absolute hegemony of the North American state and the North American bourgeoisie. It was within this framework that the new trends in business organizations and in modes of accumulation developed.

While these trends were maturing, the principal national-imperialist state's policy was aimed not only at containing and blockading the socialist countries, but also, as a function of the latter, at repressing all attempts by the dependent countries to achieve relative autonomy. This occurred even when the maintenance of capitalism and basic imperialist domination in these countries was not threatened. Later, however, the results of this same policy led to the emergence of new centers of imperialist power, with growing and relatively independent fields of action, as well as to an increase in economic and political-social difficulties within the United States.

The relative reduction of the North American *state's* hegemony in the capitalist world has not led to a reduction in the hegemony of North American *capital*. This serves to demonstrate the relative separation, though not divorce, between the official state policy of the United States and the policy of monopolies based in the United States. In this new context, in which imperialist power is redistributed at the state level as well as at the level of the firm, the policy of the principal imperialist state meets growing difficulties in exercising—in the same manner and with the same violence as before—its repressive capacity on those regimes that seek a readjustment of the terms of imperialist capital's operations in their countries.

In addition, since the principal imperialist state's policy is directed mainly toward the global defense of the system, and since this policy is constrained by the new forces conditioning international politics, this state must now face situations in which the mere defense of the interests of each North American imperialist firm operating in these countries could aggravate the contradictions and the political-social conflicts within these countries. This, in turn, could threaten the very existence of capitalism as a mode of production in these countries, owing either to the flaring up of nationalism that derives from these readjustments of imperialist domination, or to the triumph of revolutionary, socialist social forces. In the face of these conditions, the principal imperialist state in the hemisphere finds itself obligated to accept, or at least tolerate and adjust to, the political currents that under the banner of nationalism seek to reduce the internal social tensions of some countries, and obligated, as well, to maintain capitalism by readjusting its methods of operation and the very conditions of imperialist exploitation.

For this reason, both the principal and the other imperialist states must inevitably tolerate the sacrifice of the interests of this or that individual imperialist firm, especially those whose characteristics and modes of operation make them favored targets of nationalism. And, furthermore, they must often (in certain cases, unavoidably) allow the private policy of multinational firms to follow a course different from that favored by their own official administrations.

This situation is complicated by the increasing difficulties within the U.S. national economy. As a result of the international expansion of U.S. capital—which is precisely the base of the development of multinational monopolies—and of the economic consequences of the policy of a war in defense of the system (principally in Southeast Asia), the balance of trade and the balance of payments continue to run deficits for U.S. capitalism. Increasingly severe recessions (such as that of 1969–71, the lowest point of which was in 1970—when the gross national product failed to grow), unemployment (officially recorded as 6.2 percent in 1971), and an inflation that threatens to escape the state's short-term capacity to control, all reflect the difficulties U.S. national-imperialist capitalism has in competing, as a national economy, with the expansive capitalisms of Japan and West Germany, and with the international network of multinational firms generated by U.S.-originated capital itself.

In the face of these difficulties, which in the short run could aggravate the new strong tendencies toward political-social conflict within the United States, the North American state is forced to adopt measures in defense of its national capitalism. To date, however, measures such as manipulation of the value of the dollar and protective tariffs have met with little success. Not only is the internationalization of the U.S. market unchecked, but international capital enters the United States even more easily as a result of the devaluation of the dollar.

This situation suggests that the hegemonic imperialist state seems to be trapped in the crosscurrents of profoundly contradictory needs:

1. The need to defend U.S. national capitalism from the effects on the United States of the international expansion of capital generated in

this same economy—that is, from the multinational firms controlled by U.S. capital.

2. The need to defend U.S. national capitalism from the other national-imperialist capitalisms, principally those of Japan and Germany.

3. The need to defend the world-capitalist system as a whole, in the face of the economic and political advance of the socialist camp, and in the face of the deepening class struggle within the system itself.

4. The need to defend the bourgeoisie's domination within the United States in the face of the increasing questioning of the system, currently taking the form of rebellion by ethnic and social minorities (Blacks, Indians, Puerto Ricans, and Chicanos), and the ideological rebellion of vast sectors of the young, principally university students (and as well, if the situation were to worsen, the U.S. proletariat itself).

The first of these needs presupposes arbitration between two categories of bourgeois interests: national-imperialist, and multinational-imperialist. The former interests are those of that sector of the U.S. bourgeoisie whose scale of operations is either totally national or less than 25 percent multinational. The latter interests are those of that fraction of the North American bourgeoisie whose scale of operations is predominantly multinational; these interests imply the defense of the North American bourgeoisie with multinational connections against the national-imperialist bourgeoisies of other countries, be they national or multinational. It is apparent, however, that the need to defend the world-capitalist system as a whole also implies arbitration between the need to defend the interests of the U.S. bourgeoisie from other bourgeoisies, on the one hand, and the need to defend the entire capitalist system, on the other.

In the face of the aggravation of the contradictions and social conflicts within U.S. society itself in the overall context of the sharpening crisis in the entire system, the state can temporarily pursue measures of arbitration that are unevenly balanced between bourgeoisie and workers. However, the deepening of the crisis of the entire system, within which the U.S. bourgeoisie is the principal protagonist, will most probably oblige the U.S. Government to develop an increasingly harsh repressive policy against workers and against currents of rebellion within other dominated social sectors in the society.

Thus, the problem of the social base of the hegemonic imperialist state involves not only the internal dynamics of North American society, but also the total imperialist bourgeoisie of the entire world system. And it is precisely here that the conflicts with which the North American state must deal manifest themselves most clearly. It is not possible to explore this particular problem further here, but it is important to urge researchers to take up the task. As for our concerns, however, we should at least be aware that in the realm of U.S.-Latin American relations, these problems exist and deserve to be studied.

In closing, it should be noted that although the North American state can arbitrate among the various elements of its bourgeoisie within U.S. society, in its relations with Latin America it clearly defends that element of its bourgeoisie that operates on a multinational scale. It favors these interests over those of other national-imperialist bourgeoisies, despite the limitations placed on this policy by (1) the need of global defense of the system and thus of the interests of the imperialist bourgeoisie as a whole and (2) the fact that multinational corporations are powerful enough to operate, at times, outside the bounds of their country's official policy.

The New Imperialist Context: The Latin American Political Crisis

In what follows, we shall begin to explore the implications, for the issues of class conflict and international relations, of the new model of imperialist accumulation in the current international setting.

We have previously observed that the Latin American countries do not all enter into the current world context in the same manner. I have thus suggested grouping them in three levels of integration with imperialist capitalism, according to the predominant mode of production and reproduction of capital. The next step would be to set up specific analytical frameworks for each group of countries. This, however, exceeds my purpose and the limits of this paper. For this reason, I should make clear that the empirical frame of reference for the general propositions presented here applies principally to the countries now becoming integrated into the international system of expanded reproduction and to those that have now begun the domestic realization and accumulation of surplus value on the basis of urban-industrial production. Such countries have gone beyond the early stage of simple production of surplus value in the primary sector, toward surplus value largely destined to be realized and accumulated beyond their borders.

Three trends in the current Latin American process deserve to be mentioned, all having to do with the problem of imperialism and international relations. Each will be discussed in turn:

1. The crystallization and intensification of the class struggle.

2. The crisis of political hegemony.

3. The relative autonomization of the state within the national framework.

Crystallization and intensification of the class struggle. This trend consists basically of the interaction of three elements: (a) the progressive crystallization of the class content of the coalition of dominant interests, owing to the decline in power of the feudal-mercantile landowners and of those groups of capitalist bourgeoisie whose interests were based on the most primitive modes of accumulation, and to the growth in power of the more modern elements of the bourgeoisie within the economy and the state; (b) the numerical expansion of the proletariat, the changes in its internal structure, and its rise to a central class position among the dominated sectors of the society; and (c) the redefinition of the position and functions of the middle sectors as they assume an intermediary role between the capitalist bourgeoisie and the proletariat, both in production and in the political sphere.

The expansion and diversification of capitalism in those countries under the control of imperialist capital, and in particular the emergence of urban-industrial bases of accumulation as the core of the economic structure, have led to the progressive eclipse of feudal-mercantile relations in the economy and the consequent deterioration of the power base of the feudal-mercantile landowning class. These trends have persisted sufficiently long that this class has begun to disappear, especially with respect to its access to the central mechanisms of the state. At the same time, the capitalist bourgeoisie (imperialist and dependent-associated) is becoming dominant in every sphere of economic activity, imposing its style and ideology on the culture and struggling to control the state.

Within this context and for these very reasons, the working class has become increasingly proletarianized at every level of dependent capitalism. It is becoming the central class among the dominated sectors, modifying the internal relationships among its various elements in each sector of the economy, and struggling to achieve political autonomy, in relation both to the middle sector's ideological influence and organic control, and to the bourgeois state. From a basically agro-extractive proletariat with a small urban-industrial sector, the working class has become primarily urban-industrial, and its elements in the more modern, industrial fields and the fields with the most technological and productive industries have begun to develop some social and political clout.

Although in the period immediately preceding 1950, the proletariat waged more of an anti-oligarchic than anti-bourgeois struggle, since it was pitted against a power coalition combining the dependent capitalist bourgeoisie and a sector of the declining feudal landowners, the proletariat is now confronted with domination by a new and modern bourgeoisie and only minimally by this bourgeoisie's former allies. In this manner class relations and the class struggle have been crystallized and intensified.

This new situation results also from the experience of the middle sectors. These sectors—especially the professional and bureaucratic groups that joined the proletariat in a popular anti-oligarchic coalition, owing to their lacking a field of action under the old model of accumulation, politics, and the economy—have now begun to exercise their role as intermediaries. To a large extent they have become integrated into the system and have had therefore to abandon their role as "opposers." The middle sectors have gradually lost interest in, and capacity to maintain, their former alliance with the dominated sectors, and with the proletariat in particular, and have thus been unable to maintain their ideological influence and organic political control over the workers.

This trend undoubtedly varies in its intensity and rhythm in Latin America, from one level of capitalist development to another, as previously discussed. Although the countries becoming sectorally integrated into the international system of expanded reproduction have undergone this process slowly, over a long time and in great depth, in those nations in which capitalism has only recently acquired an urban-industrial base for accumulation the trend is still maturing. By contrast, in the countries in which capitalism still consists primarily of the simple generation of surplus value to be realized and accumulated abroad, this trend is probably only now entering its first stages. Nevertheless, it is important to note that the process is likely to evolve faster in the latter countries, and for this reason the structural contradictions of dependent capitalism, as well as social conflicts, could be more intense there. That this should be so is due, above all, to the fact that these processes now take place in the new context of imperialist capitalism with all of its implications.

The crisis of political hegemony. The trend toward the crystallization and intensification of the class struggle has made and will continue to make itself felt within a framework that accentuates the uneven character of dependent capitalism in Latin America. As I have pointed out above, all modes of capitalist accumulation from the most primitive to the most recent exist in these countries, interconnecting, combining, and superimposing themselves on one another. These patterns vary not only from country to country, but also within each country.

As I have indicated elsewhere,[6] this variation results from the fact that the capitalist process in our countries derives not from the maturation of a single mode or stage of production within the national framework, but rather from the injection from without, by imperialist capital, of each form of production or reproduction of capital. The result, therefore, is not the elimination of the elements of one mode in a thorough and homogeneous manner throughout the economy of the country, but rather the lessening of the relative importance of that mode and the domination of the most recent mode—while the scope of operations of previous modes and the forms of precapitalist production do in fact diminish

---

[6] See Aníbal Quijano Obregón, *Polo marginal y mano de obra marginal en la economía latinoamericana* (Santiago: 1971), mimeographed edition.

within the economy in the process. When this occurs, the respective social interests, classes, and social sectors generated in the predominant
stages of each mode of accumulation shift their relative positions in the
social-economic and political spectrum, and increase or reduce their
weight in a quite heterogeneous manner.

Under these circumstances, the crystallization and intensification of
class relations and the class struggle become uneven and irregular rather
than massive and homogeneous. In this context, the reduction of power
exerted by the feudal-mercantile landowning class, and of the sectors of
the capitalist bourgeoisie whose interests were based on previous forms
of accumulation—all proceeding in the face of the ascendency of bourgeois sectors connected to the more recent forms of accumulation—gave
rise from the start to a process in which all these interests competed for
hegemony over one another while at the same time tending to coalesce.

Nevertheless, as capitalism has expanded and become modernized, the
new bourgeois sectors have made their intention to gain power ever more
explicit. In doing so, they have increasingly found themselves aligned
with the middle sectors, which in turn have grown in number and increasingly act as intermediaries. Moreover, so long as the proletariat was ideologically and politically dominated by these middle sectors, the new
bourgeoisie joined them both in anti-oligarchic political alliances. The political phenomenon called "populism" in Latin America, which can constitute both a movement and a political regime, has been the political
expression of this process of change in the concrete social bases of the
state.

This process had a relatively early beginning and long duration, as well
as a more complete and clear development, in the countries of the first
group (Argentina, Brazil, etc.). Among the countries of the second group
(Peru, Colombia, etc.), the process began after the 1950s and had a brief
and precarious duration. In the remaining countries, it appears that oligarchic rule, with its typical repressive features, though combined with
elements of this process, still predominates. In all of these countries,
"populism" has been a peculiar expression of the growing differentiation of interests and styles of domination among the principal dominant
groups. But it has also been the expression of the inability of the new
bourgeois sectors to impose their interests and style of domination on
the other dominant groups.

The inability of these new bourgeois sectors to establish hegemony
has not been limited to their contacts with the oligarchic, bourgeois elements and the rest of the feudal-mercantile landowning class. Although
this particular failure was undoubtedly important, the decisive factors lie
elsewhere: at the very moment that the new bourgeois sectors acquired

decisive economic power, and the middle sectors tied their expectations to the new capitalist forms, the contradictions that arose both from the heightened asymmetry in the character of this economy and from the ideological-political effects of the class struggle on the international level were pushing the dominated sectors (first the peasants and almost immediately thereafter the proletariat) toward a confrontation with the dominating landowners (both feudal-mercantile and capitalist) and exploitative urban-industrial capital. At the same time, middle-sector youths, principally university students and intellectuals, all influenced by the Cuban revolution, were becoming more radical in their ideology and political conduct and had begun questioning not simply the oligarchic rule but the legitimacy of the entire system. The doubts they raised soon created a crisis among the institutions and groups accorded the function of legitimation and ideological control in the system: the universities and the Church.

The massive mobilizations of *campesinos,* now pressing not just for institutionalized channels in which to voice their economic demands, but also for abolishing the property and the power of the landowners, threatened the whole existence of the system in an even more profound manner. The threat arose not as an explicit purpose of the *campesino* movements, but because of their political implications for the basic structure of power. Though the mobilizations of the proletariat failed to reach a level of political development that might threaten political power, they nevertheless demonstrated sufficient strength to threaten the bases of accumulation. Most important, these mobilizations began to free the working-class movement from the domination of the anti-oligarchic middle sectors, for the proletariat's demands and mobilizations went quite beyond the expectations of these middle sectors.

In this convulsive context, which characterized the decade from the middle 1950s to the middle 1960s, populism entered into open crisis. That is to say, the modernized bourgeois sectors and their middle-sector allies found themselves obliged to retreat in the face of mobilizations by the dominated classes and the crisis in their own institutions of ideological legitimation. The crisis of intra-bourgeois hegemony had not been resolved, and the skies were heavy with popular storms threatening the domination of the entire power coalition. Though their mobilizations were consistently met by systematic, bloody, and massive repression, the dominated classes only gained in strength. Concomitantly, the political bankruptcy of the contradictory populist or para-populist political alliances aggravated the crisis of political hegemony.

Within this framework, it was inevitable that the groups and institutions playing an intermediary role within the political order would expand the margin of relative autonomy accruing to them from the power crisis. The groups playing this role were the armed forces and the increasingly techno-professional bureaucracy. Owing to their nature and function the armed forces had in most of these countries acquired a closed structure that encouraged independence in internal affairs and in the use of their resources. In short, the military became a sort of sub-state within the state. Thus, in all of the countries in which the dominated classes had failed to reach a sufficient level of organization and political competence, owing to specific historic factors, but could be expected to take on a quicker pace, the armed forces were well situated to take control of the state's administrative and repressive apparatus—given the political bankruptcy of the bourgeoisie and the political weakness of the dominated classes.

The relative autonomization of the state. The deeper the crisis of political hegemony, and the weaker the dominated class's political development, the larger the margin of relative autonomy achieved by the military-technocratic regimes. At the same time, the state—controlled by these social forces—was increasing its relative autonomy with respect to the basic classes of the national society.

Here, however, a crucial distinction must be made. In some of these countries the dependent bourgeois groups, drawing upon an early and extended process of capitalist expansion, had attained a substantial level of power. In other countries, by contrast, these groups had reached only a very shaky status—had not effectively become a class with nationwide power. For this reason, popular mobilizations were also quite well developed in the first countries, and were a more immediate threat to bourgeois domination (even when they simply took an anti-oligarchic form); whereas in the smaller countries the political development of the dominated classes was as weak as the development of the dependent bourgeoisie itself.

In each of these political-social contexts, therefore, the military-techno-professional-bureaucratic coalition's relative autonomy vis-à-vis the bourgeoisie, and thus the relative autonomy of the state vis-à-vis the bourgeoisie, was quite different. In Brazil, for example, especially in the first phase of military rule, the state enjoyed a significant margin of autonomy. Politically, however, with respect to the bourgeoisie this margin was much smaller. To be sure, the military regime did away with the bourgeoisie's political cadres and groups, but the economic policy was from the start rooted firmly in the clearest interests of the more "modern" sectors of the bourgeoisie, that is, in the interests of deeper and more organic integration into the new context of imperialist capitalism.

In Peru, however, the weakness of the dependent bourgeoisie, its political bankruptcy just prior to the military coup, and the defeat of the *campesino* and workers' movements (by means of bloody repression persisting for almost a decade) allowed the military-technocratic regime to come to power with a virtually free hand—that is, with considerable political autonomy vis-à-vis society's basic classes. It was this situation, more than any other circumstance, that permitted the military regime to attempt the construction of a "model" of class conciliation shortly after taking power. In such a model, the state was obliged to be autonomous and to play the role mainly of arbitrator. Obviously, however, the system could not endure for long. Shortly thereafter, despite minor conflicts with certain bourgeois groups over the expansion of state capitalism, the military regime initiated a process of total readjustment of the country's economic integration into the sphere of imperialist capitalism. As a result, the regime's autonomy with respect to the bourgeoisie has tended to diminish, and its conflict with the dominated classes to increase.

But in Chile, where the political development of popular movements provoked an overt power struggle between the bourgeoisie and the workers, owing to the growing crisis of political hegemony, the state—because it is shared and disputed by antagonistic classes—probably enjoys less autonomy than the Peruvian state. In any case, one cannot ignore the fact that the state, under whatever specific modality in whatever country (including Chile), has in a very short time altered its role and its functions in the economy and politics of Latin America, moving in the direction of relative autonomization, and also creating its own base of economic power through state capitalism.

This shift accounts for the fact that profound changes have taken place in relations among classes, and also between classes and the state, deepening the crisis of political hegemony. Despite the seeming strength and stability of certain military regimes today, in their efforts to readjust the system of domination, it is doubtful that the system can be relegitimized. It must therefore be imposed through increasing dosages of naked force.

A New Power Elite?

The new situation is manipulated, and the new functions of the state are carried out, by those groups now in direct control of the state: the armed forces, the techno-professional bureaucracy, and business circles. Under the slogan of "participatorianism" some union bureaucrats are exploring the possibility of their incorporation into this power orbit—until now without results. But remembering the Vandor case in Onganía's Argentina, and the recent invention of "participatory, nondemanding unionism" on the part of the military regime in Peru, we should thus not find it very surprising if, eventually, one or another union bureaucrat is incorporated into the system to "participate."

Thus, a new power elite seems to be emerging on the scene. In representing themselves as defenders of the interests of capital, the members of this elite have very clear interests: to control and appropriate the vast resources at the disposal of state capitalism—in association with the large international monopolies.

This potential power elite is more autonomous the weaker the dependent bourgeoisie and the weaker the political development of the working class; and it can become quite powerful, as it has in Peru. Although the argument also holds to some extent in the Brazilian situation, it appears that here the key to the state's position within the society is the private bourgeoisie's control over the state's economic policy.

In order to operate and to develop, the power coalition is forced to integrate state capital with imperialist capital, subordinating the weakest private groups of the bourgeoisie to this alliance. At the same time, however, the coalition can and does enter into conflict with private imperialist firms, principally with those that are still tied to former modes of accumulation and are therefore centers of tension that the new state can tolerate only at the risk of weakening its present position.

Though this type of regime would prefer to integrate workers into its power base, it is objectively unable to do so. For it must operate under the typical conditions of economies that are not only underdeveloped, but integrated into the needs of imperialist accumulation under its new forms—forms that require a broadened base and an increase in the rate of profits. Thus, such a regime usually attempts to control workers by means of corporative mechanisms and organizations, at first using populist techniques of manipulation, but later broadening and increasingly systematizing a process of violent repression. For their part, the workers are forced to defend their standard of living and at the same time defend the class autonomy of their organizations from corporativism.

The real social bases of such a regime are thus much less consistent than they seem, and only systematic repression can maintain the status quo for any length of time. The intensifying of the crisis of imperialism, the growth of class struggle within the metropolitan countries themselves, and the deepening of the contradictions in dependent capitalism's unevenly combined development are middle-run factors that can only continue to undermine the fragile stability of these regimes.

Latin America's international relations have already begun to be molded by these factors. The class struggle, which changes the social bases of the national-dependent state within the new context of imperialism in crisis, should thus be made the focus of all attempts to explore systematically the trends and the alternatives of the international relations of these countries.

Commentary on Quijano

PHILIPPE C. SCHMITTER

Quijano's essay is an impressive, indeed a superb, example of the extent to which Marxism can become more a rhetorical language than an analytical instrument. Those who believe that Marxism can be revised and renewed in a creative manner to understand critically the changing reality of capitalist development are likely to be somewhat disappointed by his essay; those who regard Marxism primarily as providing a language of disputation for oppressed classes and radical political movements will no doubt find it of considerable interest and, perhaps, praxiological value.

Of course, these two aspects of contemporary Marxism need not conflict—they did not in Marx's own work. There is no intrinsic reason why analytical Marxism must be as overintellectualized and obscurantist as, say, Althusser would make it; or as routinized and sloganeering as, say, the Communist Party of the Soviet Union would prefer it. Nevertheless, I do not find that Quijano has managed to combine these different priorities and objectives particularly well in his essay.[1]

The reader himself can furnish some proof of this. I invite him simply to translate large portions of it verbatim, as I have done, into the contrasting rhetoric of bourgeois social science. By merely substituting key phrases—"developed economies" for "economía capitalista metropolitana," "international or foreign entrepreneurs" for "burguesía imperialista," "dominant power position" for "posición hegemónica," and so forth—it

Philippe Schmitter is with the Department of Political Science, University of Chicago.

[1] When I presented an initial criticism of the first draft of Quijano's paper at the Lima conference, I also rather foolishly agreed to do the same for its second and final version. Now, some nine months later, I find myself confronted with a substantially revised essay and a one-week deadline for submission of comments. To make matters worse, I have since moved to Geneva and left all my notes and books on the topic in Chicago. Therefore, I apologize at the outset to Professor Quijano for not having had the opportunity to discuss this critique with him. Had I been able to do so, I might have avoided some of the misunderstandings and misplaced emphases that no doubt remain. I also apologize to the reader for its obviously hurried composition and for its complete lack of the protective scholarly apparatus of references and footnotes.

should be possible to obtain a descriptive correspondence for perhaps 50 to 60 percent of the content of the essay. For example, selecting at random, we find that on p. 72 Quijano says:

Moreover, to the extent that the foreign policies of the principal national-imperialist states were not guided by a global strategy of defense of the system, but rather by the goal of expanding the domination of national-imperialism, these policies usually corresponded closely to the concrete concerns of the imperialist firms having interests in Latin America.

Our hypothetical bourgeois social scientist would say:

On the other hand, to the extent that the foreign policies of the greater powers—in the case of Latin America, that of the United States—were not dictated by the global constraints of the existing international system, but by its narrower national interests, these policies were closely linked to the concrete concerns of the various foreign firms with interests in Latin America.

Despite the sharp rhetorical difference, the descriptive content of the statements is quite similar. If not afforded a mutual opportunity to explore their assertions further, one might even say there existed a consensus between them on this and on numerous other passages in Quijano's essay.

Of course, this obscured descriptive consensus could be taken as a sign of strength, rather than as evidence of weakness. In this case, all we would have to do to establish the "facts" of imperialism cum inter-American relations would be to consult such an "ideological glossary." Bourgeois and Marxist scholars would, of course, go on using their different rhetorics in speaking to their respective audiences, but would be in substantive agreement concerning what "really" happened or is happening. Such a "solution" is tantamount to admitting that neither is capable of analyzing and understanding the structures of society and the outcomes of societal transformation. Both can only label them and (in the case of Marxists) denounce them or (in the case of bourgeois social scientists) apologize for them.

An additional but still substantial portion of what Quijano has said in the essay can be shown to be true by definition, or can easily be made "true" by further extrapolation. For example, if I were to suggest that not all dominated classes in Latin America have opposed imperialism, that some have actually supported it or remained indifferent to the nationality of their exploiter or the ultimate destination of their surplus value, and, hence, that the struggle against imperialism cannot be, even descriptively, based exclusively on a class model, my observation can easily be dismissed as irrelevant, since those were not "really" oppressed classes—or, as we could more likely expect to hear, since those classes suffered from "false consciousness." If I were to point out that one must consider the relatively autonomous role of status ("sectores medios"), ethnic, linguistic, cultural, and purely political factors in understanding nationalistic responses to imperial domination, I could simply be told either that "in the last instance" these were reducible to economic causes or that "in any case" challenges to imperialism rooted in these superstructural elements never "really" changed the system of domination. If I were to argue, like the North American authors in this volume *a capella,* that bureaucratic routines make it difficult if not impossible for U.S. foreign policy to obey flexibly "the concrete concerns of each of the foreign firms with interests in Latin America," I could be dismissed with the assertion that the central political system of *the* (unitary) imperialist order is really acting in the long-term interests of capitalist domination while ignoring the short-term demands of individual firms.

This point is perhaps worth exploring further, since it is where I diverge most sharply from Quijano. Repeatedly in his essay he expresses great faith in the singular purposiveness, the concerted intelligence, and the capacity for long-range planning and execution of capitalist political institutions. This global system of domination appears to him to be so well articulated and polished that it can reconcile apparently clashing national positions, co-opt and convert ostensible opponents into agents at its service, and assert its long-term, strategic goals over short-term tactical interests. Quijano does acknowledge some contradictions in this impressive performance (and I shall discuss these), but we must recognize that he has moved a long way from the classical Marxist position (which I confess to share) that it was precisely the absence of these capabilities that made the capitalist state so weak and so potentially transient. At best, it can be said that there is considerable vacillation in Quijano's assessment of the present and future viability of domestic and imperial political relations under capitalism, and that this detracts from the essay's praxiological clarity. For heuristic purposes, it might be useful to admit that one is in doubt about whether a given mode of domination is or is not becoming more unified, more flexible, or more adaptable; but if one's purpose is to assert "scientific truths" for the purpose of guiding radical praxis, then such ambiguity is simply confusing.

But also, if rhetoric is to be effective, its terminology should be more or less clearly defined and consistently applied. Here, I am not suggesting that general assertions must be accompanied by empirical evidence or even concrete illustrations (although I admit I would prefer that to be the case), but that they must be labeled with words that are intelligible within the general theoretical tradition one is using and consistent in meaning from one sentence or paragraph to the next. Quijano repeatedly brings into his account expressions drawn from other theoretical paradigms (i.e. from bourgeois social science), such as "sectores medios," "capas medias o sociales," "clases [Quijano uses the plural] dominadas," "sector urbano-industrial," "minorías étnico-sociales," "grupos generacionales," etc. I would be the least qualified to criticize such conceptual eclecticism (I practise it myself), but it seems to me these expressions deserve at least to be defined and to be accorded some effort at theoretical integration, since they hint at the important role of stratification systems and social cleavages based on structural principles other than property. Making the effort is made all the more imperative by Quijano's frequently implying that these groups provide much of the conflict potential in both metropolitan and peripheral societies.

I could also have benefited from more explicit definitions and consistent usage in the Marxist terms he uses. Take, for example, "hegemony." On p. 72, we are told that the international policies of Latin American societies "without a bourgeois class" have always been a reflection of one or more hegemonic national-imperialist states. The meaning of hegemonic here is linked to "explicit submission to the dictates of the interests of imperialist firms." Elsewhere (especially pp. 86ff) we find the same concept used in its more Gramscian sense of the capacity of a given mode of class domination to elicit voluntary, "legitimate" compliance from subordinate groups through mechanisms of ideological manipulation and political socialization. I am not suggesting which of these meanings is intrinsically "correct," only pointing out that attaching both to the same concept detracts from rhetorical elegance and, more important, may lead to praxiological confusion over how to exploit different "crises of hegemony." Finally I confess, still at the rhetorical level, to some difficulty in following the logical consistency of Quijano's argument. This was particularly the case with his central argument that owing to "profound alterations in the technical and organic composition of imperialist capital" (pp. 76ff), the system has entered a crisis of "overaccumulation." Here Quijano does not seem to be invoking the classic argument about the declining rate and/or volume of profit (difficult to sustain in the face of the recent balance sheets of large North American and Western European firms), but a "technicist" argument based on greater capital intensity and scale of production. I have no quarrel here. Quijano is simply saying in a different language what innumerable bourgeois theorists of the multinational enterprise have said. What I cannot understand is the inference he draws—namely, that this inexorably results in a sharpening of the contradictions of capitalism—especially when he, himself, quite clearly points to a number of structural changes that have occurred in both metropolitan centers and peripheral "subcenters" to accommodate and encourage this shifting structure. Is the reader simply supposed to accept on faith that contradictions are intensifying, and, hence, that the whole structure of imperialist domination is in some new prospect of destroying itself?

Here, plainly, we have left the level of descriptive rhetoric and truistic assertion and begun to deal with analysis itself. If I have earlier given the impression that Quijano's essay is "just" or "only" an exercise in rhetoric— even conceding that I regard such verbal expositions as praxiologically important (if a bit wasted on cynical academics like me)—I have misled the reader. The essay does contain passages in which Quijano attempts to bring a sort of dialectical mode of analysis to bear on the problem.

I confess that I have encountered considerable difficulty in criticizing, even in understanding, these more analytical passages in the essay. As mentioned above, I occasionally found it impossible to follow the argument or line of reasoning and, hence, was often startled or unprepared for the conclusions he drew from it. Undoubtedly, the fault here lies chiefly with me; not being sufficiently familiar with Quijano's other works or with the specific tradition of Marxism from which he is developing these ideas, I simply cannot grasp the "theoretical shorthand" the author has been compelled to use by the brevity and breadth of the present essay. Partly, however, my comprehension is impeded by the fact that, while Quijano thinks and writes dialectically, he does not explicitly employ the instruments of dialectical reasoning. One searches in vain for a sense of the unity of opposites, for the relational mechanisms whereby comprehensive social structures determine specific social formations or historical outcomes, for distinctions between primary and secondary contradictions, for statements about the critical limits at which negation occurs, for the possible role of overdetermination in establishing at what point the existing mode of production or domination is no longer capable of assuring its own reproduction, etc. Only when these intermediary steps have been explicitly taken would it be possible to evaluate adequately the logical consistency of the argument and, eventually, its correspondence with empirical reality.

If, however, I have understood and can reconstruct the originality of Quijano's analytical argument, it consists of two parts. In the first, he offers an enumeration and description of recent structural changes in metropolitan and peripheral capitalist countries, or, as he puts it, "tendencies toward change in the modes of imperialist domination." Whatever reservations I may have expressed above, they are quite secondary to the fundamental importance of this part of Quijano's essay. One might complain that his summary of changes is too comprehensive or not comprehensive enough, that some of the transformations are deduced too abstractly while others are induced too concretely, but what is significant is that Quijano for the first time to my knowledge in the *dependencia* literature has systematically attempted to analyze capitalism as a dynamic and constantly changing set of institutions and practices—at the service, of course, of the same basic mode of exploitation. This constitutes a radical break with the sort of stagnant, post hoc analysis that postulated capitalism as a fixed and immutable system imposed on Latin America some five hundred years ago and evolving—once and finally—from an "old" to a "new" form of *dependencia*. With it, we return to a much more Marxist theory of capitalist international relations in which the "imperialist chain" not only is changing at its periphery but also is being constantly transformed at its metropolitan origin. In fact, although Quijano himself does not explicitly state it, one gathers from his list that the weakest links in contemporary capitalism have moved closer and closer to the center. In particular, the future viability of capitalism is seen as highly dependent upon certain special weaknesses of capitalism in the United States. This approach, in my view a much more subtle and more realistic one, is quite a change from the literature of a few years ago that postulated the hegemony and omnipotence of the United States as the "historically necessary" and ineluctable product of capitalist development in its more concentrated phase.

Having identified these recent structural changes in the "imperialist chain" (e.g., the preponderant role of multinational firms and internationalized capital, and their special combination of horizontal and vertical integration and growing independence from national control; the expansion of public policy and state capitalism in both central and peripheral economies; the displacement of industrial production of intermediate and even capital goods to certain dependent economies and the subsequent creation of "imperialist subcenters"; an increasing degree of competition between central capitalist economies and the consequent amplification of margins of policy maneuverability in dependent countries; the emergence of regional and subregional blocs and alliances, especially among dependent countries; etc.), the next step is to analyze the new patterns of change and conflict, within and between nations, that ensue from these. It seems clear (to me, at any rate) that the class, sectoral, and international conflicts postulated by the former, static model of imperialist domination require respecification, and that revolutionary praxis based on those former assumptions is increasingly likely to be ineffectual, if not counterproductive.

Here, again, I must express some disappointment with Quijano's essay. Though his summary of structural changes strikes me as of major importance (but not, I must also insist, very different in substance from that offered by several bourgeois theorists of so-called transnational politics), his subsequent analysis seems to me not to fulfill this initial promise.

What, then, *are* the contradictions of this restructured imperialist system with its multiple centers and subcenters, its increasingly autonomous giant enterprises and state apparatuses, its wider margins of political tolerance and capacity for policy differentiation? Quijano offers three principal candidates. Two of these are, I submit, ritualistic incantations left over from the earlier, static model and quite unconvincing on either logical or empirical grounds. His argument that "the global confrontation of the capitalist international system and the emerging socialist camp" is a "fundamental determination" in the "intensifying crises within capitalism" at a time when the economic and political interpenetration of the major powers—the United States, Europe, and the Soviet Union—is sharply increasing, and when China is showing clear signs of joining "the concert of powers," strikes me as not very compelling. Similarly, his invocation of "the purifying and intensifying of class struggle within the capitalist system" seems based more on wishful thinking than on available empirical evidence or logically derivable trends into the near future. Granted that there are signs of a new militancy in the trade union movements and spontaneous extra-union activity of the proletariat in developed economies, but most of this is concentrated on sectoral-type defenses of existing structures against further rationalization of production or relative deterioration due to inflation. Nor do I find much evidence that the proletariat in dependent capitalist societies is behaving differently, especially where it is dominated by its metropolitan, "aristocratic" component (as, for example, in Argentina) or by solidly entrenched state-corporatist structures (as, for example, in Brazil).

We are left, then, with intra- or inter-bourgeois "contradictions." Quijano devotes a great deal more of his attention to these than to a systematic exposition of conflicts between classes or between modes of production. It does not seem excessive to suggest that he considers these the most dynamic elements in his "model," the source of ultimate negation. Despite his originality and subtlety in discovering and diagnosing these clashes of interest between fractions of a single bourgeoisie or between central and peripheral bourgeoisies, I fail to see how these, even the sum total of these, constitute a threat to capitalism itself. Surely, if we have learned anything from the political history of capitalism, especially since the middle of the nineteenth century, it is that it has shown an extraordinary capacity for survival despite repeated and varying differences of interest within the bourgeoisie. Somehow, when the basic structure of property and institutions of domination appear threatened, those "contradictions" are set aside. This may involve, as Marx argued in the *Eigh-*

teenth Brumaire, temporary abrogations of national political hegemony —an exchange of "the right to rule for the right to make money"—or, in the more interdependent world of the twentieth century, the creation of new international arrangements to redefine statuses and redistribute marginal benefits between national bourgeoisies. But these hardly seem to be paving the way for the transition to socialism—as have defeat in international war, complete absence of bourgeois hegemony, and/or the presence of a radical proletarian movement.

Much as I would agree with Quijano that the analysis of intra- and inter-bourgeois conflicts of interest is important for understanding the direction of political change *within* capitalist society, it seems to me to be an inflation of rhetoric to elevate these to the status of contradictions, by which, I think, Marx meant structural incompatibilities that cannot be resolved *without* a fundamental change in the mode of exploitation/ domination. To mistake one for the other, even verbally, is to convert Marxist analysis into a "mere" theory of interest conflict.

A commentary as brief and as hurried as this can hardly expect to do justice to an essay as comprehensive in substance and as innovative in theoretical terms as that by Quijano. The temptation is great (and I have succumbed to it) to dwell exclusively if superficially on those aspects that seem most easy to criticize. It is more difficult to praise effectively those aspects one finds most original and admirable.

What confused me in reading Quijano's essay was to find that though I could agree with a good deal of his substantive and descriptive comment on the recent evolution of capitalist institutions in both the center and the periphery of the global system, I could not at all agree with the analytical inferences he drew from these observations. At the risk of oversimplification, I shall propose that our analytical differences can be reduced to two quite paradoxical points. On the one hand, I am *less* impressed than Quijano with the purposiveness, unity, and long-term directive capacity of the *domestic* political institutions of capitalist societies. I believe they are in a very fundamental crisis that has its origins not in purely economic contradictions, e.g. "overaccumulation," but in more purely political, military, and ideological factors. On the other hand, I am much *more* impressed than Quijano with the extent to which transformations in the *international* economic and political institutions of capitalism (especially in its relations with socialist societies) have added new elements of flexibility and viability to that mode of exploitation and domination. Less and less capable of assuring the conditions of its reproduction at the domestic or national level, capitalism seems to me more and more capable of guaranteeing its survival and expansion at the inter-societal or international level.

Economic Relations Between Latin America and the United States: Some Implications and Perspectives

ANÍBAL PINTO

In the course of the past decade, and especially during the past few years, some clear trends have been emerging in the economic relations of Latin America and the United States. Some of the results of these trends are well known, but the trends also obscure facts that are rarely considered and rather surprising. To facilitate this exposition, I shall examine commercial and financial relations separately, and then attempt an overall summary.[1]

Relative Marginalization of Latin America from the U.S. Market

If one first considers the flow of exports, it is easy to verify the decrease in relative importance of the sales of the periphery (the third world) in general, and of Latin America in particular within the U.S. market, despite the fact that these sales are at the same time expanding in absolute terms (see Table 1). As is apparent from Table 1, our region's exports have increased at a slower rate than those of the third world as a whole (5 percent, as compared to 7 percent). This lag was due fundamentally to the minimal increase of Latin America's exports to the United States, a mere 2.1 percent annual increase from 1960 to 1970 (excluding Cuba). As a result, Latin America's share of total U.S. imports decreased from 24 percent to 11 percent from the first to the last years of the decade, a drop much sharper than the net drop of the third world as a whole— 40 percent to 25 percent (see the table).

The same trend could be seen, though less dramatically, in the declining importance of the U.S. market for Latin American exports. Although

Aníbal Pinto is a member of the Economic Commission for Latin America (ECLA), Santiago.

[1]The opinions expressed in this paper are my own, and not necessarily those of ECLA (CEPAL). The materials that will be presented derive from Aníbal Pinto and Jan Kñakal, "El sistema centro-periferia, 20 años después" (Santiago: CEPAL, mimeographed); and Jan Kñakal, "Las relaciones económicas entre América Latina y los Estados Unidos en los años sesenta" (Santiago: CEPAL). A substantial part of the first of these documents appeared in *Estudio Económico de América Latina* (Santiago: CEPAL, 1971).

TABLE 1
Marginalization of Latin America from the U.S. Market

		Percent	
Exports	Year	To all center nations[a]	To the United States
Average annual rate of increase (1960-70)			
All third world nations		7.4%	5.3%
Latin America		5.0	2.1
Share in center's total imports			
All third world nations	1960	24	40
	1965	21	32
	1970	18	25
Latin America	1960	8	24 (22[b])
	1965	6	17 (17[b])
	1970	5	11 (11[b])
Share in third world's total exports			
Total third world	1960	72	22
	1965	72	19
	1970	74	18
Latin America	1960	79	42
	1965	72	32
	1970	74	30

Source: UN Statistical Yearbook and *Monthly Bulletin of Statistics* (New York: United Nations, 1961-71).
[a]According to the UN classification system, the nations of the center are "developed nations with market economies"; the nations of the third world are "developing nations with market economies."
[b]Excluding Cuba.

the United States absorbed a little over 40 percent of Latin America's exports at the beginning of the 1960s, this proportion had dropped to 30 percent by the end of the decade. The decline in importance of the U.S. market for the third world as a whole was less marked, however— from 22 percent to 18 percent in the same period. Latin America's share of the total exports from the United States during the decade decreased from 17.4 percent to 13.3 percent.

The reasons for these phenomena are well known. On the one hand, there has been a decreased dynamism in the exchange of raw materials for manufactured goods; that is, there has been more expansion within the sector of producers/exporters of industrial goods than between this sector and the nations that produce and export raw materials and food-stuffs.[2] In other words, the crucial factor is essentially the preservation

[2]Trade between the central countries represented 64 percent of all transactions in 1958 and

of what Dr. Raúl Prebish called "the past framework of the international division of labor" between the center and the periphery. It is also evident that Latin America's position relative to other parts of the third world has worsened, even though everyone's share in U.S. trade has been reduced. It is not possible to discuss here the causes of this particular trend, in which—as is sometimes stressed—more than Latin America's foreign trade policy has been influential.[3]

On the other hand, the behavior of the flows of imports and exports led to very significant changes in the balance of trade. Although the balance has traditionally been favorable to Latin America (see Table 4) and averaged $186 million per year between 1961 and 1965, it turned unfavorable to Latin America during the last five years of the 1960s, with a deficit averaging $251 million annually. The situation grew more serious in 1969 and 1970, with the deficit reaching $795 million in the latter year. This, as will be seen further on, was decisive in the accentuated disequilibrium of the total balance of payments for Latin America during these years. In addition to indicating a clear weakening of trade ties, these data indicate a trend toward the worsening of Latin America's commercial position.

Some Signs to the Contrary

The "relative marginalization" of Latin America should be examined critically in the light of other factors that, if not directly contradicting this phenomenon, condition it to an extent that is significant but difficult to evaluate (we are of course concerned here solely with matters connected with trade). From Latin America's viewpoint, the most important consideration here is that in spite of the above-mentioned shifts, the United States is still its principal client and supplier, more the latter than the former. The situation of course differs from one country to the next. The exceptions to the rule are the limited group of nations including Argentina, Uruguay, Chile, Bolivia, and Paraguay (although for the last three the United States continued to be the most important supplier until the late 1960s[4]). By contrast, there are economies such as Mexico, Colombia, Venezuela, the majority of the Central American nations, and the

---

reached 74 percent in 1968. Moreover, the increase in the contribution of manufactured products to inter-center trade was similar (see Pinto and Kñakal, "El sistema centro-periferia," Table 2).

[3] According to a recent OAS study (CIAP, March 1969), one-third of the relative marginalization of Latin America from the U.S. market during the 1960s can be explained by the region's displacement in favor of other exporters, and two-thirds by the change in the composition of U.S. imports in favor of manufactured products.

[4] For more precise details on this subject, see CEPAL, "Tendencias y estructuras de las economías latinoamericanas," *Estudio Económico de América Latina* (Santiago: 1970).

Dominican Republic in which trade with the United States is overwhelmingly important.[5]

The second aspect to consider is the long-term importance of the U.S. market to the development of the region's manufactured exports. Between 1960 and 1969 this sector overall grew at quite a high rate—16.7 percent annually. The greatest dynamism occurred in sales within the region and between the region and Western Europe, while sales to the United States—14 percent of the annual increase—were somewhat less dynamic (see Table 2). In 1969, the latest year recorded, the United States absorbed 30 percent of Latin America's manufactured exports, with a total value of $328 million, easily outstripping the total share of the other nations of the center.

TABLE 2
Exports of Latin American Manufactured Products,[a]
By Destination

Destination	Millions of US$		Average annual growth rate in percent, 1960–69	Percent of total	
	1960	1969		1960	1969
Center nations	197	536	11.8%	73%	50%
United States	–	328	14.1[b]	–	30
Western Europe	–	177	22.2[b]	–	16
Latin America	58	500	27.5	22	46
Other	14	44			

Source: Monthly Bulletin of Statistics (New York: United Nations), March and May, 1967 and 1971, and June 1971; and CEPAL, *América Latina y la tercera UNCTAD* (Santiago, DOC. E/CN. 12/L/74), January 1972, p. 82.
[a] As defined by Sections 5–8, excluding Chapter 68, of the CUCI classification.
[b] 1961–69.

The present and potential significance of the United States with respect to certain goods (cotton fiber or thread, rods and spindles, iron tubes, adding machines and other electrical equipment) exported almost exclusively to this market should also be stressed. Understandably, the future of this trade depends to a great extent on the policy of U.S.-owned international firms operating in Latin America.[6] I shall return to this issue.

If the problem is now analyzed from the point of view of the United

[5] Mexico, for example, until 1968 realized about 65 percent of its exchange with the United States. See CEPAL, "Tendencias y estructuras."
[6] Between 1957 and 1966, the manufactured exports of North American subsidiaries in the region grew from 83 to 688 million dollars. In the latter year, 169 million were returned to the United States. See H. K. May, "The Effects of the United States' and Other Foreign Investment in Latin America" (The Council for Latin America, January 1970).

States, other factors influencing the trend toward relative marginalization or distancing can be identified. Of course there should be no over-
looking the fact that while U.S. sales to Latin America decreased in comparison to total U.S. sales, they increased appreciably in absolute terms,
rising from some $3,520 million in 1960 to $5,650 million in 1970 (see
Table 4), outstripping U.S. sales to Africa and Asia. In addition, as will
be seen below, these exports play an important role in the U.S. balance
of payments.

But perhaps more significant than the absolute statistics are some qualitative features related to the importance of the Latin American market
for certain U.S. exports. If we take the year 1968, we see that purchases
of U.S. chemical products by Latin America reached $620 million, far
exceeding the respective purchases of Canada, Japan, or the European
Free Trade nations, and comparing favorably with the value of the European Common Market's purchases ($750 million). In the same year, our
region acquired $2,210 million in machinery and equipment from the
United States, a figure surpassing the respective figures of the European
Common Market ($1,970 million), the European Free Trade nations
($1,260 million), and Japan. Finally, we should bear in mind that with
regard to "diverse manufactured items" Latin America was outstripped
as a purchaser only by Canada and the European Common Market. It is
important to note also that Latin America's imports in these and other
categories are concentrated in a relatively small number of large firms—
firms that wield strategic power in the U.S. economy.

Though these data make clear the importance of the United States as
a provider of vital ingredients for the region's economies, it is also apparent that the markets of the Latin American nations are of unquestionable
importance to the functioning of the U.S. system. This fact is underscored
if we evaluate the role of Latin America as a supplier of raw materials.
As can be seen in Table 3, near the end of the 1960s the region provided
the United States with 42 percent of its total imports of 14 basic products. This percentage fluctuated between 57 percent and 80 percent for
coffee, sugar, fruits, and vegetables; between 31 percent and 45 percent
for cacao, iron ore, copper, lead, and oil products; and between 18 percent and 26 percent for fresh and canned meats, nonferrous minerals,
and wool. These 14 products represented 32 percent of worldwide U.S.
imports (of whatever sort) in 1961–65, but only 23 percent in 1966–70.
They also accounted for 80 percent of total U.S. imports from Latin
America in 1961–65 and 76 percent in 1966–70.

In summary, then, a more qualitative analysis reveals that the decrease
in the share of global exports and imports goes hand in hand with the
maintenance of certain basic or strategic bonds between the two areas—

TABLE 3
U.S. Imports of 14 Basic Products from Latin America

Product	Millions of US$ (yearly average)		Average percent growth or decline	Percent of total U.S. imports of product		
	1961–65	1966–70	1961–65/1966–70	1961–65	1966–70	1970
Foods	1,568	1,830[a]	3.5%	–	–	–
Coffee	828	739	–2.3	80%	69%	66%
Sugar	266	385	7.7	50	58	57
Fruits	130	221	11.1	65	69	70
Cacao	50	75	8.5	32	40	36
Canned meats	41	77	13.8	26	26	26
Fresh meats	40	82	15.6	14	17	18
Vegetables	32	90	22.0	50	75	80
Raw materials	514	515[a]	0.1	–	–	–
Iron	136	143	1.0	38	32	32
Nonferrous minerals	104	94	–2.1	29	20	21
Wool	61	39	–8.7	24	21	22
Copper[a]	182	256	7.0	58	41	45
Lead[a]	21	30	7.2	40	39	36
Oil and by-products	872	988[a]	2.9	–	–	–
Unrefined oil	547	496	–2.0	50	38	31
By-products	358	475	5.8	50	45	43
Total of 14 products	2,798	3,203	2.7	50	44	42
Total U.S. imports from Latin America	3,496	4,216	3.8%	20%	13%	12%

Source: CEPAL, *América Latina y la tercera UNCTAD* (Santiago, DOC. E/CN. 12/L/74), January 1972, pp. 169 and 171.
  [a]1966–69.

bonds that at the very least do not support extreme hypotheses concerning the distancing or the increasing or irreversible "dispensability" of these relations.

Financial Relations

Financial relations between Latin America and the United States exhibit trends and contradictions similar to those outlined for trade transactions, and the two undoubtedly influence one another reciprocally. Of course, if the flows of capital from the United States to our region are compared through time, Latin America's relative position can be seen to have dropped in spite of absolute increases in this capital flow (see

TABLE 4

Summary of Latin America's Balance of Payments
with the United States[a]

(Millions of dollars)

| Flow category | Annual average | | | | Index of growth or decline, 1961–65/1966–70 (1961–65 = 100) |
	1961–65	1966–70	1969	1970	
1. Export of goods	3,706	4,420	4,470	4,855	119
2. Import of goods	-3,520	-4,671	-4,822	-5,650	133
3. Comm'l balance (1-2)	186	-251	-352	-795	–
4. Balance of travel and transport	30	-72	-47	-76	–
5. Servicing of investments					
a. private	-1,165	-1,638	-1,753	-1,693	141
b. by the U.S. Gov't	-122	-138	-149	-160	123
c. total	-1,277	-1,776	-1,902	-1,853	153
6. Payments for Latin American investment in the United States	75	249	312	332	332
7. Other services	34	-25	-18	-37	–
8. Direct U.S. defense exp.	77	106	112	118	138
9. Balance of services (4+5c+6+7+8)	-1,061	-1,518	-1,543	-1,516	143
10. Flow of private capital					
a. through direct investment and purchase of securities (stock)	149	399	341	478	267
b. through loans	289	276	-13	558	96
c. total	438	675	338	1,036	154
11. Flows of "official" U.S. capital	432	494	540	506	114
12. Unilateral transfers					
a. by the U.S. Gov't	244	272	247	292	111
b. private	120	163	178	189	136
c. total	364	435	425	481	120
13. Latin American capital in the United States	-12	-27	-25	-48	225
14. Total transfers and flows of capital (10c+11+12c+13)	1,222	1,577	1,278	1,975	129
15. Net balance of payments (3+9+14)	347	-192	-612	-336	–

Source: Departments of Commerce and Treasury, U.S. Government. See also "United States Co-operation with Latin America Within the Framework of the Alliance for Progress" (OAS/Ser. H/ XIV, CIAP, 530 corr. 1), Nov. 2, 1971, Tables IV-1, IV-4, IV-5, and IV-6.

[a]In this table, figures for the balance of payments between the two regions are in all cases presented from Latin America's viewpoint: positive figures are inflows for Latin America (outflows for the United States); figures preceded by a minus sign (-) represent outflows for Latin America and inflows of capital for the U.S.

Table 4). Thus, for example, the flow of private U.S. capital rose from $438 to $675 million as an annual average between 1961–65 and 1966–70; during the same period, the flow of "official" (or public) capital rose from $432 to $494 million per year, while "unilateral transfers" rose from $364 to $435 million (see items 10, 11, and 12 in Table 4). Nevertheless, if we take into account Latin America's role as the recipient of direct investment from the United States, we see that this investment dropped sharply in relative terms during the two past decades. At the beginning of the 1950s, direct investments constituted 38 percent of the total, whereas in the late 1960s (1968) this figure dropped to 16 percent. The same shift occurred for the third world as a whole, although less markedly. By contrast, Canada and the European Common Market became relatively more important to Latin America during this period.[7]

As can be seen, transfers of capital through U.S. Government loans and credits (Table 4, item 11) have been somewhat lower than those of private capital (item 10). The latter increased by 54 percent during the two five-year periods considered, whereas government loans and credits rose at a lower rate (14 percent), and actually fell between 1969 and 1970.[8] The situation changes if we consider also Latin America's payments on these loans and credits (a look at the situation from Latin America's viewpoint is given in Table 5). It is evident that whereas transactions of private capital leave a negative annual balance, U.S. Government capital flows produce the reverse. Nevertheless, the positive balance of the latter does not cover the negative balance of the former; that is, the U.S. Government capital is not enough to finance the servicing of private investment. Furthermore, the gap tended to widen in the second half of the decade, rising from $43 to $172 million annually.

Balance of Direct Investment

Because the servicing of direct investments (not of total private capital) has been the most important element of financial transactions between Latin America and the United States, we shall examine its components in some detail. As the figures in Table 6 indicate, total payments increased by 28 percent (index = 128) during the two five-year periods considered, the most dynamic category being the outflow for patents and licenses, which rose by 50 percent. This category, moreover, constituted more than one-fourth of the total outflow in the second five years of the

---

[7] Between 1950 and 1968, North American investments in the developed countries increased from 45 percent of the total to 67 percent.

[8] This trend probably intensified in 1971. But at the same time, it should be borne in mind that neither U.S. Government capital, which is channeled through the IBRD or the BID, nor the servicing of these credits is being considered here.

TABLE 5

Flows of Government and Private Capital from the United States to Latin America

(Millions of dollars)

	Annual average	
Flow category	1961–65	1966–70
U.S. Government capital plus unilateral transfers	676	766
Servicing of investments of U.S. Government	–112	–138
Difference	564	628
Investments of private capital plus unilateral transfers	558	838
Servicing of total private investments	–1,165	–1,638
Difference	–607	–800
Net balance	–43	–172

Source: See Table 4.

TABLE 6

Direct U.S. Investment in Latin America

(Millions of dollars)

	Annual average				Index of growth or decline, 1961–65/1966–70
Transaction	1961–65	1966–70	1969	1970	(1961–65 = 100)
Outflows					
Patents and licenses	–167	–251	–272	–282	150
Interests, dividends, and profits	–811	–997	–1,049	–899	123
Total	–978	–1,248	–1,321	–1,181	128
Net inflows					
Direct investment	75	301	299	349	401
Purchase of securities	74	98	52	129	132
Total	149	399	351	478	270
Net balance	–829	–849	–970	–713	102
Balance of all transactions	347	–192	–617	–336	–

Source: See Table 4.

decade. In other words, the cost of "technological transfer" has been taking on increasing importance.

With capital inflow, direct investment is paramount, owing less to its rate of expansion than to its magnitude—which greatly outstrips increases in purchases of securities. Nevertheless, the increase in total inflow, no less than 170 percent during the two five-year periods, does not modify the traditional negative balance, which remained at more than $800 million annually, and which was accordingly decisive in contributing to the overall negative balance in total financial transactions.

But another element is crucial in all of this: the apparent increases of direct investment in the region are financed to a great extent by undistributed profits and other local funds and not by "fresh money" from abroad. In some periods from 1963 to 1965, this type of resource constituted 90 percent of the recorded direct investment.

Relations and Contradictions Between Capital Flows in Finance and Trade

When the structure and deficit tendencies in the financial transactions of the two regions are examined in light of the facts concerning trade relations just discussed, some contradictions become apparent. One of these contradictions arises from the discontinuity between the growth of Latin America's financial commitments and the region's relative marginalization from the U.S. market. During the two five-year periods in the 1960s, Latin America's exports to the United States increased by 19 percent, while total payments on U.S. investments in the region increased by 39 percent. In other words, as Kñakal points out, "Latin America had to 'return' to the United States an increasing part of the income derived from its exports to that country (34 percent in 1961–65 and more than 40 percent in 1966–70) to cover the servicing of U.S. investments in its territory."[9]

The other aspect of this trade-finance contradiction lies in the fact that Latin America increased its imports from the United States considerably more than its exports to the United States. Thus, the traditionally favorable balance of trade for Latin America reversed in the second part of the decade, with a clear tendency toward greater deterioration in the more recent years. As a result, Latin America found it impossible to redress the unfavorable balance by using its trade surplus, and was thus obliged to rely on greater indebtedness and/or lowering of reserves to handle its overall disequilibrium.

[9]Kñakal, "Las relaciones económicas."

Significance of Transactions for the Two Regions

The significance for Latin America of transactions with the United States is obvious. For one thing, direct investments are crucial to the rhythm and the "style" or mode of Latin America's development.[10] For another, Government capital from the United States provided 80 and 50 percent, respectively, of foreign public financing during the first and second halves of the 1960s—excluding what was channeled through international loan agencies. And these global statistics do not reveal the substantial concentration of the two types of capital flow in a handful of countries, particularly Brazil and Mexico, during the past few years.

From the U.S. point of view, it would seem at first glance that the financial and total transactions are relatively less important. If the cited figures are compared to the gross national product of the United States or to its ties with other developed nations, this assessment is undoubtedly valid—despite arguments to the contrary in certain circles.

Nevertheless, a different situation becomes apparent if certain qualitative aspects are examined—such as the contribution made to the U.S. balance of payments by the favorable balance of economic relations with Latin America. From 1961 to 1965 this contribution averaged 10 percent, and in the second decade, 25 percent, of the positive balance of the total exchange of goods and services of the United States during these periods.[11] In short, Latin America has provided substantial support to the United States in its recent balance-of-payments crisis, a support that has far exceeded the benefits to Latin America devolving from direct U.S. investment. It is a fact that Latin America received only 5 and 10 percent of the total U.S. investments made in the first and second halves of the 1960s. In other words, while Latin America during the closing years of the decade was contributing more than a third of total U.S. income derived from the exchange of goods and services, it was receiving only about one-tenth of the United States' direct investment and one-fourth of its Government loans.

A Summary of U.S.-Latin American Financial Relations

An overview of the trade and financial relations between the two regions leads to the following conclusions. In the first place, notwithstanding the appreciable absolute expansion of transactions, there is an evident relative weakening of financial ties between Latin America and the United States.

[10] See Aníbal Pinto, "El modelo de desarrollo reciente de la América Latina," *Trimestre Económico* (Mexico City), no. 150, April–June 1971.

[11] The proportion reached 39 percent in 1969 and 34 percent in 1970.

Second, this weakening influences the "strategic" significance that certain ties have both for Latin America and for the United States. For Latin America, the United States is still the principal commercial client and supplier, and the major source of public and private capital. For the United States, the Latin American economies play an important role as suppliers of a number of basic products and at the same time are important clients for certain industrial goods. More important, transactions with Latin America have provided considerable support for the U.S. net balance of payments.

Finally, the impact of trade and financial disequilibria should be stressed. Rather than providing a means to deal with these disequilibria, trends in trade have tended to exacerbate the problem in recent years, as the balance has shifted against Latin America.

Prospects for the Future: Elements of Tension and Conflict

Against this background, I shall discuss some possibilities, as they seem now and as they might develop in the near future—say, in the late 1970s. It is important at the outset to place the subject in a wider context, one embracing the options and trends that can be discerned in the world's economic (and political) realignment. In my judgment, the "new world order" that is now emerging will have great significance for the subject. The question was discussed in a recent ECLA (CEPAL) document.[12] The salient points are as follows:

One possibility is that, after a certain adjustment of mechanisms and practices, the process of "horizontal integration" among the developed market economies will begin anew. . . . Clearly, the opportunities to continue and expand "horizontal integration" among the developed economies will be strengthened by the entrance of new and important members to the European Common Market; and, eventually, by future negotiations among the United States, the European Economic Community, and Japan. But that is not all. Relatively recent events have revealed broad possibilities, still difficult to assess, for extending this process to the major socialist countries or their regional groupings. On this point, it is important to bear in mind not just the economic agreements reached with Russia by Western Europe, Japan, and the United States, but also the opportunities opened up by the new framework of relations with China. . . .

Other tendencies lead to greater pessimism regarding the possibilities for increasing and prolonging this "horizontal integration" of the great industrial economies. . . . This second point of view tends to the general theory that the close of this period will be marked by a reconstitution—even though on a different basis—of "vertical" groupings or blocs, a tendency moreover that has already shown signs of appearing.[13]

---

[12]For this and the following quotations, see CEPAL, *Estudio Económico de América Latina* (Santiago: 1971), vol. I, part 1.

[13]See also T. Greigh, "Toward a World of Trade Blocs," in *U.S. Foreign Policy in the '70s* (Washington: National Planning Association, 1971).

What significance or implications do these alternatives have for Latin America? From a general viewpoint—and one that would involve the entire third world—it seems clear that the first option would result in new impulses toward transactions within the industrial center, which would now fully include the socialist economies. But it is equally clear that although further "horizontal integration" of the developed economies might increase exports from the third world to the centers, it would also increase the phenomenon of relative marginalization of the underdeveloped countries—and thus the unequal and unbalanced development of the two great spheres, maintaining the old pattern of an international division of labor.[14] A shift toward "vertical integration" would have different consequences. It might relatively weaken the conciliation of the centers and, in turn, strengthen the links between the central nations (or sectors of each group) and their dependent economies, with the almost inevitable intensification of the latter's subordination.

Reconsidering the question in terms of the problem confronting us, it would be reasonable to deduce that the first option would involve fewer possibilities of conflict, for the simple reason that the economic ties linking Latin America with the United States—ties that are still very significant—would become weaker. The second option, by contrast, might bring about an increased level of interchange and financial ties, with wider possibilities for tension and disagreements. It is legitimate to object that such an analysis suffers from a "damned if you do and damned if you don't" implication, but it is well to bear in mind that this reality faithfully reflects the contradictions inherent in the alternatives. For just this reason, it is understandable that the nations of the third world— though with little success and at times with too little vigor—are struggling for another type of world order. The major features of this world order are described by CEPAL thus:

> In any event, the interest of the third world would be better served if the new order implied progress toward a true "international integration," . . . one which neither isolates the developing economies from the dynamic influences of material, scientific, and technological progress originating in the advanced nations, nor increases the new modes of dependency, which are so evident in the scheme that today generates crisis.
>
> This approach would not have to oppose itself to the groupings of countries already formed. Neither would it ignore the manifest inequality of different areas— concretely, the differences in the objective positions of the industrialized and developing economies, differences which demand preferential treatment for the nations of the third world within a global context. In short: "international integration"

---

[14]Note that the development of "horizontal integration" in new areas, e.g. the socialist economies, and especially the USSR, implies access to a great "storehouse" of raw materials, which in many cases (copper, petroleum, etc.) provide alternative sources of supply to those of Latin America.

necessarily assumes rules of arrangements which substantially improve the latter's position in the world arena.

On the other hand, it is also clear that a new international arrangement would depend to a high degree on the energetic continuation and success of regional and subregional groupings of the developing nations' economies. With time, it will be seen with greater clarity that these steps are vital, as much to utilize fully the development potential of the peripheral nations, as to raise their bargaining power vis-à-vis the industrialized economies.

The growing cooperation and complementation of all or part of the peripheral countries has a very special and positive meaning. This movement, far from implying an attempt to separate the peripheral nations from the developed economies or to divide the world economic system, signifies a way to effectively integrate the peripheral nations under just and propitious circumstances into the world economic system, putting their ties with the industrialized economies on a more solid and growth-oriented basis.[15]

The New Agencies of Relationship: Multinational Corporations

The second topic to be examined here concerns the growing—and, in the long run, dominant—role of multinational corporations as agencies or mechanisms of relationship between the third world economies (especially those that are semi-industrialized and of greater weight) and the developed capitalist nations. This relationship assumes a countertrend: a reduction in the relative importance of "traditional" investments (for example, in the primary-export sector: copper, petroleum, etc.) and also of investments from government or institutional sources (these assumptions do not, of course, apply to the case of genuine socialist experiments).

The question posed by this assumption is the following: Will the new mechanism of relationship produce more or less conflict than the old? Suffice it to say, there are no answers that are final or of universal application. Nevertheless, it is possible to make some reasonable speculations. Though we cannot address here the diverse reservations and criticisms leveled against (and earned by) the multinational corporations, it is useful to keep several elements in mind.[16]

A primary "operational" element derives from the "international" character of those entities that, while not negating the "national" roots of the home offices, undoubtedly gives them far greater flexibility than the traditional foreign enterprise has. Numerous instances demonstrate that flexibility; among them are their agreements with "socialistic" countries or countries "in transition to socialism."

A second point—particularly important for the various Latin American nations—is that these corporations are prone to more or less active competition with others of their kind. Contrary to the experience of "tradi-

[15] CEPAL, *Estudio Económico,* 1971.

[16] See, for example, Aníbal Pinto, "El sistema centro-periferia, 20 años después," pp. 27ff.

tional" investors, the "international" corporations of, say, North American origin coexist and compete with other enterprises of diverse origin: Italian, Japanese, German, French, Dutch, etc.

These circumstances unquestionably increase the capacity for maneuvering or negotiation of the economies where the corporations are located, and provide a powerful and objective stimulus to expansion. What is more, their activity is comparatively "integrated" into the internal productive system and subordinated, in various degrees, to the general and special directives of the local political economy.

Clearly, one might protest that in many cases the power of these corporations is such that they can shape decisions according to their interests. Even so, it cannot be denied that their general position—and the potential reach of national policies—differs notably from the situation formerly held by the "traditional" enterprise, exporting raw materials. This does not imply a "harmony of interests" or an absence of friction and conflicts. Quite the contrary. We would venture to claim only that the degree of contradiction is probably less than in the past and that the *potential* opportunities for negotiation and control by the countries involved are greater.

The truth is that the multinational corporations, especially those organized as conglomerates, constitute a "fact of life" in the world—surely, another phase of "the highest stage of capitalism." As the Secretary of the European Economic Commission, Janos Stanovnik, remarked: "The multinational corporations have ceased to be something you are for or against. These corporations produce $300 billion annually, something close to the total value of world trade. That is a fact. A great part of the underlying strength of Europe comes from these companies."[17]

Projections and the Political Reality of Ties

The closing aspect of this summary examination of tension and conflict in the relations between Latin America and the United States concerns the political implications of these relations and the general framework of international "power politics." Though I treated this topic some time ago in another work, it will be useful to review the major points discussed there.[18]

The first point to be made is that nowhere in the world where there is an American political presence does the influence of American private enterprises seem to be as large as it is in Latin America. Although American business is not a prime or decisive variable in areas where investment is not heavy (in Asia, for example) or where general political considera-

[17] In *The Delegates World Bulletin* (New York: United Nations, 1972).
[18] See "La 'crisis latinoamericana' y su marco externo," *Desarrollo Económico* (Buenos Aires), July-December 1966, pp. 319-54.

tions are fundamental (Western Europe), in Latin America it carries enormous weight; and often business interests outweigh the interests of the United States as a nation. In these matters, much depends on the conditions of the moment. If the United States is checkmated at a given moment—say, during World War II, or in the first phase of the Cuban revolution—"macropolitical" or "national" criteria carry more relative force. But in more normal circumstances, the "private micro-view" tends to prevail. This hypothesis draws together two aspects of the situation already mentioned, which in turn suggest a prediction for the near future: other things being equal, a greater relative weight will be given to "macro-vision" on the part of the United States. One of these two aspects is the strengthening of "peaceful coexistence" with the socialist world, which reduces the priority of "national security" and also moderates the tendency to consolidate ties with private interests. The other aspect is the change in the nature and composition of those interests. In other words, it might be deduced that the new type of enterprise is less "conflictive" than the traditional type and at the same time, because of its own "transnational" character, has less potential for bringing pressure upon or identifying its interests with the global interests of the United States.

The second major point to be made involves the future implications of possible political-ideological conflict between the multinational enterprises and their home countries. For the purpose of analysis, one might postulate two extreme alternatives: that there would be no such confrontation, or that, by design or in the course of events, such conflict would come to be fundamental. I explored the question in my earlier study in the following manner:

Aside from the particular circumstances in Latin America (differing, for example, from those in Egypt or Algeria), in which transformations of a revolutionary character do not imply a major breach in the relations of the superpowers, it is a central fact that some connection exists between domestic orientation and external politics. The problem lies in delineating those connections—different in each country—that will be modified as the internal and external framework for each country shifts.

To pursue this analysis, we might suppose that in a certain country conditions are created that are propitious for substantive change—change that will, beyond doubt, have some impact on external politics. The question to consider is whether such rectification involves or necessitates a break with the ruling superpower and a commitment to the opposing ranks.

To examine the existing alternatives, it is necessary to lower the level of abstractions and introduce more specific elements. Let us examine first some economic factors. In certain countries—though not necessarily in all—a politics of fundamental transformation might require decisions that affect foreign interests, which, in order to simplify things, we shall identify as North American. In these circumstances, as we have already seen, the private interests affected will try to fuse their particular problem with that of the United States as a nation. Whether they are successful or not will depend on various factors, which can work separately or together.

The outcome depends, first, on the extent of those interests and their power to bring pressure to bear on the United States. Second, it depends on the significance of the investments for the present or future supplying of the United States. It is sufficient to note that the expropriation of a soft-drink plant or a textile factory will not have the same repercussions as an attempt to nationalize the oil wells in Venezuela or the copper mines in Chile. Finally, the outcome depends on the means used to transfer the foreign assets to national control; that is, whether the means is a confiscation, some form of expropriation, or simply a purchase.

Now, let us look at some political variables. Here we might reduce the possibilities to two main categories. In the first—which might be called a national-development stance—conduct toward the foreign enclaves would be dictated mainly by judgments regarding their importance to the economic and social development of the country. In the second category, such steps would be derived mainly from ideological considerations—that is, from the logic of anti-imperialist action—and directed toward the final goal of harassing and damaging the regime in power.

Obviously, it is unlikely that we shall find those two types of alternatives in pure form; nevertheless, a greater or lesser proportion of one or the other motivation is decisive to the analysis.[19]

I shall not venture a hypothesis on the manner in which this situation might develop in the near future. Some elements would seem to indicate that, under present circumstances, it would be more expeditious to divide the topic into two parts—that is, conflict on the concrete and economic level, and conflict that can be projected into the political-ideological realm. But such a division would obviously be open to criticism as simplistic or limited by "economism." Moreover, if one introduces the general problem of "power politics," those conditions that justify a relatively optimistic estimate might be shown to be in danger of being swamped by much more powerful and more pertinent strategic-military considerations; though I am in no position to discuss that fact adequately, I must acknowledge it.[20]

However that may be, I shall draw no major conclusions about the problem, although it seems to me that any reasonable hypothesis must take into account the elements I have tried to outline here.

[19] Ibid., pp. 337–38.
[20] One perspective on the problem is offered by the following analysis: "Despite the considerably diminished strategic importance [of nuclear weapons], hegemony over clearly circumscribed areas continues to be a basic principle, as much for the United States as for the USSR. The very fact that the 'balance of terror' enormously limits the likelihood that nuclear weapons would be used necessitates the deployment of well-equipped conventional forces on the broadest geographical scale. The maintenance by the superpowers of bases and military forces on foreign territory demonstrates this fact dramatically. At the same time, maintaining troops on foreign soil guarantees that regimes loyal to the respective superpowers will continue to govern. A policy of geopolitics, formulated many years ago, is based on the need to unify a bloc of 'satellites' or allies who enhance the dominance and central status of the superpowers." Edy Kaufman, "Los Estados Unidos y la URSS en América Latina y en Europa Oriente." *Aportes* (Paris), no. 24, April 1972.

Commentary on Pinto

OSVALDO SUNKEL

Aníbal Pinto's study provides an excellent base from which to examine and interpret some of the changes that have taken place in U.S.-Latin American economic and political relationships in recent years, and to assess perspectives for the future. Opinions to the contrary, it is evident that U.S. perspectives on these relationships have been undergoing significant changes. There have also been major changes in Latin Americans' attitudes toward their own capacity to order their affairs.

At the same time that the United States has recommended—and, to a great degree, implemented—a "low profile" or "benign neglect" policy in Latin America, the continent itself has shown an increasing interest in diversifying its international relations, mainly toward Europe, Japan, and the socialist countries. Growing emphasis has been placed on economic and political relations among the Latin American countries themselves, and on more concrete contacts between them and other third world nations because of common interests in foreign investment, commercial policies, and certain primary products. These and other tendencies constitute a generally recognized pattern of growing Latin American nationalism, and these economic relationships, which we shall examine more closely below, have developed in a manner quite similar to that of military-security considerations, which are themselves a decisive factor in U.S.-Latin American relations.

It is not surprising that these two factors, which could be considered mutually independent, have followed such similar paths of development. Both are products of the huge worldwide transformations that have taken place during the last 10 or 15 years in consequence of the degeneration of the bipolar world system that emerged after World War II. The gradual abandonment of cold war thinking and ideologies has greatly affected notions of security and economic relations, giving way to a relaxation of

Osvaldo Sunkel is a member of the Latin American Faculty of the Social Sciences (FLACSO), Santiago.

hegemonic relations within each system, as well as to a growing diversification and fluidity in relations among the once rigidly aligned countries within each sphere of influence. Thus, one of the causes for the important changes taking place in recent years in U.S.-Latin American economic relations must be sought in the context of the radical transformation of these relations on a worldwide level—a context that has seen the gradual closing of military, political, economic, and cultural gaps, and the development of new and diverse forms of peaceful coexistence between the socialist and capitalist worlds.

Nothing could be farther from my intention than to argue the thesis of "convergence" or of "the end of ideology." It simply seems necessary to recognize that the world has been moving away from bipolar confrontation and toward multipolar coexistence. Surely the new situation will produce conflict, but it is nonetheless far from that earlier apocalyptic vision of a final confrontation between the two nuclear giants. For one thing, there are now at least three such giants. All of this is of great importance to U.S.-Latin American economic relations. We are not dealing here only with the different emphases that the United States places on security considerations and economic interests—that is to say, on the predominance of a "national macro-vision" or a "private micro-vision," depending upon the current demands of the global situation. I agree with Pinto's evaluation of these varying emphases, but there are two other important points to be considered.

First, U.S. interests with respect to "hemispheric security" are now relatively guaranteed not only by general agreement between the superpowers, but also by the development within the Latin American countries of police and military forces with considerable capability for repressing and controlling internal subversion. This development, which Stepan alludes to as the "new militarism," has manifested itself in the military's assuming a political role in many countries of the region; and though it does guarantee the United States control of internal security, it also represents a new element of power in Latin American societies. This is a nationalist militarism that has taken an increasingly autonomous position toward the United States. Disputes and conflicts that have arisen between the United States and Latin American countries over the acquisition of arms have led to arms being purchased in part in Europe and have even stimulated the development—with European support—of arms industries in Brazil and Argentina. These shipments constitute clear proof of this new and surprising factor in U.S.-Latin American relations.

Second, there have been interesting modifications in economic relations. As Pinto affirms, economic interests have been relatively more important in U.S.-Latin American relations than in U.S. policy toward

Africa, Europe, the Middle East, or Western Europe, particularly in periods of international détente. Nevertheless, the situation could be subject to important changes.

As can be deduced from the figures presented by Pinto, the expansion of U.S. trade has been oriented first toward the other developed countries, second toward the other underdeveloped regions of the world in general, and only last toward Latin America. To this finding must be added the strong possibilities of growing trade between the United States and the socialist countries, particularly the Soviet Union. To make matters worse, the Soviet Union will enter into competition principally in the market of certain primary products.

This tendency toward regional diversification of U.S. commercial activities is also seen in North American investments. Actually, American investments abroad in the postwar period have grown from $12 billion in 1950 to $65 billion in 1968. In the same period, investment in Canada grew from $3.6 billion to $19.4 billion, in Europe from $1.7 billion to $19.4 billion, and in the rest of the world (excluding Latin America) from $1.8 billion to $14.9 billion. In contrast, U.S. investment in Latin America grew only from $4.7 billion to $11 billion. In fact, from being the individually most important region, representing 40 percent of all American private foreign investment, Latin America has become the least important in absolute terms, and its relative importance has fallen to 17 percent. This notable change in the world distribution of U.S. economic interests, as it has continued to develop—signifying for Latin America a drop to less than one-half its previous relative importance—obviously had to have an impact on the reformulation of American policy toward this region, and on the significance and influence of American economic groups with interests in Latin America.

But there is more to the problem, because these groups are not even the same ones that traditionally were identified as investors in Latin America. Without doubt, United Fruit, Standard Oil, Kennecott, Anaconda, and other familiar names are still present, but the protagonists are now companies like ITT, Xerox, GM, Westinghouse, DuPont, and others.

The relative stagnation of foreign investments in Latin America has overshadowed a profound structural change. The traditional investments in agriculture and export mining (except oil), as well as in public services, have scarcely grown, while those in manufacturing, commerce, and private services have expanded considerably. Between 1946 and 1968, the proportion of manufacturing and commerce within the total amount of American investment in Latin America grew from 15.5 to 45 percent and in oil from 22.9 to 27 percent. In other areas, principally agriculture and mining, where investment had traditionally been concentrated, the percentage fell from 61.7 to 28 percent. This phenomenon, yet another manifestation of the well-known process of relative stagnation of international trade in primary products, of the policy of industrialization by import substitution with which Latin America has had to confront the loss of the dynamic of "export oriented growth," and of the colossal postwar expansion of international monopoly capitalism first in the United States and later in Europe and Japan, constitutes another crucially important factor in the transformation of U.S.-Latin American economic relations.

We shall touch only on two of the most important aspects of this process. In the first place, in the United States, the composition of the economic groups with an interest in U.S. hemispheric policy has changed. Those enterprises interested in assuring themselves of favorable conditions for the production of primary products for export in Latin America have had to share their influence with groups involved in manufacturing and related areas—that is, those groups fundamentally interested in the development of the internal markets of the Latin American countries and also in the regional markets that are the result of programs of economic integration. Furthermore, both groups have decided to expand their investments and trade with other regions.

Second, in Latin America, owing to the decline in the development of the traditional export sectors and the considerable expansion of the manufacturing sectors and public and private services, social structures have undergone important changes, particularly in the relatively more developed countries. Replacing, or at least accompanying, the traditional landed oligarchy involved in exporting, have been the rising new social and political groups whose leaders are the legitimate new spokesmen for the transnational manufacturing interests of the United States. As I have demonstrated on another occasion, ". . . in this way a new complex of economic, social, and political interests has been created that involves entrepreneurial and governmental groups, both U.S. and Latin American, including to a great extent the international financial institutions and the 'foreign aid' programs. These groups have formulated a new set of norms and mechanisms of inter-American policy whose highest expression was reached during the Kennedy Administration with the conference at Punta del Este and the establishment of the Alliance for Progress. . . . Seen from this aspect, the Alliance really was an alliance, but between modern American industrial groups and the new industrialists, public and private, that had sprung up from the process of import substitution and state expansion in the more developed and advanced countries of Latin America."[1]

[1] "Esperando a Godot: América Latina ante la nueva administración republicana de los Estados Unidos," *Estudios Internacionales* (Santiago), April/June 1969.

Nevertheless, the Alliance for Progress was not just the result of the convergent socio-economic transformation in Latin America and the United States—as might be deduced from the preceding paragraphs. Here again, world relations between the two superpowers had a decisive influence. In effect, the Cuban Revolution—perhaps not at the outset, but certainly after it took on socialist coloration and received the support of the Soviet Union—introduced social revolution and the socialist world into Latin America. This development forced the United States and the other Latin American nations to undertake an accelerated program of capitalist modernization and social reforms that fell naturally in line with the changes already under way in U.S.-Latin American relations. These changes were a consequence of the colossal expansion of transnational monopoly capitalism and of the process of import-substitution industrialization in Latin America. Here again, the influence that changes in the international situation have on U.S.-Latin American relations is clear and concrete. The situation also points up the influence that economic, social, and political transformations have on the policies adopted in the Latin American countries themselves.

So it becomes clear that it is not realistic to analyze various perspectives on U.S.-Latin American relations without placing them in the wider context of the probable evolution of the international situation as a whole, at least in terms of its more fundamental features. It is also important that we concentrate on the more immediate determinants of these relations and study them with some precision.

One way of getting down to cases is to examine the tendencies in U.S.-Latin American trade relations. For this purpose, Pinto's work is very useful. Examination of his figures reveals that the participation of Latin American exports in total U.S. imports, and the proportion of total U.S. exports going to Latin American markets—notwithstanding the substantial absolute increases in these trade flows—show a severe relative deterioration: 24 to 11 percent and 17 to 13 percent, respectively, between 1960 and 1970. These indicators, among others, encourage Pinto to postulate a process of "relative marginalization" of Latin America in its economic relations with the United States, a process that could be a key factor in understanding the lesser importance that the United States is currently attributing to its hemispheric relations.

Nevertheless, by his own account Pinto demonstrates, despite the process of diversification of American exports to other regions and of the American purchases from other suppliers—which is what his statistics imply—that a close examination of U.S.-Latin American trade reveals the continuing crucial importance of Latin America in supplying the United States with numerous primary products (in 1970 more than 40 percent of 14 principal products required by the United States). Moreover, U.S. sales to Latin America of certain types of manufactured goods (chemical products, machinery, equipment, and various other manufactured items) are, in general, comparable to exports of the same goods to Canada, the Common Market, and Japan, according to data included in Pinto's analysis.

In light of this overview, which accentuates the importance of certain strategic trade products, the relative marginalization pointed to by general statistics requires a sharper interpretation in order to isolate (1) those interest groups that gain or lose influence in the shaping of U.S. international economic policy; (2) those changes that can be seen in the levels of concentration and control of the internal and external markets; and (3) those changes that all of this introduces into the competitive capability and the negotiative capacity of Latin America vis-à-vis the United States, etc.

In other words, we have here a key phenomenon, one correctly revealed by Pinto's work. However, its real importance, from the point of view of the foreign policy of the several countries and of the continent as a whole, requires a more careful and more detailed study of the structure of the international markets of certain key primary products (oil, copper, wheat, meat, coffee, sugar, etc.), and of certain branches of manufacturing (chemical products, capital goods, etc.). Furthermore, we must examine the financial, technological, and political conditions that determine each nation's participation in international trade flows, and, naturally, the interrelations of power and national and international interests.

The asymmetry exhibited in the knowledge of these characteristics and conditions, between the Latin American nations on the one hand and the United States and her transnational companies on the other, is frankly abysmal. Therefore, pursuit of the necessary research—not in terms of the surrealistic and irrelevant categories of the neoclassical theory of international trade, but rather in terms of real international economic policies—could make a positive contribution to the bettering of the negotiative capacity of Latin America as a whole and of each of its component countries.

The figures cited by Pinto constitute a good starting point for a demonstration of an important change that has occurred recently in U.S.-Latin American relations—one that will surely have an enormous influence on the future of these relations. As we have seen, Latin America diversified its exports to a much greater degree than its imports; in other words, while the Latin American component of total American exports fell only from 17 to 13 percent, the Latin American component of total American imports fell from 24 to 11 percent. Two phenomena here are worthy of attention. First, U.S. exporters were more successful in maintaining their Latin American markets than Latin American exporters were in retaining their U.S. markets. Second, the trade balance between Latin America and the United States has reversed: whereas Latin America formerly exported more to the United States than the United States exported to Latin America, in this way contributing to the growth of Latin American international financial capacity, this relationship has been turned around. Now, Latin America is in effect helping to finance America's balance-of-payment deficit. These phenomena, adequately covered in Pinto's work, constitute manifestations of a new crisis, inherent in the relations between both regions; and it seems necessary to me to emphasize this crisis because of its importance for future relations.

The model of industrialization by import substitution was able, without doubt, to instill in Latin American nations a new and prolonged dynamism when the primary-export model entered into definite crisis in the Great Depression. From the 1930s to the 1960s, most Latin American nations showed positive signs of modernization and economic development. Nevertheless, import-substitution industrialization carried with it profound contradictions, many of which have surfaced fully and dramatically during the last decade. These contradictions contain the germs of a new and profound readjustment in U.S.-Latin American relations, especially since they have already intruded themselves in a particularly sharp manner in external economic relations.

In effect, the two phenomena noted above are the direct expression of the crisis. The policy of import substitution encouraged the establishment in Latin America of industries that were highly dependent upon imports of capital goods, primary materials, intermediary goods, technology, specialized human resources, organizational forms and financial aid. As long as the growing external commitments stemming from the needs of this policy could be financed by the foreign currency saved by ceasing to import finished goods, the situation presented no insurmountable problems. But when the scarcity of foreign currency became more acute, and when it was realized that neither the traditional exports nor the new manufactured exports were capable of generating the capital needed to finance the growing demands for industrial imports, private foreign investment and external public financing began to increase rapidly. Since neither the former nor the latter contributed to the expansion of exports, while growing external commitments in the form of financial services began to mount up, the foreign debt of the Latin American nations took on enormous dimensions. At the same time, because imports expanded faster than exports, the formerly favorable balance in commercial relations with the United States was reversed.

The situation confronted by most Latin American countries in their foreign economic relations was thus critical. In the face of this situation, vigorous demands—some old, some new—have arisen that suggest, in my judgment, a new stage of difficult and conflictive U.S.-Latin American relations. I shall attempt in what follows to set forth briefly the elements that will probably play a major role in this phase.

The United States constitutes the most important market for Latin America's traditional export products, but also the least dynamic one. At the same time, subsidiaries of American enterprises control the production and marketing of many of these exports. The pressures exercised by Latin American governments to reduce the margin of profits remitted abroad, to demand a higher percentage of local processing, to achieve greater use of national raw and processed materials, to replace foreign personnel with national personnel, to solicit the diversification of external markets, to intervene in the setting of prices, to have access to technology, etc., can only increase, given the balance-of-payments problem and growing internal social pressures. The degree of local pressure will inevitably lead to more direct government intervention and national control of productive resources, and probably will accelerate the process of nationalization initiated in recent years as well as the attendant economic and political conflicts.

The critical necessity of encouraging exports will also cause Latin America to take an increasingly united and aggressive stand in demanding greater access to the markets of the developed countries, in particular the United States—the largest of them all. We are dealing with a question not only of primary products, but also of manufactured products toward which the developed nations have erected a formidable network of institutional, tariff, and tax barriers. In view of the failure of general negotiations, be they bilateral or multilateral, and of organizations such as the UNCTAD, the Latin American nations can be expected to revert to less orthodox but perhaps more effective means. One obvious target is the foreign subsidiaries whose access to natural resources and Latin American markets might be made to depend on counterpart access to the U.S. market. The recent agreement between the Soviet Government and Pepsi-Cola, in which the latter promises to distribute Russian liquors and wines in the United States in exchange for access to the markets of the Soviet Union, demonstrates the validity of the idea. The diversification of economic, political, cultural, and even military relations with other developed countries, with the socialist countries, and among the Latin American countries themselves is another obvious course, one that to a greater or lesser degree is already being pursued.

All of the North American apparatus designed to promote manufactured exports that are tied to Latin America's industrialization through foreign subsidiaries—in which foreign aid programs, credits, investment guarantees, and American and international financial institutions play an important role—will be increasingly criticized and questioned by the Latin American nations. The crude utilization of these mechanisms as clubs to be held over the heads of Latin American governments, as has recently been the case in Peru and Chile, as well as the increased cost of imports financed through these mechanisms, will sooner or later force the Latin American governments to demand changes. Such changes have already been initiated, with some success, as for example with the "tied" credits and the U.S. import surcharge, both of which have been dropped.

One of the major causes of conflict in certain countries in recent years has been the considerable penetration of foreign subsidiaries into manufacturing, commerce, banking, telecommunications, and mass communications: major firms in the most dynamic sectors are appropriated by foreign subsidiaries, resulting in the displacement of national entrepreneurs; coordination between subsidiaries produces powerful economic and political influence, indeed an oligopoly; the subsidiaries tend to finance their expansion with few external resources and a very high proportion of local resources; extensive resources—including payments to the parent corporation for technical assistance, and the patents, services, and charges levied by the parent corporations themselves—are remitted abroad, and imports are vastly overpriced; the subsidiaries come to have decisive influence on the question of what private consumption and public investment will be; that is to say, in general, the subsidiaries influence the assignment of productive resources and the control of surpluses.

Depending on how fully Latin American governments have recognized these phenomena, the policies of many of them toward foreign investment have been changing from indiscriminate concessions with a broad range of advantages, to the creation of more restrictive policies that encourage the channeling of investment into areas of government priority and require the negotiation of financial conditions that redound to the benefit of the country. The common policy toward foreign investments adopted by the countries of the Andean Pact, which so angered the U.S. international corporations in the Council of the Americas, is an outstanding example of those changes; and the reaction of the Council is an example of the corresponding tensions and conflicts.

Many other, more concrete, examples can be cited of areas in which U.S.-Latin American economic and political relations will have to undergo profound readjustments. But I do not intend to overextend this commentary, and I have still not touched upon a central point of my argument: What internal socio-political forces in Latin America will affect these nationalist revisions in relations with the United States? As has become obvious, the situation differs from country to country, depending on degree of economic development and social diversification, nature of political regime, degree of foreign penetration, geopolitical situation, size, etc. But given all these factors, there are some common characteristics that are shared at least by the larger and more developed countries.

First, as the model of industrialization by import substitution entered into crisis, causing breaks in the harmony of interests between dominant local groups and foreign groups, the profoundly asymmetrical nature of the relations between the United States and Latin America became more and more evident. Over the past few years, the explosion of literature on dependency, imperialism, and colonialism attests very clearly to this trend.

Second, the crisis of the import-substitution industrialization model also sharpened the conflicts between classes and internal social groups, as unemployment, marginality, concentration of income, expropriation of national activities by foreign interests, and the lack of opportunities even for technicians and professionals grew. The consequent mobilization of the new social forces that have emerged from the process of industrialization, urbanization, state intervention, and increased education—and even those sectors that are marginal to these processes—has led in some cases to the overthrow of the traditional dominant classes (sometimes by military regimes), or at least has wrested from them internal reforms and a renegotiation of their international relations. In some countries these traditional dominant classes have opposed such pressures by increasing coercion and internal repression and by seeking even more outside support. Nevertheless, in most cases, certain internal reforms have been tried, reforms that almost necessarily imply the adoption of "revisionist" positions with respect to the United States.

Finally, a few countries have greatly accelerated their processes of internal transformation and the reformulation of their external ties, advancing frankly toward socialization of their economies. In these cases, confrontations with the United States and its economic interests are, of course, the sharpest.

Part Two
Some North American Perspectives

The 'Bureaucratic Politics' Approach: U.S.-Argentine Relations, 1942-47

ERNEST R. MAY

In 1971 Graham T. Allison published a seminal book.[1] In it he developed the thesis that events such as the 1962 U.S.-Soviet crisis over Soviet missile emplacements in Cuba could be explained in three substantially different ways, depending on the paradigm of governmental behavior in the back of the explainer's mind.

The Allison Paradigms

In the first and most widely employed paradigm, the nation figures as a unitary actor. This paradigm underpins many generalizations about politics and political history and nearly all generalizations about international relations. The literature often conflates the nation, the state, the government, the administration, and the chief executive. Some writings treat of a "ruling class" or an ideological entity such as "the Communists" or "the Wall Street imperialists." The logic, however, is the same. A single entity is assumed to be capable of having ideals, perceiving interests, reacting to events, laying plans, having purposes, making decisions, taking actions, and following policies just as might an incorporate individual.

Allison points out that there are at least two alternative paradigms. Underlying one is an assumption that actions of a government are not actions of a nation but rather those of the semiautonomous organizations making up the government. The relatively meager research relevant to this paradigm suggests that even in a well-fitted dictatorship the activities of government are more likely to be products of organizations than reflections of the decisions or purposes of any central mind or minds. The point is developed by Peterson,[2] and, in broader perspective, by Bracher.[3]

Ernest May is a member of the Institute of Politics, Harvard University, Cambridge, Massachusetts.

[1] *Essence of Decision: Explaining the Cuban Missile Crisis* (Boston).

[2] Edward N. Peterson, *The Limits of Hitler's Power* (Princeton: 1969).

[3] Karl Dietrich Bracher, *Die deutsche Diktatur* (Köln: 1969) [English Translation: *The German Dictatorship* (New York: 1970)].

Thinking of medieval Europe, we perceive France and the Holy Roman Empire as fictions, the true sovereignties being more localized. In sketching his second paradigm, Allison invites us to think likewise of modern nations, with departments, bureaus, service arms, and the like as counterparts of olden duchies, counties, and cities.

Moreover, research on various types of organizations has suggested that their behavior is somewhat different from that ordinarily imputed to individuals. They have narrowly conceived missions, limited repertoires, set routines for responding to stimuli, and the characteristic of "satisficing" rather than maximizing—that is, of stopping with the discovery of the first satisfactory solution to a problem rather than identifying a range of possible solutions and selecting the best. Thus, when resorting to Allison's second paradigm, one must not only visualize a state composed of many feudal entities but also bear in mind that these entities do not behave like men.

Yet a third paradigm is one that Allison describes under the rubric "governmental politics." One who explains events with this paradigm in mind conceives of government as neither a unitary actor nor an aggregation of organizations but as an arena of competition among individuals. Although generalizations in much of the literature represent the nation as a unitary actor, detailed narratives almost always portray dispute, strife, and intrigue of one kind or another among officeholders. By laying out the "governmental politics" paradigm, Allison proposes that this process be conceived as analogous not to that by which an individual makes up his mind but to that by which the so-called international system comes to be what it is at a given moment in time—that is, a function of the balance among the various powers that make it up. An alternative analogue might be a legislative body, the enactments of which are not products of a corporate will but compromises bargained out by men with differing attitudes, interests, and constituencies.

Allison's analytic distinctions have come to be characterized as the "bureaucratic politics" approach to study of international relations. Although the label is not altogether appropriate, it has acquired enough currency that it must be used.

A Case: U.S.-Argentine Relations, 1942–47

Allison illustrates how the three modes of explanation yield different answers to questions about the Cuban missile crisis. I wish here to explore their applicability to a quite different set of events, specifically those in U.S.-Argentine relations during and just after World War II. These events extend over a long period of time, involve no true crisis, and concern not two great powers but one great and one lesser power. The case serves therefore as a test of the broader applicability of Allison's insights. It also provides a basis for building upon them a synthetic model suscep- tible to testing against other bodies of data. Since inter-American rela- tions are not a central concern of many social scientists or historians, it is necessary, however, to commence with a brief chronicle.

After Japanese forces attacked the U.S. Naval Base at Pearl Harbor, Hawaii, and the United States formally went to war with Japan and her European allies, Germany and Italy, the foreign ministers of the Ameri- can republics held a special meeting at Rio de Janeiro. The chief U.S. del- egate, Undersecretary of State Sumner Welles, asked that all American republics at least sever relations with these so-called Axis states.

The chief Argentine delegate, Foreign Minister Enrique Ruiz Guiñazú, objected to the draft resolution that Welles put forward. The two then compromised on an ambiguous text, recommending that all the republics display solidarity with the United States but leaving an opening for their preserving ties with the Axis. Subsequently, Argentina's acting President, Ramón S. Castillo, announced that for the time being Argentina would maintain diplomatic and commercial relations with the three states with which the United States was at war.

At first, U.S. officials expressed little open criticism of the Argentine action. As it happened, the Chilean government took the same action that Argentina had. Welles explained in a speech that "unfortunate cir- cumstances" temporarily prevented the two from following the example of the other Latin American states. As time passed, however, comments by U.S. officials became more reproachful. In October 1942, Welles pro- tested publicly that agents in Argentina were broadcasting to German submarines the location of merchant vessels. The United States and six other American republics had meanwhile formed an inter-American Com- mittee for Political Defense to gather information about Axis espionage and the like in the hemisphere and to coordinate countermeasures. As- sembling some documentary evidence that Axis agents were conducting un-neutral activities in Argentina and Chile, this committee first trans- mitted the documents to the two governments and then published them to the world.

On June 4, 1943, Argentine army units occupied the Casa Rosada and ousted Castillo. General Arturo Rawson briefly assumed the presidency, followed after twenty-eight hours by General Pedro P. Ramírez. U.S. dip- lomats and journalists in Buenos Aires at first supposed this coup to have been the work of forces desirous of a breach with the Axis and collabo- ration with Britain and the United States. But nothing done in the early months of the new Argentine government bore out this assumption. On the contrary, the Ramírez cabinet adopted a series of measures that

North American observers interpreted as imitative of the Fascists and Nazis. For example, all Jewish and Masonic organizations were dissolved. At the same time, German agents and German-financed organizations and newspapers reportedly continued unmolested.

In January 1944, however, Ramírez announced the severance of diplomatic relations with Germany and Japan (Italy had by this time surrendered to the Allies). This action was greeted with guarded approval by U.S. Secretary of State Cordell Hull. He responded by itemizing particular measures that Argentine authorities might take to curb activities of German agents. Few of these actions were taken. When Ramírez shortly afterward stepped down, Hull refused to acknowledge General Edelmiro Farrell as a legitimate successor. He recalled the U.S. ambassador, leaving only a chargé d'affaires to conduct relations with Argentine ministries.

During 1944, Hull progressively adopted a harsher and harsher line toward the Farrell regime. He filed diplomatic notes protesting not only the continued presence of German agents in Argentina but also the encouragement given by Farrell and his new Vice-President, Juan Domingo Perón, to allegedly pro-Axis revolutionary groups in other South American states. In September, Hull issued a public statement branding Argentina "the Nazi Headquarters of the Western Hemisphere." Meanwhile, the U.S. Treasury Department froze Argentine gold reserves in the United States, and other U.S. agencies clamped special controls on trade with Argentina. The U.S. Government appeared to have adopted a position of unrelenting hostility to the Farrell-Perón administration.

Then, suddenly, the U.S. posture seemed to change. Hull, aging and in ill health, resigned. A little more than a year earlier, Welles had left the undersecretaryship, being replaced by Edward R. Stettinius, Jr., and Stettinius now stepped up into Hull's post. At first, official statements about Argentina preserved the earlier tone. Then, in February 1945, Stettinius conferred at Chapultepec Palace in Mexico City with foreign ministers of most other American republics and there agreed to a resolution inviting the Argentine government to declare war on the now tottering Axis powers and by doing so to restore itself to full fellowship in the interAmerican community. On March 27, Farrell did as requested. U.S. President Franklin D. Roosevelt promptly acknowledged Farrell as a legitimate chief of state and dispatched a new ambassador to Buenos Aires. The Treasury and other U.S. agencies modified the orders that had constrained financial and commercial relations. At the San Francisco conference in April, where the United Nations organization was formally created, Stettinius and his fellow U.S. delegates supported Argentina's admission as a full member. Despite vehement opposition from the Soviet delegation, the motion carried. Meanwhile, a mission headed by Avra

Warren of the U.S. State Department visited Buenos Aires to discuss not only improvement of diplomatic, economic, and cultural relations but also the possibility of U.S. military aid. Commentators in both the United States and Argentina reported the two governments as well on the way to effecting a rapprochement.

This appearance proved short-lived. The new U.S. ambassador was Spruille Braden. Hardly had he reached Buenos Aires before he began publicly to condemn the Farrell regime as Fascist and to charge it with sheltering Nazis. Braden's charges were endorsed by James F. Byrnes, who had recently succeeded Stettinius as Secretary of State. They were also endorsed in a public speech by Nelson Rockefeller, Assistant Secretary of State for American Republics Affairs, who was widely regarded as the engineer of the earlier effort to achieve a rapprochement. In August, shortly after the surrender of Japan, Byrnes recalled Braden to Washington to take Rockefeller's post. Although recognition was not formally withdrawn, diplomatic relations were left—as in the interval between Farrell's accession and the Argentine declaration of war—in the hands of a chargé d'affaires. And Braden in Washington continued denunciation of the Argentine goverment.

In the meantime, Argentine politics went into turmoil. In August 1945, Farrell eased bans on political activity, and huge rallies resulted, some supporting the government and some attacking it. At the beginning of October, students in the nation's eight universities staged a concerted strike. For the better part of a week, the suppression of this strike engaged all available troops and police. At the same time, a coalition of naval officers and out-of-office politicians petitioned the Supreme Court to declare the Farrell regime illegal. In a surprising move, Farrell discharged Perón from the three posts he had come to hold—Vice-President, Minister of War, and Minister of Labor. He also placed Perón under arrest. There ensued gigantic and militant demonstrations against the President and the army. These demonstrations did not come to an end until October 17, when Farrell released Perón, restored his offices, and publicly embraced him.

Thanking the *"descamisados"* who had rallied to his support, Perón announced that he would voluntarily leave the government. It seemed evident that he would seek the presidency in the national elections scheduled for the following year, and, indeed, Perón soon declared himself the candidate of a new Workers Party and of a splinter faction of the old Radical Party. The Radicals, Socialists, and Communists, with tacit support from the quiescent Conservative Party, formed a Democratic Union to oppose Perón, nominating as their joint candidate Dr. José P. Tamborini.

On February 12, 1946, less than two weeks before the Argentinians were to go to the polls, the U.S. Department of State released a so-called "Blue Book." Consisting in large part of cables and memoranda from captured German archives, it documented collaboration between the Farrell government and the Nazis. Several items demonstrated that Perón had enjoyed close relations with German agents and had, in fact, made an effort in 1944 to arrange the exchange of Argentine meat and wheat for German-made armaments. Charging that the United States was intervening in the election, Perón declared that the voter's choice was no longer Perón or Tamborini but Perón or Braden.

In what foreign observers and even Tamborini's supporters judged to be the most honest election in Argentine history, Perón won decisively. In June 1946, he took office as President.

The apparent posture of the U.S. Government, however, remained unaltered. At the Chapultepec conference of February 1945, it had been agreed that the American republics should promptly hold another conference to negotiate an inter-American security treaty. It was scheduled to convene in Rio de Janeiro in October of the same year. The U.S. State Department, however, refused to permit Farrell's representatives to take part, and the meeting was postponed. After the Argentine elections, discussion of rescheduling the meeting revived, but the State Department remained adamant against participation by Argentina. The conference was therefore put off to an unspecified future date. In a speech on April 8, 1946, Secretary of State Byrnes declared that the United States would not welcome Argentina as a partner in the inter-American system until its government demonstrated by deeds its willingness to purge the nation of Nazi and Fascist elements.

Not all U.S. officials spoke as Braden and Byrnes had. After an interval of several months, George S. Messersmith was sent to Buenos Aires to succeed Braden as ambassador. Both publicly and privately, Messersmith indicated that he would welcome improvement in relations. Various other Americans did likewise. But the posture of the principal officials in Washington remained unbending.

In 1947, this posture once again changed. In January, General George C. Marshall succeeded Byrnes as Secretary of State. A few months later, Marshall and the Secretaries of War and the Navy agreed to include Argentina among the nations that might receive U.S. military aid. In June, both Braden and Messersmith retired. Soon thereafter, a date was set for the long-deferred inter-American security conference, with Argentine representatives to be included. Harry S Truman, who had succeeded to the U.S. presidency in 1945 upon Roosevelt's death, meanwhile indicated that he was now prepared to regard Argentina as a friendly and cooperative state.

How are the twists and turns in U.S.-Argentine relations to be explained? Why did U.S. officials express so little criticism of Argentina in 1942–43? Why did they resort to both denunciation and economic coercion *after* Argentina severed relations with the Axis? Why did the U.S. stance appear to change during the early part of 1945? Why did it then revert to what it had been earlier? The period 1945–47 is usually thought to be that in which the United States turned to preoccupation with a Soviet and Communist threat. Certainly, U.S. officials and agents actively supported anti-Communist elements in Europe. Perón seemed ardently anti-Communist. His opponent in the presidential election had Communist support, whereas Perón had the endorsement of Argentina's Roman Catholic hierarchy. Why did the United States oppose him? Once he had won in an apparently democratic election, why did the United States continue its opposition? And why a year later did it make another about-face and embrace him as an ally?

Unitary Actor Explanations: Three Versions

From the existing literature, one can extract explanations framed in terms of Allison's first paradigm—that is, explanations in which the nation figures as a unitary actor. In fact, one can identify several versions. In one, the unitary actor is assumed to be moved primarily by ideals; in another, by external political interests (considerations of security, power, prestige, and the like); and in yet another, by internal political and economic interests (specifically, its own stability and prosperity).

The first variant, assuming an idealistic unitary actor, is exemplified in most of the North American literature dealing with these events.[4] It also emerges in one work by a Venezuelan scholar.[5] In brief, these authors depict the United States in the 1940s as torn between two sets of beliefs not easily reconciled: one, that Nazism or anything like it was a poison from which the people of the hemisphere needed to be protected; the other, that the independence of all American republics was precious, that U.S. intervention in their internal affairs was wrong, and, in addition, that the states of the New World should always act in unanimous concert. Seeing Argentina as a nation infected with Fascism, the United States wanted it to be purified. At the same time, it wanted to avoid both intervention and disruption of inter-American solidarity.

In 1942–43 the United States assigned priority to maintaining hemispheric unity and avoiding any appearance of intervention. But its priority

---

[4] J. Lloyd Mecham, *The United States and Inter-American Security, 1889–1960* (Austin: 1961); Harold F. Peterson, *Argentina and the United States, 1810–1960* (New York: 1964); and O. Edmund Smith, Jr., *Yankee Diplomacy: U.S. Intervention in Argentina* (Dallas: 1953).

[5] Francisco M. Cuevas Cancino, *Del Congreso de Panamá a la Conferencia de Caracas, 1826–1954* (Caracas: Editorial Ragon, 1955).

changed when it concluded that Argentinians in collaboration with Nazis were plotting the overthrow of various governments in South America and had, in fact, inspired the revolution in Bolivia of December 1943. It was not therefore moved by the Argentine severance of relations with the Axis. Instead, judging Farrell and Perón to be leaders of a pro-Axis faction opposed by the majority of the Argentine people, the United States resolved to do what it could to bring them down and hence resorted to public denunciation and to economic coercion.

These policies, however, aroused disquiet in a number of friendly Latin American capitals. They seemed a departure from the principle of nonintervention. Furthermore, many Latin American governments indicated fear lest the formation of the UN signify abandonment by the United States of the historic special relationship with other American republics. Sensitive to Latin American opinion and desiring both to establish an effective UN and to preserve the inter-American system, the United States relented. At Chapultepec, it agreed to offer Argentina a means of redeeming itself, and at San Francisco it kept its bargain.

The United States had, however, lost none of its loathing for Fascism. It perceived Argentina as making only token gestures to deal with the Nazis whom it harbored. Worse still, U.S. reporters in Buenos Aires in June 1945 described Farrell and Perón as launching a "reign of terror." A *New York Times* correspondent declared conditions worse than any he had seen during long service in Fascist Italy. In these circumstances, the United States returned to a policy of denouncing the Argentine regime as Fascist and encouraging the Argentine people to overturn it.

The victory of Perón in a fair election was unsettling, for it suggested that a major premise of U.S. policy had been mistaken. Whatever the ideological complexion of the Argentine regime, it was not holding power against the will of the masses. It had popular support. Gradually, the United States began to modify its position. Meanwhile, it came to view Communism as an evil and as a menace equal to Fascism, and it saw reason to fear that, if it continued to treat Argentina as a pariah, the result might be to drive the Argentinians into Communist arms. Consequently, the nation decided to let bygones be bygones, revert to a policy of nonintervention, and put its emphasis once again on hemispheric unity.

The second variant of the unitary actor paradigm, representing the nation as a calculating player of power politics, appears commonly in writing by non-North American scholars. One can see it, for example, in two works by the Peruvian, Ezequiel Ramírez Novoa.[6] In this version the United States figures as an imperial nation concerned with its own safety

---

[6] *La farsa del panamericanismo y la unidad indoamericana* (Buenos Aires: Editorial Indoamérica, 1955); and *La política yanqui en América Latina* (Lima: T. Scheuch, 1962–63).

and its opportunities for expansion at the expense of other states. From its standpoint, Latin America served as the functional equivalent of a colonial empire—an area providing a protected market for U.S. goods and capital, strategic raw materials, and a reservoir of manpower for its own defense or its wars of conquest. So that it might make full use of the area's resources, it strove to maintain subservient governments. It was content to have military dictators such as Fulgencio Batista in Cuba, Rafael Leonidas Trujillo in the Dominican Republic, and Anastasio Somoza in Nicaragua, or quasi-Fascist dictators such as Getúlio Vargas in Brazil, so long as they did what the United States wanted.

Long before World War II, Argentina had been a source of concern for the United States. It traded more with Europe than with the United States. It imported European and especially British capital and with these capital imports struggled to build industries potentially competitive with those of the United States. Moreover, it acted with some degree of independence and even threatened on occasion to become leader of an autonomous southern bloc.

When the United States entered World War II, its immediate preoccupation was to use the resources of Latin America for war purposes. That was the objective of its seeking common action by the American republics at the Rio conference of 1942. Although the noncooperation of Argentina was vexatious, the United States for the moment could do nothing except tolerate the fact, for it was too completely engaged in coping with the Axis threat to its interests in Europe and Asia.

By 1944, however, the United States possessed greater freedom of action. Owing partly to its exploitation of Latin American raw materials, it had gained the upper hand in the war and could turn its attention to Argentina. By adopting measures of political and economic coercion, it could hope to achieve a number of ends. It could end the danger of Argentina's forming a southern bloc, force upon the Argentinians a government that would in the future serve U.S. interests, reorient the Argentine economy, and, by so doing, make not only Argentina but also Great Britain more dependent on the United States. It made the most of the opportunity.

As the war drew to an end, however, the United States had to look to the future. It had to ensure that Latin American resources would be available to it in postwar competition with Britain and the Soviet Union, and it had to face the fact that not all Latin American governments were completely under its dominion. Some were insistent that the United States pay compensation in the form of economic aid or tariff concessions. Furthermore, the United States regarded it as important that there be a UN organization it could control. To this end, it needed a solid bloc of

Latin American votes at the San Francisco conference and in subsequent meetings of the General Assembly. Hence, for the time being, it compromised, yielding to Latin American governments on the single point that Argentina be invited back into the so-called inter-American community. When the San Francisco conference was over, the United States resumed its previous policy.

Before long, this policy came to seem unproductive. The British renewed their commercial ties with Argentina. More important, the Soviet Union commenced a flirtation with the government in Buenos Aires. Now entering the cold war, concerned about the strength of Communist parties throughout Latin America, and needing Argentine food supplies for its effort to stabilize Europe, the United States concluded that its safest and most profitable course of action was to come to terms with Argentina and bring it into the anti-Soviet alliance.

The third variant, in which the nation figures as a self-preoccupied unitary actor, is the paradigm underlying interpretations by the U.S. "New Left." The best example is that of David Green.[7] Here, the United States is seen as centrally concerned with preserving its own social order. It perceives that this social order depends on continual economic growth at home and that this growth in turn depends on the continual expansion of opportunities for the export of goods and capital. This being the case, the United States cannot afford to have foreign markets closed to it by the socialistic or nationalistic policies of other governments. As a result, it opposes by every means not only Communism but also "revolutionary nationalism."

Before and during World War II, the United States had been concerned about Argentina's relative economic independence. After the military coup of June 1943, it became further alarmed by evidence that Argentina was turning to revolutionary nationalism. This alarm grew when the upheaval in Bolivia in December and reports of plots in Chile and Peru suggested that such revolutionary nationalism might sweep the whole southern tier of South America. In 1944, therefore, it exerted itself to uproot the source of this danger by applying pressures designed to force the Argentinian nationalists out of office.

Toward the end of the war, however, the United States came to perceive as the greatest threat to its own internal order the possibility that Communism would engulf its markets in Europe, the Middle East, and Asia. As a tactical maneuver, it effected a temporary truce with Argentina so as to have support from all the American republics in its efforts to preserve the open door elsewhere in the world. It had not, however, lost its fear of Argentina's revolutionary nationalism, and it persisted in

[7] *The Containment of Latin America* (New York: 1971).

efforts to overturn the Argentinian government. Although Perón's election appeared to be a defeat for the United States, in fact it was not, for Perón proved willing not only to leave Argentina open for U.S. economic penetration but to buy large quantities of goods from U.S. war industries. Since he also professed hostility to Communism, his government seemed one that suited the ends of the United States, and a rapprochement therefore became easy.

Of course, the foregoing summaries greatly oversimplify what these various authors say, for none relies wholly on a single paradigm. Each work that includes any kind of detailed narrative mentions differences of opinion within the U.S. Government and concedes that particular decisions were at least marginally influenced by the preferences of individuals who happened to hold certain offices at critical times. Nevertheless, I think these summaries state with fairness the generalizations to be found in most of the literature.

Explanation in Terms of Organizational Processes

If one can inject into his thinking the second of Allison's paradigms, some rather different generalizations emerge.

Prior to the war, formal U.S. relations with Argentina appeared to be managed by the Department of State. The U.S. embassy in Buenos Aires communicated with the Argentine foreign ministry, while the Argentine Ambassador in Washington communicated with the Secretary of State or his aides. The language used by North Americans in both capitals was vetted by the State Department's Division of Latin American Affairs. This division was organized to handle U.S. diplomatic dealings with all Latin American republics other than Mexico. Within it, one officer supervised correspondence with all three River Plate nations. It was his function to see that nothing said to Argentinians complicated communications with Uruguayans or Paraguayans. Another officer had the Brazilian portfolio; a third, that for North and West Coast affairs. Each had an opportunity to examine anything in writing destined for the U.S. embassy in Buenos Aires or the Argentine embassy in Washington. In doing so, their concern was naturally to ensure that there were no initiatives that could not be matched in dealings with "their" countries. The existence of a separate division for Mexico, as for Western Europe, Eastern Europe, the Near East and Africa, and the Far East, facilitated the development of policies for Mexico and the Caribbean area that were somewhat different from those for the rest of Latin America. The fact that a single division dealt with all the remaining American republics contributed to a presumption that the United States should pursue an undifferentiated policy toward all of them.

In practice, however, the Division of Latin American Affairs had only marginal influence on U.S. Government actions materially affecting Argentina. Prior to World War II, such actions all had to do with economic relationships, and the practical management of these relationships lay with other agencies. There was, for example, a flat prohibition on importation into the United States of Argentina's prime export—beef. This prohibition had been imposed in the 1920s when foot-and-mouth disease had developed on the Argentine range. It was imposed by the Bureau of Animal Industry of the Department of Agriculture. An organization employing more people than the entire Department of State, this Bureau had been created by Congress to control or prevent diseases that might affect meat produced or consumed by Americans. Its chief officials were all veterinarians or pathologists with high standing in their professions. Its procedures and routines were designed to reduce to an absolute minimum the incidence of disease among animals arriving at U.S. stockyards. Formally or informally, officers of the Bureau might be told by the State Department or the Commerce Department that admission of Argentine beef could improve political relations or enlarge U.S. exports, but, so long as they had reason to fear that any such beef might be contaminated, they had no incentive to change their position. And State and Commerce had no capacity for coercing them, for neither the President nor the leadership in Congress could hope to win a row with veterinarians who could represent themselves as simply protecting the healthiness of American meat.

With regard to trade in other products, power lay with an interdepartmental committee on reciprocity agreements. By legislation passed in 1934, this committee oversaw negotiations for reciprocal trade agreements. On its recommendation, the President could lower tariffs on imports by as much as 50 percent.

The Secretary of State was chairman of this committee, and State Department officers presided over subcommittees set up to work out detailed trade agreements with individual countries. The overall committee and its subcommittees also included representatives of the Bureau of Foreign and Domestic Commerce of the Department of Commerce. Having the mission of expanding U.S. export trade, they were in general partisans of lowering barriers to imports so that foreign countries might earn dollars with which to buy U.S. goods. Aware of Argentina's relatively large volume of importation from Britain and Western Europe, they were especially interested in improving Argentine sales to the United States.

Offsetting State and Commerce participants, however, were representatives of the Treasury and of the Agriculture Department's Office of Foreign Agricultural Relations and Agricultural Marketing Service. Conscious that a favorable balance of trade with Argentina contributed importantly to protecting the overall U.S. balance of payments, Treasury spokesmen were not keen on having Americans spend more dollars on Argentine goods. Representatives of the two branches of the Agriculture Department of course had uppermost in their minds protection of the American farmers who might receive lower prices if the United States imported larger quantities of Argentine agricultural produce. Men from the Agricultural Marketing Service had an additional concern, for their agency purchased surpluses in order to maintain farmers' incomes. If imports drove down free-market prices, the Service would have to buy more and hence have to seek larger appropriations from Congress.

Determinative power within the committee and its subcommittees lay with representatives of yet another agency—the independent Tariff Commission. An outgrowth of the Progressive Era movement for a "scientific tariff," the Commission's staff consisted of economists expert in estimating comparative domestic and foreign production costs. This staff had gradually acquired the confidence of protectionist businessmen and Congressmen by the thoroughness of their investigations and the conservatism of their recommendations for tariff revision. Within the reciprocity committee and its subcommittee, the pace of movement toward any new trade arrangements with Argentina was wholly up to the Tariff Commission representatives, for other members could do nothing until its experts completed detailed commodity-by-commodity studies of all products that might be involved. And their findings on allowable tariff concessions were ordinarily conclusive.

As of the last years of peace, therefore, one can construe U.S. Government relations with Argentina as functions of the way in which various bureaucracies had defined their missions and developed structures to carry them out. Formal diplomacy was supervised by the State Department Division of Latin American Affairs, organized to deal indiscriminately with all republics south of Mexico. Terms for trade were controlled in part by a Bureau of Animal Industry devoted to minimizing any danger of foot-and-mouth disease and in part by a Tariff Commission concerned primarily with preventing any perceptible decline in prices received in the domestic market by U.S. producers.

With the onset of war in Europe in 1939, other organizations in the U.S. Government acquired ability to influence relations with Argentina. As early as 1933, Congress began to authorize larger sums for defense. With actual war on the other side of the Atlantic, followed by the German conquest of France, the near-defeat of Britain, and the signing by Japan of a virtual alliance with Germany and Italy, these allocations soared. The changing proportions of money and civilian personnel at the disposal of the armed services are indicated in Fig. 1.

Earlier, the services had interpreted their missions relatively narrowly.

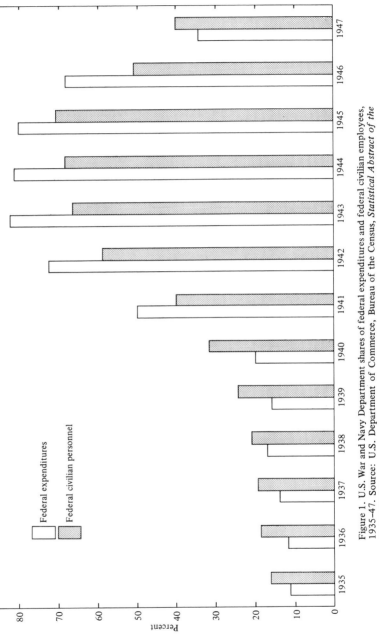

Figure 1. U.S. War and Navy Department shares of federal expenditures and federal civilian employees, 1935–47. Source: U.S. Department of Commerce, Bureau of the Census, *Statistical Abstract of the United States.*

The Army had sought to develop a small professional cadre suitable as a base for expansion should the United States again mobilize for a large war. The Navy had had the same objective, plus that of maintaining a sufficient naval force to defeat any other navy attempting to gain control of the western North Atlantic, the Caribbean, or the eastern Pacific. Although the Army and Navy had both maintained attachés at embassies and legations in South America, neither service had actually paid much attention to the continent. According to Spruille Braden, the Army intelligence file for Colombia in 1941 contained nothing more than excerpts from a tourist guide.

With the growth of German and Japanese military power and accompanying increases in Congressional allocations for military purposes, the U.S. armed services developed larger conceptions of the threats to the United States and the requirements for combatting those threats. Among contingencies envisioned by Army, Army Air Corps, and Navy planners were efforts by the Axis powers to acquire bases in southern South America from which they would then seek control of the air and sea bases in the Caribbean and North Atlantic, disrupt traffic through the Panama Canal, and perhaps even bomb or invade the continental United States. As time passed, these imagined dangers became increasingly the basis for the planning of forces, the design of aircraft and ships, and petitions to Congress for funds and for such legislation as that of 1940 introducing conscription.

Latin American affairs became the preoccupation of various units within the armed services. In the War Department General Staff, the dominant Operations Division formed an American Theater Section which developed and advocated plans for building up the self-defense forces of South American republics, coordinating U.S. and Latin American forces by standardization of equipment and provision of U.S. officers to advise on plans and tactics, and acquiring bases for U.S. air and army units assigned the mission of protecting the hemisphere.

In the Navy, similar developments took place. Indeed, so prominent did Latin America become that, in a reorganization immediately after Pearl Harbor, a Pan American Division was established on a par with Communications and Intelligence Divisions, all immediately under a Sub-Chief of Naval Operations. This Division processed information about Axis activities in the hemisphere and worked out proposals for supplying and advising Latin American navies, training Latin American officers, and securing base rights in South America for the recently created South Atlantic Fleet.

By 1941, the armed services had added new dimensions to relations with Latin American republics. Either directly or through State Department channels, they could offer or withhold military equipment and various supplies, including lend-lease materials available at little or no cost. They could also offer or withhold invitations to Latin American officers to attend U.S. service schools, the dispatch of training and advisory missions to Latin America, and bids for base facilities for U.S. ships or aircraft or both.

Furthermore, spokesmen for the armed services had a voice—sometimes a decisive voice—in trade relations. A Joint Advisory Board on American Republics, composed entirely of military and naval men, made recommendations to the Munitions Assignment Board concerning quantities of military materiel that Latin Americans in each republic might be permitted to purchase. Other military bodies advised the agencies that determined quantities of raw materials, civilian industrial production, and food releasable for export to Latin America and quantities of merchant-vessel tonnage allocable to runs between U.S. and Latin American ports.

Military and naval organizations concerned with Latin America acquired an influence in bureaucratic structures within which they had no direct representation. In particular, they had an effect upon the Interdepartmental Committee on Reciprocal Trade Agreements. They prompted representatives of the State Department to speak more forcefully about the need for improved political relationships, those from Commerce to stress the importance of importing more raw materials from Latin America, and those from Agriculture to perceive that demand for food would be sufficient to permit increased importation without injury to U.S. producers. The coincidental economic boom produced by preparation for war meanwhile eased the consciences of Tariff Commission representatives. One result was the conclusion in October 1941 of a reciprocal trade agreement with Argentina. Though never ratified by Argentina, it would have lowered barriers to Argentine trade with the United States.

After Pearl Harbor and the actual involvement of the United States in World War II, the situation within the military establishment gradually changed. While the influence of the military within the Government continued to grow, the influence upon the services of groups concerned with Latin America steadily diminished. Their places were usurped by units dealing with the vast operations that began to be projected and carried out in North Africa, the Mediterranean, Western Europe, the Central Pacific, and the Southwest Pacific.

The concerns expressed by military spokesmen between 1939 and 1941 continued nevertheless to exert a controlling influence within the U.S. Government. In the first place, the information sought about Latin

America had to do primarily with the supposed Axis threat. Most military and naval intelligence officers and FBI agents assigned to Latin America had this as their sole mission, and State Department representatives were continually enjoined to report on the subject. In the second place, efforts to encourage Latin American cooperation in hemispheric defense not only continued but gained momentum. Military and naval aid and advisory missions remained in place. Despite their steadily diminishing importance in the eyes of upper-level Army, Army Air Corps, and Navy officers, most of them secured at least marginal increases in allocations of weapons, supplies, and personnel. Such an effort in Rio de Janeiro secured for Brazil more than $361 million worth of lend-lease equipment.

Largely in response to military representations regarding the importance of Latin American defense cooperation, the President created a special organization, the Office of the Coordinator of Inter-American Affairs. It swiftly grew to be an agency larger than the prewar State Department, with vast suborganizations assuming such functions as the promotion of agriculture, industry, transportation, education, and health, and the dissemination of pro-U.S. and pro-UN propaganda in Latin America. Sitting in interagency committees, representatives of this office increasingly took on the task of arguing that some portion of lend-lease and other supplies should be allocated to Latin America.

Meanwhile, still other emergency organizations became involved. Corporations controlled by the Reconstruction Finance Corporation engaged in preclusive buying of Latin American products that, it was feared, might otherwise go to Axis agents. A Board of Economic Warfare gave advice on such buying and also located and arranged for purchase in Latin America of scarce commodities needed in the U.S. war effort. A War Food Administration sought additional food supplies in Latin America.

U.S. tolerance of Argentine neutrality up to 1944 may be explicable as a product of the new position of the military services within the U.S. Government and the bureaucratic institutionalization of the interests to which the services gave voice. Similarly, the stiffening U.S. attitude during 1944 could be interpreted as a belated product of, first, the declining military concern about defense of Latin America and, second, the concentration of intelligence collection on evidence of activity by Axis agents. The continued momentum of agencies engaged in preclusive buying and purchases of raw materials and food was reflected in trade statistics that, despite the diplomatic notes and coercive decrees issuing from the State and Treasury departments, showed U.S. imports from Argentina in 1944 to be at a record level ($177 million, as contrasted with $144.9 million for 1943 and $168.7 million for 1945).

The abrupt shift from coercion to conciliation in the spring of 1945 can perhaps be explained in part by the emergence of additional organizations that attached priority to acquiring Argentine produces. As victory came nearer, the Board of Economic Warfare was transformed into a Foreign Economic Administration within which the most important subunits became those concerned with securing supplies for relief and reconstruction. Meanwhile, the giant U.S. military commands in Europe filed increasingly urgent requests for provisions to feed the millions of civilians in liberated and conquered areas. Concerned with protecting consumption levels at home, the War Food Administration resisted meeting foreign needs by drawing on domestic stocks. In combination, the Foreign Economic Administration, the military establishment, and the War Food Administration all exerted pressure therefore for turning to Argentina as a major supplier of food for Europe.

Within the State Department there had meanwhile grown up a cluster of new units concerned primarily with creating a United Nations organization to replace the defunct League of Nations. Their planning assumed that the Latin American republics would form a solid bloc with the United States. Learning that some of these republics might make difficulties if U.S.-Argentine relations were not meanwhile conciliated, these elements in State lobbied for a resumption of diplomatic relations and an invitation to Argentina to become an ally. In view of the interests expressed by the Foreign Economic Administration, the military, and the War Food Administration, the UN planners prevailed within their own department. The results were evident at Chapultepec and San Francisco.

The ascendency of the UN planners in State was short-lived. Once the San Francisco conference ended, they no longer controlled the most important agenda items in the Secretary's staff committee or other such coordinating groups. Moreover, the death of Roosevelt had brought into the White House a new President who looked to the Department, as Roosevelt had not, as a principal source of information and advice about the whole range of U.S. international relations. In short order, Truman transferred to State such functions as supervising occupied areas and disposing of surplus U.S. military equipment abroad. Suddenly, the regional offices and desks had functions and stature they had not had since at least the late 1930s.

As the Department was by then organized, one Assistant Secretary of State dealt with affairs in all parts of the world except Latin America. Another Assistant Secretary concerned himself with the American republics, now including Mexico and Central America. Since the most important business after the San Francisco conference was negotiations with the USSR about liberated areas and peace treaties for the defeated Axis states, the former of these two Assistant Secretaries occupied the dominant position.

On the whole, officers of the Department were suspicious of and hostile toward the Soviets. Nevertheless, their organizational mission was to secure agreements with them. At San Francisco, the Russian delegation had opposed and voted against admission of Argentina to the UN. At meetings of the Council of Foreign Ministers in 1945 and 1946, Soviet representatives repeatedly chided the United States for permitting the continued existence of a Fascist state within the Western Hemisphere. To organizations in the State Department preoccupied with the terms of possible bargains for Eastern Europe, Germany, Italy, the Middle East, China, Korea, and Japan, this Argentine question was a nuisance. Their concern was that the Office of American Republics Affairs handle the matter in such a way as to deprive the Soviets of a talking point.

At the same time, other important organizations in the Department and elsewhere in the Government developed a parallel interest. While State had worked on the UN, units in the War Department, with some unwelcome assistance from the Treasury and other agencies, had prepared plans for the occupation of Germany and Japan. Truman moved these units wholesale into State, placing them under an Assistant Secretary of State for Occupied Areas. Under this official's supervision, a vast network of military and civilian agencies effectuated decisions that had been made in principle during the war. German and Japanese officials were rounded up for trial as war criminals; factories were dismantled; purges and propaganda campaigns were pressed forward with a view to "de-Nazifying" Germany and "demilitarizing" Japan. On occasion, agencies involved in this work called attention to the possibility that some German war criminals were in refuge in Argentina and to the fact that Germans in Argentina retained positions or property they would have been deprived of in other allied states. In 1945 and 1946, therefore, the Office of American Republics Affairs was under continual organizational pressure to be outspokenly critical of the Argentine regime and to agitate about the continued presence of former Nazis within the country.

Once again, however, circumstances changed. The President, the Secretary of State, and lesser officials gradually became convinced that a genuine peace could not be negotiated with the Soviets. Privately, they concluded as early as August 1946 that the Russians were bent on expansion and could be checked only by a threat of war. Publicly, Truman announced this doctrine of "containment" in a speech to Congress in March 1947 proposing economic and military aid to Greece and Turkey. Meanwhile, concern grew lest Western Europe suffer such economic misery as to enable Soviet-sponsored Communist parties to seize power.

The dominant bureaus of the State Department saw Argentina as a potential source of food and raw materials to avert hunger and chaos in Europe. Some units in the military establishment meanwhile perceived that Argentina, possessing large surplus funds, might be a purchaser of guns, tanks, ships, aircraft, and other equipment left over from the war. Others saw that preparation for future defense of the hemisphere would be greatly advanced if the American republics should integrate their planning and standardize their armaments and military doctrine.

In the Department of Commerce, there was a feeling that Argentina represented a profitable market that U.S. firms could not adequately exploit because of the state of diplomatic relations. One Commerce Department official remarked to a reporter, "I can just see that damn pile of pink pesos down there waiting for American business." Hence, interested organizations in the War, Navy, and Commerce departments joined the European and Near Eastern bureaus of State in pressing for accommodation with Argentina.

State's Office of American Republics Affairs (known familiarly as ARA) resisted these pressures for an interval. By 1947, however, it capitulated. Thus, one can explain the twists in U.S. relations with Argentina in terms of the relationships, perceptions, interests, capabilities, procedures, and tendencies toward inaction of semi-sovereign entities within the U.S. bureaucracy.

Explanation in Terms of Governmental Politics

Now, thinking in terms of Allison's third paradigm, we can attempt a somewhat different explanation by assuming that the critical actors were neither the nation as a unit nor bureaucratic organizations but rather strategically placed individuals, each of whom had his own perceptions and interests.

We must recall that from 1933 to 1943 the official who had the greatest personal stake in U.S. relations with Latin America was Undersecretary of State Sumner Welles. A onetime career diplomat, the author of an exhaustive study criticizing past U.S. intervention in the Dominican Republic, and an old friend of Roosevelt's, Welles had gained the reputation in 1933–34 of being the President's principal adviser on Latin America and the architect of the so-called "Good Neighbor Policy." In dealing with Roosevelt, the Congress, the public, U.S. missions in Latin America, and Latin American diplomats, Welles often consulted only pro forma with his nominal chief, Cordell Hull.

As World War II approached, Welles invested his energies in obtaining unanimous Latin American support of the United States. In inter-American conferences at Panama, Havana, and Rio in 1939, 1940, and early 1942, he made verbal concessions to the Argentine delegates in order to ensure unanimity. Although he expected the agreement at Rio to produce an Argentine break with the Axis, he defended Argentina's failure so to act as permissible according to the language he had accepted. Throughout 1942 and 1943 he argued that no action should be taken other than quietly to urge the Argentine government to sever relations with Rome, Berlin, and Tokyo. Although he had to accept the decisions of the agencies controlling lend-lease, shipping, and exports and imports, he insisted that any economic coercion or even any public representations against Argentina would run counter to the principle of unanimity and, worse, would constitute intervention in Argentine affairs and hence a breach of the Good Neighbor doctrine. His status, influence, and power were all bound up in this position.

There were many who wanted to displace Welles. Hull in particular resented his Undersecretary's independence and closeness to the President. Over time, Hull had proved able to get rid of others who acted as Welles did, but Welles had remained invulnerable, largely because of the fame of the Good Neighbor principle. When Welles at the Rio conference allowed Argentina to escape a commitment to break relations with the Axis, Hull saw an opening for attack. To the President and others, he denounced the compromise resolution to which Welles, on his own initiative, had agreed. Aware that a turn by Roosevelt toward a harder line would be tantamount to repudiation of Welles, Hull seized every chance to forward evidence that Argentina was a Fascist state that ought to be treated as an enemy.

Outside the State Department were others who differed in principle with Welles and stood to gain if he were ousted. Secretary of the Treasury Henry Morgenthau was another old friend of Roosevelt's. He craved the role of chief presidential adviser on foreign affairs. Moreover, the period preceding U.S. entry into the war had convinced him that most of his rivals for that assignment had insufficient understanding of the evil of Fascist and Nazi doctrine and the danger that it would represent if not wholly rooted out and put to the torch. Welles's conciliation of the Argentinians outraged Morgenthau, and from early 1942 onward he pressed Roosevelt to reverse the action and, in effect, remove Welles and turn to the Treasury as a substitute.

Morgenthau, it should be noted, was a rival not only of Welles but also of Hull, and was so perceived by the Secretary of State. His maneuvers had the objective of persuading the President to act against Argentina primarily by measures of economic coercion manageable by his department. Hull's maneuvers had the end of ensuring that, if Welles went, Morgenthau would not take his place. Hence, the Secretary of the Treasury and the Secretary of State battled one another even as each worked to bring down Hull's Undersecretary.

Probably, there were people interested in this goal who were even better placed to effect it than was Morgenthau or Hull. The principal figure in Roosevelt's entourage, Harry Hopkins, was too busy with Europe to think about the Western Hemisphere, and well into 1943 he was too sure of the President's confidence to worry about someone like Welles. But it is likely that others near to Roosevelt were jealous of the Undersecretary. William C. Bullitt, who had been Ambassador to France up to 1940, believed himself entitled to be Undersecretary of State. It was actually he who finally forced Welles's resignation, not by getting the President to make a policy decision but by collecting, presenting to Roosevelt, and threatening to make public evidence that Welles was a homosexual. It did Bullitt no good, for Roosevelt would thereafter not even admit him to his presence. For a long time, however, Bullitt was the organizer of intrigue against the Undersecretary; and during that time he was something of a White House insider.

When Bullitt's disclosures forced Roosevelt to ask for Welles's resignation, the political situation changed altogether. Those who had been advocating courses of action contrary to what had been espoused by Welles no longer faced high-level opposition. Moreover, they were so committed that they could not easily retreat. Neither Hull on the one hand nor Morgenthau on the other could without embarassment adopt the position that Argentina's severance of relations with the Axis in January 1944 nullified the recommendations they had been advancing earlier. On the contrary, each had to assume that any show of hesitancy would have the effect of abandoning the field to the other. Hence, the Secretary of State and the Secretary of the Treasury competed in trying to demonstrate which department could most effectively lead in the new direction, with Hull advising ever sterner notes and speeches and Morgenthau matching him stride for stride with proposals for economic coercion.

The end of 1944 brought a new change in the political situation, for ill health forced Hull to abdicate. His successor, Stettinius, had had no part in making a success of plans for the UN organization. Although his new Assistant Secretary for American Republics Affairs, Nelson Rockefeller, had been the Coordinator of Inter-American Affairs and, as such, may have worked against Welles in 1942 and 1943, hoping to succeed to Welles's influence, he had been left far behind in the race of 1944, for his apparatus had been capable chiefly of designing proposals to help friendly countries rather than plans for hurting an enemy. Having no worrisome past to live down and appreciating that his own prospects might depend on how well he served Stettinius's needs, Rockefeller could readily abandon the Hull line and give priority to winning Latin American votes for the UN Charter.

Meanwhile, Morgenthau was occupied on another front. In the autumn of 1944 he had succeeded in winning Roosevelt's approval for his own scheme for dealing with Germany. It involved destroying industry and converting Germany into a country primarily agricultural and pastoral in character. Morgenthau's triumph was, however, short-lived. Facing the prospect of paying occupation costs out of funds that might otherwise go to other purposes, the armed services wanted to make use of whatever productive capacity the defeated nations still possessed. Some civilians in the military establishment and some professional diplomats in State feared, moreover, that the Morgenthau plan would render Germany and perhaps the rest of Europe unduly vulnerable to takeover by Communists. Hardly had the ink dried on Roosevelt's "OK" before elements in the War and State departments opened a massive campaign to change his mind. Throughout the winter of 1944–45, this issue and certain others having to do with agreements to create the World Bank and the International Monetary Fund served as the principal tests of Morgenthau's influence and, indeed, of the ability of Morgenthau to remain in office. So long as there remained hope that Stettinius would be neutral in the German controversy or perhaps even throw his weight onto Morgenthau's side, the Secretary of the Treasury could not afford a dispute with the new Secretary of State. Thus, when the Stettinius regime altered course with regard to Argentina, Morgenthau kept his peace. And when Stettinius and Rockefeller proposed the lifting of economic sanctions, he acquiesced.

The replacement of Roosevelt by Truman, of course, altered the political scene far more than had the departure of either Welles or Hull. With it came a tidying up of the lines of influence running to the White House, with the State Department being assigned a much larger role. Furthermore, Truman replaced Roosevelt's people. He substituted Byrnes for Stettinius and the relatively unaggressive Fred M. Vinson for Morgenthau.

For Byrnes, Argentina held only peripheral interest. An expert technician in political mediation, he was handicapped by few convictions or principles. As he interpreted his job, it was to work out a peace settlement with the Soviets that would win acceptance inside the U.S. Government, by the Congress, and by U.S. public opinion. From his standpoint, the Argentine policy of his predecessor was a liability, for it provided the Soviets with an irrelevant talking point and it drew widespread criticism at home. During the San Francisco conference, one left-wing journal had published a cartoon portraying Hitler and Hirohito examining the bulletin, "Argentina Goes to San Francisco"; in the caption, the Japanese emperor is saying to the German Führer, "You declare war on me, I declare war on you, and we both go to San Francisco." With less pungency, such staid periodicals as the *New York Times* and *Washington Post* voiced similar attitudes. Since there had been no counterbalancing acclaim for Stettinius's actions except from the out-of-office Sumner Welles and from politicians and journalists in Latin America who influenced few if any voters in the United States, Byrnes probably saw almost no utility in continuing his predecessor's course and every advantage in seeming to be the author of a change.

Being not only a new Secretary of State but also the appointee of a new President, Byrnes felt relatively free to make personnel changes. Although Rockefeller, perhaps sensing Byrnes's needs, surprised the world with a speech sharply critical of the Argentine regime, he was a symbol of the policy of conciliation. By getting front-page publicity in the United States for his anti-Farrell and anti-Perón utterances in Buenos Aires, Braden became at the same time the symbol of an alternative policy. Moreover, although Braden's own background was that of an engineer and executive in large U.S. corporations active in Latin America, he was thought to have friends in precisely those circles where an infighting attack on the Truman Administration was most likely to start, for he had in the past enjoyed help from Harry Hopkins and from Eleanor Roosevelt, the late President's wife. The appointment of Braden must have seemed to Byrnes not only to solve a minor diplomatic problem but more importantly to contribute to coping with a major domestic problem.

In fact, Byrnes's expedient failed to be fully successful. The Braden appointment drew some opposition, especially from Arthur Vandenberg and Tom Conally, the two powerful Senators who had been members of the delegation at San Francisco and who were therefore sensitive about criticism of the decision to recognize Argentina and sponsor its admission to the UN. The "Blue Book" provoked angry comment not only from Welles but also from many other sources, for its publication was almost universally interpreted as an attempt to influence the Argentine elections and hence as intervention out of keeping with the Good Neighbor doctrine. And when Perón nevertheless won the election, the chorus of criticism swelled, for many people who were prepared to overlook a sin could not forgive a failure. In *Time* magazine, "shrewd, jolly Spruille Braden" became "hulking, excitable Spruille Braden." He became a liability to Byrnes but not one that Byrnes could write off without reviving the very problems he had hoped initially to solve.

Meanwhile, Byrnes's position worsened in other ways. President Truman had begun listening to other advisers. And Byrnes, frequently away from Washington for prolonged sessions of the Council of Foreign Ministers, could not adequately protect his personal interests.

Policy toward Argentina served as one point of attack for those in the capital eager to gain some share of the influence and power that Truman had originally conferred on his Secretary of State. Among civilians in the military establishment, there were individuals who believed Truman basically wrong in wanting to centralize foreign affairs in the State Department. Secretary of the Navy James Forrestal and some of his colleagues pressed upon the President the argument that it was inimical to U.S. security interests to exclude Argentina from the inter-American system and thus force the Argentinians to look to Europe, perhaps even to the Soviet bloc, for arms and technical aid. Given the fact that Braden was irrevocably opposed to providing military equipment or advice to a Perón-dominated Argentina, their recommendation implied that Braden should go. And Byrnes was sufficiently committed to Braden that, if Braden went, the Secretary himself might be the next to go. At any rate, his apparent influence would be much diminished.

Argentine policy was nowhere near the center of high-level politics in Washington. It was merely a minor zone of weakness in Byrnes's defenses. But it was simultaneously a focus of lower-level politics within the Department of State, for Braden was there a target of men who conscientiously differed with him and who at the same time saw themselves as better fitted than he to manage U.S. relations wtih Argentina or with Latin America as a whole.

When Braden was appointed, Norman Armour announced his resignation from the U.S. Foreign Service. Throughout Braden's tenure, U.S. newspapers reported anonymous "old Latin American hands" as critical of his conduct, and it seems likely that Armour was one of these. In fact, when Braden was eventually removed, Armour was brought back to take his post.

A more open rival of Braden was George S. Messersmith, whom Braden himself selected as his successor in the Buenos Aires embassy. A onetime school administrator in Delaware, Messersmith had risen in the Foreign Service via the consular corps, which had much lower social and professional standing than the elite diplomatic corps. As Consul General in Berlin in the 1930s he had, however, distinguished himself as an outspoken critic of the Nazis. Hull had eventually made him an Assistant Secretary of State. He had then spent the war as Ambassador to Mexico. Braden probably assumed that, with his anti-Nazi record, Messersmith would be a helpful agent in Perón's Argentina. In fact, however, Messersmith hardly reached the country before he became an impassioned advocate of rapprochement, appealing to Byrnes and on occasion directly to the President for repudiation of all that Braden had stood for. Doubtless, Messersmith believed in his case. Doubtless, too, he recognized that, if his appeals succeeded, he would at least be confirmed an independent authority in Buenos Aires and conceivably summoned back to Washington to take Braden's place.

As in 1943–44, so in 1946–47 the question of what U.S. policy toward

Argentina should be involved issues of principle and alternative definitions of national interest, but those issues were inseparably bound up
with matters crucial to the private egos of individuals in the U.S. Government: Who would have or would appear to have the President's ear? Who
would stand ahead of whom in the Washington pecking order? And who
would hold which prestigious job?

At the beginning of 1947, Truman replaced Byrnes with Marshall. As
a new man, Marshall had a grace period in which to choose his own team.
Owing to his background as a professional soldier, some Congressmen
and some journals identified with the left wing of the Democratic Party
had questioned his appointment. Specifically, some had asked whether
it might spell more militant opposition to the USSR, coupled with a more
forgiving attitude toward the Germans and such states as Spain and Argentina. Marshall could foresee that he would stir criticism if he promptly
fired Braden. On the other hand, he could also perceive the danger to his
primacy as presidential adviser if he had to defend Braden. The solution
for Marshall was to take in public the position that Braden had his support but in private to disassociate himself from the Assistant Secretary.

I write "the solution for Marshall" rather than "Marshall's solution"
because there is reason to suppose that these tactics were devised not by
the general himself but by Dean Acheson. The Undersecretary of State
throughout Byrnes's tenure, Acheson was, like Byrnes, so closely identified with Braden that he could not easily have repudiated him. Also, he
had a strong sense of loyalty to subordinates who came under fire from
Congress or the public. At the same time, however, Acheson was a cool-
headed and pragmatic lawyer who had no difficulty in perceiving that
he and Byrnes would have been politically stronger if they had not been
obligated to defend Braden's position. When Marshall asked him to stay
on for a few months to aid in the transition, Acheson saw that the interests of his new client, Marshall, would be best served by disembarassment
of both Braden and Braden's policy. Hence, either advising Marshall or
acting for him, Acheson proceeded to concede the points that had been
at issue earlier, ruling that Argentina should be permitted to purchase
arms and obtain U.S. military advisers and directing that arrangements
proceed for the long-delayed inter-American security conference. Then
in June 1947 when the headlines were full of Marshall's proposal for a
massive aid program to Europe, Acheson requested simultaneous resigna-
tions from both Braden *and* Messersmith.

With this action, Marshall became able to carry forward a different
policy. Since Armour had been involved in both the conciliation of Argentina by Welles and the coercion of its government by Hull, his selection as Braden's successor drew little criticism. By not only choosing

Armour but giving him the lofty title of Assistant Secretary for Political Affairs, Marshall made some headway toward solving a problem that was probably more important for him than anything having to do with Argentina, namely, that of reassuring the corps of career Foreign Service officers that he respected their professionalism and merited their support and cooperation. The choice, as Messersmith's successor, of James Bruce, a businessman untainted by prior involvement in Argentine affairs, further freed the new Secretary from the hand of the past. In short order, Marshall could preside over a new rapprochement with the Argentine government.

Consistently with the third of Allison's paradigms, one can thus explain the course of U.S. relations with Argentina not as a product of national purposes or of bureaucratic momentum but rather as a set of side effects resulting from competition for status, influence, and power within the United States.

A Synthetic Model of Governmental Action

The preceding pages suggest that there are alternative modes of explanation, each involving different premises and implicit propositions. Which most nearly approximates the truth about the past? To reply is difficult, because each of the three, including each variant of the one that assumes a unitary national actor, has to it a ring of solid truth. Each is consistent with what little we understand about the motivation and behavior of both individuals and organizations; each can be confirmed rather than controverted if one tests it against the evidence in particular cases.

It follows that each mode of explanation captures a segment of reality. Some statements about the truth of the past will most appropriately have as subjects in their grammar the nation as a collectivity; others concern people in power; still others concern bureaucratic organizations that function for the nation. By distinguishing such statements and noticing their logical relationships with one another, one can perhaps improvise a model of governmental behavior that, even if crude, may be more satisfactory than the random resort to essentially different paradigms that is so often characteristic of historical reconstruction.

What statements can properly be made about the collectivity—that is, about the nation? One cannot realistically speak of a nation deciding or acting, but one can say that a nation holds certain beliefs, since notions of right and wrong, visions of national interest, and even judgments on what are and are not prudent courses of action are not the peculiar property of people who hold office. On the contrary, people in high office continually look outside their own circle for validation of their suppositions.

The sources to which they look may vary from system to system. In one that is rigid and hierarchical, the rulers may be sensitive principally to opinion among an aristocracy or the elite of a governing party. The Ottoman Sultans may, as Hume suggested, have listened only to their Mamelukes. Germany's leaders in the 1930s apparently found in the Nazi Party, and in an acquiescent or terrorized public, adequate reinforcement for their hideous beliefs. In a more fluid and pluralistic society such as that of the United States, the men or women who exercise power attend to opinion among a variety of elites, presumably representative of or providing leadership for different social classes, ethnic or religious groups, or aggregations of people with common interests or attitudes.

Whatever the composition of the collectivity, its beliefs are neither homogeneous nor fixed. There are always powerful contradictory currents within the collectivity, and whatever there is of consensus at one time may be different at another time. Nevertheless, at any given point there will probably be a discernible set of beliefs sufficiently widely shared both inside and outside government that they can be characterized as beliefs of the nation.

In regard to the particular case described here, one can conjecture that the following beliefs were widely held by people in the United States during 1942–44: (1) that Fascism and Nazism were loathsome ideologies; (2) that any Fascist or Nazi state was dangerous to its neighbors because inherently it had an insatiable need to expand; (3) that a Fascist or Nazi state would therefore be dangerous to the peace of the United States because its aggression would eventually threaten the United States itself; (4) that any anti-U.S. government in Latin America, even if not Fascist or Nazi in character, might endanger the security of the United States because it might serve in this or a future war as an ally of or base for an enemy; (5) that unlimited opportunity for the export of U.S. goods and capital was mutually beneficial to the United States and to the rest of the world; (6) that autarchic policies on the part of any foreign government were therefore injurious to the interests of both North Americans and the rest of humanity (this especially the case in Latin America, which had absorbed 20.6 percent of U.S. prewar foreign trade and 42.4 percent of U.S. prewar foreign investment); (7) that if the United States did not expand foreign trade and foreign investment after the war it might suffer a new economic depression, and that such a depression might have disruptive political and social effects; but (8) that the United States should not intervene in Latin America but should, on the contrary, be a "good neighbor."

These beliefs implied certain specific concerns. In fact, "the nation" had ways of indicating the hierarchy of its concerns. Newspaper editors decided which subjects to feature on page one, column eight, and which to consign to page fourteen. Columnists, broadcasters, and book pub-lishers similarly called attention to particular issues, and private citizens did likewise by writing to periodicals or public officials or by answering questions put by opinion polltakers. The Congress and its committees then functioned to goad the executive branch into taking up the concerns then expressed. In these ways, "the nation" made manifest in 1942–44 its fear that Argentina was or was becoming Fascist or Nazi in orienta-tion or, at any rate, anti-U.S. in attitude and autarchic in policy and, as a result, potentially a threat to the safety or well-being of the United States.

The people in power necessarily shared the beliefs and concerns of "the nation." The President had to ensure that he or members of his Admin-istration were prepared to answer congressional or press inquiries about Argentina. Those of his staff and cabinet with any responsibility for for-eign affairs had to make ready to fulfill this need. The duty then devolved from them to subordinates whose province was Western Hemisphere af-fairs and in turn to others down the line.

At this stage, the President and his high-level subordinates acted as both members of and agents for "the nation." They had the special func-tion, however, of mobilizing governmental resources to deal with con-cerns of "the nation." In doing so, they did not act as automata. Their own perceptions of what was important and not important, their sense of their own interests, and perhaps above all their skill in statecraft here entered the process, much as the perceptions, interests, and skills of ar-chitects and contractors might enter the process of fulfilling someone's specified need for a dwelling or place of business.

First of all, people in high offices incited the bureaucracy to supply or develop information. Within limits, they could choose how to put their questions and to whom. Had members of the Roosevelt Administration displayed more interest in Argentina's capabilities for injuring U.S. in-terests than in the extent of Fascist or Nazi influences, they might have obtained somewhat different data. Almost certainly, they would have elicited slightly different reports if they had relied chiefly on State De-partment desk officers rather than military intelligence and FBI agents.

The discretion of people in power was not unlimited. They could only pick and choose among information-gathering agencies already existing, and these agencies could deal only with questions that they were, in a sense, preprogrammed to answer. Of course, these bureaucratic organi-zations were made up of people who had no less individuality than those who sat in the Oval Office of the White House or presided over cabinet departments; but the organizations themselves, and the people within them, necessarily had limited perspectives and functions. Like piecework seamstresses in sweatshops, they worked to produce certain patterns, assuming that someone else understood how the whole garment was to come together. Thus, officers in Army G-2 and the Office of Naval Intelligence and legal attachés reporting to the FBI carried out their mission of gathering information about Fascists and Nazis in Argentina. If they thought about the matter at all, they assumed that others had the chore of providing supplementary data that would put their reports into perspective.

Information supplied by the bureaucracy flowed back to people in high office. Potentially, it could influence opinion within the nation as a whole. In this case, had the large majority of the specialists reported an inability to find what they had been commissioned to find, high officials might have fed such reports to Congress and the press and thus undertaken to communicate their own altered opinion of the dimensions of the alleged Argentine problem. As it was, they had to perceive themselves as likely sooner or later to face the question: what is the government doing about Argentina? They therefore turned back to the bureaucracy for recommendations on what might be done.

Once again, they had some latitude in defining the problem to be solved and in selecting the agencies to which to turn. At this juncture, individual differences in perception and interest acquired even greater importance. Morgenthau's view of Argentina, for example, owed something to his whole set of attitudes about Fascism and Nazism, to his judgment that the organization over which he presided could develop proposals for effective action, and to his estimate that he could profit politically by making the cause of action against Argentina his own. Secretary of the Interior Harold Ickes had an identical set of attitudes, but he did not have the wherewithal to enter the competition. The Secretary of War and Secretary of the Navy, each of whom had vastly greater resources than Morgenthau, lacked his passionate feeling that Fascism or Nazism was as much a threat in South America as in Europe or Asia. Which temperaments happened to be where within the hierarchy thus had a good deal to do with decisions about which parts of the bureaucracy were called upon to translate concern into action.

Again, however, elements of the bureaucracy performed piecework. Each had certain capabilities and certain standard products. Those in the Treasury and other economic agencies could draw up decrees dealing with Argentine gold reserves, shipping, and trade. Those in the Department of State could manufacture instructions to missions in Latin America, diplomatic notes to Latin American governments, and speeches to be delivered by departmental officials. Presumably, all of these organizations "satisficed," or settled on the first attractive recommendation that their routines developed.

Proposals from the bureaucracy then flowed back, level by level, to people in higher office. Each person in direct touch with a relevant organization faced at this stage the question of whether to say yes or no. This fact is important, for too often we reconstruct or explain as if statesmen made deliberate choices among all the options perceptible to a retrospective analyst with unlimited time and no other subject on his mind. In ninety-nine cases out of a hundred, the statesmen had only the alternatives of accepting or not accepting the single solution that "satisficing" processes had brought forth. It is also important to bear in mind the fact that the decision point was somewhat removed in time from the initiation of search for a solution. The proposal to which they had to react was therefore tailored to circumstances existing at some past time rather than to the exact circumstances at the moment of choice. The solution fitted a problem as that problem was perceived at some earlier juncture.

In judging whether to say yes or no, high-level officials had to consider the extent to which the answer not only met the concerns of "the nation" but also served their own personal interests. Indeed, in any given case, the working distinction between the bureaucrat and the official at the political level may well turn on whether the individual has a personal stake in the decision. The man who helps produce an organization's memorandum has something to lose only if his colleagues think ill of his contribution or if superiors think ill of the whole organization's performance. The man who must attach his own signature to an endorsement or dissent has more at risk. He may have to consider the possibility that his signing or refusing to sign may cost him his job and the esteem and sense of power and influence that go with it. And no person holding high office is invulnerable to such considerations, for he would not be where he is were he not convinced of his fitness to do what he is doing—and perhaps more—and of doing it better than any other eligible person he can think of. At the juncture of yes-or-no decision, in fact, the official's sense of the implications of his action for his own status and position probably becomes controlling.

At the very highest levels in the Government, the range of choice is wider, and the relevant considerations are more complex. In this instance, the President did not face simple yes-or-no decisions regarding proposals from the bureaucracy, for Welles, Hull, and Morgenthau, and later Hull and Morgenthau, put before him competing proposals. Though he had even less capacity than they for identifying alternatives to the recommendations of the bureaucracy, Roosevelt had to decide which cabinet officer to support and which to desert or, with the aid of his staff, how to effect a compromise. In other instances, officials lower down could confront comparable dilemmas—as Byrnes and Marshall did, for example,

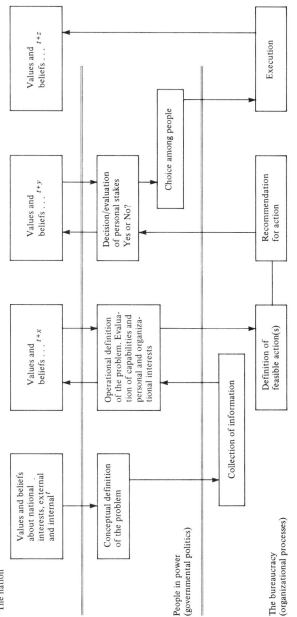

Figure 2. A flow chart of governmental action.

when having to choose between Braden and Messersmith. In such a situa-tion, the high official may still have uppermost in mind his own personal stake, but the stake is apt to be conceived in larger terms, as, for example, in terms of the consequences for his relations with the friends and sup-porters of his rival advisers, or of the consequences for credit or loss with Senators or Representatives or individual barons in the press or the worlds of business or labor. Of course, each man is also continually influenced by his sense of what "the nation" thinks or wants and by his own pecu-liar psychological makeup. Nevertheless, his choice of action at this junc-ture is probably determined less by his perception of the national will or interest than by his sense of his own interest.

Once the decision is made, responsibility usually returns to the bu-reaucracy. Bureaucratic organizations work out what follows from a Treasury directive, a diplomatic cable, or a speech by a President or cabi-net officer. Just as the decision point may come well after the definition of the problem, so the outcome of a decision may emerge only after a considerable interval. It may not take the form that the decision-maker visualized, for he may neither have foreseen the delay nor appreciated exactly what his bureaucracy could and could not do. In any case, some-thing irreversible will have occurred out in the world beyond the walls of government buildings, and some evaluation of what has occurred will then feed back into the value and interest perceptions of "the nation."

The sequence thus sketched can perhaps be diagrammed as in Fig. 2. If this "model" captures reality, the different stages call for differing as-sumptions, hypotheses, and types of data. For "the nation" at any given moment, the appropriate propositions have to do with what people out-side and inside the Government believed. Clues have to be sought in news-papers, periodicals, pamphlets, books, and, to the extent that they can be located, broadcast transcripts and letters by private citizens, as well as in the speeches, letters, and reminiscences of people in public life. Al-though the objective is in some sense to understand public opinion, the focus here is not on bloc or pressure-group opinion so much as on values and beliefs widely shared—perhaps even so widely shared that they were seldom articulated.

It is messy subject matter, the investigation of which does not lend it-self to a scientific approach. In the United States on any one day, tens of millions of words are published or otherwise recorded. What collects over a few years' time contains data to support almost any conceivable thesis. It is important, therefore, that serious research on beliefs of "the nation" be designed with a specified model of opinion formation in mind and with rigorous standards of proof. Thus, for example, my intuitive hypotheses about beliefs in 1942–44 relevant to U.S.-Argentine relations should be tested by seeking first to discover which publications or individuals were thought by people in government to speak for or lead opinion among that segment of the public specially attentive to Latin American affairs. What appeared in those publications or was written or said by those individuals should then be scrutinized with an eye to determining the frequency and force with which a given attitude found explicit or implicit expression and the frequency with which any definably contradictory attitudes appeared. If used with sensitivity and discretion, mathematical content analysis can here be a useful auxiliary to research.

For what takes place at the level of the bureaucracy, the sources are to be found primarily in public archives. It is a common fault among historians to center their research in archives and to assume that they can reconstruct the entire governmental process from documents found there. This is not the case. On the whole, people in the bureaucracy have only dim perceptions of "the nation" outside the government. This is especially true of diplomats who spend most of their lives mixing with their own kind in foreign capitals. Also, while bureaucrats may sense the concerns and interests of officials above them, they are apt to be careful not to acknowledge the fact, bearing in mind that such officials change and that it may not be good for the organization if the files indicate that it exerted itself to help one political figure against another.

Most documents in official archives are therefore poor sources for answering questions about beliefs or purposes of "the nation" or about personal motives entering into governmental choices. The scholar using such evidence should ask instead what assignment the author or authors of a given document were carrying out, why they, rather than others, received the assignment, what procedures they followed, what repertoire they possessed, and why certain choices from the repertoire were the first satisfactory ones to turn up.

To understand how higher officials defined and perceived problems and made yes-or-no decisions or choices among people, one has to search private records—letters, diaries, autobiographies, and, if the events are recent enough, the oral testimony of survivors. And just as one must draw on theories concerning public opinion, social psychology, and organizational behavior for aid in understanding the nation and the bureaucracy, so here one must borrow—with equal skepticism and caution—from the body of literature that generalizes about human psychology.

Unfinished Work

This essay is, in effect, a preliminary sketch for a monograph. When completed, the monograph will not only elaborate the alternative explanations of U.S. behavior but will "test" the synthetic paradigm just outlined by employing it for stage-by-stage analysis of actions by the Argentine Government. This should prove particularly rewarding, for the conventional unitary actor explanation supposes that Argentina acted in response to what was done by the United States. I believe that closer examination will show Argentine behavior to be explicable instead in terms of the general values and beliefs of the Argentine "nation," the perceptions of their own political interests entertained by key actors in Buenos Aires, and the development of options and yes-no choices by the Argentine bureaucracy.

Once this is accomplished, the next step is to ask how the behavior of one government actually influenced processes of decision and action in the other. This will involve an effort to specify at what points in the cycle Argentinians or North Americans in Argentina made a difference, and vice versa. For example, it seems likely that Argentine exiles in New York, U.S. newspaper and magazine reporters in Buenos Aires, and U.S. businessmen in Argentina influenced U.S. perceptions of the successive Argentine regimes. Was this influence greatest at the level of "the nation," at that of the U.S. political leadership, or at that of the U.S. bureaucracy? Similarly, it seems probable that the measures of political and economic coercion that were outcomes of the U.S. Government process in 1944 had some impact in Argentina. But what, when, where, upon whom? From exploration of such questions, I hope to derive some general hypotheses about how two political systems interact.

A final word should be added to emphasize the possible utility of this line of approach to all scholars concerned with inter-American relations or indeed any set of international relationships. For this approach can profitably be employed, I believe, as a complement to almost any mode of analysis, specifically including those rooted in Marxism. By systematically according some weight to the political interests of governmental managers and the behavioral characteristics of bureaucratic organizations, analysts of almost any persuasion ought to become better able to account for real-world phenomena that might otherwise seem incompatible with their framework of explanation, prediction, and prescription. "Bureaucratic politics" is not an alternative macropolitical theory. It is rather a body of micro-level findings, apparently verifiable empirically, that larger theories of imperialism or *dependencia* should not ignore.

Commentary on May

GUILLERMO O'DONNELL

Everyday opinion and a fair number of studies on international relations conceive of governments (and also states and nations) as unitary actors to whom intentions, acts, and omissions can be attributed. This conception allows for *a posteriori* interpretations of important events in which the actor is seen as the analogue of the "rational man," able to make transitive orderings of his preferences, able to consider all possible consequences of his alternatives, and consistently working to achieve his goals through a complex sequence of events. The "explanation" of the decisions (or lack of decisions) of such an actor consists of interpreting each of his acts—assuming rational, optimizing calculations—as conducive to achieving the goals that dominate his scale of preferences. It is not clear whether this is a conscious process on the part of the actor or whether, on the contrary, the logic is *constructed post facto* by the scholar so that the facts will correspond to his *a priori* conception of the government-actor's unity and rationality. This is a crucial distinction, for only if we are dealing with the first situation can the norm of explanation (or even description) be said to be met.

The Allison and May Models

In studies that have had a well-deserved impact, Graham Allison[1] argues that this traditional conception ignores fundamental aspects of the problem. Among these aspects are the restrictions that cognitive limitations impose on rationality, the cognitive and evaluative biases that accompany specialization, the high marginal cost that analysis and deliberation imply in certain situations, the frequently nonoperational nature of the

---

Guillermo O'Donnell is a member of the Center for Research in Public Administration (CIAP), Instituto Torcuato Di Tella, Buenos Aires.

[1] Graham T. Allison, *Essence of Decision: Explaining the Cuban Missile Crisis* (Boston: 1971); and "Conceptual Models and the Cuban Missile Crisis," *American Political Science Review,* vol. 43, no. 3, 1969, pp. 689–718. All future references to Allison are to the second of these works.

dominant goals in a given scale of preferences, the intransitivity of individual preferences, and—partly as a consequence of all this—the internal differentiation of actors, coalitions, and goals in interactions as complex as those that for convenience we call "governments." As alternatives to the traditional criteria (which, following Allison, I shall call "Model I"), he proposes two others, one that stresses the organizational component ("Model II") and one that stresses the individual ("Model III"); both are well synthesized by Professor May. According to the conclusions of Herbert Simon and his colleagues,[2] the rejection of Model I opens the way to considering government as a complex aggregate composed of complex organizations specialized in terms of recruitment, repertoires, programs, and perceptions. These organizations can enter into coalitions oriented toward achieving "satisfactory" solutions (given a certain level of aspirations) to problems presented by their environments (ranging from other organizations within the same government all the way to the international system). According to Allison and May, this model can be disaggregated even more, becoming "Model III," centered on the capacity, will, perceptions of personal interest, and other characteristics of individuals who hold positions from which they can influence the content of the decisions adopted by the "government." As opposed to Model I, both Models II and III imply that the decisions under study do not tend to be determined by any one individual but are rather processes of accommodation between organizations (Model II) or between individuals (Model III). For future reference, it is interesting to note that according to Allison and May, these three models are not exclusive: each can support an alternative *explanation* of the events and they can be combined in different ways and forms as a *heuristic* resource for the study of concrete cases. In this commentary, however, I shall limit myself to arguing that the substantive validity (and consequently the explanatory capacity) of the three "models" cannot be demonstrated. And thus the sharp distinction that is implied between the models—although it has heuristic value—by its own logic makes it impossible to identify the set of conditions that are necessary and/or sufficient for the events under consideration to take place. I shall conclude by suggesting a new criterion that may lead to a more systematic use of Allison's and May's contributions, illustrating this by using the same historical material presented by May.

[2] See especially Herbert Simon and James March, *Organizations* (New York: 1958); James March and J. Cyert, *A Behavioral Theory of the Firm* (Englewood Cliffs: 1963); and Herbert Simon, "The Changing Theory and the Changing Practice of Public Administration," in Ithiel de Sola Pool, ed., *Contemporary Political Science: Toward Empirical Theory* (New York: 1967). See also J. Thompson, *Organizations in Action* (New York: 1967), and Anthony Downs, *Inside Bureaucracy* (Boston: 1966). In this commentary it is assumed that the concepts and terminology of these authors are known to the reader.

Difficulties with the Allison and May Models

To take a look "below" the seemingly monolithic actors, to detect the interests (in a broad sense) of their participants, to understand the decisions attributed to government as the result of the complicated decision-making procedures of a complex group of actors—all this is good advice, successfully followed by Allison and May in their respective studies.[3] But if the difference between Model I and the others is evident and defensible, I confess my doubts that such will be the case between Models II and III as proposed by both authors. As they point out, we are dealing with a relative emphasis, either on the organizations that compose a government's institutional structure (official and nonofficial), or on the individuals who occupy governmental posts. One aspect that should not be lost sight of is that these "posts" generally correspond to the highest levels of those organizations. And it is on the basis of the study of the individuals that occupy these posts that we can formulate expressions that—following the style of Simon et al. and "Model III"—elliptically assert that "the organizations do not try to optimize but rather 'satisfice,'" or that "the organizations develop repertoires and programs." It is obvious that in this type of proposition there exists—though at a lesser level—a risk similar to that of Model I, namely, the "reification" of the subject with respect to which certain propositions are formulated. Simon et al. avoid this risk because they do not think it is necessary to postulate a third level, "individual," that would be as clearly distinguishable from the "organizational" as Model I is from the other two. The risk of reification of the organizations seems large when we try to express the clear division between this level and the individual, in order to be able to affirm that any one of these levels (aside from Model I) can be the basis for alternative explanations.[4]

It is evident that if on one level it is the organizations that "act" and on other levels the individuals, the operative factors at this latter level are those that constitute the "personality" of the actors. Thus, Allison affirms that "The core of bureaucratic politics (Model III) is the personality (of the actors)."[5] There is little doubt that the individual personality

---

[3] As May points out, his argument differs in important ways from Allison's (especially in the very different level of centrality of the problem for the highest authorities in the U.S. Government, and in the much longer timespan of the decisions studied by May). This permits a more rigorous "test" of the analytical framework of both authors.

[4] The risk of reification is apparent in expressions such as ". . . one must not only visualize a state composed of many feudal entities but also bear in mind that these entities do not behave like men." On the contrary, the argument of Simon et al. is that the cognitive limitations on individuals lead to patterns of decision that can be imputed to the organizations themselves only elliptically.

[5] It should be pointed out that the term "personality" is not used by these authors in the

can provoke important variations in the content of decisions. But the problem consists in identifying the conditions under which those factors have greater or lesser degrees of freedom in which to operate. The possibilities for individual variation are introduced with regard to more or less rigid situational parameters—goals shared and debated contextually, the type of problem, known and relevant antecedents, relative power positions, etc.[6] Nevertheless, the "reification" of the organization seems to imply, reciprocally and necessarily, the imputation of all contextual factors as independent variables, operating on the "organization" as a different kind of actor. Symmetrically, in Model III it must be postulated that the decisions studied *can also* be attributed to the actor's individual makeup and inclinations—characteristics that are no longer controlled by contextual factors or by situational parameters that have been postulated and pertain to a *different and alternative* potential explanation. For that reason, the proposed distinction between Models II and III seems to lead to a reification of the organization in the first case and a psychological interpretation of the individual in the second. The problem seems soluble to me by way of the affirmation made by May that in the final stage of analysis what we have learned from each one of these perspectives can be recombined into a single explanation. Aside from the fact that it is not indicated how one should proceed to do this, it is difficult to see in what way a reified analysis and another that is psychological can be combined into an explanation.

If these problems seem insoluble on the abstract level—where up until now they have been discussed—a scholar can elude them on the basis of the very fineness and richness of his perception of the empirical case. This can be accomplished by reinserting, *as components of Model III,* the factors previously postulated as characteristic and distinctive of Model II. This is just as true when we are trying theoretically to explicate Model III's[7] components as when we are presenting the analysis of a con-

---

usual sense of permanent dispositions manifested in the total set of the actor's behavior. Rather, what is meant is the capacity, will, and perception of one's own interests brought into play by an individual holding a position in government.

[6] Fred Greenstein, in *Personality and Politics* (Chicago: 1969, especially pp. 40–62) synthesizes the type of structural conditions that make it more or less probable that the individual characteristics of an actor will have an important impact on his political decisions. It is interesting to note that the episode of the installation of the Russian missiles in Cuba belongs very clearly to those situations that Greenstein's work suggests permit the actor's individual characteristics to have a substantial impact. The case studied by May seems to be of just the opposite sort.

[7] Thus, in presenting Model III, Allison affirms that "The positions (roles?) define what the players can and cannot do," and in general, "on the position that one occupies depend the attitudes that one adopts." These affirmations are difficult to reconcile with the basic proposition previously mentioned to the effect that "the core [of Model III] . . . is the personality [of the

concrete case.[8] We are dealing with a double reinsertion: first, the reinsertion of the individual into organizations (his own and the ones with which he interacts) that compose the government; second, the reinsertion of the interests and strictly individual preferences of other individuals and of those involved in the organizations' repertoires and the totality (government) to which they belong into a multidimensional set of goals (operational or not). That accomplished, we will have reinserted the context (including—and principally—the organizational context) into the formulation and application of Model III. But this serves only to reexpress Model II. And this latter model, according to the propositions of Simon et al. and the contributions of Greenstein, allows by its own logic varying degrees of liberty for individual factors—according to the degree of "programming" of possible activities and the precise expectations of other actors involved. Fundamentally, the reexpression of Model II does not seem useful if one considers that it is analogous to the "original," and for that reason incapable of forming the basis for an *alternative* explanation. Most important, this is the case if the structural or situational factors are not introduced systematically, but rather as residuals that limit the inferences of Model III, one by one.

The most comprehensive formulation of the organizational factors allowed by Model II, together with the (empirically variable) degrees of freedom allowed the strictly individual factors, should establish the basis for a more complete and economical explanation of why certain decisions are adopted, others rejected, and still others not even considered by a government. To be brief, the three models seem to me not to be three possible alternatives for explanation. If such were the case, it would be equivalent to the formal problem of subidentification of explanatory models in which nothing guarantees that one of the three (or four . . .) possible models approaches a valid explanation of the phenomenon studied. As I see it, in the first place Allison and May make the important contribution of showing the *invalidity* of Model I. Second, on the basis of the authors' contributions, if Model I is invalid and Model III could conveniently be reexpressed in terms of Model II, it seems worthwhile to ask if the segmentation of explanations (and the consequent problems of sub-

---

actors] ." According to Allison, every "position" implies different responsibilities toward different co-actors, and the negotiations among these actors take place through "channels of action, that is, regularized ways of generating actions related to types of problems [programs] ." Translating these expressions to the language of Model II, it seems evident that they are equatable, and that—furthermore—Model II embeds the expressions in a much more comprehensive theoretical system.

[8] In May's work, the definition of individual interests (Model III) is explicitly linked to the definition of organizational interests and to those of the government in its entirety. We shall return to this point.

identification of each of them) could not be solved by concentrating on Model II. To do this, however, one must take into account two important aspects of the formulations of Simon et al. that have not retained their original role in Allison and May's formulation of Model II.

The Formulations of Simon et al.

The first of these aspects was mentioned above in connection with the risk of reification. The second is connected to the absence of a necessary distinction in Allison and May's critique of Model I. Governments are not omniscient or consistent optimizers of transitively ordered goals. *But this does not mean that dominant goals do not exist* (that is, goals that are hierarchically ordered with respect to others), *goals that whether consistent or not among themselves profoundly influence the decisions under study.* As formulated, Model II gives the impression that all that is at stake in the relations between organizations and in the decisions they make is the satisfaction of interests that are strictly organizational— as if common, overriding goals did not exist.[9] In any given instance this may or may not hold true, but for precisely that reason, it ought to be empirically determined, and not form an *a priori* element of Model II. It would seem that the inadequate conception of goals (and of the strategies to achieve them) postulated in Model I has led Allison and May to a non sequitur: to deny the *possible* existence of dominant, shared goals among the actors who comprise a "government." Here it is possible to detect an important difference from the propositions of Simon et al., who suggest that the members of complex organizations probably do agree on goals, whether operational or not. The level of agreement admits of gradations, which in turn influence patterns of coalition formation, the definition of problems, and the search for solutions. There can be agreement on goals that are higher in the hierarchy, such as "capture X percent of the market" or "earn Y percent interest on invested capital." These goals are not operational (they do not indicate how they should be achieved), and they give rise to differences among members of the organization who tend to define—according to the biases that derive from their specialty and their position in the organization—subgoals that are presumably appropriate for achieving the primary goals.[10] Whatever "solution" seems conducive to achieving these goals will be considered "satisfactory," and the search for other solutions will cease without further

---

[9]See, for example, "thus, one can explain the changes in U.S. relations with Argentina in terms of the perceptions, interests, capacities, backgrounds, and tendencies toward inaction of semi-sovereign entities within the North American bureaucracy" [Editors' note: This quotation is from an earlier draft of the May paper].

[10]This subject is treated in detail in March and Cyert, *Behavioral Theory.*

attempts to optimize. It is in this sense that Simon et al. speak of goals as "restrictions": they are criteria that have to be satisfied for a "solution" to be considered acceptable. Even though different internal coalitions perceive "solutions" in accord with their own particular cognitive limitations and interests, if there exists a high level of agreement on the dominant goals, this latter fact will exercise a great deal of influence over the behavior and the decisions of each of the members and coalitions of the total group.

Returning to May's paper, it is interesting to note that the most general goals mentioned are expressed in terms of "the nation" and not in terms of the government. This distinction accords well with the conceptualization of Model II, in the sense that the component organizations of the government seem only to be able to propose goals that are directly linked to their perception of their own organizational interests. Moreover, the low level of centrality and attention given by public opinion to the "problems" that governments decide—above all, problems like the ones studied here that are not even central to the government itself—is well known.[11] Thus, it is necessary to posit something akin to concentric circles of opinion (from public opinion in general to the demands formulated by the pressure groups directly interested in the "problem") in which preferences are articulated with increasing intensity and specificity. Once this position is taken, *we cannot avoid the search for the goals that the government,* as a group of "individuals in organizations," *could have had.* In the event they exist, these goals would operate as restrictions that each decision would have to satisfy, both in the view of those who make the decision and in the view of those who—in the context defined by the "government" and the concentric circles of opinion—interact with the decision-makers. The existence of such goals can be explored using the same historical material presented by May.

Basic Beliefs and Dominant Goals

The "basic beliefs" formulated by May can be expressed as dominant goals (or, equivalently, as restrictions) in the following manner:[12]

1. Fascism and Nazism are repugnant ideologies (movements, governments) that ought to be eliminated.

---

[11] See especially Phillip Converse, "The Nature of Belief Systems in Mass Publics," in David Apter, ed., *Ideology and Discontent* (New York: 1964).

[12] For reasons of brevity, I have reformulated the "beliefs" identified by May, eliminating those that are specific instances of the more generic. The only one that is not reducible to those I propose is the theme of the "good neighbor." It is not included here because, as May's study itself clearly shows, it was far from being shared by all the actors. Furthermore, its tangential character is demonstrated by the ease with which it was set aside as soon as it was seen to be in conflict with the dominant goals listed here.

2. Any Latin American government, whether Nazi or Fascist or not, if hostile to the United States, threatens the latter's security and ought to be eliminated.

3. Widespread opportunities for the export of U.S. goods and capital ought to exist (reciprocally: the "nationalist" economic policies of other countries are bad).

One other important goal can also be inferred from May's paper:

4. Latin America should be an area of incontestable U.S. hegemony. Corollary: any Latin American government that is seen as being under the influence of other foreign interests (1 and 2), and/or undertakes "nationalistic" policies (3), is bad and ought to be eliminated.

Following Simon et al., it is possible to hypothesize that these dominant goals play a decisive role in determining the set of "problems" that can fall within the focus of attention of the highest government leaders. We can elaborate this perspective as follows:

1. From 1943 to 1947, the focus of attention of the highest U.S. leaders was centered on the following themes: (i) win the war against the Axis and eliminate movements and governments sympathetic to the enemy; (ii) later, create the United Nations and assure control of the majority of UN votes—for which the control of Latin American votes is decisive; (iii) still later, contain the expansion of the USSR and "Communism."

2. Other themes are marginal; they come to the attention of the highest government leaders only to the extent they are perceived capable of making an important contribution (positive or negative) to achieving the dominant goals.

3. To the extent that these other themes are not so perceived, they are handled and resolved by less important and more specialized personnel. Who handles what problem is determined in large measure by the original definition of the marginal issue. This in turn leads to biases in the information and interpretation that will be available to the highest leaders if and when the marginal problem is seen as capable of having an important impact on one of the dominant goals.[13] In general, the members of the specialized organizations will behave in the way postulated by Model II and by Simon et al.

With this in mind, we can return to May's paper, interpreting the events described therein in terms of Model II, but now also in the light of having sketched the dominant, shared goals that the actors try to "satisfice," each in his own way and each according to his own biases. This can be done quite briefly:

1942-43: War with the Axis, outcome not determined. Detection of "hostile" activities in Argentina. Consequent concern originating in the potential use of Argentina by the Axis. First definition of the situation in these terms.

---

[13] Thus, for example, once the situation in Argentina was defined as tending toward "Nazi-Fascism" and as encouraging similar coups in other countries (Bolivia), as May notes, intelligence organizations (first the FBI and then the CIA) came to play an important role both in the type of information that was collected and in the way in which it was interpreted.

1943: Coup d'état in Argentina by sectors with apparent sympathies for the Axis and with "nationalist" tendencies that seem to be confirmed by the domestic actions taken. "Confirmation" by the U.S. Government of its first definition of the situation.

1944: Outcome of the war now determined; dominant U.S. concern becomes the creation of the UN and the control of Latin American votes. Because a worsening of relations with Argentina could endanger this goal, the U.S. attitude changes.

1945: The above-mentioned goal is achieved, and the Argentine question is again handled at lower levels of the U.S. Government, where officials continue to act on the basis of the hostile vision developed earlier. Among other things, the intelligence agencies have continued collecting information about presumed "Nazi" activities, and the "Blue Book" is published. Furthermore, a soft position toward "Nazi Argentina" could be an impediment to the agreements with the USSR that are still thought possible. Thus, returning to a hostile attitude implies removing possible roadblocks to the achievement of higher-order goals.

1946–47: The two previous dominant goals have been achieved (defeating the Nazis and founding the UN), and they are replaced by the containment of the USSR and "Communism." The continuation of the hostile attitude toward Argentina is now seen as endangering the following operational subgoals: (i) the strengthening of Western Europe against the USSR, for which food exports from Argentina seem necessary; (ii) the maintenance of unchallenged U.S. hegemony in Latin America, given the possibility that Argentina would receive support from Europe and eventually from the USSR. One consequence of (ii) is the emergence of new, specialized North American organizations with specific goals such as the sale of armaments and the consolidation of "anti-Communist" Latin American sectors (the military). This development also requires an opening of relations.

1946–47, and after: The normalization of relations means that Argentina is once again perceived as not capable of affecting the dominant goals of the U.S. Government. Thus, to date, relations with Argentina have not intruded into the focus of attention of the highest levels of the U.S. Government.

Implications of the Argument

From what has been said above, we can make several observations:

First, each one of the stages sketched in the previous section is supported by information presented by May *throughout his paper,* whether he is analyzing the case from the point of view of Model I, or from that of Model II or Model III. According to what is suggested here, the "organizations" of Model II and the "individuals" of Model III appear as motivated by their "specific" interests and by the aim of "satisficing" (and convincing other actors to "satisfice") the dominant goals. In other words, we share with Allison and May the criticism of the unitary actor of Model I, omniscient and optimizing. But this does not prevent us from recognizing dominant goals that are shared by the actors who constitute the government and for which each one seeks—according to his biases—"satisfactory" solutions. The centrality of the goals related to the Axis, the UN, the USSR, and U.S. hegemony in Latin America restrict the range of "satisfactory" solutions for each actor and for each coalition of actors.

Second, each organization behaves in conformity with the postulates of Model II: it conforms to the patterns preprogrammed by its specialization, and with respect to its more specific goals it can (and frequently does) enter into conflict with other organizations and groups. But, following Simon et al., we must expand Allison's Model II to include: (i) the dominant goals already mentioned; (ii) the corollary that the decisions studied are the result of complex decisional functions into which specific operational goals (subgoals in Simon's terminology) certainly enter along with the obviously important dominant goals (in other words, to take into account only the subgoals inevitably weakens the explanation when there are shared, dominant goals); (iii) the crucial influence that the dominant goals have in the determination of the focus of attention of the highest levels of government—such that marginal questions intrude only when they are seen as capable of affecting the achievement of the dominant goals; (iv) the corollary that if a marginal question is explicitly connected to the dominant goals,[14] important changes in the specialized patterns of handling this question at lower governmental levels are probable.

Third, the (few) elements that can be attributed to strictly individual motivations (that is, that are not derived from the dominant goals nor from the responsibilities of those who lead complex governmental organizations) in this case seem neither necessary nor sufficient to explain the set of decisions under study. These elements do seem necessary to explain some relatively secondary characteristics of the decisions, such as the delay in the taking of actions that Model II—as reformulated—allows us to predict. (An example would be the delay in changing the hostile attitude toward Argentina, in good measure attributable to the performance of ex-Ambassador Braden who was then Undersecretary of State for Latin American Affairs.)

Fourth, it is clear that—as Allison and May certainly emphasize—Model I is invalid both as description and as explanation. Furthermore, however, the distinction between Model II and Model III—as each was formulated—does not aid in explaining the sequence of decisions under study.[15] For reasons that have now been analyzed, neither Model II nor Model III, standing alone, can specify the necessary and/or sufficient conditions. As an alternative possibility, we have here suggested that one ought to take advantage of Allison and May's contribution, redefining their Model II in a way that is closer to the original formulations of Simon et al.

Fifth, if this is to be a useful suggestion, we must also insist on the ne-

---

[14] This sort of connection—as is well illustrated in May's work—is established by means of the kind of "rudimentary causal theory" that is also analyzed by Simon et al.

[15] See May's affirmations regarding the explanatory capacity of each model.

cessity of empirically determining the levels of importance of and agreement on the dominant goals.[16] Similarly, it is also necessary to distinguish among the types of situations that result in greater or lesser degrees of freedom for the strictly individual characteristics of the actors.[17]

Sixth and finally, to refute the image of an omniscient and unitary actor calls into question the bases of any and all Manichean views of international politics. This is fortunate, but it is not all to the good if the alternative conceptualizations are reduced to hypothesizing decisions tied to specifically organizational and individual goals of the sort proposed by Models II and III. Despite the important internal conflicts emphasized by these models, the set of "individuals in organizations" that constitutes a government *can* agree on nonoperational goals that in turn define the parameters within which a conception of national interest and an attempt to establish hegemony over other participants in the international system are developed. These factors suggest that decision-making is severely limited by cognitive factors which, not infrequently, are noncongruent among themselves and very different from the analytical framework used by the scholar, *post facto,* to reconstruct the situation. In short, these factors imply decisions that are not optimizing, but rather "satisficing," following the terminology used by Allison, May, and Simon et al. But following the interpretation proposed here, what they attempt to "satisfice" is the achieving of shared, dominant goals that derive from a definition of the national interest and an attempt to establish hemispheric hegemony—all of which is well illustrated in the historical material presented by May. The reformulation of Model II that is suggested here permits the specification of this type of factor, without prejudicing the study of the more specifically organizational and even individual factors that the model emphasizes. Inversely, the omission of the dominant goals in those cases where they seem to have been important has twin consequences: on the one hand, it leads to a weakening of any explanation based on the other relevant factors; and, on the other hand, it makes it difficult to detect decisions that are designed to achieve "sat-

[16] According to the information presented by May, it seems reasonable to conclude that the dominant goals outlined above existed and were shared by U.S. Government actors. It could happen, of course, that dominant goals exist but are not shared, or that—in the extreme case—a government disintegrates into sectors that only perceive their own, specific interests. Here also Simon's works (cited above) offer valuable insights that cannot be followed up at this time.

[17] The previously mentioned example of the case studied by Allison (a crisis situation, which developed and was resolved quickly, and which did not have antecedents that the participants could consider "obviously" analogous) would be typical of those cases—as opposed to the one studied by May—that permit important margins of liberty for the expression of strictly individual characteristics. In spite of this, Allison's reconstruction of the case from the perspective of Model III is still heavily influenced by the dominant goals and by organizational interests and biases.

isfactory" degrees of presence, consolidation, and control in the asymmetrical power relations between nation-states.

One issue remains to be presented—one that it would be unjust to link to the individual intentions of the scholars who propose or adopt the conceptualizations on which I have been commenting: if Model I is thrown out as obviously in error, along with Models II and III as formulated, then neither the decisions of governments nor their consequences correspond to the intentions of any actor. Such a conclusion makes it impossible to attribute any ethical or political responsibility to those who occupy positions from which they can mobilize enormous resources to support the decisions of the "government" of which they form a part. In this fashion, one of the basic issues of politics as human activity is simply ignored—with little profit for a nation that is now beginning to discover some of the consequences of its own attempt at world domination.

Dominance and Fragmentation in U.S. Latin American Policy

CHRISTOPHER MITCHELL

Two facts stand out when one looks at U.S. policy toward Latin America over the past 20 years: since the early 1950s, the United States has often been insensitive and inflexible in dealing with the hemisphere, and more particularly in attempting to dominate Latin America; at the same time, her policy has frequently been fragmented, poorly coordinated, and even confused.

Of these two policy characteristics—dominance and poor coordination—the first is widely recognized. North American influence is clearly preponderant in many fields of inter-American relations, among them finance, military affairs, trade, aid, and communications. Politically, U.S. dominance has exhibited two principal aspects during the post-World War II period: conservatism and intervention. Conservatism has meant a general U.S. aversion to political change in Latin American nations—and if change seemed inevitable, the United States has always preferred incremental to radical innovation. Traditional "intervention" (the sending of troops) has been relatively rare in recent decades. But in a broader sense, the United States has intervened almost constantly in Latin America: U.S. agencies have exercised direct and often powerful influence in the domestic politics of Latin American states. Conservatism and intervention (possible analytical distinctions aside) have become justifiably linked in Latin American eyes with U.S. political dominance.

But the second characteristic of U.S. policy—its generally poor coordination—is seldom noted. Most critical observers have assumed that since the United States has been the dominant hemispheric power, her policies have also been centrally determined, rationally interlaced, and

Christopher Mitchell is a member of the Department of Political Science, New York University, Bronx, New York. This is the revised version (January 1973) of a paper originally delivered at the seminar held in Lima.

coherently executed.[1] Dale L. Johnson, for example, has argued along these lines:

> Foreign policy flows naturally, and by and large rationally, from the structure ["of the international system . . . a stratified system of power relations"]. The basis of United States foreign policy is a conception of national interest as inherently involved in the strengthening of international capitalism against the threats of socialism and nationalism. . . . United States private investment, aid programs, foreign policy, military assistance, and international interventions, and international agencies, under the influence or control of the international business community, are interwoven and oriented toward the promotion and maintenance of influence and control in other countries. These are the dimensions of imperialism.[2]

But the record of the past 20 years indicates, I think, that North American policy ("U.S. imperialism") has not been as unified as many have maintained. It may be more accurate to view U.S. policy as a set of imperialisms:[3] a number of policy themes pursued by the U.S. Government with little interconnection and even a good deal of contradiction. This lack of coordination has taken different forms. In some instances, goals have been quite clear, but disparate actions pursuing them have tended to cancel each other out. In other cases, the U.S. has aimed at various incompatible goals simultaneously, making her policy appear hypocritical or uncontrolled. And at times North American concepts have been so vague, and national actions so confused, that U.S. Latin American policy could only be termed incoherent.[4]

During the past 20 years, three separate and distinct policy themes (or goals) have been evident in U.S. hemispheric policy: (1) military and ideological security, (2) U.S. supervision of Latin American economic development, and (3) promotion and protection of U.S. private investments. The exact definition of these themes has varied over the years, as has their relative importance, but the lines of policy are clear. It is clear, as well, that each goal (backed by a segment of the U.S. Government) has often been pursued in isolation from the other themes of U.S. Latin American policy. Let me briefly sketch these themes:

---

[1] See Lowenthal (this volume) for a discussion of other critical views on U.S. policy.

[2] Dale L. Johnson, "Dependence and the International System," in James D. Cockcroft, André Gunder Frank, and Dale L. Johnson, *Dependence and Underdevelopment* (New York: 1972), pp. 98–100; bracketed phrases from p. 91.

[3] If, I must add, one wants to use the term "imperialism" to describe North American dominance at all. I find the word unclear, and crippled by its historical and theoretical associations; thus I shall not use it elsewhere in this essay.

[4] The test for "coherence" in policy proposed by I. M. Destler is a useful one: "We want the various things we do to be consistent with one another and with our broader purposes." See his *Presidents, Bureaucrats and Foreign Policy* (Princeton, N.J.: 1972), p. 4. U.S. Latin American policy has too often failed this test during the past 20 years.

1. *Military and ideological security.* In the best-known crises of recent inter-American relations—Guatemala in 1954, Cuba in 1961 and 1962, and the Dominican Republic crisis of 1965—the United States has been motivated by a policy concern that demands the hemisphere be kept "secure." It is not that the Pentagon considers Latin America vulnerable to a conventional outside attack, though the Caribbean is still thought of as strategically vital. What the U.S. *has* sought to avoid, in Hugh Thomas's phrase, is the presence in the hemisphere of "a state actively hostile to the United States."[5] Such a state, the reasoning went, while not threatening North America directly, might voluntarily open a military and political "hemispheric beachhead" to the Communist powers. Thus the United States has consistently pictured adherence to radical ideologies by Latin American nations as necessarily threatening hemispheric security.

2. *U.S. supervision of Latin American economic development.* North American policy-makers have sought to sit in judgment on the models of economic development adopted by Latin American nations, and have shaped U.S. economic assistance policies in accord with "acceptable" doctrines. However, the definition of what the U.S. considers acceptable has changed considerably over the past two decades.

Under Truman and during most of the Eisenhower Administration, the engine of Latin American development was assumed to be the private sector, especially U.S. private investment. U.S. economic assistance was to play a complementary but minor role. Abandonment of this line of policy began under Eisenhower. A new willingness to grant large amounts of direct economic aid under the Alliance for Progress was complemented and justified by acceptance of a reduced private and an expanded public role in Latin American development efforts. Some of the early faith in outside economic assistance has since been lost (together with many of the funds), and the influence of private investment interests has increased under the Nixon Administration. But the North American image of a "proper" Latin American development model has permanently shifted toward formerly unacceptable statist ideas.

3. *Promotion and protection of U.S. private investment.* American policy in relation to U.S. private investments in Latin America has been remarkably consistent since the 1950s. Overseas investment has been encouraged, and the U.S. Government has proclaimed the benefits of this investment to prospective recipients. Also, the U.S. has pressed for "equitable and speedy compensation,"[6] when Latin American nationalizations

---

[5] Hugh Thomas, *Cuba: The Pursuit of Freedom* (New York: 1971), p. 1061.

[6] This phrase is the one used in the Hickenlooper Amendment; quoted in Charles T. Goodsell, "Diplomatic Protection of U.S. Business in Peru," in Daniel A. Sharp, ed., *U.S. Foreign Policy and Peru* (Austin: 1972), p. 247.

could not be deterred. There has been considerable variation, however, in the prominence of the foreign-investment theme during the last four administrations.

At times, when the White House was keenly pro-investor or allowed pro-investor public officials a free hand, sympathy for North American businessmen overseas has ranked high among U.S. policy themes. This sympathy, for example, has been marked since 1969. During other periods (e.g., for most of the Kennedy years) investor interests were not stressed. North America's investment concern, in short, has been poorly integrated with her other two policy themes. In a number of cases of North American military intervention in Latin America, for example, there is clear evidence that security concerns—not investment interests as is often thought—prompted U.S. actions.[7]

Bureaucratic Pluralism as a Source of Policy Fragmentation

What underlies the frequent separation among these themes in U.S. hemispheric policy? Basically, the roots of poor coordination lie in the pluralism and fragmentation of the U.S. Government, where power is to a significant degree dispersed among a number of agencies and individual decision-makers. The State and Treasury Departments, diplomats, generals, CIA directors, and USAID administrators—many of these enjoy considerable autonomy in making hemispheric policy, or can exert substantial influence on those occasions when the President himself makes a decision on U.S. Latin American actions. Just as scholars are finding that many transnational actors now compete with the nation-state for influence in the world arena,[8] a parallel pluralism is being noted (or rediscovered) within the nation-state itself. Isolated and/or competing fragments of the bureaucracy, we are finding, often do much to shape foreign policy actions that were previously traced to a centralized governmental decision, and often to the President.

This point of view draws on the paradigms suggested by Graham Allison, which are analyzed in detail by Ernest May (this volume). The making

[7] See Abraham F. Lowenthal, *The Dominican Intervention* (Cambridge, Mass.: 1972), pp. 18–19. He observes (p. 18): "The whole record of American involvement in [the Caribbean] . . . suggests that the main interest of the U.S. Government has not been economic. Security concerns and traditional axioms, not simple conquest or profit, have motivated American involvement in the Dominican Republic and the rest of the Caribbean for many decades." Further evidence to this effect emerges in my discussion (below) of the United Fruit Company's relative lack of influence on Eisenhower's action in Guatemala. This is not to say, of course, that corporations are never persuasive pressure groups; see, for example, my discussion of IPC's influence on U.S. policy toward Peru.

[8] See Robert Keohane and Joseph S. Nye, eds., *Transnational Relations and World Politics* (Cambridge, Mass.: 1972), especially the Introduction by the editors. Contemporary transnational actors include world religions, multinational corporations, philanthropic foundations, and guerrilla movements.

of foreign policy, Allison argues, may be described by at least three models. The Rational Actor or "Classical" Model (Model I) views governmental actions as the result of centralized and fully rational decisions by unified national governments. In the Organizational Process Model (Model II), foreign policy is the output of diverse, narrow, and routinized organizations. These "blunt instruments" may not maximize the national interest with respect to "the problem," but may further their own interests with respect to a partial conception of the problem instead. Finally, the Governmental Politics Model (Model III) puts its emphasis on influential individuals and on competition among them; policy, according to this model, results from the conflicts and negotiations among decision-makers strategically located in the foreign-policy mechanism.[9] One of the main theses of this essay is that Model II and Model III are more helpful than Model I in explaining U.S. policy toward Latin America over the past 20 years.

This approach—stressing the problem of policy coordination as well as the fact of U.S. hemispheric dominance—has a number of advantages. First and most basic, it gets us closer to the facts. By relieving us of the assumption that there must be some single motive that guides all the actions of the United States, it frees us to look carefully at the particular causes of particular U.S. policies. Why did the U.S. embassy in Havana act as it did toward U.S. investors in 1960? What effect did Thomas C. Mann have on U.S. hemispheric policy? Why did White House and State Department staffers support Latin American economic integration efforts in 1965–67? A Model I analysis not only would give rather misleading answers to these significant questions; it might well not even ask them.

Although my approach stresses the problem of policy coordination, it does not commit the error of assuming that U.S. hemispheric policy is necessarily unintended, or unconscious, or accidental. Clearly there are many interests in North American society and government consciously committed to dominance over Latin America. Each interest contributes, however, only part of a policy mosaic, a mosaic that is (often) not con-

---

[9] See Graham T. Allison, *Essence of Decision: Explaining the Cuban Missile Crisis* (Boston: 1971), *passim.* Other discussions of bureaucratic politics and foreign policy are: Allison's own earlier formulation of his analysis: "Conceptual Models and the Cuban Missile Crisis," *American Political Science Review,* vol. 53, September 1969; Destler, *Presidents, Bureaucrats;* Allison and Morton H. Halperin, "Bureaucratic Politics: A Paradigm and Some Policy Implications," in Raymond Tanter and Richard H. Ullman, eds., "Theory and Policy in International Relations," Supplement to *World Politics,* vol. 24, Spring 1972; and Morton H. Halperin, "Sources of Power in the Foreign Affairs Bureaucracy," paper prepared for delivery at the 1972 annual meeting of the American Political Science Association. Halperin's analysis will appear in expanded form in his forthcoming *Bureaucratic Politics and Foreign Policy,* the Brookings Institution (Washington, D.C.).

trolled by any unified central will. The key here is pluralism: to stress it is to clarify, not to obscure, the tricky problem of responsibility in a fragmented government.

Greater accuracy is certainly desirable, but are the explanations afforded by the analysis of bureaucratic politics relevant to any important questions? I believe they are. So far from describing simply minor perturbations in U.S. hemispheric dominance, they help describe the political dynamics of that dominance itself. In particular, they offer useful insights into the question of change in U.S. Latin American policy, both past and future.

With regard to the past, the evidence I shall present suggests that an often unrecognized *political* factor has acted to keep U.S. Latin American policy generally static: the difficulty of assessing and revising a fragmented policy. With many different interests and agencies committed to different forms of U.S. dominance over Latin America, it has been hard for the White House to review whether the many assumptions behind U.S. policy were still relevant. Instead, diverse images and plans have often gone unchanged (and sometimes even unrecognized) until hasty government action based on them has revealed their weaknesses. This seems to have been true, for example, in the case of security assumptions and the Dominican intervention.

This analysis may help us toward a clearer view of change in the future as well. It suggests that altering the U.S. policy of conservative intervention will prove difficult—again, for a political reason having to do with the structure and dynamics of the U.S. Government. To change hemispheric policy, the President would have to coordinate and discipline the line agencies; and to recoup the political capital thus invested, he would be very likely to undertake an interventionist and activist policy toward Latin America. A number of U.S. observers have urged, in effect, that the President take control of U.S. activities in Latin America in order to limit them. My argument suggests that this is quite unlikely to happen, because of the political imperatives that any president faces.

My emphasis on policy coordination, in sum, leaves us little less pessimistic about U.S. policy than does the "centralized imperialism" approach, but it may leave us rather better informed. In the discussion that follows, I shall first review the record of North American policy since the early 1950s, discussing the Eisenhower, Alliance for Progress, and Nixon eras in turn. The essay will then look more thoroughly into the sources of fragmentation and poor coordination in U.S. hemispheric policy. Finally, I shall discuss policy change in more detail, together with my own pessimistic view of the prospects for change.

Eisenhower: The Illusion of Coordination

There was a superficial consistency about the Eisenhower Administration's policies toward Latin America. Continuing trends begun under
Truman,[10] the new administration stressed military and ideological security over other policy themes. The enemy, of course, was the "international
Communist apparatus."[11] The chief defenses were to be (1) U.S.-assisted
armed forces to repel a conventional attack, and (2) inter-American solidarity through the O.A.S. to coordinate political and military defense,
including that against "subversion" from within.[12]

North America's approaches to economic development and private investment–developed in the State Department and the Treasury–seemed
in harmony with the Pentagon's security premises. As a "safe" area, Latin
America was free to follow the liberal road–the only proper route–to
economic development. The area's governments, U.S. agencies argued,
needed to play little role in economic development. Nor did the United
States believe that North American public economic aid for Latin America was necessary; in any case, European recovery and the Korean War
had priority.

"The entrance of foreign capital," Milton Eisenhower wrote in 1953,
was "essential to development" in Latin America, but he added that most
of that foreign capital must be private. Only a marginal role, he recommended, should be reserved for World Bank and Export-Import Bank
loans.[13]

However, there was considerable latent inconsistency among these
strands of policy, and between them and the interests of Latin American
nations. The "reciprocity" that had defined the Good Neighbor policy–
North America's promise not to intervene militarily, and a reduction in
the United States' support for her investors, in return for Latin American
cooperation on defense and expropriation[14]–had been eroded from both

[10] For a critical account of the Truman policies toward Latin America, see David Green, "The
Cold War Comes to Latin America," in Barton J. Bernstein, ed., *Politics and Policies of the Truman Administration* (Chicago: 1972).

[11] Dulles, quoted in U.S. Department of State, *The Intervention of International Communism
in Guatemala* (Washington, D.C.: August 1954), p. 2.

[12] See Edwin Lieuwen, *Arms and Politics in Latin America* (New York: rev. ed., 1963), pp.
203, 241. Reitzel et al. also discuss U.S. security policy with relation to the hemisphere: "From
the point of view of the United States, here was a very special regional structure that, in terms
of the world situation, contributed directly to the security of the United States." William Reitzel, Morton A. Kaplan, and Constance G. Cobbenz, *United States Foreign Policy, 1945-1955*,
the Brookings Institution (Washington, D.C.: 1966), p. 77.

[13] Milton S. Eisenhower, "U.S.-Latin American Relations: Report to the President," Department of State (Washington, D.C.: 1953), pp. 8, 17-18.

[14] See Bryce Wood, *The Making of the Good Neighbor Policy* (New York: 1961), pp. 7-8,
and Chapter 13.

sides since World War II. The United States sought Latin American compliance in many areas—security should be maintained, investors welcomed, economic orthodoxy preserved—but she offered few concessions or contributions in return. To the Latin Americans, nonintervention pledges seemed irrelevant. If the United States wanted cooperation in security efforts, she should provide extensive assistance to state-supervised development, and recognize that foreign investors were (1) widely distrusted, and (2) of little help in basic development schemes. But the United States did not see herself as inconsistent or unreasonable. At meeting after meeting of inter-American organs, the Latin Americans pointed out the contradictions in North American actions, but "the final agreements reached at these meetings were unsatisfactory and everything was left in the form of studies, promises, recommendations, good wishes, and noncommittal declarations."[15]

The 1954 U.S. intervention-by-proxy in Guatemala illustrates both Eisenhower's concern with security and the resentments in Latin America that his diverse policies caused. The desire for ideological security made Guatemala of major concern to such principal policy-makers as the President and Secretary of State John Foster Dulles, and it determined North American opposition to Col. Jacobo Arbenz. The fate of the United Fruit Company, though it certainly concerned Washington, mattered principally as an indication of Arbenz's aims and capacities. "If the United Fruit matter were settled," Dulles told a press conference before Arbenz was overthrown, "if they gave a gold piece for every banana, the problem would remain just as it is today as far as the presence of Communist infiltration in Guatemala is concerned."[16] The State Department and the CIA used United Fruit's protest against land seizures as part of their political barrage against Arbenz, but they appear not to have been, themselves, instruments of the company.[17]

But though White House intervention coordinated North American actions in Guatemala, contradictions were evident in U.S. dealings with

[15] Alonso Aguilar, *Pan-Americanism from Monroe to the Present: A View from the Other Side* (New York: 1968), p. 107. On these frustrating inter-American conferences, see also Jerome Levinson and Juan de Onis's excellent *The Alliance That Lost Its Way* (Chicago: 1971), pp. 36-44.

[16] John Foster Dulles, "International Unity," U.S. Department of State *Bulletin,* vol. 30, 1954, p. 951 (press conference, June 8, 1954).

[17] It is also perfectly plausible, as Richard Barnet suggests, that United Fruit used the anti-Communist theme in its public relations campaign against Arbenz to cloak its mercenary interests. This campaign simply does not seem to have determined U.S. *official* policy. See Barnet, *Intervention and Revolution* (New York: 1968), p. 231. On the details of the UFCO claim presented by the State Department to Arbenz, see U.S. Department of State *Bulletin,* vol. 30, no. 775, May 3, 1954, pp. 678-79; also see Fredrick B. Pike, "Guatemala, the United States, and Communism in the Americas," *Review of Politics,* vol. 17, 1955, pp. 237-41, on the extent of U.S. investment in Guatemala in 1954, and its role in the Guatemalan economy.

other Latin American nations *concerning* Guatemala.[18] In inter-American conferences, the United States sought open, collective intervention against Arbenz; in fact, she carried out covert subversion of his regime, aided (in secret) only by Honduras and Nicaragua.[19] Many Latin American states hoped that the 1954 Caracas meeting would deal principally with economic matters, either on their merits or as a *quid pro quo* for support of the United States against Guatemala. But economic programs were shelved once political negotiations had produced paper agreements —accords that, without economic backing, could only be superficial.[20] The Guatemala affair made the United States appear not only cynically interventionist, but hypocritical as well, and unwilling to make up in economic assistance for some of her overemphasis on ideological security.

In the late 1950s, many U.S. officials recognized the divisions beneath the surface of U.S. policy, and the frictions with Latin America caused by these lines of action. Milton Eisenhower, C. Douglas Dillon (Undersecretary of State for Economic Affairs), Thomas C. Mann (Assistant Secretary of State for Economic Affairs), and Roy Rubottom (Assistant Secretary of State for Inter-American Affairs) discussed sympathetically such policy changes as support for an inter-American development bank, for commodity-price stabilization, and for social reform.[21] But these suggestions were vague, and Secretarial and Presidential attention could seldom be garnered to sort out Latin American problems.[22] Although a number of their proposals were adopted, the policy reformers tended to be simply one contending bureaucratic group among many. They became part of a larger pattern of discord and confusion among decision-making agencies in the late Eisenhower years.

[18] For an interesting analysis of this aspect of U.S. Guatemalan policy, which has influenced my own, see Karl M. Schmitt, "Contradictions and Conflicts in U.S. Foreign Policy: The Case of Latin America," in J. B. Gabbert, ed., *American Foreign Policy and Revolutionary Change* (Pullman, Washington: 1968), pp. 37–38.

[19] Assistant Secretary Holland, who pleaded against re-equipping Castillo Armas with planes on grounds of nonintervention, was overruled by Eisenhower, who felt that the Caracas resolution of the O.A.S. obliged him to grant this aid! Eisenhower implies that John Foster Dulles agreed with him, and with his brother Allen of the CIA, who pushed the Castillo Armas plan enthusiastically. See Dwight D. Eisenhower, *Mandate for Change, 1953-1956* (New York: 1963), pp. 424–27. Philip B. Taylor's "The Guatemala Affair: A Critique of United States Foreign Policy," *American Political Science Review,* vol. 50, 1956, pp. 787–806, stresses U.S. maneuvers in the O.A.S. and UN. David Wise and Thomas B. Ross's *The Invisible Government* (New York: 1964), pp. 177–96, drawing on more recent information, provides the best narrative in a disappointing literature on the Guatemala affair.

[20] See Taylor, *Guatemala Affair*, pp. 790–92; also Federico G. Gil, *Latin American-United States Relations* (New York: 1971), pp. 211–12.

[21] Milton S. Eisenhower, *The Wine is Bitter: The United States and Latin America* (New York: 1963), pp. 162–63, 209.

[22] E.g., Milton Eisenhower reports that Rubottom's junior standing in the State Department made it difficult for him to initiate policy changes in 1956–57; *Wine is Bitter*, pp. 204–5.

The case of Cuba demonstrates this pattern of fragmented policy. Perhaps ultimate U.S. hostility toward Castro was preordained, but it is striking how divided and vacillating North American policy was, as the United States assessed and reacted to Cuba's (inevitable?) move toward socialism. Whatever its attitude toward Castro, the U.S. embassy in Havana frequently disagreed with agencies in Washington, and these organizations in turn often left the ambassador uninformed of planned policy steps. Ambassador Earl E. T. Smith, who staunchly opposed Castro's revolution, charged that the State Department's uncertain actions, its "leftist" doctrine, and its blindness to possible solutions without Castro helped bring Fidel to power.[23]

Philip Bonsal, on the other hand, succeeded Smith and recommended a policy of firm but sympathetic watchful waiting toward Castro. He opposed the cancellation of Cuba's sugar quota in 1960, but was alerted only a few hours before it took place.[24] Both Bonsal and the State Department itself, in turn, were largely in the dark about Eisenhower's authorization (March 1960) to the CIA to plan Castro's overthrow.[25]

U.S. actions toward her investors, as well, were conflicting. When the U.S.-owned Cuban Telephone Company was expropriated in 1959, Bonsal received no instructions and did not protest.[26] Later, however, the U.S. Treasury took an independent hand in the dispute over whether two U.S. oil companies would refine Soviet crude oil in Cuba. Though the companies were inclined to comply with the Cuban order, Secretary of the Treasury Robert B. Anderson successfully urged them to refuse— which led to their expropriation.[27]

It is small wonder that Eisenhower's Cuban policy was so fragmented; no clear and coordinated guidelines for *general* U.S. hemispheric policy had emerged from the bureaucratic tangle in the late 1950s. Security was still important, but the conventional military threat was fading. The United States had finally agreed to establish and fund an inter-American development bank, but had not revised its "acceptable" development model for Latin America, nor related this model to security needs. American investors' interests seemed to matter less than in the early 1950s,

[23] See Earl E. T. Smith, *The Fourth Floor: An Account of the Castro Communist Revolution* (New York: 1962), pp. 58–62, 71, 159–60. Smith was apparently himself confused, sometimes backing Batista firmly, at other times working to bring an anti-Castro military or civilian junta to power. His book, which describes these varying positions unselfconsciously, is marred by dreary repetitiveness and a jumbling of events out of their sequence in time.

[24] Philip W. Bonsal, *Cuba, Castro, and the United States* (Pittsburgh: 1971), p. 151.

[25] Ibid., pp. 134–35.

[26] Ibid., pp. 46–47.

[27] Ibid., pp. 149–50, and Thomas, *Cuba*, p. 1288. It is likely that the oil refineries would have been expropriated soon anyway, but the Guatemalan pattern recurs here: a U.S. Government agency using the claims of U.S. corporations to further its political purposes. In Peru after 1963, we will observe a different pattern.

but their role in economic development had not been written out of the script. As Hugh Thomas observes, "The United States had at the turn of 1958–59 no policy toward Cuba or really toward Latin America. Attacks on Vice-President Nixon had suggested that something was wrong, but it was unclear what. There were so many other problems."[28]

The Alliance for Progress: An Effort to Coordinate Policy

The Alliance for Progress was a major attempt to make U.S. Latin American policy coherent, and to make its elements interdependent. Implicitly, the Kennedy Administration sought to go beyond piecemeal changes; the old hemisphere policies were seen not only as outworn, but hopelessly disconnected. The new administration would not only alter them, but would knit them together under central control. The failure of the Alliance was due largely to the resistance of the governmental foreign-policy agencies, each seeking to retain significant autonomy and some favoring policies of the past. There are indications, too, that President Kennedy's pursuit of key Alliance goals had slowed before his death in 1963. Certainly his successor carried on only the activism of the Alliance, combining it with policy aims that had become, once more, fragmented and diverse.

Changes were made within most U.S. policy themes during the early 1960s. The most basic (and also the most lasting) alterations came in U.S. policy toward economic development. The Alliance planners argued that a new model of economic development was needed in Latin America, one that stressed public-sector guidance and incentives, not private initiative.[29] Further, they urged that the United States give unprecedented attention and assistance to the drive for economic development. In doing so, Kennedy would be supplying the "conspicuous omission" of the Good Neighbor policy,[30] and would aid Latin American governments to duplicate what were seen as the domestic accomplishments of Roosevelt's New Deal.[31]

The new economic development policy was closely linked to (and in part justified by) the Kennedy Administration's view of hemispheric security. Communist methods, it was agreed, had changed and grown more

[28] Thomas, *Cuba,* p. 1061. On the Nixon trip, see Richard M. Nixon, *Six Crises* (New York: 1962); and James C. Carey, *Peru and the United States, 1900-1962* (South Bend, Ind.: 1964), pp. 186–207.

[29] Arthur M. Schlesinger, Jr., described the doctrine accepted by Eisenhower as the "theory of development as an act of immaculate private conception." *A Thousand Days: John F. Kennedy in the White House* (Boston: 1965), p. 174.

[30] Schlesinger, *Thousand Days,* p. 171.

[31] Note the title, for example, of Lincoln Gordon's *A New Deal for Latin America: The Alliance for Progress* (Cambridge, Mass.: 1963).

dangerous; a minor conventional menace from outside had become an important threat of domestic rebellion in Latin America. Through Cuba's example and international efforts, "subversion" and "insurgency" might spread to other parts of the hemisphere.[32] It was fashionable to view Latin America apocalyptically: in a fast-changing hemisphere, only two outcomes were possible—reform or revolution—and the United States raced against time to see that the first prevailed.[33] Economic development, spurred by North American aid, could blunt the appeal of radicalism; counter-guerrilla assistance, and possibly American military intervention,[34] could stop the Communists at the tactical level.[35]

Support for North American investors in Latin America played little role in the rhetoric of the Alliance for Progress, and indeed the "new economic model" implied that private investment had not performed as expected. But though the salience of investment had declined, the basic policy in this issue area had not changed. The United States still urged entrepreneurs to invest in Latin America (though few chose to, following expropriations in Cuba), and she still urged Latin American governments to accord them "fair treatment." Indeed at times (as I shall discuss below) the Kennedy Administration lent more governmental leverage to U.S. businessmen than its predecessor had.

The Kennedy Administration also stressed the goal of social reform: Latin American internal change toward a more just society—this goal would serve to coordinate U.S. economic, security, and investment policies. As social and political structures gradually changed in Latin America, it was also hoped, other U.S. goals would come closer to realization. Economic growth would be easier, and its benefits better shared; internal security would not become internal suppression; U.S. investment would be sought by more self-confident governments.[36]

---

[32] This fear pervades the public documents and academic analyses of the period. Mario Monteforte agrees that the United States' definition of the threat changed about 1961, but does not consider this change significant: "La política militar de los Estados Unidos en Centroamérica," *Cuadernos Americanos,* vol. 28, no. 3, May/June 1969, pp. 35–36, 40.

[33] See Milton S. Eisenhower, *Wine is Bitter,* p. 39, and Schlesinger, *Thousand Days,* pp. 186–87, for examples.

[34] Kennedy discussed the possibility of unilateral North American military intervention following the Bay of Pigs invasion: ". . . let the record show that our restraint is not inexhaustible. Should it ever appear that the inter-American doctrine of noninterference merely conceals or excuses a policy of non-action—if the nations of this Hemisphere should fail to meet their commitments against outside Communist penetration—then I want it clearly understood that this Government will not hesitate in meeting its primary obligations which are to the security of our Nation!" (Quoted in Schlesinger, *A Thousand Days,* pp. 287–88.)

[35] For a "hard-nosed" exposition of this theme, see Adolph A. Berle, *Latin America: Diplomacy and Reality,* Council on Foreign Relations (New York: 1962), p. 114.

[36] Theodore C. Sorensen stresses reform as a goal in his discussion of the Alliance: *Kennedy* (New York: 1965), pp. 533–37. William D. Rogers notes, though, that by "focusing attention on

The Alliance, launched with much idealism and an unusual breadth of view, scored successes in a number of fields. It won the apparent acceptance of Latin American governments, it generated enthusiasm in the hemisphere at first, and it did contribute to economic and social change. But efforts to coordinate North American policy under the Alliance were soon thwarted. The story of this frustration is essentially the story of a Presidential resolve that was inadequate to withstand the fragmenting social and intragovernmental pressures working against it. Diplomats, military men, and private pressure groups (especially investors and exporters) all pressed for and regained considerable margin for independent action. As they succeeded, and as policy coordination diminished, many Alliance policy aims were abandoned.[37]

In their efforts to reduce White House discipline, critics of the Alliance took full advantage of the confrontation between an often simplistic policy and a complex hemisphere. The problematic relationship between reform and the military in Latin America, for example, created a dilemma for Kennedy's "coordinated" policy, a dilemma that benefitted advocates of traditional U.S. security aims. The new administration favored reform and favored democracy; thus it initially opposed military takeovers. In Peru, Honduras, Guatemala, and the Dominican Republic it refused recognition and assistance to governments that came to power through coups.

This opposition, however, was almost never successful; at best, the United States could elicit vague promises of future elections before resuming normal relations with the new governments. And the strongest arguments for recognition came not from the juntas themselves, but from within Washington: it was argued that the new policy undermined security and encouraged leftist rebellion. Pressures were also felt from business groups and from Congress.[38] Much of the coordinative effect of the reform idea was lost, and the "normal" U.S. tendency to treat the military positively and in isolation from other social forces reasserted itself.

U.S. investors also reestablished substantial influence in policy-making, often at the expense of other goals and of general policy coherence. Both the White House and the State Department sought to retain a free hand in dealing with aggrieved U.S. companies,[39] but their resolve weakened

---

aid, [the Alliance] obscured the critical element of self-help and reform": *The Twilight Struggle* (New York: 1967), p. 34.

[37] For further discussion of why Alliance policy aims were abandoned by the United States, see Lowenthal, this volume.

[38] On this phase of the Kennedy policy generally, see Rogers, *Twilight Struggle,* pp. 119–29; he records that Kennedy had "resolved to resume aid" to the anti-Bosch junta in late 1963. On the Dominican Republic problem, see also John Bartlow Martin's extraordinary memoir, *Overtaken by Events* (New York: 1966), pp. 610–14.

[39] See, for example, the State Department's position against the Hickenlooper Amendment,

after the 1962 passage of the Hickenlooper Amendment. At that time, the State Department began once again to give strong support to threatened North American companies.[40]

This aid to investors, and the damage it did to the effort to coordinate policy, were shown most clearly in the protracted dispute between Peru and the International Petroleum Company (IPC). Teodoro Moscoso's title of "United States Coordinator of the Alliance," actually exceeded his powers. He was not given the authority needed to knit together the many strands of U.S. policy, and sought instead to bargain with and persuade influential agencies and constituencies. Perhaps to improve his standing with the U.S. business community, Moscoso froze U.S. economic assistance to Peru in late 1963 in order to induce Peruvian President Belaunde to settle his government's dispute with the American-controlled IPC. This freeze against the reformist Belaunde government was intended by Moscoso to be temporary; instead, it lasted for more than two years.[41]

Meanwhile, the State Department made no effort to assess the merits of the case independently, and the U.S. embassy in Lima took no part in the Peru-IPC negotiations. "So, in effect," as Richard Goodwin observed in 1969, "we placed American policy in Peru in the hands of negotiators for IPC. For if they didn't agree there would be no aid."[42] The halt in U.S. assistance contributed to economic difficulties that weakened Belaunde, just as IPC's intransigence encouraged the military intervention that finally took place in 1968. It is doubtful that any U.S. President would deliberately have sought these results. But, to quote a concise recent judgment: "Of greatest significance is the fact that the U.S. Government seems to have made little attempt to evaluate the IPC situation in light of other, broader foreign policy considerations."[43]

Hearings Before the Committee on Foreign Relations, U.S. Senate, 87th Congress, Second Session, pp. 557–58. See also Levinson and de Onis, *Alliance,* pp. 143–46, which discusses the White House position. Congress was generally sympathetic to complaining American investors. For Senate speeches supporting United Fruit in a 1962 dispute with Honduras, see " 'We Have the Sovereign Right to Protect our Investors Abroad': A Case and a Commentary," in Marvin D. Bernstein, ed., *Foreign Investment in Latin America: Cases and Attitudes* (New York: 1966), pp. 192–208.

[40] Sometimes, on the other hand, companies deliberately avoided involving the U.S. Government on their side; this was true in the negotiations between U.S. oil companies and Venezuela in 1965–67. See Gertrud G. Edwards, "Foreign Petroleum Companies and the State in Venezuela," in Raymond F. Mikesell, ed., *Foreign Investment in the Petroleum and Mineral Industries: Case Studies of Investor-Host Country Relations* (Baltimore: 1971), pp. 101–28.

[41] See Levinson and de Onis, *Alliance,* pp. 146–56.

[42] Testimony of Richard Goodwin, in *United States Relations with Peru, Hearings Before the Subcommittee on Western Hemisphere Affairs of the Committee on Foreign Relations, U.S. Senate* (Washington, D.C.: 1969), pp. 91–92. Goodwin's "Letter from Peru," *The New Yorker,* May 17, 1969, offers an excellent discussion of the IPC case. Charles T. Goodsell is more charitable toward the U.S. embassy in Lima than Goodwin is: "Diplomatic Protection," p. 252.

[43] Bruce A. Blomstrom and W. Bowman Cutter, "The Foreign Private Sector in Peru," in Sharp, ed., *U.S. Foreign Policy,* pp. 265–66.

A third indication of the Alliance's loss of coherence was the accumulation of special conditions, provisos, and prohibitions attached to economic aid. These restrictions responded to many interests: those of pressure groups in American society, those of Congressional committees, and those of interested executive departments.[44] Senator Church probably exaggerated when he stated that the foreign aid program had been "twisted into a parody and a farce," intended "primarily to serve private business interests at the expense of the American people."[45] But certainly the original unity of the aid effort was considerably eroded, in relation to Latin America, by the many domestic interests that claimed a share in its operations and benefits.

The decay in Alliance policy coordination that began with Kennedy was accelerated by his successor; Lyndon Johnson was unwilling to incur significant political costs by imposing new and common goals on U.S. actions in Latin America. Instead, he relaxed pressure on diverse interests, speeding up the drift back to conservative aims. But Johnson did not, unfortunately, abandon another feature of the Alliance: its interventionism. One may well criticize the activist role played by the United States even in the Alliance's more reformist heyday—and many Latin Americans were already doing so in the early 1960s.[46] But the Johnson Administration offered an even more objectionable combination: activism coupled with conservatism.

Thomas C. Mann, appointed as both Alliance Coordinator and Assistant Secretary of State by the new President, set forth his policy views in March 1966. His speech signaled his chief's return to a fragmented and conservative policy; as Levinson and de Onis observe,

What became known as the Mann doctrine consisted of four basic objectives: (1) to foster economic growth and be neutral on internal social reform; (2) to protect U.S. private investments in the hemisphere; (3) to show no preference, through aid or otherwise, for representative democratic institutions; and (4) to oppose Communism.[47]

---

[44] On these restrictions, see the excellent discussion in Levinson and de Onis, *Alliance,* pp. 112–28, detailing the hindrances they created for economic assistance efforts in Brazil and Chile. See also *United States Relations with Peru,* pp. 47–51, for a list of "all the prohibitions now [1969] attached to the giving of aid, under present law."

[45] Church, quoted in John W. Finney, "Foreign Aid Alive But Not Well," *New York Times,* March 4, 1972. See also Church's 1970 speech, "Toward a New Policy for Latin America," reprinted in Richard B. Gray, ed., *Latin America and the United States in the 1970's* (Itasca, Ill.: 1971), pp. 339–52.

[46] Cf. Albert O. Hirschman's timely warning that such criticism was probably inevitable: "Second Thoughts on the Alliance for Progress," originally published in 1961, reprinted in Hirschman, *A Bias for Hope* (New Haven, Conn.: 1971), pp. 175–82.

[47] Levinson and de Onis, *Alliance,* p. 88.

Abandonment of reform as a goal, in favor of concentration on economic development and ideological security, was clearly shown in U.S.
policy toward Brazil. Even under Kennedy, North American aid administrators in Northeast Brazil favored "high-impact" programs in health and
education over the more calculated but less glamorous reformism of Celso Furtado's SUDENE.[48] This bias derived from the United States' seeking
to win votes for individual "reformist" state governors whom it favored.
The results were to undermine SUDENE's coalition of support, to spend
USAID money for paper projects, and to strengthen conservative forces
in the region.[49] Johnson's search for reform in Brazil was even more perfunctory; he welcomed the Castelo Branco coup of 1964, which the
United States apparently knew of in advance and encouraged without
promising support.[50]

The North American drive for economic development—in Brazil and
elsewhere—thus became separated from reformism, creating disillusion-
ment in Latin America. Somewhat later, the United States briefly gave
great emphasis to another isolated policy theme, and created suspicion
in Latin America. This theme was economic integration.

In August 1965, President Johnson for the first time heartily endorsed
Latin American economic integration efforts.[51] Previously, when the
United States had given attention to Latin American integration (which
was seldom, except in Central America), she had shown more interest in
quibbling over plans than in offering assistance.[52] Thus the suspicions of
many Latin Americans were stirred by this "sudden conversion" in North
American policy, culminating in Johnson's appearance at the 1967 Presidents' meeting in Uruguay. Some critics warned that the concerns of U.S.-
based multinational corporations, anxious to dominate an enlarged regional market, lay behind Johnson's moves.[53]

---

[48] See Riordan Roett, *The Politics of Foreign Aid in the Brazilian Northeast* (Nashville, Tenn.:
1972), Chapter 5. Roett's book is one of the best available discussions of the impact of Alliance
aid programs on the politics of a Latin American state.
[49] Ibid., Chapter 7.
[50] See Thomas Skidmore, *Politics in Brazil* (New York: 1967), pp. 322–30.
[51] Johnson's speech is quoted in Joseph Grunwald, Miguel S. Wionczek, and Martin Carnoy,
Latin American Economic Integration and U.S. Policy, the Brookings Institution (Washington,
D.C.: 1972), pp. 78–79.
[52] On U.S. policy toward CACM, see James D. Cochrane, "U.S. Attitudes Toward Central
American Economic Integration," *Inter-American Economic Affairs,* vol. 18, no. 2 (Autumn
1964). U.S. lack of attention to LAFTA was quite evident. In July 1965—a month before Johnson's speech—the only direct U.S. contact with LAFTA was maintained by one foreign service
officer in the Montevideo embassy, who covered LAFTA affairs as half of his assignment.
[53] This thesis, for example, is part of the argument presented by Celso Furtado's article, "U.S.
Hegemony and the Future of Latin America," *The World Today,* vol. 22 (September 1966), especially pp. 384–85. See also Aguilar, *Pan-Americanism,* pp. 11–12.

These fears were easily understood, but, ironically, businessmen had had little to do with Johnson's initiative. At most, U.S. business had relaxed its opposition to integration, and was tentatively exploring the benefits it might bring.[54] The pressure came, instead, from a small group of State Department and White House functionaries who had chosen integrationism as an attractive new name for a largely unchanged policy: the old Alliance concern for supervising economic development. Some novelty, they believed, was needed to counteract the (reasonable) impressions left by Vietnamese and Dominican events: that the United States cared little for reform in Latin America, and that only "threats to security" could attract Presidential attention there.

Certainly there was some substance as well as fanfare in Johnson's visit to Punta del Este. Had the Latin American states strengthened LAFTA and CACM, pressing for U.S. performance as well as promises, the years 1965–67 might have marked a basic change in U.S. policy. In fact, of course, a strong commitment to integration did not appear in Latin America, and the United States quickly returned to more traditional ideas and policies in relation to economic development.

The point is this: North American policy-makers should have known in 1965 that strong Latin American support for integration was quite unlikely. Instead, they plunged ahead, following the pattern that was typical of Johnson's Latin American actions: activist but confused, with very poor control over the use of U.S. power. This pattern—not peculiar to the Johnson Administration but exaggerated by it—was also clear in North America's Dominican intervention.

The most obvious lesson of the landing of U.S. troops in the Dominican Republic in April 1965 was that the United States still sought security—military and ideological—in Latin America. But the full lesson of the Dominican intervention is brought out only when we recognize the deep division that had developed between the United States' security interest and the rest of her hemispheric policy. The United States chose the direct pursuit of security in the Dominican Republic, acting on largely unexamined assumptions and neglecting her possibly countervailing interests elsewhere in Latin America. The Dominican affair raises, in short, the question of whether the U.S. policy machine—poorly coordinated as it is—is capable of making fully rational decisions.

Two recent accounts of the crisis—Jerome Slater's *Intervention and Negotiation* and Abraham Lowenthal's *The Dominican Intervention*—answer this question in very different ways, and their debate is instructive. Slater searches for a rationale behind American policy, a guiding and reasoning political will that orders and explains all particular policy acts. The

[54]See Grunwald, et al., *Latir American,* pp. 75–78.

prevention of a "second Cuba," he argues, was only part of the clear U.S. purpose in the Dominican Republic. This goal was complemented by a resolve to foster democracy in the island:

... despite some apparent ambiguities and inconsistencies here and there, the evidence, both positive and negative, overwhelmingly points to an early and firm U.S. decision to avoid a return to the pre- and post-Bosch status quo in the Dominican Republic and, on the contrary, to use the opportunity to work for democratic and progressive government.[55]

Slater does observe that the "no second Cuba" policy had become anachronistic by 1965, and that the Communist threat in the Dominican Republic was overestimated.[56] But, given these limitations, he finds that the bulk of U.S. policy actions were mutually consistent and rationally deduced from accepted premises.

A very different picture emerges from Lowenthal's account. He details the actions taken by a number of U.S. Government agencies—the embassy in Santo Domingo, the Pentagon, the CIA, the State Department, and the White House—that constituted the Dominican intervention. Each agency had its own organizational quirks, its own prejudices and interests. As these agencies interacted in April and May 1965, policy actions frequently represented uneasy compromise, or parochial triumph, or evasive postponement. The Dominican case indicates, Lowenthal suggests, that

foreign policy actions ... are shaped not so much by the purposes in terms of which they are usually discussed, but by perceptions and information, by the priorities and procedures of differing actors in the policy-making process, by bargaining and politics, by external pressures and internal strains, by conflict resolution and consensus-building. Competition, compromise, coalition, and confusion combine in uncertain ways to produce the occurrences we term foreign policy.[57]

Certain "assumptions and preconceptions" *were* shared, Lowenthal points out, by virtually all U.S. policy-makers. These assumptions were that a Communist takeover in Santo Domingo must be prevented, but that U.S. involvement in Dominican politics beyond that goal should be minimized.[58] The lesson, if it can be that, of the Dominican episode is here: outdated assumptions are seldom examined or related to other goals by the "particularly fragmented and incremental processes of American foreign policy-making."[59] Slater imputes wholly rational motivation to

---

[55] Jerome Slater, *Intervention and Negotiation: The United States and the Dominican Revolution* (New York: 1970), p. 70; see also pp. 48–49.

[56] Ibid., pp. 194–202.

[57] Lowenthal, *Dominican Intervention*, p. 149.

[58] Ibid., pp. 150–52.

[59] Ibid., p. 162.

the U.S. Government in the Dominican case. But the Administration's basic motives, while real, were diffuse and difficult for the Government itself to perceive, judge, and control. The United States was willing to place the interests of military and ideological security above all others in the Dominican affair; but it did not do so with the coordination that makes both control and correction possible. Would the United States land troops in the Caribbean again? Was the Dominican adventure an end, a beginning, or an aberration? It is hard to say. There has been little basic change since 1965 in the way the United States makes foreign policy. Given that fact, it is as difficult for the observer to predict the future as for the policy-maker to learn from the past.

Nixon: The Play of Interests

President Nixon assigns a low priority to the problems of the hemisphere, and activism in Latin American affairs has not been a proclaimed Presidential goal in his administration.[60] Yet the last four years demonstrate that simply because the White House is inattentive to Latin America, the United States is not necessarily inactive in the area. On the contrary, the free play of a number of interests—both governmental and private—has created an impressive record of activity, intervention, and inconsistency.

Owing in part to investors' pressure, the protection of U.S. enterprises is once again an important theme in American policy, especially during a period when few new initiatives are being taken in other policy fields. U.S. entrepreneurs have become more influential in Washington, and newly active on their own behalf in Latin America.

Following the 1968 nationalization of the IPC in Peru, for example, the Nixon Administration decided against formal enforcement of the Hickenlooper Amendment. But the *substance* of Hickenlooper was applied: normal U.S. economic aid was cut off,[61] and international lending agencies have been discouraged by the United States from granting loans to Peru.[62]

In Chile, the International Telephone and Telegraph Company (ITT) apparently acted with considerable autonomy in opposing the Congressional election and inauguration of President Allende. ITT reportedly consulted with local CIA agents on plans to "bring on economic chaos" and

---

[60] See Luciano Martins, this volume, on this point.

[61] In 1971, the United States did announce a $30 million earthquake relief loan to Peru, and Peru's sugar quota has not been cut substantially. These moves may represent a post-1970 North American effort to woo Peru, thus isolating Chile. James F. Petras and Robert LaPorte, Jr., suggest so, in "Can We Do Business with Radical Nationalists?—Chile: No," *Foreign Policy*, no. 7 (Summer 1972), pp. 138–39.

[62] See "An Exchange on Chile," *Foreign Policy*, no. 8 (Fall 1972), pp. 156–65.

to have "select members of the armed forces . . . lead some sort of upris-ing."[63] It is not clear from available documents whether these plans origi-nated with ITT or with the CIA; at all events, neither effort succeeded.[64] In Washington, ITT and other U.S. investors with Chilean interests (in-cluding the large copper companies) pressed the State Department and the White House to deny U.S. assistance to expropriating regimes.[65] ITT in 1970 reportedly went so far as to offer to "assist [the U.S. Government] financially in sums up to seven figures" to prevent Allende's inauguration. The White House, which is said to have received this message, apparently showed little enthusiasm for the plan.[66]

Investor pressure, however, did succeed in eliciting a major Presiden-tial policy statement in January 1972, reaffirming the basic principle of the Hickenlooper Amendment:

When a country expropriates a significant United States interest without making reasonable provision for . . . compensation to United States citizens, we will presume that the United States will not extend new bilateral economic benefits to the expro-priating country unless and until it is determined that the country is taking reason-able steps to provide adequate compensation or that there are major factors affecting United States interests which require continuance of all or part of these benefits.[67]

The last, qualifying clause of Nixon's statement reflected the State De-partment's desire for a flexible policy toward nationalizing governments. The statement's harsh general tone reflected the fact that investors had acquired a powerful bureaucratic ally in Washington: the Treasury De-partment. Secretary of the Treasury John B. Connally, in influencing the President and acting within his own competence, consistently favored investors' interests.[68] Nixon's statement on investment was only one re-sult of this unprecedented Treasury influence; it was shown as well in U.S. policy toward Latin American economic development.

[63] Quotes are from purported ITT memoranda published by columnist Jack Anderson, and reported in "I.T.T. and C.I.A. Tried to Stop Allende's Election, Anderson Says," *New York Times,* March 21, 1972. See also "I.T.T. Said to Seek Chile Coup in '70," *New York Times,* March 22, 1972, p. 25.

[64] I discuss further the U.S. Government's possible role in secret anti-Allende efforts below.

[65] For example, in October 1971, Secretary of State Rogers met with representatives of ITT, Anaconda, Ford Motor Company, Ralston Purina, the First National City Bank of New York, and the Bank of America. Pressed by the companies to take action against Chile, Rogers is re-ported to have replied that "Washington would take steps to cut off aid to Chile unless she pro-vided prompt, fair compensation" for nationalized properties. Quote and report are from Ben-jamin Welles, "Rogers Threatens Chilean Aid Cutoff in Expropriations," *New York Times,* Octo-ber 23, 1971, pp. 1, 6.

[66] See "I.T.T. Said to Seek Chile Coup in '70," *New York Times,* March 22, 1972, p. 25.

[67] Petras and LaPorte, "Can We Do Business," p. 155, quoting Nixon statement.

[68] See, for example, Benjamin Welles, "Aides Say Chile's Move Will Spur U.S. to 'Get Tough'," *New York Times,* September 30, 1971, p. 3; see also the interview with Secretary Connally in *Business Week,* July 10, 1971; this interview is the original source for Connally's "We have no friends left there [in Latin America] anymore" statement.

The incoming administration announced in 1969 two broad changes in economic-assistance policy: a stress on multilateral rather than bilateral channels for development aid, and an improvement in Latin America's benefits from trade, particularly through industrial exports.[69] Both would be sensible steps, backed by experience and by Latin American opinion. But practice has not matched proposal in the areas of aid and trade. Only narrow and immediate North American advantage has been pursued, at the urging of the Treasury. In the Inter-American Development Bank, the United States has used her influence to minimize loans to Chile and Peru, while failing to provide promised increases in her Bank contributions.[70]

In the field of trade, the United States has sought to persuade *all* developed nations to extend tariff preferences to *all* modernizing nations;[71] these efforts have failed. Instead of extending unilateral preferences to Latin America as a substitute measure, the Treasury applied the temporary 10-percent import surcharge to Latin American goods in 1971, despite a favorable U.S. trade balance with the region.[72] In short, though in the abstract the United States accepts Latin American governments' efforts at economic development, it does little to support and a good deal to hinder those efforts.

In the area of military security, some change is evident in U.S. concepts and actions. While the Nixon Administration has reaffirmed hostility to Soviet strategic weapons in the Caribbean,[73] guerrilla rebellions are no longer considered very dangerous. Actions have, for once, followed this change in perceptions; U.S. arms sales have been sharply reduced, as has the size of U.S. training-and-advice missions to Latin American armies.[74]

[69] See Nixon 1969 speech in Gray, ed., *Latin America,* pp. 264–65.
[70] Cf. H.J. Maidenberg, "Anger Marks Convention of Inter-American Bank." *New York Times,* May 9, 1972, pp. 55, 59; see also Connally, *Business Week* interview. David A. Baldwin argues that all forms of aid—including multilateral assistance—imply a certain degree of political intervention. See his article, "Foreign Aid, Intervention, and Influence," *World Politics,* vol. 21, no. 3 (April 1969), pp. 425–47.
[71] See Nixon Trade Message to Congress, quoted in excerpt form, *New York Times,* November 19, 1969, p. 38.
[72] See H.J. Maidenberg, "Latin America is Denied Exemption from Surtax," *New York Times,* September 18, 1971, pp. 37, 39.
[73] In warning the Russians on their use of Cuba's naval base at Cienfuegos as a base for nuclear-weapons-carrying submarines. On recent U.S.-Cuban relations, see Edward González, "The United States and Castro: Breaking the Deadlock," *Foreign Affairs,* vol. 50, no. 4 (July 1972), pp. 722–37.
[74] Arms sales have been vigorously opposed by Congressional committees. The Senate Foreign Relations Committee's latest version of the currently pending military assistance bill sets a limit of $150 million on sales and military aid to Latin America. See *New York Times,* September 20, 1972.

In the field of ideological security, however, the Nixon Administration has continued its predecessors' tradition of anti-radicalism. The proclaimed U.S. position has been this:

We have a clear preference for free and democratic processes. We hope that governments will evolve toward constitutional procedures. But it is not our mission to try to provide—except by example—the answers to such questions for other sovereign nations. We deal with governments as they are.[75]

U.S. hostility toward Chile, despite this statement of policy, has been clear. Only occasionally has a U.S. agency or individual policy-maker sought to treat Allende's Chile normally—as when the Navy and the Defense Department sought to have the carrier *Enterprise* visit Valparaíso, or when Ambassador Edward M. Korry reportedly "developed effective working relations with key members of Dr. Allende's government."[76] And the only case of (limited) U.S. assistance to Allende remains the agreement to renegotiate Chile's long-term debt to the U.S. Government ($900 million) and to U.S. banks ($160 million).[77]

There is also strong reason to believe that U.S. opposition to Allende has gone beyond the announced aid and loan cutoffs and diplomatic rebuffs. The State Department, of course, has denied that the U.S. Government supported any covert anti-Allende moves, stating that any such ideas were "firmly rejected" by the Administration.[78] But the "ITT Papers" suggest that the CIA did try to foment an anti-Allende army revolt, as the Chilean Government has repeatedly asserted. Moreover, President Nixon may in this case have left his usual role of simply tolerating the actions of governmental and private agencies in Latin America, becoming more active himself. Again according to the "ITT Papers," the White House gave Ambassador Korry a "green light" to oppose Allende's inauguration by any means short of a coup d'état.[79]

[75] Richard M. Nɪxon, *U.S. Foreign Policy for the 1970's: Building for Peace: A Report to the Congress by Richard Nixon, February 25, 1971* (Washington, D.C.: 1971), p. 53.

[76] See Benjamin Welles, "U.S. Declines Invitation for Visit by Warship," *New York Times,* February 28, 1971, and Juan de Onis, "U.S. Cancellation of a Visit by *Enterprise* Stirs Chile," *New York Times,* March 7, 1971. In a dispatch following the latter article, the *Enterprise* affair is described by an unnamed official as a "bureaucratic mess," in which Mr. Nixon and Dr. Kissinger, allied with State Department officials, overruled Secretary of Defense Melvin Laird. On the other hand, Richard E. Feinberg views the State Department as "willing to be flexible" toward Allende, and only the White House as intransigent: *The Triumph of Allende: Chile's Legal Revolution* (New York: 1972), pp. 189–92. On Ambassador Korry, the quote is from Juan de Onis, "Chile Confirms U.S. Will Replace Ambassador Korry," *New York Times,* April 8, 1971, p. 2.

[77] "Chile's $160 Million Debt at U.S. Banks Refinanced," *New York Times,* June 13, 1972, pp. 61, 71.

[78] Tad Szulc, "State Department Denies Any Move to Block Allende," *New York Times,* March 24, 1972, pp. 1, 7.

[79] See articles listed in notes 63 and 78 above.

Paths of Policy: Past and Future

In the discussion so far, I have tried to separate two ideas—the recognition of U.S. hemispheric dominance and the assumption that U.S. policy is unitary. In place of the second, I have argued that U.S. policy has often been fragmented, and sometimes even confused. U.S. interests have long regarded Latin America as an area subordinate to their power. They have cast Latin America in several different roles: as offering North America favorable trade relations, as echoing her political ideals, as supporting her in world councils, and as welcoming her investors. But just as U.S. society and government have been plural, her policy has been divided, with lines of action quite often crossing one another in poorly coordinated patterns.

Here at the essay's close, I shall not spend time on the clear fact of U.S. dominance, nor on its recognized social sources. Instead, I shall stress what the record has shown us about the nature, sources, and implications of poor coordination in U.S. policy. The study of policy fragmentation offers insights into both the political dynamics and the future of U.S. hemispheric dominance.

Forms of Inadequate Policy Coordination

Lack of order and organization in U.S. policy, we found, has taken at least three different forms:

1. *Poor coordination among aims and actions.* Sometimes U.S. goals were relatively clear, but actions "pursuing" them did not all contribute to their attainment. An example is given by the early Eisenhower years, when security policy held at least formal precedence over other U.S. policy themes. The United States sought and expected strong Latin American support in the cold war—but her approach to economic development prevented her from offering much in the way of inducement or reward for this help.

A second example is afforded by the case of U.S. actions toward Peru during the Alliance era. The overall U.S. Government goal was to encourage reformist civilian rule in Peru, yet the U.S. Government's actions made that goal harder to achieve. The State Department endorsed the IPC's rigid position; in part as a result of this pressure, President Belaunde's prestige crumbled, and nationalist military reformers took power in 1968.

2. *Plural goals.* Often the United States pursued several different policy goals, each leading to a series of actions—actions that, considered together, were incongruous or incompatible. Such a contradiction appeared between Johnson's stress on hemispheric security (e.g., the proposal for

a permanent "inter-American Peace Force"), and his administration's enthusiasm for Latin American economic integration. The latter implied a willingness to strengthen Latin American autonomy; the former was a form of U.S. cold war dominance that not even Dulles had dared to propose. This sort of competition among policy concepts and their attendant actions is often caused by the influence of North American private groups on official U.S. policy. Pressures from U.S. corporations, for example, have bred chaos in Nixon's Latin American policies.

3. *Incoherence.* There have been times when the uncertainty of U.S. policy has been even more important than its pluralism. Lack of coordination here crossed the line into incoherence, and the U.S. Government appeared not so much schizophrenic as bewildered. The late Eisenhower Administration was such a time. North America's view of economic development was changing in important ways, her view of security was changing in ways that seemed important, and no one seemed to know what these changes meant for the relevant policy themes, much less for an overall concept of U.S. goals and tactics. The Nixon Administration has at times shown the same uncertainty concerning its basic aims in Latin America.

Two Sources of Poor Policy Coordination

The record of the past 20 years indicates that poor coordination in U.S. hemispheric policy has two interacting sources in the structure of the U.S. Government: plural bureaucratic interests and scant Presidential attention to Latin American affairs.

1. *Competing interests in the U.S. bureaucracy.* Bureaucratic pluralism and competition within the U.S. Government encourage fragmentation in policy. Governmental agencies tend to adopt narrow views of what is important in U.S.-Latin American relations, and they tend to argue that these views should dominate *all* U.S. hemispheric policy. At times, departments hold several perspectives and try to reconcile them; the State Department, to give an example, is concerned with all three policy themes.[80] But each of the policy themes has generally been closely identified with a bureaucratic constituency: the security perspective has been favored by the Department of Defense, the CIA, and conservative members of Congress. Supervision of development has been of major concern to USAID, and to the Commerce and Agriculture Departments. Investors' interests have traditionally been supported by the Treasury Department.

---

[80] A department may in some cases change its basic policy aims. This happened during the 1960s at the Treasury; at the beginning of the decade under C. Douglas Dillon, Treasury strongly favored the Alliance for Progress and U.S. development aid. By the early 1970s, Treasury, under new leadership and new national economic conditions, had become reluctant to grant aid and was very supportive to United States investors in Latin America.

Poor coordination among policy themes—as during the late Eisenhower and the Nixon Administrations—generally indicates that these fragments of the bureaucracy have gained a good deal of autonomy from the potential coordinative power of the White House.

In studying diverging agency interests, it is important to remember that they often do not appear in stark contrast, but are blurred together by a superficial compromise. Yet the outlines of disagreement remain. For example, the State Department has never welcomed the idea of mandatory termination of aid to Latin American countries that nationalize U.S. investments without meeting North American demands for compensation. The Department believes the Hickenlooper Amendment restricts its diplomatic options excessively, and Dean Rusk testified against the legislation when it was first proposed. But to placate the agencies that came to favor Hickenlooper—Congress and the Treasury—State changed its attitude toward the new law, and Rusk even said that it had been helpful to the conduct of diplomacy.[81] At the end of the 1960s, however, this uneasy compromise came under new strains.

North American enterprises began to be expropriated more frequently, and applying Hickenlooper was no longer an academic matter. Specifically, the State Department did not want to apply the amendment openly to Peru and Bolivia.[82] At the same time, the Treasury's opposition to expropriation intensified, and it demanded that the United States take vigorous measures. The old compromise broke down, and the dispute was carried to President Nixon, who imposed a new interagency agreement—an agreement that may prove, in time, to be just as superficial as the old one. As Roger Hilsman has written:

> Very often policy is the sum of a congeries of separate or only vaguely related actions. On other occasions, it is an uneasy, even internally inconsistent compromise among competing goals or an incompatible mixture of alternative means for achieving a single goal.[83]

2. A low level of Presidential attention to Latin America. U.S. Presidents certainly have the power to improve coordination in foreign policy; though their success in these efforts is never complete, they *can* tighten discipline over competing fragments of the bureaucracy.[84] But they tend

---

[81] See Statement of Professor Richard B. Lillich, *United States Relations with Peru, Senate Hearings*, p. 62, on Rusk's initial opposition.

[82] Ibid., p. 139. After about 1968, the State Department equivocated in its general appraisal of the legislation. Senator Church aptly described Assistant Secretary Meyer's 1969 testimony on Hickenlooper as "an artful assumption of a nonposition."

[83] Roger Hilsman, *To Move a Nation: The Politics of Foreign Policy in the Administration of John F. Kennedy* (New York: 1967), p. 5.

[84] Various detailed plans have been suggested to make the U.S. policy-making machine more responsive and rational. The key element they all require is an energetic and engaged chief execu-

to hoard this power, to conserve it for issues they consider of deep importance. In the period since 1950, Korea, Europe, the Middle East, and Vietnam all were usually felt to warrant greater Presidential commitment than Latin America.

It has been argued that the United States is often uninterested in Latin America, and that this inattention breeds poorly coordinated and unrealistic policy.[85] There is a good deal of truth to this argument, but it is somewhat misdirected. Our acquaintance with the internal pluralism of the U.S. Government should alert us to this fact: the problem is not so much one of U.S. inattention to Latin America, as of Presidential inattention to what U.S. public and private agencies are doing in Latin America.

When Latin American policy has a "low priority" at the White House, this does not mean that U.S. agencies are inactive in dealing with Latin America. It means, in Theodore Sorensen's words, that there is "no single overriding program to submerge the dissonant attitudes of the Congress, corporations, and competing executive departments, no . . . concepts of cooperation to replace the constant haggling over bits and pieces of policy."[86] The Eisenhower, Johnson, and Nixon Administrations attributed little importance to what happened in Latin America, and thus none was willing to spend much political energy to make U.S. policy toward the region coherent and responsive. Under these administrations, the Pentagon, the Treasury, and the State Department did not lose interest in Latin America; the confusion among their actions was due, instead, to executive unwillingness to discipline the agencies' actions.

Policy Fragmentation as a Source of U.S. Dominance

Certainly the fact that U.S. hemispheric policy is poorly coordinated affects the style of U.S. dominance, helping to make it fragmented and unselfconscious, compartmentalized, and hypocritical. But the U.S. style is often viewed as a secondary matter by Latin Americans.[87] And indeed the more basic importance of studying policy coordination lies elsewhere,

---

tive. See, for example, John Franklin Campbell, *The Foreign Affairs Fudge Factory* (New York: 1971). Campbell recommends a smaller, more authoritative, and younger State Department. See also Destler, *Presidents,* who proposes a strengthening of and reliance on the Secretary of State, while building "lines of confidence" downward to his subordinates (pp. 261–65). Coordination of course does not guarantee that a policy will be politically or morally desirable. For a chilling view of U.S. policy in Vietnam as being coordinated but nonetheless disastrous, see Leslie Gelb, "Vietnam: The System Worked," *Foreign Policy,* no. 3 (Summer 1971).

[85] For an expression of this theory, see Robert N. Burr, *Our Troubled Hemisphere,* the Brookings Institution (Washington, D.C.: 1967), p. 23.

[86] Theodore C. Sorensen, " 'We Don't Have Any Friends There'," *New York Times,* October 1, 1971, p. 41.

[87] See, for example, Jorge Graciarena's views, as expressed in his commentary following this essay.

in the insights it offers into the origins—and particularly the permanence—of U.S. hemispheric dominance. It presents us with distinctly *political* reasons (1) why the U.S. policy of conservative intervention has changed so little during the past 20 years, and (2) why it may well be difficult to turn the United States away from the pursuit of future dominance.

In the immediate past, poor governmental coordination helped to cause and perpetuate the U.S. search for dominance over Latin America. First, lack of coordination gave many private and official interest groups nearly direct access to fragments of governmental power. These groups included not only the U.S. investors and exporters whose influence is often noted. They embraced, as well, generals anxious to maintain "good working relations" with Latin American armies, USAID officials eager to maintain staff size, and information officers with surplus truth to communicate. A few of these groups—such as liberal Senators anxious to make reputations in foreign affairs—were committed to the control or even the restraint of U.S. intervention in the hemisphere. But most were concerned to maintain conditions in Latin America with little change, and to maximize the role of the United States there.

Poor coordination helped preserve the policy of dominance by obscuring the vision of the President and by placing political obstacles in his path. With the making of hemispheric policy dispersed among so many Government agencies, it was difficult for the President to carry out a critical comparison among all U.S. actions toward Latin America. Often, only a foreign policy crisis—such as the 1965 Dominican affair—could reveal (to some) the biases and weaknesses of many policy maxims. At other times, irrelevant or mutually antagonistic lines of policy were seldom compared, and thus seldom revised.

But if there was some political cost attached to getting a complete picture of U.S. hemispheric policy, changing that policy required much more Presidential commitment. The President might well have to forgo other long-sought policy goals, in order to impose centralized priorities on U.S. actions in the hemisphere. To disappoint aggrieved investors and their Congressional allies, for example, a President would have to be willing to brave criticism as "anti-business." To supervise U.S. military aid or intervention in Latin America more closely might require acceptance of Pentagon priorities elsewhere in the world. In order to achieve policy change, one had first to pay the price for governmental coordination—and few Presidents considered such a political investment in hemispheric policy profitable. Only Kennedy, of the four Presidents we have examined, sought to coordinate U.S. actions and thus to change them.

The policy of President Kennedy is particularly relevant here, since it suggests that change in U.S. dominance will be quite limited in the future. The Alliance for Progress was certainly quite coordinated, and innovative as well in several themes; but the point to notice is that it was activist and interventionist as well. To justify the political cost of coordinating U.S. actions, domestic political benefits from the new policy were needed; activism seemed to offer the shortest route to those benefits. Preventing the spread of Communism was a useful negative goal, but beyond that, "tangible" achievements were sought: a road or reservoir built, a budget spent, a government saved. In addition, potentially feuding agencies submit best to central discipline when their budgets and tasks are expanding–and when the President has the financial leeway to create new agencies that share his special policy views (e.g., USAID under Kennedy). As a result of these political factors, almost every aspect of Latin American life became the object of U.S. policy during the New Frontier period. This may be the most basic effect of U.S. Government structure on U.S. hemispheric aims: it helps to force an administration to choose between fragmented interventionism, and coordinated interventionism.

If these observations are sensible, they question the likelihood of key policy changes currently being recommended by some North American critics of U.S. hemispheric policy. Some of these observers believe that the United States can disengage from her Latin American involvements relatively easily. Others argue that a considerable amount of North American influence is inevitable, and that the United States must choose proper aims for an influence of which she cannot divest herself. What these detailed aims might be–types of governments encouraged, aid offered, and so forth–are also matters of debate.[88]

But behind the debate there is a rough consensus. Most critics of current policy agree that (1) North American agencies, public and private, should be less active overall in Latin America, and (2) when they do act, it should be with more restraint, empathy, and sophistication than in the past. An American policy based on these views would make *self-restraint* its principal goal. It would require the executive to coordinate government agencies in order to restrain them; it would call on the President to give considerable attention to Latin America, in order that the United States should do *less* there.

This aim seems unlikely to appeal to a President of the United States. Faced with a resistant policy-making mechanism, he would be likely to

---

[88] For recent discussions of future U.S. policy toward Latin America, see Peter T. Knight and John Plank, "United States Policy Toward Latin America in the 1970's," draft essay, the Brookings Institution, 1971; Lawrence Harrison, "Waking from the Pan-American Dream," *Foreign Policy*, no. 5 (Winter 1971–72). Cf. the exchange between Harrison and Abraham F. Lowenthal, in *Foreign Policy*, no. 7 (Summer 1972), and John Plank, "Latin America," in Abdul A. Said, ed., *America's World Role in the 70s* (Englewood Cliffs, N.J.: 1970), pp. 66–74.

decide that control for the sake of restraint would not be worth the political energy it would cost. He might choose, as Kennedy did, to combine coordination with intervention. However, especially during the coming four years, a policy of Presidential laissez-faire and divided bureaucratic intervention is much more probable. My central thesis in this essay—that both dominance and fragmentation have characterized U.S. hemispheric policy, and that the latter has helped cause the former—may well apply to the future as well as to the past.

Commentary on Mitchell

JORGE GRACIARENA

Christopher Mitchell is committed to demonstrating the inconsistency of United States policy in Latin America: "For the most part, we (the United States) have not followed one centrally set policy toward the rest of the hemisphere; instead we have pursued a number of policy themes that were often unrelated or even incompatible with one another. . . . Our effort to subordinate Latin America to North American interests, though real, has been neither coordinated nor conspiratorial." Later, he adds, "Our 'policy,' instead of being one conservative course consistently controlled by rational decision-makers, has been a collection of actions, concepts, and attitudes, with little interconnection and many contradictions." To demonstrate this, Mitchell distinguishes "three distinct policy themes during the past 20 years," these being "military and ideological security, economic development, and promotion and protection of U.S. private investment." Then, in examining the evolution of these themes during four administrations, he finds "a peculiar combination of traits in North American policy: a tendency toward conservative domination, a reluctance to change, and a frequent inconsistency." Finally, he presents an extensive and well-informed analysis of North American policy in Latin America after 1950—emphasizing particularly the behavior of the United States in various episodes of great political significance during the period.

Mitchell's analytic model derives from Graham Allison. The "govern-

Jorge Graciarena is a member of the Economic Commission for Latin America (ECLA), Santiago. This commentary reflects the views of the author and not necessarily of the institution of which he is a member.

Editor's Note: This commentary was written in response to the earlier draft of the Mitchell paper presented at the Lima conference. Subsequently, after receiving this commentary, Mitchell revised and shortened his paper. The commentary, however, was not subsequently revised, and thus some of the direct quotations used by Graciarena will not be found in the version of Mitchell's paper published here. We feel, however, that the main burden of the commentary remains relevant to Mitchell's thesis, even in its revised form.

mental politics paradigm" is quite similar to the structure and (more so) to the dynamic of the market model of classical liberal economics from which so many "paradigms" have already been derived for sociology, political science, and other social sciences. In the Mitchell-Allison paradigm, it is assumed that a series of actors (officials with diverse interests and unequal influence) compete among themselves (by bargaining) through regular political channels as individual members of the Government, and that as a result these actors produce one or more policies that are chosen not so much as solutions to a particular problem as the result of compromise, conflict, and confusion among the functionaries (or bureaucrats). Competition among the functionaries appears to be perfect, in that no limits or structures are indicated to qualify it, with the exception of a vague reference to values. Thus, foreign policy is formed through a competitive process in which Government agencies (enterprises) and individual functionaries (entrepreneurs) participate; and the result is a policy (price) that varies continuously within certain themes (parameters). The analogy between the two models seems evident if we omit the specific differences that derive from the different processes involved.

Certainly, we find here the presupposition of a social dynamic that is, by nature, atomistic, ahistorical, and not structured or conditioned by concrete determinants. That the United States is the dominant capitalist power and follows, in its foreign policy, an imperialist tradition that has been applied implacably over a long period in accord with quite evident national interests, appears not to be very important in this explanation of fluctuations in Latin American policy during the last two decades. Nevertheless, Mitchell introduces some exceptions to the paradigm, as I shall indicate later.

The paradigm suggests that foreign policy results from the actions of a limited public composed of bureaucrats (civilian and military) who act in accord with "diverse interests." Up to what point these interests are *really diverse* is something that is not clarified in any part of the paper, and there are reasons to doubt the extent of actual divergence among them. The author himself offers us evidence that this diversity is not great—that it is confined within well-defined parameters. For example, he indicates that during the nearly quarter-century under study, the central themes of U.S. Latin American policy have been consistently maintained, even though they may have been *incoherently implemented.*

It seems to me there exists here an important confusion between two distinct problems that are insufficiently differentiated in Mitchell's treatment. One problem involves defining the goals and general interests that a policy serves; and the other, quite different problem involves the implementation of that policy—the way it is put into practice. It is obvious that what the functionaries and bureaucrats discuss refers to matters of implementation and concrete policy, and their differences are merely at the level of application—for example, how to overthrow Arbenz in Guatemala or invade Cuba, or what to do when North American fishing boats are detained by the Écuadorian Navy. But within the existing configuration of power in the United States, it is impossible to imagine that functionaries can discuss the possibility of alternatives contrary to the preservation of capitalism and private North American investment in the hemisphere, or actions that support popular revolutions of a socialist or anti-imperialist nature.

In reality, the values and vital interests of U.S. policy are not matters for divergence in the decision-making centers of the Government, however much its executive agencies appear to be Balkanized. In one paragraph, the author recognizes these constants as existing quite apart from the possible differences among the functionaries: "At least since her expanding economy and growing population brought her into world politics at the end of the nineteenth century, the United States has regarded Latin America as an area subordinated to her power. Latin America came to play several roles: as offering North America favorable trade relations, as echoing her political ideals, as supporting her in world councils, and as welcoming her investors." Even though the terms used here by Mitchell are more refined, what he affirms in substance is approximately that which he called into question concerning the "radical view." The difference, that is, is principally one of tone and emphasis. Where Dale Johnson affirms that North American diplomacy strengthens international capitalism through the implementation of an imperialist policy, Mitchell limits himself to pointing out that the policy is conservative and interventionist, without attributing to it a particular motive force. Nevertheless, he rejects the idea of an "imperialist logic" and makes no judgment on the relation between U.S. Latin American policy and the dominant role played by the United States since the end of World War I in the international strategy of capitalism. Later, I shall return to this point.

In my opinion, the fundamental interests of the United States as a nation and leader of the capitalist world rarely enter into the debates of the political functionaries and bureaucrats, since these interests are shared among them as a common assumption; and thus the commitment that homogenizes the diverse groups has to do with policy execution and implementation. It is clear that as historical conditions vary, these fundamental interests are continually redefined—not so much in their substantive aspects as in their formalization through concrete courses of political action. The fact that these interests remain constant implies that they are strongly encrusted as values of the power structure within which the

individuals act. A change of values depends, therefore, on a transformation of the structure—and on the historic setting—and much less on the
will of individuals.

The already noted lack of a unifying principle leads Mitchell to emphasize a certain level of inconsistent irrationalism in U.S. Latin American
policy. I see the problem in the following statement: "Conscious executive coordination among policy themes has been rare, and if there is an
unconscious 'logic of imperialism,' it is only very imperfectly reflected
in the interrelations among lines of policy." Once again, here, there appears the confusion between rational formulation and executive coordination of policies, a confusion that underlies the entire paper. All the
problems involving lack of coordination and inconsistency that Mitchell
notes refer to the second level and not to the first—a point clearly indicated both in the preceding quotation and in the data invoked throughout his paper.

As to whether the general goals of North American policies are constants (that is to say, "themes"), the answer must be affirmative, once
their continuity throughout the period is demonstrated. Whether they
are conscious or unconscious, or respond to an inherent "logic of imperialism," forms another set of problems that must be interpreted using
concepts inevitably entailing personal preferences and ideological frames
of reference. Nevertheless, the plain fact is that there is manifest asymmetry between U.S. foreign relations toward Latin America and the subordination of Latin America to North American interests, and to the political models and ideologies the United States imposes. The exceptions
of Cuba and Chile—and in another sense, of Peru—to the effective exercise of American hegemony in Latin America do not alter the essence of
the problem; in the last instance, these cases confirm the rule—especially
if one takes into account the subsequent reaction of the United States
to the change of political-social regimes in the two countries.

Thus, what Mitchell analyzes is the application and coordination of
policies rather than the general ends that are pursued through them. To
a great extent, this second area lies outside the focus of his analysis. For
example, "The Dominican affair raises, in short, the question of whether
the U.S. policy machine—poorly coordinated as it is—is capable of making fully rational decisions." In this episode, the need to prevent a possible revolutionary transformation of Dominican society was the basic
goal. This does not appear to have ever been in question; what was a matter of discussion and dissent seems to have been the most appropriate
procedures to avoid a revolution and maintain the Dominican Republic
within the capitalist orbit and subject to the leadership of the United
States.

Discussion about whether or not actions and concrete policies have been coherent and well coordinated is a matter that has some intellectual interest; but historically and politically it appears to be secondary to the admitted continuity of general goals. It might be added that all history, on the level of concrete events, shows a series of misadjustments and contradictions of the type indicated. These are always the consequence of incoherencies, vacillations, and conflicts among the individual actors. Nevertheless, in order to understand the course of social as well as historical processes, it is necessary to climb above the trees in order to see the forest. For this, it is necessary to try to discover the behavior and the logic of systems, not of individuals, no matter how central these individuals may have been to the events under consideration. It is clear that if one conceives of society as an atomistic grouping formed by unstructured units—or with a low level of structure—what necessarily stands out in the analysis are concrete units (whether they are individuals, cliques, groups) and not global, historical formations. Moving from that position to denying that the nation can be a social actor is only a short jump, one that is easily made by affirming that no one—not even the Government—really represents the nation and that the nation lacks the capacity to act as a unit. This image of political society inevitably leads to giving priority to individualistic action in the observation, articulation, and implementation of policies—while treating the ends and interests that these policies serve as assumptions and constants.

At the beginning of his paper, Mitchell declares, "This is not to say that our conservatism has been unconscious, nor that our domination of Latin America has been wholly unintentional. It *is* to say, however, that we have exercised dominion in the hemisphere in an uncertain, fragmented, and sometimes confused way." Faced with this statement, as a Latin American, I ask myself, of what importance is the discovery that North American policy in the region has at times been implemented in an incoherent or contradictory manner? One could assume that in today's historic circumstances Latin Americans must inevitably be dominated by the great hemispheric power; and that, in order to make plans and establish fields of action and margins of liberty, they are better off confronting a rationally applied policy of domination, with its ends and means well harmonized. For my own part, I am not sure that if U.S. Latin American policy were articulated and implemented in a coordinated and coherent manner this would be advantageous to the interests of Latin America—in fact, quite the contrary. There is some basis for thinking that from these very inconsistencies arise more opportunities to better our position at the negotiating table. The existence of fissures and contradictions, resulting from a lack of unity in the policies put into practice by the hegemonic power, provides us with greater possibilities for maneuver.

Finally, I want to make a few rapid observations on the "themes" of

U.S. Latin American policy. In the first place, we know nothing of the reasons why Mitchell selected those themes and not different ones. He says simply, "We can discern three distinct policy themes during the past 20 years, three issue areas in inter-American relations that have attracted the attention of the United States." It is possible to imagine that one of the reasons, perhaps the principal reason, why Mitchell provides no key to his selection of those themes is that, in order to do so, he would have to make explicit a general theory—the utility of which he criticizes and rejects in various parts of his work (see, for example, his criticism of Slater, who "searches for a rationale behind American policy, a guiding and reasoning political will that orders and explains all particular policy acts"). Nevertheless, the fact remains that a selection of themes took place; and this necessarily assumes—however reluctant the author—a theory of North American policy, a theory that is implicit in the criteria used for that selection.

In the second place, the three themes, looked at together, seem relatively arbitrary in two senses—in their capacity to describe accurately the general features of U.S. Latin American policy; and in their interrelation and mutual compatibility. The first theme (military or ideological security) and the third (promotion and protection of North American investors) are closely related. In this sense, one can assume that the military or ideological security of the United States not only refers to its security as a nation but extends to include its responsibility for the defense and promotion of capitalism as a social system. The strategic conception of North American security is very broad. It is obvious that in Vietnam the national security of the United States was not at stake, but rather the survival of capitalism in Southeast Asia. The protection of North American investors is closely meshed with the logic of protecting capitalism.

What appears quite unrelated to these other points is the supposition that the United States is concerned with the promotion of economic development in Latin America—unless this economic growth is conceived of as occurring within the framework of "counterinsurgency," on the basis of the conviction, now fading, that there is an inverse relationship between per-capita income and popular revolution. Mitchell, however, does not seem to be reflecting this conviction, but rather a more altruistic interest on the part of the United States in the economic future of the countries of the hemisphere.[1] If this is the case, he would have to acknowledge that in this area U.S. policy is even less contradictory. Personally, I think that the United States does not have much interest in the economic growth of Latin America, except to the degree necessary

---

[1] In the first version of Mitchell's paper the second theme was simply "Latin American economic development," not the "U.S. supervision of Latin American economic development" that appears in the final version [Ed.].

for its own national economic interests and those of its multinational corporations. There is much empirical evidence, including that documented in several papers published in this book, that North American exploitation has functioned as a serious obstacle to economic growth in the majority of the countries in the region, whether it be through the extraction of natural resources and capital or through the creation of discriminatory conditions with respect to prices, quotas, preferential tariffs, etc. The United States has also functioned as a very serious obstacle to economic and social development through helping to consolidate and maintain structural distortions and archaic institutions.

I conclude with a last point that relates to U.S. Latin American policy and to the guidelines for its interpretation. The author examines the implementation of the three "themes" in a totally autonomous manner— that is to say, with no relation to the changes in the international situation that occurred in this period, and also without regard to the totality of North American international policy. Moreover, nothing is said about the influence the internal situation of the United States might have exercised, aside from the change of Presidential administrations. The idea that U.S. Latin American policy is independent of the internal economic and political dynamic of the United States, and of its international global policy, appears quite questionable from several points of view. The most important is whether this postulated autonomy really exists; it is difficult to believe that there are no implications or interdependencies among the various internal and external policies. There is only one departure from this general neglect, and that in a brief comment—interjected somewhat casually and without reference to the period under study—in which Mitchell alludes to the influence of Nazism on Roosevelt's "Good Neighbor" policy.

If he had adopted this perspective in a general manner and had established a relation between levels and types of policy, his explanation of U.S. Latin American policy would probably have been more useful and meaningful. Perhaps what he sometimes considers as inconsistencies and discontinuities are nothing more than necessary "tactical adjustments" within certain configurations of general policy, both international and domestic. A purely domestic analysis of a policy has limitations that prevent one from seeing this; still more is this the case if—as here—the analysis is based on a theoretical paradigm that emphasizes primarily a dynamic of opposition between interest groups at the expense of the analysis of relations between policies and historical forces. Moreover, these limitations emerge clearly when one attempts to move from description and formal discussion to an historical explanation of the causes and structural factors that determine concrete policies, aside from the interests and mentalities of the individuals who animate them.

'Liberal,' 'Radical,' and 'Bureaucratic'
Perspectives on U.S. Latin American Policy:
The Alliance for Progress in Retrospect

ABRAHAM F. LOWENTHAL

This paper reviews and analyzes recent North American writing on U.S.-Latin American relations, particularly on the Alliance for Progress. It does not attempt to summaıize or evaluate the Alliance's history as such, nor does it deal with Latin American perspectives on the Alliance (or more generally on inter-American relations), though I hope to treat these subjects in future works. Rather, it analyzes the dwindling North American literature on the Alliance for Progress as a means of illuminating the state of scholarship in this country on U.S.-Latin American relations. I shall draw on available writings to illustrate my major theme: that U.S. analysts of inter-American relations tend to adopt either of two alternative (and inadequate) perspectives. These perspectives, which I shall call "liberal" and "radical," differ sharply in their sets of assumptions about the nature of U.S.-Latin American relations and more generally about politics in America, North and South.[1] Each provides insights for interpreting the Alliance and for explaining other aspects of inter-American relations; neither, by itself, seems to me satisfactory. In the final section of this essay, I shall attempt to sketch out a complementary "bureaucratic politics" perspective, a perspective usually missing from both liberal and radical accounts, and to suggest that this third perspective may be useful for analyzing U.S. Latin American policy.

When President John F. Kennedy proclaimed the Alliance for Progress in 1961, North American reaction to his initiative was almost unanimously favorable. The Alliance program (as announced by Kennedy and as

Abraham Lowenthal is with the Center for International Studies, Princeton University, Princeton, New Jersey. He wishes to express his appreciation to the Center and to the Council on Foreign Relations for support during the period when this paper was written, to the sponsors and organizers of the Lima seminar for the opportunity to reflect on this theme, and to the participants in the seminar and other colleagues for their critical suggestions on the first draft. An earlier version of this essay was published in the *Latin American Research Review,* vol. 8, no. 3, 1973, pp. 3–25, under the title "United States Policy Toward Latin America: "Liberal," "Radical," and "Bureaucratic" Perspectives."

[1] I shall not continue to use quotation marks around these terms; but I invite the reader to imagine that they have been retained.

agreed upon internationally at Punta del Este) reflected, in fact, a virtual consensus among U.S. specialists on Latin America regarding the nature of Latin America's needs, North American interests and responsibilities, and the steps to be taken by the United States to improve inter-American relations. The consensus was far from accidental, for those who drafted the Alliance commitment drew extensively on scholarly critiques of U.S. policy in framing their approach, and relied particularly on what prominent Latin American economists and political leaders had been suggesting.[2] ECLA doctrines, dismissed by official Washington for years, suddenly appeared to be accepted, as the U.S. Government embraced such concepts as economic planning, regional trade agreements, and international commodity arrangements. After years of resistance, the U.S. Government committed itself publicly to a long-term and substantial transfer of U.S. resources, including public aid, to assist Latin American development. Long-standing debates about proper U.S. policy toward Latin American dictatorships seemed to have been resolved as Washington (moving forward in this respect, as in several others, along a trend actually begun during the second Eisenhower Administration) pledged to encourage democratic governments. Perhaps most important, the Alliance program appeared to represent a U.S. Government decision to support, even to foster, major social and economic transformations in Latin America. The U.S. Government seemed to be backing those who called for revolutionary change in the hemisphere (albeit through peaceful processes) and those who would tackle what were perceived in Washington as the major obstacles to development in Latin America.[3] The Alliance program was acclaimed by U.S. specialists on Latin American affairs as "an innovation of tremendous significance in inter-American relations," a "dramatic and fundamental reorientation of Washington's policy," "a major turning point in the history of U.S.-Latin American relations."[4]

Acclaimed by almost all at the start, the Alliance for Progress quickly became the object of controversy, and the controversy has outlived the Alliance itself. An extensive literature (vast compared to what was written on inter-American relations in the three decades before 1961) burgeoned, arguing many points of view.[5]

---

[2] See Lincoln Gordon, *A New Deal for Latin America* (Cambridge, Mass.: 1963), p. 5; Jerome Levinson and Juan de Onis, *The Alliance That Lost Its Way: A Critical Report on the Alliance for Progress* (Chicago: 1970), pp. 52–56.

[3] According to Federico Gil, for instance, the United States was "offering to underwrite a social revolution in Latin America." *Latin American-United States Relations* (New York: 1971), p. 240.

[4] The three phrases quoted are from Herbert K. May, *Problems and Prospects of the Alliance for Progress* (New York: 1968), p. 33; Levinson and de Onis, *Alliance*, p. 5; and Gil, *Latin American*, p. 227.

[5] A useful listing, fairly complete through 1969, is Paquita Vivó, "A Guide to Writings on the Alliance for Progress" Press Division, Organization of American States (Washington: January 1970).

Amid all the controversy, however, agreement has emerged on one key point, which we may accept as stipulated for the purpose of discussion: that during the 1960s a substantial gap arose between what Washington's early rhetoric promised and what the U.S. Government actually did. U.S. economic assistance failed to reach projected levels; debt service requirements and other capital transfers may even have produced a net outflow of financial resources from Latin America to the United States. American "aid" not only was insufficient in magnitude but often turned out to be misdirected from the standpoint of advancing Latin American development; it became a "substantial device for profiteering at public risk" as various conditions were imposed to serve various U.S. special interests.[5]

Noneconomic aspects of the Alliance fared no better. The supposed U.S. resolve to back constitutional regimes and oppose military takeovers did not stand up, as a new wave of military regimes swept to power, several with apparent U.S. support. (A cartoonist for the *San Francisco Chronicle* even mused, "The Alliance for Progress is very successful; we're getting a much better class of military dictatorship."[7]) Examples of repeated U.S. intervention in Latin American politics—particularly in the Bay of Pigs episode, the Dominican invasion, and the Camelot affair—contradicted the pledges U.S. officials had made. Perhaps most important, the supposed U.S. commitment to peaceful revolutionary change went unredeemed. So unrevolutionary an observer as the Republican George Cabot Lodge concluded by 1969 that "the total effect of the Alliance has been to solidify the status quo, to entrench the oligarchy, and to heighten the obstacles to change."[8]

That the Alliance did not achieve its original stated objectives is widely accepted. Analyzing why the Alliance failed would involve not only an examination of American aims but an investigation and explanation of the effects of American actions in Latin America—a fascinating subject that is beyond the scope of this paper. What I want to emphasize as a point of departure is the general agreement among North American analysts that the Alliance's rhetoric was not even a reliable guide to American actions in Latin America during the 1960s, let alone an adequate predictor of their effects. By the end of the 1960s, indeed, the actions of the U.S. Government in and toward Latin America bore so little resemblance to the declarations of national intent Washington had enunciated in 1961 that virtually all agreed the Alliance was dead, if it had ever lived.

---

[6] The phrase quoted is from Simon G. Hanson, *Five Years of the Alliance for Progress: An Appraisal* (Washington: 1967), p. 13.

[7] Ibid., p. 121.

[8] George Cabot Lodge, *Engines of Change: United States Interests and Revolution in Latin America* (New York: 1970), p. 345.

What happened to the Alliance? Was it thwarted, sabotaged, or simply abandoned? Or was it never what it seemed at the start, but rather a verbal façade, cloaking "real" American aims?

Two main categories of explanation dominate the extensive North American literature on the Alliance. Each reflects a major tradition in U.S. thinking about inter-American relations.[9] Each perspective has also been influenced by recent, more general writings on foreign affairs: a similar liberal/radical split divides most scholars now writing on Vietnam and the cold war.[10] Because of both Latin American and more general events, the liberal perspective is less pervasive than it was in the early 1960s, although it probably still informs a majority of books and articles on inter-American affairs. The radical perspective, in turn, has gained much more acceptance in recent years, especially among younger scholars. Whatever its appeal, however, each view leaves unanswered some significant questions about U.S. Latin American policy.

The "Liberal" Perspective

The liberal approach, which underlay the Alliance itself, assumes an essential compatibility of interest between the United States and Latin America.[11] Additional key liberal assumptions are that the United States has a national interest, with respect to Latin America, "different from and superior to the private interests of any sector of American enterprise or of business enterprise as a whole," and that the U.S. Government is capable of defining and pursuing that interest.[12]

According to the liberal interpretation, historic difficulties between

---

[9] The liberal tradition is discussed extensively below. The radical approach was largely dormant during World War II and much of the cold war but had exercised a major influence on U.S. scholarship during the 1920s and earlier. See for instance the various works on U.S. imperialism published in the 1920s, such as Scott Nearing and Joseph Freeman, *Dollar Diplomacy: A Study in American Imperialism* (New York: 1925) and Melvin M. Knight, *The Americans in Santo Domingo* (New York: 1928).

[10] For an excellent discussion of recent writings on U.S. foreign policy, especially regarding Vietnam, see Robert W. Tucker, *The Radical Left and American Foreign Policy* (Baltimore: 1971). On the cold war literature, see J. L. Richardson, "Cold War Revisionism: A Critique," *World Politics,* July 1972, pp. 578–612.

[11] Among the writings I would classify as "liberal" are the cited works by Gordon, Gil, Levinson and de Onis, May, and Lodge. See also Adolf Berle, Jr., *Latin America Diplomacy and Reality* (New York: 1962); Harvey S. Perloff, *Alliance for Progress: A Social Invention in the Making* (Baltimore: 1969); William D. Rogers, *The Twilight Struggle: The Alliance for Progress and the Politics of Development in Latin America* (New York: 1967); Martin C. Needler, *The United States and the Latin American Revolution* (Boston: 1972); J. Warren Nystrom and Nathan A. Haverstock, *The Alliance for Progress: Key to Latin American Development* (Princeton, N.J.. 1966); and Paul Rosenstein Rodan, "Latin America in the Light of Reports on Development" Working Paper No. 66, Department of Economics, Massachusetts Institute of Technology (December 1970).

[12] Bryce Wood, *The Making of the Good Neighbor Policy* (New York: 1961), p. 167.

the United States and Latin America have arisen because of past U.S. policies now assumed to be nonrecurrent ("gunboat" and "dollar" diplomacy, especially), temporary confusions of private U.S. interests with the national public interest, North American neglect of Latin America, and "pervasive, serious and persistent misunderstanding" between the United States and Latin America, attributed to cultural differences and inadequate information.[13] The liberal view asserts that President Franklin D. Roosevelt's "Good Neighbor" policy dealt successfully with all four causes of inter-American tension; the U.S. Government directed its attention to Latin America, ended unacceptable governmental actions, subordinated private interests to national concern (as in the case of the Mexican oil expropriation), and worked to enhance mutual understanding throughout the Americas. In undertaking these efforts, "The Roosevelt Administration, fortunately for the United States, was doing much to prepare Latin America psychologically for joining in a hemisphere-wide defense program to meet an external threat," but this important result of Roosevelt's initiative is regarded by most liberal writers as largely fortuitous, not as a clue to the U.S. Government's intentions.[14]

Following World War II, American concern focused sharply on Europe and particularly on Russia, erstwhile ally of the United States but by then regarded as its natural rival. U.S. officials once again paid scant attention to Latin American problems and issues, except for arranging regional defense measures. Latin American hopes that the United States would extend its Marshall Plan concept to the Western Hemisphere were disappointed, and Latin American attempts through the O.A.S. to win U.S. trade concessions made little headway. U.S. Latin American policy during this period was not particularly exploitive, according to the liberal view, but simply ignored regional matters, which were not salient in Washington.

[13]The phrase quoted is from Milton Eisenhower, *The Wine is Bitter: The United States and Latin America* (Garden City, N.Y.: 1963), p. 6. Eisenhower's earnest book, based explicitly on the premise that "our welfare and the welfare of other American Republics are inextricably bound together" (p. 45) is a classic liberal statement. Another example, very influential as a text for a whole generation of North American students of U.S.-Latin American relations, is Samuel Flagg Bemis, *The Latin American Policy of the United States: An Historical Interpretation* (New York: 1943). Bemis's argument, which was the conventional wisdom in North American universities when the Alliance was proclaimed, suggested that North American imperialism had been a temporary aberration. "A careful and conscientious appraisal of United States imperialism shows, I am convinced, that it was never deep-rooted in the character of the people, that it was essentially a protective imperialism, designed to protect first the security of the Continental Republic, next the security of the entire New World, against intervention by the imperialistic powers of the Old World. It was, if you will, an imperialism against imperialism. It did not last long and it was not really bad" (pp. 385–86).

[14]The phrase quoted is from Edwin Lieuwen, *U.S. Policy in Latin America: A Short History* (New York: 1965), p. 72. Cf. Donald Dozer, *Are We Good Neighbors? Three Decades of Inter-American Relations, 1930–1960* (Gainesville, Fla.: 1959), p. 37.

By the late 1950s, however, Latin American problems forced themselves back toward the top of the U.S. foreign policy agenda. Among the specific reasons for Washington's increased attention to Latin America were the hostile reception accorded to Vice-President Nixon on his 1958 trip to South America, the less dramatic but nevertheless important impressions of Latin America gathered by Milton Eisenhower, the President's brother, and especially the accession to power in nearby Cuba of a regime perceived as a threat to U.S. interests. Also influential were the increasingly forceful writings by Latin Americans, Raúl Prebisch most prominent among them, who argued that the United States and other industrial powers were largely responsible for Latin America's development problems because the terms on which Latin American countries (and other "peripheral" areas) traded with the "central" powers were structured to the "periphery's" disadvantage.[15]

Slowly but surely, according to the liberal account, the reasons for Latin American discontent with U.S. policy came to be understood in Washington. Steps began to be taken to assist Latin America, starting with the U.S. Government's long-delayed decisions to welcome the establishment of the Inter-American Development Bank and to pledge $500 million in soft-term capital to its Social Progress Trust Fund. Out of these steps, given increased impetus by the Kennedy campaign's political thrust and by the influence of Kennedy's advisers on Latin American affairs, came the Alliance for Progress. The Alliance is seen by liberal writers as a genuine U.S. Government commitment to cooperate with Latin American countries in pursuing the ambitious political, social, and economic objectives proclaimed at Punta del Este.[16] Liberal writers agree that the Alliance was ultimately intended to promote U.S. security and private economic interests, both of which were thought compatible with, indeed largely dependent upon, social and economic progress in Latin America.[17] Liberal writers do not pretend that U.S. policy was selfless and disinterested, but assert that the promotion of genuine Latin American economic

[15] See, for example, Prebisch's well-known article "Commercial Policy in the Underdeveloped Countries," *American Economic Review,* May 1959, pp. 251–73. See also Levinson and de Onis, *Alliance,* p. 39.

[16] The Punta del Este Charter pledged the signers to pursue the goals of sustained economic growth, more equitable income distribution, economic diversification, industrialization, increased agricultural production, reformed land tenure, extended education and reduced illiteracy, improved health services, expanded housing, price stability, regional economic integration, and multilateral agreements to diminish the adverse effects on Latin America of its dependence on export commodities subject to extreme price fluctuations; it made implicit the goal of promoting democratic government in the hemisphere.

[17] See, for instance, Lincoln Gordon's argument, based on the assumptions that "economic development and social progress are 'Siamese twins' " and that the United States has "a national interest which converges with that of our Latin American neighbors" in promoting social and economic progress. Gordon, *New Deal,* pp. 11, 112.

and social development was central to the Alliance as a mutual aim of the United States and the other countries of the hemisphere.

Specific liberal explanations of separate aspects of the Alliance's overall failure (or abandonment) differ. All have in common, however, the assertion of a dichotomy between benevolent U.S. intentions and unfortunate actions; the latter are attributed to particular causes, even sometimes to accidental or contingent forces. The Alliance's disappointing record tends to be chalked up to "halfhearted execution" or to "lack of implementation" (either from the outset or following President Kennedy's death and Teodoro Moscoso's replacement as Alliance Coordinator).[18] It is argued that the Alliance's original aims were attenuated, and some even dropped, because of a series of intense short-term pressures to which responsible U.S. officials understandably but "erroneously" succumbed: pressures to score immediate political impact, to gain Congressional support for foreign aid by serving local and special interests, and to help alleviate the U.S. balance of payments difficulties.[19] Objectives apparently assumed to be consistent at first—economic growth, social equity, political stability, constitutional democracy, the promotion of U.S. private economic interests, and the protection of U.S. national security—turned out to be in conflict, and some were necessarily subordinated to others; liberal writers usually argue that the "wrong" aims were given preference.

Another reason for the Alliance's failure, according to liberal writers, was inadequate North American understanding of the nature of Latin American politics. The Alliance had been based on a "consensus model" of Latin American politics, which supposed that the traditional oligarchic pattern in Latin America was being replaced by a process of struggle and compromise among conflicting interest groups not unlike the U.S. political process.[20] "Middle sector" elements were believed to be the leading

[18] Harvey Perloff, for instance, argues that the Alliance was "a truly magnificent concept . . . carried out in a halfhearted way with a weak, underfinanced, and poorly designed mechanism" (*Alliance*, p. ix). Paul Rosenstein Rodan, one of the Alliance's original "Nine Wise Men," suggests that "while the Alliance failed, it is important to realize that it failed because of lack of implementation, not because of faulty objectives." See Rosenstein Rodan, "Latin America," p. 2.

[19] The most detailed and persuasive exposition of the Alliance's history in these terms is the aforementioned study by Levinson and de Onis, which draws particularly on Levinson's firsthand experience (and frustrations) as a USAID official in Brazil and in Washington. See also *Colombia—A Case History of U.S. Aid* (A Study Prepared at the Request of the Subcommittee on American Republic Affairs), Committee on Foreign Relations, United States Senate, 91st Congress, 1st Session, and Abraham F. Lowenthal, "Foreign Aid As a Political Instrument: The Case of the Dominican Republic," *Public Policy,* vol. 14, 1965, pp. 141–60.

[20] For an interesting exposition of the "consensus" and "conflict" models of Latin American politics, and an argument that the Alliance was based on assumption of the former, see N. Joseph Cayer, "Political Development: The Case of Latin America," unpublished doctoral dissertation, University of Massachusetts, May 1972. See also Susanne Jonas Bodenheimer, *The Ideology of*

actors in Latin American politics by 1960, and to be committed to the Alliance's political, economic, and social goals.[21] But the hoped-for democratic and progressive commitment of the "middle sectors" turned out to be largely illusory, as middle-class politicians showed themselves to be committed chiefly to their own advancement. Often they allied with the traditional elites, whose values, attitudes, and consumption patterns they tended to emulate; they were not suitable "allies for progress."[22]

Liberal writers are not uncritical of U.S. policy toward Latin America during the Alliance period; some, indeed, are devastatingly critical. Their attacks, however, are generally limited to questioning the efficacy of individual officials (or, at most, of sets of officials) and the appropriateness of their decisions, which are seen as "mistakes," based on erroneous judgments or calculations, inadequate information, or faulty understanding. Some liberal writers appreciate that the repeated pattern of American actions suggests a more systematic explanation, but even they see the Alliance's abandonment as essentially unnecessary and invariably conclude their expositions with exhortations to American officials henceforth to resist extraneous pressures and to pursue the Alliance's original goals. The emphasis in liberal critiques is on the supposed discontinuities and contradictions between the aims of American policy, specific American actions, and their consequences.

Perhaps it would be useful here to illustrate the liberal approach by drawing on Riordan Roett's *The Politics of Foreign Aid in Northeast Brazil.*[23] Brazil's vast, drought-stricken, bitterly poor Northeast provinces seemed ready in the early 1960s to become the arena for a major attempt to undertake regional development based on structural changes: agrarian reform, industrialization, and a general realignment of political power. Dedicated and astute leadership was available for this attempt in the person of Celso Furtado. Administrative flexibility and power were furnished by the Superintendency for the Development of the Northeast (SUDENE). Political clout had been achieved by bringing together a broadly based coalition drawing on reformist politicians, urban workers, politi-

---

Developmentalism: The American Paradigm-Surrogate for Latin American Studies (Beverly Hills, Calif.: Sage Professional Papers), Comparative Politics Series, vol. 2, no. 15, 1971.

[21] The classic formulation of this view was John J. Johnson's *Political Change in Latin America: The Growth of the Middle Sectors* (Stanford, Cal.: 1958), a book that was very influential when the Alliance program was being formulated. See also Robert J. Alexander, *Today's Latin America* (Garden City, N.Y.: 1962).

[22] A considerable literature emerged during the 1960s on the political role of Latin American middle sectors. See, for instance, Claudio Véliz, ed., *Obstacles to Change in Latin America* (New York: 1965); Véliz, ed., *The Politics of Conformity in Latin America* (New York: 1967); Seymour M. Lipset and Aldo Solari, eds., *Elites in Latin America* (New York: 1967); and Victor Alba, *Alliance Without Allies: The Mythology of Progress in Latin America* (New York: 1965).

[23] Riordan Roett, *The Politics of Foreign Aid in Northeast Brazil* (Nashville, Tenn.: 1972).

cized students, and the new Church. All that was lacking, or so it seemed, was material resources, which could be provided from abroad if external donors were willing to back the comprehensive development scheme Furtado and SUDENE proposed.

By July 1961, when President Kennedy received Furtado personally at the White House and attentively discussed SUDENE's needs, the stage seemed set for a major U.S. effort to assist economic, social, and political change in a particularly needy region of Latin America. By early 1962, when USAID's Northeast Survey Mission Team reported to President Kennedy—supporting SUDENE and Furtado and accepting the latter's views on the preferred nature, scope, and modalities of U.S. assistance—all appeared ready for a major test of the Alliance. AID proceeded to set up its only regional mission anywhere in the world in Recife, capital of Brazil's Northeast, and prepared to help SUDENE.

Professor Roett's careful, well-documented study shows, however, that AID's effects on Northeast Brazil during the next few years "counteracted" the Alliance's stated goals of supporting social and economic change. AID's overall impact, Roett argues, was to undermine Furtado, to bypass SUDENE, and to help dissipate the coalition for structural change Furtado and SUDENE had so painstakingly assembled. The Northeast Survey Mission Team's alignment with Furtado turned out not to be binding on the U.S. Government as a whole: USAID/Recife, USAID/Rio, and the political section of the American embassy in Rio de Janeiro were all more interested that AID should have an immediate political impact in Northeast Brazil (to combat supposed Communist influence there) than in longer-term, more fundamental programs. This emphasis on short-term political gain, in turn, induced AID to rely on direct agreements with state governments for school construction and similar projects rather than to work through SUDENE on more basic, change-oriented plans. AID's funds, channeled through the entrenched power brokers, thus wound up strengthening the traditional oligarchy's hold on Northeast Brazil. American development assistance in Northeast Brazil consequently hampered Brazil's modernization efforts, and suggested that "foreign aid can have a deleterious effect on a developing nation."[24]

Why was the proclaimed U.S. interest in supporting structural change abandoned in practice? Roett attributes this twist to a "basic misunderstanding"[25] between Furtado and American officials on the nature of the problem: "Furtado saw the Northeast as a national economic and social problem; the United States viewed the region as an international security problem and foreign economic assistance as a weapon against a threat

[24] Ibid., p. 175.   [25] Ibid., p. 10.

Brazil did not unanimously recognize."[26] Thus USAID moved away from SUDENE's priorities and eventually came to regard SUDENE as an obstacle. In concentrating on immediate political impact, Roett argues, the U.S. Government was "short-sighted"; failing to comprehend Furtado's priorities and needs and to perceive the political balance in the Northeast, the United States "misjudged."[27] Such flaws, Roett suggests, produced the Alliance's "failure" in Northeast Brazil. Roett, in short, takes at face value all the Alliance's professed goals and the expressed intent of the early Kennedy Administration's originally enunciated foreign-aid philosophy, which he thinks were unnecessarily abandoned in Northeast Brazil and elsewhere.[28]

The "Radical" Perspective

The radical perspective on U.S. Latin American policy, and specifically on the Alliance for Progress, differs sharply from that embodied in liberal accounts.[29] Increasingly plausible to a generation of North Americans painfully seeking to make sense of this country's destructive acts abroad, especially in Asia but also in this hemisphere, the radical perspective offers a clear and understandable, if disturbing, vision of recent and contemporary U.S. foreign policy. Stated with different levels of subtlety by different authors, the radical view characteristically includes one theme: that U.S. foreign policies primarily serve the expansive interests of North American capitalism.

What liberals regard as mistakes, accidents, and discontinuities, radicals interpret as a rational, coherent, and continuous pattern. What lib-

[26] Ibid., p. 92. [27] Ibid., especially pp. 173–74.
[28] Ibid., p. 177.

[29] Among the writings I would term radical are the aforementioned article by Bodenheimer and also her "Dependency and Imperialism: The Roots of Latin American Underdevelopment," *Politics and Society,* vol. 1, no. 3, May 1971. See also André Gunder Frank, *Latin America: Underdevelopment or Revolution* (New York: 1969); James D. Cockcroft, André Gunder Frank, and Dale L. Johnson, *Dependence and Underdevelopment: Latin America's Political Economy* (Garden City, N.Y.: 1972); James Petras, *Politics and Social Structure in Latin America* (New York: 1970); Petras and Robert LaPorte, Jr., "Modernization from Above Versus Reform from Below: U.S. Policy Toward Latin American Agricultural Development," *Journal of Development Studies,* April 1970, pp. 248–66; David Horowitz, "The Alliance for Progress," in Robert Rhodes, ed., *Imperialism and Underdevelopment: A Reader* (New York: 1970), pp. 45–61; and various articles in James Petras and Maurice Zeitlin, eds., *Latin America: Reform or Revolution?* (Greenwich, Conn.: 1968), especially J. P. Morray, "The United States and Latin America," pp. 99–119. See also K. T. Fann and Donald C. Hodges, eds., *Readings in U.S. Imperialism* (Boston: 1971) and North American Congress on Latin America (NACLA), *Yanqui Dollar: The Contribution of U.S. Private Investment to Underdevelopment in Latin America* (New York: 1971). C. Wright Mills, *Listen, Yankee: The Revolution in Cuba* (New York: 1960) should also be consulted for its radical perspective. More general works relevant to Latin American policy include: Harry Magdoff, *The Age of Imperialism: The Economics of U.S. Foreign Policy* (New York: 1969); Paul Baran, *The Political Economy of Growth* (New York: 1969); and Gabriel Kolko, *The Roots of American Foreign Policy: An Analysis of Power and Purpose* (Boston: 1969).

erals ascribe to misunderstandings and misjudgments, radicals tend to attribute to the designs of American officials, or at least to the predictable actions officials undertake, wittingly or unwittingly, in furtherance of their institutional and class interests. Whereas liberals puzzle over apparent contradictions between U.S. purposes and the instruments chosen to advance them, radicals see clear linkages. What liberal writers believe unnecessary, radicals think determined by the requirements of the North American system. What liberals find surprising, radicals regard as predictable.

More fundamentally, whereas liberal critics presume an essential compatibility of interests between the United States and the countries of Latin America, radicals explain inter-American relations in terms of a basic conflict between the U.S. aim to dominate Latin America and the Latin Americans' urge to achieve sovereignty. And while liberals distinguish between a broader U.S. national interest and the interests of American business enterprises, radicals understand the latter to dictate the objectives of U.S. foreign policy, at least as a general rule. The U.S. Government is believed to be capable of perceiving clearly and pursuing single-mindedly what is in the interests of American business—and to do so.

What is seen as a long-standing pattern of insistent U.S. political, military, and economic intervention in Latin America—epitomized during the first three decades of this century—is regarded by radicals as intrinsic to U.S.-Latin American relations. The Good Neighbor policy is viewed, not as a substantive shift of U.S. policy, but simply as the choice of a new instrument to pursue the traditional U.S. aim: containing and exploiting Latin America. The United States, it is argued, prefers allies in the Western Hemisphere to be dependable and weak; the Good Neighbor policy was allegedly established and structured with that goal in mind.[30]

Following World War II, with its effect of submerging U.S.-Latin American differences in common defense against the extra-hemispheric threat, the fundamental antagonism between the United States and Latin America emerged again, according to the radical interpretation. Nations that questioned North American hegemony—Argentina, Guatemala, and Cuba being the most dramatic examples—suffered U.S. intervention. The O.A.S. and other inter-American institutions were used systematically to reinforce Latin American dependence on the United States. The driving force behind North American policy, radicals suggest, has always been the expansive need of private capitalism, which has adopted one means after

---

[30]This argument is developed most fully by David Green in *The Containment of Latin America: A History of the Myths and Realities of the Good Neighbor Policy* (Chicago: 1971). See also Alonso Aguilar, *Pan Americanism from Monroe to the Present: A View from the Other Side* (New York: 1968).

another to protect and extend its stake in Latin America (and elsewhere). A typical statement is Dale Johnson's:

Foreign policy flows naturally, and by and large rationally, from the structure described. The basis of U.S. foreign policy is a conception of national interest as inherently involved in the strengthening of international capitalism against the threats of socialism and nationalism. . . . U.S. private investment, aid programs, foreign policy, military assistance, military interventions, and international agencies, under the influence or control of the international business community, are interwoven and oriented toward the promotion and maintenance of influence and control in other countries.[31]

The Alliance for Progress, in the radical view, was perhaps the most sophisticated instrument of U.S. Latin American policy fashioned to date. It is argued that the Alliance was, from the start and in concept, a means to advance U.S. private economic interests in Latin America.[32] U.S. interests were to be served specifically by reopening the area to U.S. investors and facilitating inter-American trade and, more generally, by preserving and reinforcing the socioeconomic status quo in Latin America in order to preclude structural changes that might restrict the scope for U.S. business. Since North American "development" and Latin American "underdevelopment" have always been causally linked, radicals contend, the United States necessarily sees its interest in the preservation of Latin American dependence.[33] The Alliance was "merely one more means of integrating Latin America into the international system that creates dependency and hinders development in the region."[34]

Radicals regard the supposed Alliance commitments to a variety of other goals—social progress, more equitable income distribution, etc.— either as mere verbal glosses on traditional policies or else as the cynical cloaking of North American intent. Some go so far as to attribute virtually all U.S. programs, however apparently benevolent—programs to expand agricultural production or even to control malaria, for instance— to the U.S. drive to dominate.[35] Others are willing to concede some non-

---

[31] See Cockcroft, Frank, and Johnson, *Dependence and Underdevelopment,* pp. 98, 100.

[32] See, for example, Horowitz, "Alliance," pp. 56–59; Morray, "United States and Latin America," p. 108.

[33] Much of the radical critique draws directly on the extensive Latin American literature on *dependencia.* For typical examples of the literature applying "dependence" concepts to the making of U.S. policy, see Bodenheimer, "Dependency and Imperialism," and Frank, *Latin America.* For a critique of some "dependencia" literature, and specifically of Bodenheimer's article, see David Ray, "The Dependency Model of Latin American Underdevelopment: Three Basic Fallacies," *Journal of Inter-American Studies and World Affairs,* February 1973, pp. 3–21.

[34] Bodenheimer, "Dependency and Imperialism," p. 358.

[35] See, for example, Morray, "United States and Latin America," p. 108, for an assertion that anti-malaria projects are "not unrelated to a veiled strategic purpose . . . to revive faith in the potential of the existing bourgeois order to meet the problems of the hemisphere."

exploitive, even reformist, motives to American officials, but argue that these aims are always subordinated to the primary goal of assuring domination.[36]

As for the supposedly misplaced U.S. reliance on "middle sector" elements as potential allies for progress, radicals contend that the U.S. Government chose correctly those forces in Latin America that would cooperate with the North American program to reinforce the status quo. Radical critics, usually grounding their approach in Marxian analysis, generally adopt a "conflict theory" of Latin American politics, in which a fundamental struggle between classes is seen as central. So-called "middle sectors" are understood as having either joined or displaced traditional power-holders in the satisfied segment of society, and more important, as exactly that part of the satisfied segment likely to ally with external influence to solidify its position against lower-class challenge.

It would be most interesting to illustrate the radical perspective by citing a specific radical alternative to Roett's appraisal of the Alliance's experience in Northeast Brazil. Unfortunately, I have not found a good example; radical critics tend, indeed, to eschew case-study treatments, preferring usually to deal in broadbrush terms.[37] The most useful radical piece on Northeast Brazil I could find, Joseph Page's recently published volume, concentrates much more on Brazilian events and personalities than on U.S. policies, and relies mainly on Roett's study for material on American attitudes and actions.[38] Drawing on Page and on the radical perspective generally, one can speculate however, that a full-blown radical account would deny that the Alliance was a failure in Northeast Brazil, given its "real" objectives. It would suggest that, far from revealing faulty judgment and lack of understanding in undercutting SUDENE, the U.S. Government displayed thereby its acumen and skill. Not shortsighted at all, in terms of their primary goals, U.S. officials short-circuited a structural solution to Brazil's development problems at precisely the crucial moment, thus assuring a perpetuation of Brazil's internal domination and external dependence. The Northeast Brazil case would be seen as an example of the Alliance's aim to contain Latin America by thwarting basic change. "From this perspective," according to Page, "the work of

[36]Petras and LaPorte, for instance, discuss "ambivalence" within the Kennedy Administration on the redistributionist-productionist issues of agricultural programs, but conclude that this ambivalence was inevitably resolved in favor of the "completely productionist point of view." *Modernization*, p. 260.

[37]The work promoted by the North American Congress on Latin America (NACLA) to stimulate and facilitate empirical research on inter-American relations from a radical perspective represents a potentially important contribution, although few finished research projects are available to date.

[38]Joseph Page, *The Revolution That Never Was: Northeast Brazil 1955-1964* (New York: 1972).

USAID and the CIA must be deemed a great success. The forces of radicalism were defeated, the status quo remained secure, and the Northeast did not become 'another Cuba.'"[39]

André Gunder Frank's more general view of Brazil-U.S. relations states the radical position well:

Far from contributing capital to, and improving the structure of, the Brazilian economy, the United States draws capital out of Brazil and with what remains gains control of Brazilian capital and channels it into directions that increase Brazil's dependence on the United States and hinder Brazil's economic growth. The terms of trade form neither an accidental nor an extraneous part but an integral part of this process. Far from pointing the way to Brazil's industrialization and development, the American Ambassador's recommended policies—emphasis on private enterprise, foreign investment, more raw material exports, etc.—would maintain Brazil's position as an underdeveloped, dependent economy.[40]

"Liberal" and "Radical" Perspectives Contrasted

Although sharply different, the liberal and radical perspectives on the Alliance for Progress, and on inter-American relations generally, share important traits. Each treats the Alliance as if it were a coherent policy, or set of policies, produced by a central apparatus. Each, indeed, accepts the "rational policy model" of foreign policy, assuming that policies are made by unitary, rational actors (analogous to individuals) choosing instruments in accord with established purposes.[41] Liberals tend to assume that policies are derived from stated purposes—some combination of "ideals" and "external political interests" (security, etc.)—although they usually concede that policies also respond partly to "internal political and economic interests"; radicals tend mainly to discount the significance of the first two and to highlight the third.[42] But both concur that "the Government" perceives interests, defines goals, makes decisions, and takes action in accord with identifiable aims.

Liberals, puzzled in the case of the Alliance by the evident dichotomy between stated purposes and perceived actions (and their consequences),

---

[39]Ibid., p. 220.   [40]Frank, *Latin America,* p. 160.

[41]The following discussion draws substantially on the concepts and terminology advanced by Graham Allison, though I am using the term "bureaucratic politics perspective" (as do Halperin and Kanter) to refer generally to both Allison's Model II and his Model III, i.e. "organizational process" and "governmental politics." See Graham T. Allison, *The Essence of Decision: Conceptual Models and the Cuban Missile Crisis* (Boston: 1971); Allison and Morton H. Halperin, "Bureaucratic Politics: A Paradigm and Some Policy Implications," in Raymond Tanter and Richard H. Ullman, eds., *Theory and Policy in International Relations* (Princeton, N.J.: 1972); and Halperin and Arnold Kanter, "The Bureaucratic Perspective: A Preliminary Framework," in Halperin and Kanter, eds., *Readings in American Foreign Policy: A Bureaucratic Perspective* (Boston: 1973), pp. 1–43. Ernest May (this volume) further outlines these concepts and suggests their possible usefulness for analyzing inter-American relations.

[42]See May (this volume).

explain the difference by arguing that the U.S. Government abandoned its purpose, for the kinds of reasons outlined above. Radicals, struck by the same dichotomy, tend to impute purposes from actions and results, and to argue, therefore, that the Alliance's main stated goals were not its "real" ones, or at least not its primary ones. (It may not be accidental, then, that there are so few empirical studies of the Alliance's history grounded in the radical perspective. Since the radical tends to equate results with "policy," there is little to puzzle about in examining the Alliance's demise and no reason to study in detail why things turned out as they did.)[43]

A second trait shared in liberal and radical writings on the Alliance— probably associated with their mutual reliance on the concept and language of "purpose" and their assumption of a unitary, rational actor who can be educated or blamed—is the tendency to present analysis and explanation with a strong overlay of evaluation, even exhortation. Hardly a book or article on the Alliance concludes without either an appeal to American officials to resurrect its principles and establish them as a guide for U.S. actions or a condemnation of the officials for exploiting Latin America and for their hypocrisy in announcing a "policy" so different from their real intentions. Even the most thorough and far-reaching liberal critics (de Onis and Levinson, Lodge, and Roett, for example) frame their argument in terms of particular failures and feel compelled to suggest still another Alliance effort. Similarly, few radical writers are content to "tell it like it is"; they are generally outraged that it should be so. Implicitly or explicitly, they call for a basic change in the United States (including an end to capitalism), which would presumably remove the need for North American exploitation of Latin America and the Third World. The possibility that "domination" and "dependence" might characterize U.S.-Latin American relations regardless of the intentions of U.S. officials or even of the nature of the North American economy does not appear to concern radical critics, whose indignant tone suggests they assume these relations could be transformed.[44]

A third trait that I believe is shared in liberal and radical perspectives is the inability to provide a satisfying, consistent, and concise explana-

---

[43] A second reason why the radical literature on inter-American affairs generally lacks substantial empirical support may be that the radical task so far has been largely reactive and critical, aimed at contradicting the established liberal framework. As the radical critique becomes increasingly conventional at U.S. universities, one may expect a turn toward more substantial research projects such as NACLA proposes. An interesting question is whether these will be funded by established sources of support.

[44] Cf. Howard Becker and Irving Louis Horowitz, "Radical Politics and Sociological Research: Observations on Methodology and Ideology," *American Journal of Sociology,* July 1972, pp. 48–66.

tion for both the Alliance's birth and its death. The liberal view seems to account satisfactorily for the Alliance's creation, and the more detailed and critical versions provide plausible explanations of why this or that aspect of the Alliance was abandoned. But the stark dichotomy between the Alliance's rhetoric and U.S. actions during the 1960s is too overwhelming to leave one satisfied with the liberal explanation of the Alliance as a policy adopted and then abandoned, which could (or even should) be adopted again. Why did the U.S. Government so completely abandon a policy announced with such fanfare? Liberals pose the question that way, and find no easy answer; many focus, therefore, on personalities like Lyndon Johnson and Thomas C. Mann to explain the supposed shift.[45]

The radical critique, for its part, assumes away the problem of explaining the gap between the Alliance's rhetoric and its reality by positing that U.S. actions in Latin America during the 1960s faithfully reflected "real" initial intentions, regardless of what was said. Radicals emphasize the North American aim to isolate and defeat the Cuban Revolution as central to the Alliance's content, style, and timing. They stress, too, the predominant U.S. concern with security, reflected in the counterinsurgency programs that from the start accompanied the Alliance. But why, then, all the flamboyant North American talk about transforming structures in Latin America, about revolutionary social and economic change there? Radical critics can only presume that the Alliance's rhetorical commitment to change was an elaborate put-on, intended to camouflage the traditional U.S. aim to dominate, or else evidence of minimal understanding by U.S. officials of what inter-American relations are really all about. That so many North Americans (including officials as well as the authors of liberal accounts) apparently took the Alliance's early rhetoric seriously can only be attributed to self-delusion or hypocrisy.

The "Bureaucratic" Perspective

At least part of what is inadequate about both the liberal and radical perspectives on the Alliance for Progress might be corrected by consideration of what Graham Allison and others have called the "bureaucratic politics" perspective. This approach, rare among published analyses of inter-American relations, treats U.S. policy not as the choice of a single, rational actor, but rather as the product of a series of overlapping and interlocking bargaining processes within the North American system, involving both intra-governmental and extra-governmental actors.[46] Al-

[45] See, for example, Jerome N. Slater, "Democracy Versus Stability: The Recent Latin American Policy of the United States," *Yale Review,* December 1965, pp. 169–81.

[46] Surprisingly few studies of U.S. Latin American policy adopt this approach. The best ex-

though these processes take place within established parameters and are importantly affected by extra-bureaucratic constraints, including shared values, their products are also very much influenced by events and procedures internal to governmental organizations and often minimized (or overlooked) by liberal and radical observers.

The Alliance as proclaimed in early 1961 would be seen from this perspective as the temporary outcome of internal American political processes that continued to take place thereafter and subsequently produced different results. If one focuses not on the presumed aims of the Alliance as the supposed policy of the U.S. Government as an entity but rather on how the Alliance program came to be declared and later to be implemented (and not), the history and significance of the Alliance may be better understood.

Numerous North American individuals and organizations affect Latin America in some way. The set of those directly affecting U.S. Government policies toward Latin America is much more restricted but nonetheless considerable. Private business and nonbusiness interests of different kinds and degrees of influence play their roles. Business entities—from mineral exporters to tropical-fish salesmen—want special consideration for whatever they buy, sell, or make, or else general improvement in the terms and conditions on which they work. Noncommercial private interests—religious groups, trade unions, academic specialists and institutions, groups united by common interests or causes, foundations, journalists and press associations, etc.—bring a wide variety of aims and perspectives to bear with differing degrees of effectiveness at various points in the policy-making process.

Within the U.S. Government, too, a great number of interests and views come into play. Each agency has its own clienteles and constituencies, its own personnel and recruitment, its own tasks and routines, its own piece of the mosaic. The Defense Department and the CIA busy themselves mainly with protecting what are regarded as U.S. security interests, and scour Latin America looking for potential "threats." But the Defense Department is also out to protect its various institutional interests—to sell surplus or new equipment, for instance—and no agency escapes that

---

amples are R. Harrison Wagner, *United States Policy Toward Latin America: A Study in Domestic and International Politics* (Stanford, Cal.: 1970) and Wagner, "Explaining and Judging U.S.-Latin American Policies," unpublished paper prepared for the Second National Meeting of the Latin American Studies Association, Washington, D.C. (April 16–19, 1970). Another useful illustration is Richard J. Bloomfield, "Who Makes American Foreign Policy?: Some Latin American Case Studies," unpublished paper presented at the Center for International Affairs, Harvard University (April 1972). See also Abraham F. Lowenthal, *The Dominican Intervention* (Cambridge, Mass.: 1972), and Joseph Tulchin, "Inhibitions Affecting the Formulation and Execution of the Latin American Policy of the United States," *Ventures,* Fall 1967, pp. 68–80.

tendency. The Treasury Department concerns itself with protecting the U.S. balance of payments, the Commerce Department with expanding U.S. exports, and the Agriculture Department with disposing of surplus crops. The White House staff, presumably imbued with the President's own perspective and concerned (among other matters) especially with his prestige and influence, is sensitive not only to possible threats but also to whatever opportunities are presented by Latin American issues to enhance the President's position. The White House staff is particularly aware of the partisan political implications of Latin American policy decisions and may provide the main point of access for those with political claims. The State Department, lacking its own constituency, is responsive to pressures from all sides; its institutional bias is probably toward continuity and toward accommodation with foreign governments. And aside from all these institutional interests affecting intra-governmental considerations of Latin American issues, there are the personal stakes of individuals whose views on specific matters are inevitably bound up with their own egos and ambitions and are conditioned by their psychological makeup.[47]

U.S. Latin American policy (or U.S. foreign policy generally) emerges from the interplay of many actors who take part in a political process so arranged that it "has the effect of guaranteeing that those interests and points of view that are organized and articulate are injected without much alteration right into the center of the decision-making process."[48] Each of the actors has a different weight and influence, depending on many considerations: the substance of the issue being considered, the context in which it is raised, the power, skills, stakes, and style of participants in the policy-making process and their relative access to the relevant action and implementation channels—even the order in which participants take part. Actors with varying, sometimes conflicting, aims and views may have predominant influence with respect to different but related issues. The overall outcome of the process, therefore, need not be coherent, and often is not. That agencies with differing concepts, personnel, and procedures are eventually called upon to "implement policy," and thereby to shape it, further increases the likelihood that what comes out of the policy-making process reflects at least some of the variety of interests that feed in. (There are limits, of course, to what goes in, in the sense, for example, that no individual or organization is knowingly pursuing an objective adverse to the interests of all North Americans, and

[47] See May (this volume).
[48] Wagner, "Explaining," p. 12. An additional major influence on U.S. Latin American policy-making, the subject of remarkably little research, has been the Congress and its committees, which often provide an effective channel for the expression of various private interests.

that shared premises and values importantly shape the goals and procedures of all actors.) The relative importance of various influences on policy-making may vary greatly over time, and governmental actions and "policy" may consequently change, sometimes dramatically, with or without an amendment of official pronouncements.[49]

In the case of the Alliance for Progress, one may discern several reasons why the amalgam of influences on the North American policy-making process was critically different at the moment of the Alliance's inception from what it would be at any later point. Consideration of the Alliance came early during the administration of a new president, a time when the U.S. policy-making process always is unusually centralized and therefore more accessible than usual to those who propose new measures, and more likely to frame a coherent, inclusive formulation.[50] The early Kennedy Administration, like all incipient regimes, was not only receptive to novel and comprehensive approaches to old problems, but actively interested in a new mode for dealing with Latin America, an area the Presidential candidate had cited repeatedly as an example of the Eisenhower Administration's failure in foreign affairs.[51] The new President sought a policy for Latin America, consistent with his Administration's New Frontier commitment to "get America moving again," which would visibly draw on active U.S. involvement to improve inter-American relations.

Given the nature of Kennedy's political coalition and the makeup of his immediate staff, the new Administration turned to scholars for advice in designing its Latin American policy. Specialists, many of them personally and professionally committed to "inter-American cooperation" and particularly attentive to Latin American points of view, advocated changed North American attitudes and actions in order to remove what they considered artificial obstacles to improved U.S.-Latin American relations. Other groups, in addition to academic specialists, had exceptional access to policy-makers at the time the Alliance program was designed. Puerto Rican and other Caribbean politicians (e.g., Luis Muñoz Marín, Teodoro Moscoso, Arturo Morales Carrión, Rómulo Betancourt, and José Figueres) had a channel to the White House, mainly because they were closely linked to Adolf Berle, who directed the Latin American task force, and to others of the Eastern liberal Democratic advisers (like Arthur Schlesinger, Jr.) who surrounded President Kennedy and wrote

---

[49] The "bureaucratic politics" perspective, therefore, produces some skepticism about the capacity of the U.S. Government to pursue in a sustained manner a coherent Latin American policy. See Mitchell (this volume).

[50] See Wagner, *United States Policy*, pp. 150–51.

[51] See, for instance, Arthur M. Schlesinger, Jr., *A Thousand Days: John F. Kennedy in the White House* (Boston: 1965), p. 183.

many of his speeches.[52] Some of these, plus some Washington-based South American economists, even participated closely with the White House staff in drafting President Kennedy's major speech of March 13, 1961, outlining the Alliance; the State Department, on the contrary, had little hand in it.[53]

Those with a personal and ideological stake in promoting institutional democracy thus had a great deal to do with formulating the Alliance; career diplomats, who traditionally seek nonhostile relations with all types of regimes (not just democracies) were little more than bystanders at this point, though they were later expected to put American "policy" into effect. A similar division plagued the management of Latin American policy well into the Kennedy Administration, as Latin American policy decisions were largely entrusted to Berle, Schlesinger, and Goodwin, while one candidate after another turned down the post of Assistant Secretary of State for American Republic Affairs.[54] Even after Robert F. Woodward was finally appointed, in June 1961, the struggle between "Kennedy men" and "career men" continued to shape the making of U.S. policy.[55] As the President's own concern with Latin American issues diminished, so did the influence of his personal appointees relative to that of established bureaucrats.

While academic specialists, Caribbean politicians, and Presidential assistants had considerable influence on the making of U.S. Latin American policy early in the Kennedy Administration, other actors, conversely, had extraordinarily reduced roles. Corporate influence, particularly, was unusually limited for a number of reasons. First, President Kennedy's personal concern about the supposed security threat in Latin America— a concern deepened by Castro's stance in Cuba and reinforced by Khrushchev's January 1961 announcement of Russian support for "wars of national liberation"—caused the White House early in 1961 to approach Latin America mainly in national strategic terms.

Second, while many businessmen had been among those exercising policy-making responsibilities during the Eisenhower Administration,

[52] The Latin American task force consisted of Berle, Moscoso, Morales Carrión, three U.S. professors (Lincoln Gordon, Robert Alexander, and Arthur Whitaker) and Richard Goodwin, the gifted young speech writer who had actually coined the phrase "Alianza para el Progreso," during the 1960 election campaign. Revealingly, Goodwin's first formulation of the phrase in Spanish was grammatically incorrect ("Alianza para Progreso"). See Schlesinger, *A Thousand Days,* p. 183, and Levinson and de Onis, *Alliance,* 52–55.

[53] According to Levinson and de Onis, Assistant Secretary of State Mann returned the draft speech to the White House without comment or criticism, and Secretary of State Dean Rusk made but one substantive suggestion. Levinson and de Onis, *Alliance,* p. 58.

[54] See de Lesseps S. Morrison (with Gerold Frank), *Latin American Mission: An Adventure in Hemisphere Diplomacy* (New York: 1965), pp. 28, 66.

[55] Ibid., p. 223, and Schlesinger, *A Thousand Days,* pp. 231, 696–97.

businessmen were rare among Kennedy's appointees; of his first 200 appointments, 6 percent came from business and 18 percent from universities and foundations, compared to 42 percent and 6 percent respectively for the same posts in the Eisenhower period.[56] Finally, and perhaps most important, corporate interests and leaders were not generally part of the circle to which President Kennedy's key advisers on Latin America (especially Schlesinger, Goodwin, and Ralph Dungan in the White House) naturally responded, nor did they constitute a major part of the President's domestic political constituency.[57]

Far from reflecting big-business domination of U.S. foreign policy, therefore, the Alliance commitment emerged in part because of the unusual (and temporary) reduction of corporate influence in the foreign policy-making process. The few businessmen involved in early Alliance policy-making were primarily those who favored the kind of Latin American development the Alliance as proclaimed promised to promote; the Alliance's main goals were established before they were even consulted. The Alliance was not dictated by big-business interests, nor was it a mere rhetorical pose, adopted simply to camouflage traditional North American imperial designs. Rather, the Alliance's proclamation resulted from a political and bureaucratic process stacked temporarily to weight the influence of persons and groups genuinely interested in the Alliance's stated goals. If the Alliance rhetoric camouflaged anything, it was not the intentions of the framers but rather the lack of substantial agreement throughout the U.S. bureaucracy regarding the priority and feasibility of the announced aims.

Specific review of the Alliance's birth from the bureaucratic-politics perspective tends to contradict the radical position, at least as argued in the available literature. A bureaucratic-politics approach to the Alliance's implementation phase, however, lends support—if not to the radical position as generally argued—to the basic radical contention that the U.S. Government's virtual abandonment of the Alliance's reform thrust was not accidental but rather a predictable result of the way foreign policy-making relates to the North American economy. For when the salience of Latin American security problems diminished and the normal processes and channels for considering Latin American issues were restored, the extensive U.S. business interests involved in Latin America were able to make themselves felt more forcefully again. (The confluence of

[56]From calculations done by Professor Seymour Harris as reported in Schlesinger, *A Thousand Days,* p. 199.

[57]Levinson and de Onis note, for instance, that the Administration did not invite businessmen to participate in the first Punta del Este meetings until three days before the conference, and even then only as observers (*Alliance,* p. 71).

substantial transnational relations between the United States and Latin America and the relative unimportance of security considerations in this hemisphere remains, indeed, the major fact shaping contemporary inter-American relations.)

Partly because corporate attempts to influence Latin American policies were systematic and sustained, business groups were able eventually to transform several Alliance programs into instruments for North American private gain, however far this result was from the intent of those who had drafted the Alliance's early doctrines. Partly because U.S. military attempts to assure continuing influence in Latin America were persistent and unimpeded; security aspects of the Alliance evolved from a coordinate aspect of U.S. policy into a predominant one. Partly because those who pressed for social, political, and economic reforms as the essence of the Alliance had so few bases of support in the North American political and economic system, including the bureaucracy, those parts of the Alliance program soon lost force. Asking the State Department bureaucracy to implement a policy adversely affecting U.S. private interests as well as perhaps undermining the power base of foreign governments with which the United States maintained friendly relations, without instituting major administrative and political efforts to assure that these programs would actually be carried out, was predictably ineffective. Arthur Schlesinger, Jr., took delight in his ability to take "full advantage of the White House leverage and the Presidential mandate" to assure that a document he drafted on Latin American policy emerged "substantially intact" from the bureaucracy.[58] One more sensitive to bureaucratic politics would have been concerned equally, or more, about what happened to the implementation of "policies" after such documents were cleared.[59]

Summary

What this paper suggests is that to explain or predict U.S. Government actions in and toward Latin America (whether during the Alliance period

[58] Schlesinger, *A Thousand Days*, p. 231.

[59] The usefulness of an approach focusing on organizational processes and bureaucratic politics might be further suggested by considering the case of Northeast Brazil. Available material and time do not permit me to frame an alternative interpretation of the Brazil case here, but an analyst sensitive to the foreign policy-making process would ask questions like these: Who in the U.S. Government took an interest in Northeast Brazil, how, why, when, and for how long? In what ways did the identity, stakes, and relative influence of participants in the process of making U.S. policy toward Northeast Brazil change over time? What different assumptions were made by various U.S. actors about the nature of Northeast Brazil's problems and about U.S. interests there? How did those assumptions relate to the primary missions of each of the various U.S. agencies involved? What mechanisms existed to assure that the perspective and premises of the President and the White House staff would be shared by State Department, AID, and CIA officials in Rio and Recife? What were the standard operating procedures of the United States mis-

or at any other time) one should probably not start—or at least certainly not stop—with the question "what goals account for American actions?" Nor should one make the assumption that the U.S. Government as a whole pursues an objective (or a set of objectives) that may be either presumed or imputed. Distinct organizations within the U.S. Government, and even individuals and groups within organizations, pursue their own aims in accord with varying conceptions, premises, and procedures. Clearly, some of these aims and concepts coincide (or nearly coincide) across the Government and even over time, accounting in part for some of the regularities in the international behavior of the United States. Generally accepted values, images, and premises set some of the parameters for U.S. foreign policy, and explication of all these should be central for foreign policy analysis.[60] But these common elements do not explain all foreign policy occurrences; intra-governmental differences, even conflicts, account for much of what is puzzling.

To improve our understanding of U.S. Latin American policy, we should be concerned not only with goals and results, as liberal and radical writers are, but also with other factors that determine foreign policy outcomes. In particular, we should focus more on the bureaucratic and political processes that translate (often inadequately) intents into actions.[61]

The available writings on the Alliance, and on the making of U.S. foreign policy toward Latin America generally, do not facilitate this kind of analysis. Much more work has been done comparing acts and their consequences to stated purposes (and thereby evaluating "policy") than showing how varying aims relate to each other in the decision-making and implementation processes. It would be most useful if some students of U.S. Latin American policy undertook to study the relative influence of a number of distinct actors on policy formulation and implementation, at different stages and with respect to different kinds of issues. Most, perhaps all, of the main institutional actors—inside the Government and out—have been identified, but little empirical work has been done on

---

sion in Brazil (for reporting on the use of U.S. funds, for instance), and how did these affect the concerns and actions of United States personnel?

[60] I regard as perhaps the most fruitful area for research on U.S. policy to be precisely the analysis of the various factors that structure and constrain bureaucratic consideration of alternative foreign policy actions, and of how they do so.

[61] I should perhaps emphasize that this essay addresses itself only to the study of United States Government policy toward Latin America, not more generally to U.S.-Latin American relations. The "bureaucratic politics" perspective is presumably somewhat less useful for studying the latter subject because it focuses attention on governmental decisions and actions, rather than on the series of nongovernmental national and transnational processes which so importantly affect the overall interaction between North American society and those of Latin America. Even for studying the latter, however, an approach concentrating on bureaucratic structure and behavior should be helpful.

how each contributes to the making of Latin American policy. Studies are needed, for instance, of the people who take part in the policy-making process at each of several points: their attitudes, assumptions, values, training, psychological characteristics, socioeconomic ties, etc.[62] Research is required to identify the characteristic action channels for several types of policy issues and to ascertain who has what kinds of access at what stages to those channels. It would be helpful to analyze the processes by which information about Latin American issues is sought, analyzed, and communicated in various parts of the bureaucracy, and to determine how the premises underlying the questions asked differ from agency to agency. Examination of the control and coordination mechanisms affecting U.S. Latin American policy would also be helpful.

Case studies are needed of how U.S. Government policies have been made with respect to various kinds of issues—commodity agreements, treatment of U.S. investments, military assistance, etc.—involving several different agencies and interests. Detailed studies are also needed on how the U.S. Government has managed (or failed to manage) its overall relations in such a way that various countries of the hemisphere have been affected differently by the expression of U.S. interests through different Government institutions. And research is needed on the mechanisms used by private organizations, including national and transnational institutions and especially corporate enterprises, to affect U.S. Government policy or to bypass it.

In short, improved studies of U.S. Latin American policy will require hard work, some of it focused on the American policy-making process. Obviously, other research emphases are also desirable. More must be done to analyze the specific consequences of the manifest asymmetries of various kinds of power that characterize U.S.-Latin American relations. The concepts of dependency theory must be formulated in the form of testable hypotheses and applied to particular cases. The effects in the United States and in Latin America of prevailing concepts in each region about the nature of politics in the other might be profitably studied, as might the processes by which each society informs itself about the other. Further examples abound.

Perhaps this paper, exploring some of the inadequacies of the conventional liberal and radical approaches to these tasks and suggesting the usefulness of a complementary bureaucratic-politics perspective, will be a useful contribution.

---

[62]For one interesting attempt to do this kind of research, not on Latin American policy officials but on State Department and Defense Department officials generally, see Bernard Mennis, *American Foreign Policy Officials: Who They Are and What They Believe Regarding International Politics* (Columbus, Ohio: 1971). Another attempt, less systematic but nonetheless worthwhile, is Richard Barnet, *Roots of War* (New York: 1972).

Commentary on Lowenthal

HERACLIO BONILLA

Abraham Lowenthal's essay consists of two basic parts. The first discusses the characteristics and limitations of two main approaches to the Alliance for Progress: the liberal and the radical. According to the author, despite the different nature of these two approaches, the two are based on the same faulty premise: that the Alliance is the result of a coherent policy. Lowenthal questions this premise, relying on Graham Allison's notion of "bureaucratic politics," a perspective that "treats U.S. policy not as the choice of a single, rational actor, but rather as the product of a series of overlapping and interlocking bargaining processes within the North American system. . . . Although these processes take place within established parameters and are importantly affected by extra-bureaucratic constraints, . . . their products are also very much influenced by events and procedures internal to governmental organizations." In other words, what is postulated here is the existence of a bureaucratic rationality separate from and opposed to the basic instruments of power found in every society. Specifically, it is argued that the relative success achieved in the early days of the Alliance was due to the fact that the Kennedy Administration had only recently taken office. This permitted a scope of action that was relatively broad, broad even to the point of working against the basic interests of the traditional sources of power and pressure. Consequently, the failure of the Alliance, according to this analysis, was due on the one hand to the separation that a bureaucratic organization establishes between intention and action, and on the other hand to the ultimate reconciliation of power and bureaucracy.

I must confess that I am not particularly averse to such an approach, provided that two conditions are met. First, we must be offered a far more convincing analysis of the relationship between power and bureaucracy, and of the concrete historical conditions through which a bureaucracy is actually able to obtain *relative* autonomy. To say that bureau-

Heraclio Bonilla is a member of the Institute of Peruvian Studies, Lima.

cracy separates from and later reintegrates itself to power is an excellent observation, but not an explanation. Second, the problem of U.S. policies must not be reduced to a mere problem of administering power and the Government. It is true that there is a lack of unity among ends, means, and actions, just as it is true that the system does not always process either its decisions or its actions coherently. Nevertheless, it is also apparent that there is a rationality within this irrationality. To fail to recognize this rationality, and above all to fail to analyze its structure, is to condemn thought to absolute impotence.

A specific system of power exists in all societies structured along class lines. The ruling class, through its monopoly of power, not only guarantees the subordination and the cohesion of the entire system, but also expresses and pursues its own interests. From these premises, however, it is not possible to infer that *class* and *power* are absolutely identical, for institutions mediate between the two. Examples of such institutions are the various units of a society's public administration. To consider these units, which merely administer power, as the very source of power is a great mistake. It is certainly probable in some crisis situations, or situations of stalemated power between the dominant classes or sectors of the same dominant class, that a bureaucracy (if it is stable) could acquire some autonomy in relation to the ruling class—even to the point of making decisions in opposition to the interests of that class. In this case, however, although a decision's ambivalences and failures are expressed through the organizational structure, all of this is directly rooted in the problems inherent in the consolidation, hegemony, and internal tensions of a class. It is precisely for this reason that the relative separation of the Government's bureaucratic apparatus from the class that controls the power can only be temporary. Ultimately, the compatibility between intention and action leads to the dominant class's reconquest of its bureaucracy.

The failure of the Alliance for Progress, however, cannot be satisfactorily explained in this manner. If its birth is closely linked to Cuba, that is, as a concession made by North American imperialism in the face of Latin America's challenge, and from fear of losing the sources of capitalist accumulation, then the Alliance's failure was the failure of a policy that attempted to harmonize inter-American relations while leaving the roots and mechanisms of exploitation intact. Seen in this way, the Alliance's failure had little or nothing to do with the confusions within the North American bureaucracy. These confusions were not the cause, but rather the result of hemispheric struggles and external and internal reactions to the North American system. The Alliance's failure is a sign and a symptom indicating that the explosions and the aspirations of Latin America's popular classes can no longer be checked nor satisfied by reforms, however bold they may be.

U.S. Latin American Policy in the 1970s: New Forms of Control?

LUIGI R. EINAUDI

On April 17, 1961, Cuban exiles landed at the Bay of Pigs. Among the supporting operations controlled by the Central Intelligence Agency was Radio Swan, which broadcast propaganda and instructions to saboteurs inside Cuba. Radio Swan's transmitters were located in trailers on Great Swan Island, which the United States had claimed since 1863.[1] On September 1, 1972, the then Acting U.S. Secretary of State John N. Irwin II and Roberto Alonzo Cleaves, Chargé d'Affaires *ad interim* of the Embassy of Honduras in Washington, exchanged their respective governments' instruments of ratification of a treaty providing for U.S. recognition of Honduran sovereignty over the Swan Islands.

In many ways, none quite as symbolic, but most just as unnoticed as the Swan Island ceremony, the United States has gradually begun to dismantle what had seemed to constitute an interventionist apparatus aimed at Latin America's very independence. The mere existence and nature of any such "interventionist apparatus" is, of course, open to considerable debate, and thus complicates any discussion of its "dismantling." But U.S. policy has appeared largely in this light to many observers since the U.S. interventions in Guatemala and Cuba.[2] Yet the signs of change, ranging from the 1967 National Student Association revolt against CIA financing, to the decline in U.S. military assistance programs (no equipment grants

Luigi Einaudi is a senior staff member of The RAND Corporation, Santa Monica, California. This paper, written while the author was on leave of absence to attend the Lima conference, should not be thought to represent the views of RAND or of any of its private or governmental research sponsors.

[1] Radio Swan is mentioned in most studies of the Bay of Pigs, but its history and that of Great Swan Island are most explicitly told in David Wise and Thomas B. Ross, *The Invisible Government* (New York: 1964), pp. 328–37.

[2] Of the many works along these lines that could be cited, one of the most relentless and best documented (its author is a U.S.-educated Panamanian journalist who was stationed in Washington from 1959 to 1966) is Leopoldo Aragón, *Por qué y cómo somos satélites de EEUU* (Lima: Moncloa, 1968).

to the major Latin American countries since 1968, and a reduction of overall military grant aid to less than one-fourth of the 1966 peak), are too numerous to be dismissed. Indeed, the entire range of U.S. instruments and attitudes, from covert operations to inter-governmental relationships, appears to be in flux. Nor have the ideological and paternalist justifications for intervention that characterized even the generous reforming impulses of the Alliance for Progress been unaffected. Something is clearly afoot when a U.S. President comments that:

We have sometimes imagined that we knew what was best for everyone else and that we could and should make it happen. Well, experience has taught us better. . . . Our partnership should be one in which the United States lectures less and listens more. It should be one in which . . . the shaping of the future of the nations of the Americas reflects the will of these nations.[3]

Underscoring the change in atmosphere since the early 1960s, the U.S. Government has recently shown considerable restraint when confronted with political and economic challenges to lo.,g-standing U.S. interests. The Nixon Administration, for example, avoided direct conflict with Peru over the uncompensated seizure of the International Petroleum Company in 1968, despite the pressure of Standard Oil of New Jersey and the requirements of U.S. law, which called for a termination of assistance programs and elimination of Peru's sugar quota after six months. And despite the ominous scenarios and angry representations of another corporate giant, ITT, the new flexibility was confirmed by U.S. unwillingness to become entrapped in overtly hostile acts against Chile's "Marxist" government after 1970.

U.S. policy, however, has been explained only in rather general statements like those cited above from President Nixon's 1969 speech calling for a "mature partnership." This lack of explicit definition, together with an apparent absence of consistent attention, has sustained a high degree of uncertainty, both about current U.S. policy and concerning possible future courses of action by the United States. Without clear policy guidance or general consensus on the direction of policy, the past and present mix in the habits and entrenched patterns and programs that shape bureaucratic behavior, even when the original sources of that behavior are no longer valid. Confusion about U.S. Latin American policy is compounded by the fact that intellectual observers and practicing politicians—North and South alike—sometimes still appear to be reacting with the reflexes of the past. The tendency is still strong, for example, for

[3] Richard M. Nixon, "Action for Progress for the Americas," an address made before the Inter-American Press Association at Washington, D.C., October 31, 1969, as printed in *The Department of State Bulletin,* vol. 61, no. 1586, November 17, 1969, pp. 409–14.

North Americans to consider criticisms of U.S. policy in Latin America as somehow related to "Communist" activity, or to encourage Latin America to follow U.S. prescriptions for change and "democracy." Similarly, many Latin Americans are quick to denounce U.S. activities, or even developments in their own countries they do not understand or like, as manifestations of U.S. "imperialism."[4] Though relations are in flux, the intellectual and emotional heritages of the past hinder our understanding the sources of contemporary policy—not to mention its formulation, implementation, and communication.

What *are* the sources of U.S. Latin American policy today? And how are U.S. interests and policy instruments likely to evolve in Latin America over the next five to ten years? This paper seeks a preliminary answer by examining first the recent evolution of attitudes toward foreign affairs in U.S. domestic politics, and then the emerging environment of inter-American relations and the world scene.

Two Views of the "Low Profile"

My conclusion is essentially that the lessened attention given Latin American problems in the United States today accurately reflects both a general loss of interest in Latin America as a politically strategic area and an uncertainty over what policies to adopt in a fluid world environment and in the face of substantial Latin American criticism of past U.S. policies. Preoccupied with Vietnam and with domestic issues, U.S. leaders have adopted a passive approach to all but the most pressing problems. And Latin American policy, it seems, is generally not considered among these, perhaps partly because no simple prescription seems likely to apply. The result of these profound changes in U.S. perceptions is that U.S. Government activities in the hemisphere today are considerably less interventionist than those of the 1960s were. But they are also considerably less supportive of Latin American development. For reasons discussed below, at least some of these shifts in attitude are likely to be transient; the chief problem before us is thus how to utilize the present lull to hammer out future policies that will maximize mutual rather than unilateral interests.

Before developing these arguments further, however, it is necessary to consider briefly an alternative hypothesis that is widely shared among Latin American observers of U.S. policy. According to this view, the changes in U.S. activities in Latin America do not represent fundamental

---

[4]My use of quotation marks (as in "Communism," "democracy," and "imperialism" above) reflects my belief that these concepts (each of which has several tolerably precise meanings) are commonly so abused as to become virtually meaningless, except as expressions of a state of mind, which is the sense in which they apply here.

changes in U.S. perceptions or policy, but constitute rather a tactical shift, the adoption of new (and generally more intelligent) "forms of control" by the United States over Latin America.

According to this analysis, the United States, or at least its ruling forces, has a permanent interest, largely economic, in maintaining hegemony over Latin America. The means required to maintain this domination change with changing circumstances. Thus, for instance, the emergence of the Good Neighbor policy represented a tactical shift, required by the ineffectiveness of Dollar Diplomacy and the Big Stick in advancing U.S. economic interests. The overt noninterventionism of the Good Neighbor was in time supplemented by covert intervention and finally by the strengthening of military and police forces under the screen of the "developmentalist" legitimacy provided by the Alliance for Progress. Continuing this line of reasoning, we see that the often crude interventionism of the 1950s and 1960s is also giving way to fresh tactics. Subtle new "forms of control," known generally as the "low profile," enable the United States to continue its domination. These new tactics are said to include indirect economic pressures, exercised chiefly through international financial institutions, and the delegation of direct interventionism to the more powerful Latin American nations, such as Brazil, which, having been drawn into the U.S. orbit by prior economic and military programs, are now capable of acting as indirect executors of U.S. political and military intentions.

The sweep of this argument is breathtaking, and though some might find it appealing for that very reason, I am somewhat troubled by its failure to discriminate between different U.S. interests and agencies, public and private, and by its assumptions of unified rationality and control over time.[5] To be sure, there is much in the argument that is more accurate than most North Americans would care to admit. Some forms of intervention have indeed had to be modified or abandoned, partly because they became counterproductive.[6] But I also find this a rather emotional

---

[5] One does not have to be a partisan of the work of Graham Allison to point out that policy is an outgrowth of conflict, and hence is only rarely formulated or executed consistently. Interestingly, even Allison's *Essence of Decision: Explaining the Cuban Missile Crisis* (Boston: 1971), perhaps because of the case he examined, concentrates almost exclusively on the Executive bureaucracy and overlooks the roles of political purpose, private U.S. economic interests, and Congress, all three of which are critical to an understanding of U.S.-Latin American relations.

[6] Thus, for example, Bryce Wood has documented that the U.S. withdrawal of Marines from Nicaragua in the early 1930s was due partially to the growing conviction that "the absence of Marines offered the best protection to U.S. citizens in Nicaragua." *The Making of the Good Neighbor Policy* (New York: 1961), p. 45. But then neither Wood nor another eminent American scholar of the period, Dana Munro, would agree that economic factors were the dominant reason for the Marine landings in the first place. Munro, in fact, explicitly argues that "the motives that inspired [U.S.] policy were basically political rather than economic." See Dana G. Munro, *Intervention and Dollar Diplomacy in the Caribbean, 1900-1921* (Princeton, N.J.: 1964), p. 531.

and politically impotent argument. Despite its assumption that changing Latin American conditions have forced tactical shifts on the part of the United States, it implies that Latin America has been and is likely to remain ultimately a pawn of U.S. manipulation.[7] Without minimizing the enormous differences in power between "the United States," globally considered, and the individual states of Latin America, I am convinced that Latin America's "margin of freedom" is substantial and growing, and is overlooked by an overly great concentration on "dependence." Moreover, the focus on the United States as a rationally organized and motivated power is a corollary of the equally fallacious American belief in unlimited U.S. power—a belief already challenged in Latin America by the Bay of Pigs, and now given a political *coup de grâce* by events in Vietnam. Indeed, Vietnam offers us a useful beginning from which to reconstruct something of what is actually happening to U.S. approaches to Latin America.

The Political Crisis in the United States

Vietnam has for several years been the chief problem of U.S. foreign policy and the major focus of political attention.[8] The logic of disengagement from the Vietnamese folly has now led the U.S. Government to seek more cooperative relations with both the Soviet Union and China. One result has been to accelerate a tendency toward a world political and economic multipolarity already foreshadowed by the resurgence of Europe and Japan from the devastation of World War II, by the widening differences within the "socialist bloc," and by the refusal of many countries of the "Third World" to allow themselves to be drawn into a bipolar system. Understanding and participating constructively in the new international system now gradually replacing the broken post-World War II balance, is understandably the first priority of U.S. foreign policy.

But the Vietnam war has also combined with the press of domestic problems within the United States to produce a generalized revulsion against "foreign entanglements" among the North American public. One consequence, in addition to a climate of hostility and divided opinion that bedevils all concerned with foreign policy, has been great pressure on U.S. foreign-assistance programs, economic as well as military, which have been in growing difficulty in Congress throughout the past decade.

---

[7] A historically more accurate view, reflecting "the intractability of societies, especially to outside control" is quite amply documented in Herbert Goldhamer's excellent and highly empirical *The Foreign Powers in Latin America* (Princeton, N.J.: 1972), which examines the varied interests and activities of major foreign powers, including the United States, in Latin America.

[8] Perhaps for this very reason we should be cautious about ascribing to it trends that were already developing, but for only partially related reasons. Yet Vietnam has become that political rarity: a touchstone of political and self-definition that cannot be ignored, even if one desired.

The U.S. Senate Foreign Relations Committee, to borrow from one Washington observer, seems quite unbureaucratically bent on eliminating the reasons for its existence by urging the Executive to curtail or eliminate U.S. foreign commitments.

In this environment, the Alliance for Progress, and with it much of the political-military interventionism characteristic of U.S. Latin American policy during the 1960s, has been quietly abandoned. This retreat from interventionism (no new Marines, for example, since 1965) does not require as an explanation either a sudden growth of sympathetic understanding for Latin America or the emergence of a new U.S. "imperialist master plan." Rather more prosaically, the origins of current policy are to be found in a desire to avoid problems that might divert attention and resources from more important issues. The main objective of U.S. Latin American policy today, therefore, is not positive, but negative: to avert conflict through compromise. Anything goes so long as it is quiet.[9]

Coming on the heels of the bureaucratized hyperactivism of the Alliance, this style is distinctly refreshing. It may even work relatively well for a while. But it cannot be a permanent approach to policy. Among the many issues that today require increased attention from the U.S. Government are the entire range of economic relations within the hemisphere, both bilateral and multilateral, as well as the establishment of new patterns of political and military relations outside the traditional but now slowly dissolving "assistance" framework. Specific problems that cannot be avoided much longer include the relationship between expropriation of U.S. properties and U.S. policy toward the international lending agencies, an area in which Executive indecision has already produced much Congressional heavy-handedness; trade and investment policies, including transfers of arms and technology, but essentially focused on the place of direct U.S. private investment in Latin American industries, and on the availability of U.S. markets for nontraditional Latin American exports; and a host of other issues, including relations with Cuba, the future status of the Panama Canal, and the rise of Brazilian power in South America.

But it is one thing to be aware of the need to recast policy and quite another to in fact do so. The Rockefeller Report was issued for public consideration, but not generally implemented.[10] Its fate, like the contin-

[9] Although this description is obviously something of a caricature, let me emphasize that it is not meant as criticism. I, for one, prefer inaction to imposition, no matter how well intentioned. Nonetheless, my chief interest in this paper is analytical rather than judgmental: I am more interested in understanding than in attacking, and if I occasionally use value-laden characterizations, even then my primary purpose is descriptive rather than normative.

[10] This report, fatally flawed by its use of cold war terminology and assumptions of U.S. power at a time when both were increasingly being questioned, remains an important statement of

uing debates over U.S. policies throughout the world, not just in Latin America, suggests that the process of redefining U.S. roles abroad is likely to be thoroughly agonizing. For at least the past ten years, as the post-World War II bipartisan consensus on foreign policy began to break down, North American national leaders have had great difficulty in formulating and then communicating policies commensurate with a true sense of both the limits and potentials of U.S. power and responsibilities. Once again, Vietnam serves to illustrate this weakness of the U.S. ruling class.[11] After a decade of escalating and often futile warfare, even today's (November 1972) perilous steps toward peace are being sought through lonely individual efforts, with much of the national-security bureaucracy and most political leaders of both national parties acting as helplessly disoriented bystanders.[12]

What is surprising, it should be emphasized, is not that minorities should rule, but that the minority in the United States today should be so thin and divided. The inability of the Democratic Party to mount a serious political challenge to President Nixon in the 1972 elections merely underscores this point, for in my view, Nixon (himself a lonely man with little party organization) won largely because George McGovern failed to present a coherent and credible governing alternative.[13]

The United States, in other words, is currently traversing a period of profound intellectual and moral uncertainty, internally and internationally. The Vietnam war and concern over domestic priorities have fostered

---

many problems of hemispheric relations. See, of the various editions, Nelson A. Rockefeller, *The Rockefeller Report on the Americas, The Official Report of a United States Presidential Mission for the Western Hemisphere* (Chicago: *The New York Times* edition, 1969).

[11] I do not want to be drawn into a debate over the existence or nonexistence of a U.S. "ruling class," particularly as my basic point is weakness rather than strength. In general, however, my suspicion is that de Tocqueville is a better guide to the internal diversity and failure of political leadership in the United States than either Marx or C. Wright Mills.

[12] Again, a point of clarification. Despite (and perhaps in part because of) the mutual suspicions and even hatreds engendered by American involvement in Vietnam, there is overwhelming agreement in the United States today over the need to end the war. My point here is that how to do so, and with what implications, remains remarkably obscure—at least to judge from the public debate—even among specialists in such matters, most of whom do not appear to have been drawn into the Nixon-Kissinger deliberations.

[13] This is meant, not as a partisan statement, but rather as an expression of agreement with V. O. Key's contention that "In American presidential campaigns of recent decades, the portrait of the American electorate that develops from the data is not one of an electorate straight-jacketed by social determinants or moved by subconscious urges triggered by devilishly skillful propagandists. It is rather one of an electorate moved by concern about central and relevant questions of public policy, of governmental performance, and of executive personality." V.O. Key, Jr., *The Responsible Electorate: Rationality in Presidential Voting, 1936-1960* (Cambridge, Mass.: 1966), pp. 7-8. There was undoubtedly an element of racism in the Nixon vote, as there was of blind oppositionism in the McGovern vote, but it would appear that Richard Nixon, on balance, was the better representative of the reflective as well as the darker sides of the electorate.

divisions that frequently remain beyond the capacity of U.S. leaders or political parties to articulate constructively. Lack of consensus in turn makes policy difficult to define or defend. Domestic support for the dé-tente in the cold war is matched by uncertainty over the basis and nature of emerging patterns of world politics and economics.

Short-Term Prospects

If uncertainty marks many of the central issues confronting the United States, what then can we say about the future course of U.S. policy to-ward Latin America, a region which is rightly or wrongly consigned to a low priority in the United States today? Further, does the reelection of Richard Nixon preclude changes in U.S. Latin American policy?

Two considerations force themselves upon us with some strength to suggest that it does not. The first is that even lack of attention does not necessarily imply that bureaucratic routines will take over and policy will remain unchanged. Indeed, if current trends persist unchanged, bilateral economic and military assistance programs will go out of existence, at least as we have known them since World War II. From a North American standpoint, the Alliance for Progress was in many respects a delayed ap-plication of the principles of U.S. responsibility and leadership expressed earlier in the Marshall Plan. To take another example, military assistance to Latin America is also largely a reflection of a global postwar policy of strengthening allies to enable them to operate jointly with U.S. forces in the face of a common enemy. The current process of redefinition of in-ternational relationships in all their phases will profoundly condition U.S. policies toward Latin America as well. The import surcharge of August 15, 1971, which was applied to Latin America as well as to the more developed countries, is a harbinger of this process.

The second consideration is that major changes have twice before emerged at the end of long periods of relatively inactive Republican rule. The Good Neighbor policy was hammered out during the last years of the Hoover Administration. The Alliance for Progress owes much to pre-liminary developments of the late 1950s under President Eisenhower.[14] From this perspective, the next phase of U.S. policy toward Latin Ameri-ca, whatever its name, may well be initiated toward the end of Richard Nixon's second term, and in particular after the 1974 Congressional elec-tions. Indeed, by 1976, almost regardless of intervening events short of a new world conflagration now apparently stymied by ideological and

---

[14] Those who incline toward the belief that U.S. Latin American policy is largely the fruit of partisan (Democratic versus Republican parties) considerations would do well to reread Milton S. Eisenhower's endorsement and explication of the fundamental philosophy of the Alliance for Progress in his *The Wine is Bitter: The United States and Latin America* (New York: 1963).

nuclear stalemate, the United States seems likely to reenter a period of activism under the direction of new leaders who will make political capital out of public boredom with current styles of "managerial" government. The directions this new activism will take will depend to a large extent on the intellectual and political groundwork that will have been laid before then.

What, if any, are the characteristics, that can be identified today, of a new policy? Prediction is always a risky business. It is even more hazardous to the extent that U.S. Latin American policy depends on a prior resolution of uncertainties in other areas.[15] But we do know something about the present.

To begin with, there is some consciousness in official U.S. circles of a continuing need to redefine policy. President Nixon himself recently listed inter-American relations as a "sharp disappointment," saying in his 1972 report to the Congress on U.S. foreign policy that

We have yet to work out with our friends a solution of the conflict between their desire for our help and their determination to be free of dependence upon us. The thrust for change in Latin America, and our response to it, have yet to shape themselves into a pattern permitting us to make as full a contribution as we wish and as our hemisphere friends expect.[16]

As President Nixon suggests, any effective U.S. policy toward Latin America must take into account Latin American interests. But it must also reflect North American interests. The perception of these interests in the United States is profoundly conditioned by nationalism, frequently expressed most dramatically in Congress, often in forms linked to economic issues.[17] Without a political consensus or strong Executive leadership, Congress and the national-security and foreign-policy bureaucracies tend to lapse into inertia, punctuated by an alternation of weak initiatives (and often as hasty retreats), mostly in support of "tough" policies. Rising protectionist sentiment in U.S. labor and the U.S. Congress, and recent legislation sponsored by Representative Henry B. Gonzalez, Democrat of Texas, suggest that economic nationalism may be replacing anti-Communism as the standard of "toughness." The Gonzalez Amendment extends the Hickenlooper principle to multilateral economic relations,

[15] This may be the real meaning of "dependence": depending on decisions taken elsewhere, for reasons that have little to do with one's own situation.

[16] *U.S. Foreign Policy for the 1970s: The Emerging Structure of Peace,* a report to the Congress by Richard M. Nixon, February 9, 1972 (Washington: 1972), pp. 11-12.

[17] As will become clear below, I do not mean by this formulation to sidestep the question of U.S. private economic interests. But I do mean to emphasize my belief that these interests frequently gain their political influence by manipulating the symbols of nationalism, a topic much written about in the United States with regard to Latin America, but virtually ignored in thinking about the United States.

by requiring U.S. representatives on international financial institutions to vote against loans to countries that have nationalized U.S. properties without first paying the compensation desired by the companies affected.[18] As a $26 million disaster relief loan to Peru in 1972 implies, such pressures can be partially overcome through other channels—but only at the cost of great effort.

This prominence of economic factors in U.S. policy is greatly assisted by the absence of political and security reasons to the contrary. In the past two decades, American leaders generally felt that the world situation required a friendly and developing Latin America—whether as a political ally against the USSR, or as a strategic reserve in case of actual conflict and reconstruction, or as a front line of defense against foreign Communist attempts to exploit the weaknesses of Latin American underdevelopment through subversion. For these reasons of politics and security, therefore, U.S. policy sought to foster Latin American development.

Inevitably, the United States—following a pattern that suited its resources and historical experience—sought to encourage Latin American development through "free enterprise" and U.S. private investment, as well as by providing public assistance. Sometimes, in fact, the U.S. Government actively supported private investment as a solution for political or security problems, encouraging activity even when U.S. companies seemed reluctant to act on their own. It was President John F. Kennedy who argued that

There is not enough available public capital either in the United States or in Latin America to carry development forward at the pace that is demanded. . . . *If encouraged,* private investment . . . can . . . provide the vital margin of success as it did in the development of all the nations of the West and most especially in the development of the United States of America.[19]

The point often missed in Latin American discussions of U.S. foreign policy and "imperialism" is precisely this: So long as a substantial consensus existed in the United States that development was necessary for security and that development in turn depended at least in part on U.S. private capital, the defense and even advocacy of U.S. private investment in Latin America was a concern affecting the security of the United

[18]This is, of course, not the language of the Amendment. But so long as there is no accepted external measure, the effect of the doctrine of "prompt, adequate, and effective" compensation is precisely this: to make U.S. assistance policy dependent on the attitudes of major foreign investors in their relations with foreign countries. This is clearly not the desire of many in the U.S. Executive branch—but others, with a powerful assist from Congressional nationalism, still prevail.

[19]Remarks of the President to the Inter-American Press Association, as released by the Office of the White House Press Secretary, Miami Beach, Florida, November 18, 1963 (emphasis added).

States. Of course U.S. companies sometimes sought U.S. Government protection or influence. But the driving force was frequently not the companies using the state as the implementor of their desires; it was rather the state that actively encouraged such relations in the name of security. Business is not always just "business."

Today, without compelling reasons for such policies, the U.S. Government's approach is essentially passive. Latin America, it is increasingly felt, does not threaten the United States. U.S. private investments, it is now recognized (for how often have we heard it from Latin Americans?) often create more political headaches than they resolve. So perhaps investment should no longer be encouraged. But the "rights" of U.S. investors as citizens entitled to the protection of their Government cannot be ignored either, and may no longer be counterbalanced by security considerations or the political requirement for friendly relations.[20]

U.S. Government restraint toward Chilean expropriations was almost certainly influenced by a desire to avoid a repetition of the mutual escalation that a decade earlier transformed economic and political problems with Cuba into a security crisis with the Soviet Union. But who else in Latin America can play such a card with the United States in an era of great power détente? Will what Washington considers an effort to "have with Latin America the relations it is prepared to have with us" thus turn out in practice to be a new form of mercantilism? Will U.S. policy become a hostage to the interests and activities of its private business concerns, backed by Congressional nationalism, untempered either by an understanding of Latin America or by a broader sense of U.S. national interests?

Some Thoughts on Economic Relationships

Before accepting such a gloomy prospect, we should consider several additional perspectives. First, it is entirely legitimate for the U.S. Government to seek fair treatment for its citizen-investors. Second, however, the means likely to be employed in such attempts in the future have been diminished dramatically by the decline in U.S. concern and by the collapse of the ideological rationale that had automatically linked investment to development to security. Limited economic pressures, however obnoxious, are clearly different in kind from political subversion or the

---

[20]Though it should be noted that President Nixon explicitly provided for such interests in his expropriation policy. "Henceforth, should an American firm be expropriated without reasonable steps to provide prompt, adequate, and effective compensation, there is a presumption that the expropriating country would receive no new bilateral economic benefits until such steps have been taken, *unless major factors affecting our interests require us to do otherwise." U.S. Foreign Policy for the 1970s,* p. 76 (emphasis added).

U.S. Marine Corps. Third, even in the unlikely event that the U.S. Government were to limit its interest in Latin America to economic matters, that decision would not necessarily be the automatic determinant of the content of policy. Differing economic interests frequently come into conflict. Should conflict between some companies and local governments be allowed to endanger the operations of other companies? Should trade be sacrificed to investment? Access to raw materials is not necessarily determined by the ownership of the means of production. Chilean copper is still largely marketed in the United States and other Western countries, despite the nationalization of Kennecott and Anaconda.

Finally, it is not at all clear either that U.S. private economic interests are inevitably damaging to Latin America, or that they are independent of the growing Latin American capacity for controlling any potentially damaging side-effects. Latin American governments have for some time been successfully imposing greater national control over foreign economic activities. But relations would be far easier if each side were convinced that the other did not feel it was playing a zero-sum game. This is where the practical problems begin: not only is there some question about the ability of all but the strongest governments to keep up with the constantly changing forms of international economic relations,[21] but there is a strong possibility that attempts to control foreign investors may discourage them by affecting the "investment climate" so unfavorably that new investment will dry up—not as a result of a coordinated "plot" but simply by making investment in Latin America less attractive than elsewhere, including "socialist" Eastern Europe or even China or the Soviet Union.

Many Latin Americans, influenced by the powerful impact of U.S. economic activity on their societies, give credence to the notion that the United States must export capital for its own survival, and therefore discount such possibilities. Unfortunately for Latin America, however, its relationship to the United States is so asymmetric, and opportunities for investment so varied, that even were the vague Marxist thesis on imperialism generally correct, the United States could export capital elsewhere. That part of the U.S. entrepreneurial class active in Latin America would certainly suffer, but the United States and its economy, however labeled, would just as certainly survive. As Anibal Pinto (this volume) makes clear,

---

[21] Luciano Martins (this volume) provides an excellent starting point for considering the setting within which the international business community must increasingly operate within the United States. But while many business executives complain about lessened governmental receptivity—both at home and abroad—and are indeed seeking their own "independent" policies, foreign and otherwise, most of the few with whom I am personally acquainted are not particularly sanguine about their "control" over events, and see themselves rather as trying to cut their losses as much as creating new opportunities.

Latin America's relative importance in U.S. foreign trade has already fallen. And although much of what the United States continues to import does fall into the "essential raw materials" category, I have already suggested that access may not necessarily depend on continued U.S. ownership of the means of production.

Lessening U.S. interest in controlling Latin America may, ironically, also deprive Latin Americans of means of controlling the United States. The predictable responses elicited, for example, by the fear of Communism in the past are no longer there. In fact, many Latin American leaders now complain privately that it is difficult to elicit any response at all from the U.S. Government. Why should U.S. investors, faced with what they consider hostility, behave any differently?

Despite the Alliance for Progress, U.S. commitment to the development of foreign countries in general has weakened steadily since the 1950s. To take just one dimension, now that the advent of nuclear parity and the evolution of relations with the Soviet Union have altered the strategic perceptions of a generation ago, Latin America seems less important as a reservoir of industrial capacity and raw materials for reconstruction after a potential world war. In the longer run, of course, Latin America's growing industrialization and dwindling world reserves of natural resources may lead to a reassertion of the importance of Latin American trade and raw materials to the United States. By then, however, economic relations including access to raw materials may already have been largely determined by the ground rules now emerging as Latin American countries seek to assert control over their resources before they are depleted. This is but one reason for following with care the developments in countries, like Peru, now taking the lead in exploring new forms of economic organization and cooperation.

But there is no guarantee that cooperation will come automatically, without effort on both sides. As Raymond Aron once commented, when men do not decide, events decide for them. And events seem to be slowly but inexorably driving the two Americas apart.

Forging a New Pattern of Hemispheric Relations

It should by now be clear to all of us that increased tolerance for political and economic variety within Latin America has been obtained at the cost of lessened involvement and assistance from the United States. The last few years have produced a dramatic change in the working environment of the most sensitive "Latin American experts" within the U.S. Government. Though many remain so disillusioned that they continue to urge disengagement (out of the belief that North American activism is inherently counterproductive in Latin America), a few are reversing themselves—after a decade of acting as "brakes" on their fellow citizens' heavy-handed security concerns—and becoming advocates for greater U.S. involvement. But most North Americans are now too bored with foreign affairs to listen. Interventionism has been replaced by indifference.

For intervention to be replaced by more constructive policies, an intellectual and political effort of no mean proportions will be required. For without a common understanding about purposes, *any* action can be considered intervention. On the North American side, the U.S. academic community is generally out of touch with Latin America and suspicious of the U.S. Government, a combination that lends itself more to clichés than to policy analysis. The Department of State, lacking political support both in the United States and abroad, is also hampered by traditional concepts of diplomacy, and may not be well suited to the cultural interpretation and mediation between societies that seems to be required. On both sides, despite this meeting, there is a great absence of the stubborn dialogues and professional exchanges needed to forge a common understanding.

From this viewpoint, one of the most dangerous heritages of the 1970s may well be the lack of dialogue of the 1960s. Vietnam and Cuba have not only affected direct dialogue between North and South Americans but have also damaged the links of the U.S. Government to potential interpreters in the U.S. intellectual community, and weakened both through a process of mutual alienation. In addition, the resistance, frequently but not always polarized along ideological lines, of many U.S. liberals and Latin American nationalists to what they consider an overweening American presence and a naive desire to impose American solutions—which would be a somewhat unfair but not altogether inaccurate rendering of one aspect of the Alliance—has hindered a search for alternate patterns of relations. And there has been a time-lag—in the United States as well as in Latin America—in perceiving the U.S. Government's increased awareness of this issue.

For these and other reasons, despite the incredible technological resources of the modern world, political communications between Latin America and the United States tend on the whole to be poor. Latin America's growing development, the rise of nationalism, the increased diversity of Latin America's foreign links, and the uncertainty about the exact ways in which the United States should define its interests there, all suggest a need to develop what President Nixon has called a more mature relationship. But they also create a prior requirement for an exchange of views to identify the forms this relationship should take as it is divested of the tutelary dimensions of prior policy.

The transition of Argentina and Brazil from being aid recipients to the status of aid-givers illustrates some interesting problems in communication. To some extent, Argentina and Brazil, by participating in U.S. aid programs, were thereby engaged in a dialogue with the U.S. Government. This dialogue—always somewhat conflicted—may be significantly affected by the termination of the bilateral aid relationship. In these countries (as also in Mexico, which has avoided many bilateral relationships) and in other Latin American countries, as they too become increasingly industrialized, there will be a need for the maintenance of communication in matters of common interest, including technology and economic policies generally.

Although many Latin Americans worry about the danger of U.S. "penetration," most still seek U.S. understanding and would favor strengthened professional relationships and communications among U.S. and Latin American national institutions, both public and private. Simultaneously, however, past and current controversies have frequently contributed—on both sides—to the diminished interaction that has characterized the current period of the "low profile." To the extent that the low profile is understood as the abandonment of attempts to impose U.S. solutions on Latin American problems and a determination to lay the basis for a more mature relationship, such a policy guideline is clearly desirable. To the extent, however, that it paralyzes individual initiative and contributes to a decline in the interaction necessary for understanding, it is just as clearly undesirable. To some extent, we may be faced with a practical contradiction between the goals of nonintervention and cooperation: If North Americans can cooperate only in an overbearing and counterproductive fashion, then it may be preferable not to try. But this view is probably an overreaction to criticism and to mistakes of the past. If the Western Hemisphere is to have a future conducive to the common interests of its countries, that future must be built, and the building of anything worthwhile inevitably entails a certain amount of friction.

In many ways, therefore, the central intellectual challenge of the 1970s for the United States and Latin America may well be the development of relationships outside the traditional assistance-intervention framework. These relationships should enable Latin America to shape its own paths of development and define its own interests, while encouraging a continuing rediscovery of common interests within this changing inter-American context. Only if it recognizes the changes that are taking place can a new policy consensus, when it is finally forged, incorporate the improved consciousness of mutual interests necessary to give it some stability.

In the short run, U.S. Government immobility can be positive as well as negative, in the sense that it now allows Latin America greater latitude in charting its own institutional and national development. To the extent that Latin American governments can settle their own affairs, whether by consolidating regulations over foreign economic activities within their borders, or by extending jurisdiction over their territorial seas, they may thus succeed in increasing their own control. Much depends on the intelligence and capacity of Latin America's ruling elites, and on the technical skills of the region's expanding public sector.[22] I personally believe that much can be done by Latin America acting on its own, even without U.S. support—which is not to say that some kinds of U.S. participation would be undesirable if they could be obtained. But the point is that the basis of a true "mature partnership" can be achieved only if Latin American governments are in the end better able to assert control over their own domestic and foreign affairs, and thereby define and articulate their own interests.

In this regard, the old principle of nonintervention may still prove a useful reference point—despite its unattainability—in providing Latin America greater latitude and in developing a basis for greater cooperation in the future. The cornerstone of policy would be the reaffirmation of the principle of noninterference in Latin American affairs, with the United States explicitly recognizing the right of states to give themselves whatever form of political or economic organization they see fit to give. A major corollary of this doctrine would be that the United States recognize all regimes in Latin America, whether Communist or Fascist, socialist or oligarchical, democratic or dictatorial, military or civilian. Second, the United States would do away with the discriminatory treatment embodied most vividly in the maze of restrictions currently affecting U.S. assistance programs to Latin America—even if the price were the termination of all assistance.

The outline of such a policy could be roughly as follows:

Politically, to seek constructive relations with all Latin American governments and peoples as a means of ensuring U.S. security and prosperity, and of contributing to the evolution of a more harmonious world order.

Diplomatically, to extend automatic recognition to any government in control of its national territory.

Militarily, to cooperate on a technical and commercial basis through sales of such equipment and services as the United States makes available elsewhere, but terminating concessional military and police assistance programs.

---

[22]I am in fundamental agreement with Marcos Kaplan's emphasis on the growing importance—and relative autonomy—of the state. That is one of the basic dimensions of my own emphasis on "Latin American institutional development." See, for example, the Conclusion in Luigi Einaudi, ed., *Latin America in the 1970s* (Santa Monica, California: December 1972).

Economically, to extend nondiscriminatory treatment to Latin America, but otherwise to treat trade and investment as primarily private matters, while seeking to offset major imbalances through multilateral programs and bilateral consultations.

Culturally, to foster greater understanding of Latin America in the United States, and to increase nonpartisan professional exchanges and training of governmental and private personnel from both North and South.

I do not advocate this general orientation as a panacea, even if it could be translated into practice, which seems doubtful. The problems and even direct conflicts of interest between the Americas are too many to be papered over or solved with slogans. But I believe that without an atmosphere of "respectful and correct relations" we cannot hope to approach the issues that divide us or to construct a new pattern more in harmony with our aspirations.

The Outlook

The collapse of the simplistic design of the Alliance for Progress has coincided with the erosion of the cold war and the post-World War II international political and economic system. What is left is variety, multipolarity, and a good deal of confusion. Future U.S. Latin American policy will inevitably reflect the broader principles of the post-Vietnam world. But what sense of purpose will infuse specific approaches to Latin America? Commercialism is too petty, and "the common good" doesn't sound very convincing—at least in the absence of a common enemy, and particularly in the light of accumulating evidence about conflicts of interest within the hemisphere, and the difficulties of imposing "rational" solutions.

Past U.S. policy toward Latin America, like today's relative indifference, had little to do with Latin America. Indeed, that was one of its chief problems, and a source of many contemporary tensions. Concerned with blocking the advance of Communism, U.S. leaders tended to interpret events in countries they did not understand as part of a worldwide Soviet conspiracy. Not understanding the problem, they naturally sought to resolve it by applying U.S. solutions. Today, with the urgency gone and with Vietnam-induced beginnings of wisdom about the limits of U.S. power, U.S. leaders, to the extent they are prepared to think at all about Latin America, also seem prepared to listen for Latin American initiatives and advice.

But what Latin America? Who will represent "Latin America" in the U.S. political eye? In the heyday of the Alliance, U.S. leaders had a vision of progressive and democratic governments simultaneously reforming

Latin America's outmoded social structure and allied internationally with Washington.[23] Is there a new generation of leaders who will do for Nixon what the "democratic left" of Haya, Betancourt, and Figueres did for Kennedy—that is, typify the "preferred solution"? To some extent, the answer today would probably be "Brazil." But without underestimating Brazil's power and its leaders' cleverness in exploiting their national potential to enlist U.S. support, I believe the answer is that there is no longer a "preferred solution." The direct transfer of the North American experience with "representative democracy," like any foreign model, is obviously difficult—and North Americans today have a greater appreciation than previously of the flaws in their own system. And though Brazil is important, so also are Mexico, Peru, Chile, Argentina, and even Cuba—for reasons that will be differently stated by businessmen, Catholics, and the new generations of Latin American technocrats educated in the United States and of Americans committed to Latin America.

Unfortunately, however, we all seem to share one thing: though we live in an increasingly interdependent modern world, we have lost our vision of what that world should be. Or perhaps it would be more accurate to say that as we have begun to shed our parochial world views, we have yet to replace them with a new one. The decline of the "Western Hemisphere ideal" is complete. If my own search for an *idée motrice* is any indication, we may have to wait later than 1976 for a new vision of common interests. But in that case, to the extent that politics and security have indeed been the driving force of past U.S. policies, we may also have to wait at least that long for the emergence of "new forms of control." Unless we and others like us can come up with a new vision, we shall in the interim simply stumble along together in interdependent—but separate—ways.

[23]One of the best expressions of this vision was the joint work of a liberal Congressman from Oregon and a social democratic professor, who together linked U.S. idealism to Latin America's "democratic left": Charles O. Porter and Robert J. Alexander, *The Struggle for Democracy in Latin America* (New York: 1961).

Commentary on Einaudi

RICHARD R. FAGEN

There are a number of themes running through Luigi Einaudi's paper that serve to set the stage for a more pointed discussion of U.S. Latin American policy in the 1970s. First, he argues that as "the result of . . . profound changes in U.S. perceptions, . . . U.S. Government activities in the hemisphere today are considerably less interventionist than in the 1960s. But they are also considerably less supportive of Latin American development." Second, he suggests that even with a Nixon presidency— because of trends already under way and a history of late-term Republican activism—more or less positive changes in U.S. Latin American policy are not completely precluded. Third, he is very much afraid that generalized intellectual and public indifference to Latin America will leave U.S. policy "hostage to the interests and activities of its private business concerns, backed by Congressional nationalism, untempered either by understanding of Latin America or by a broader sense of U.S. national interests"—which is to say, hostage to the most retrograde policy influences operating on the national scene. Finally, Einaudi urges that academics and intellectuals inject themselves into policy debates, clarifying the issues at stake and suggesting alternatives, lest the sectors just identified take full command of U.S. policy in the 1970s.

Although I differ sharply with Einaudi's first proposition,[1] and find the second somewhat ridiculous in this era of Watergate and Nixon, the third opens a critical area of discussion, and the fourth poses a continuing challenge for all those who profess to work on Latin American-U.S. relations.

Richard R. Fagen is Professor of Political Science at Stanford University, Stanford, California.

[1] Actually, my disagreement is with the first half of the first proposition, that dealing with U.S. intervention. After a careful program-by-program and policy-by-policy review of Nixonian "malign neglect" in the hemisphere, Yale Ferguson comments, "The policy of the low profile, as it has evolved, has clearly been merely an attempt to downplay—not to alter fundamentally— U.S. opposition to radical socioeconomic change in the hemisphere and active support for the political forces of the status quo." "An End to the 'Special Relationship': The United States and

Einaudi's third point implies a concern not only that the formulation of policy be in the "right hands" (or at least not in the wrong hands), but also that it move in certain concrete directions. Yet at the very conclusion of his paper, when he actually attempts to sketch what he calls the "outline" of a more enlightened Latin American policy, he can do no better than to assemble a general list of political, diplomatic, military, economic, and cultural suggestions that float safely above the real issues agitating the hemisphere. It is my intention, then, to cite some of these issues, to suggest some concrete policies that should form part of any U.S. Latin American policy that aspires to be called enlightened, to discuss the viability and implications of such a policy, and then—in the spirit of Einaudi's fourth point—to touch briefly on what "injecting academics and intellectuals into policy debates" really implies.

One does not have to search very long or hard to assemble a list of the kinds of issues that any realistic U.S. foreign policy for Latin America would have to confront. There are ample leads in the daily newspapers and in a host of books, articles, documents, and reports. For convenience, and with no pretensions to exhaustiveness, I have grouped these issues under the headings of sovereignty, investment, trade, aid, and international organizations.[2]

Sovereignty. From the Panama Canal to Guantánamo, from the territorial waters and seabed disputes to the salinity of the Colorado River, questions about who controls what territory and what resources, under what conditions, and for what purposes agitate the hemisphere. Directly related are disputes over Chilean copper, Ecuadorian oil, and foreign participation in ostensibly national enterprise. Problems of recognition of new governments, frontiers, asylum, extradition, and other concerns of "traditional" international law are also very much alive.

Investment. Whether Andean efforts to specify and enforce an investment code, Argentine attempts to develop a policy of controlled investment favoring European capital, Venezuelan rulings about profit remit-

---

Latin America," *Revista Interamericana Review*, vol. 2, no. 3, Fall 1972, p. 368. This is, of course, essentially the position taken by Jorge Graciarena (and others) at various points throughout this volume, and it is one with which I can very comfortably associate myself. Whether the U.S. is currently "less supportive of Latin American development" than in the heyday of Alliance for Progress activism is another question. Answers depend to a great extent on the definitions given the key terms "supportive" and "development." One thing is clear: on a per-capita basis, fewer U.S. aid dollars are flowing into Latin America than flowed in the mid-1960s. This statistic, however, sheds little light on the fundamental question involved: whether the United States has *ever* been supportive of Latin American development *in the aggregate* (rather than in isolated cases and instances).

[2] In no sense are these headings mutually exclusive; investment involves sovereignty, trade cannot be considered apart from investment, international organizations touch all issues, and so it goes.

tances, or the whole range of nationalization-expropriation-compensation issues, no package of problems is more sensitive than those involving foreign investment. As suggested above, it is almost impossible in most instances to dissociate questions of sovereignty from investment issues.

Trade. A list of trade problems is easily suggested by invoking such key terms as commodity agreements, quotas, tariffs, credits, surcharges, preferential treatment, dumping, guaranteed markets, CARIFTA, and LAFTA. As repeatedly pointed out in such forums as UNCTAD and GATT, trade issues cannot be conceptualized in an exclusively Latin American context. The problems, by definition, have a global component.

Aid. Even within so-called liberal circles, there is no longer consensus— if there ever was—on what constitutes proper aid policy. Bilateralists contest with multilateralists, "social" development vies for scarce dollars with scientific, technological, or agricultural development, and the continuing vestiges of a military-security-protect-the-foreign-investor mentality lurk in the minds of North American elites at all levels. What consensus exists is little more than agreement that current foreign-aid programs in Latin America are a mess. Widespread definition of these programs as a mess has led to serious efforts to terminate them entirely. At stake, then, is not just their substance but actually their continuance at some minimal level.

International organizations. Using a very open definition of international organizations, we can include groupings as diverse as the OAS, the World Bank, the Group of the 77, the UN, and the Club of Paris. Such being the case, everything from recognition of Cuba to debt reschedulings—as well as just about all the issues mentioned above—falls within the purview of one or more international organizations. But equally important are issues having to do with the organizations themselves and their purposes, procedures, and powers. Move the OAS out of Washington? Change the voting system in the Inter-American Development Bank and the World Bank? Treat as binding certain resolutions of duly constituted UN affiliates? Substance cannot be separated from procedure; change in the latter implies eventual if not immediate change in the former.

Note that "security" has not been accorded a place on this list, for it is an issue that is almost exclusively stamped "made in U.S.A." The other issues are truly hemispheric: they derive from a widely shared recognition of the realities of the hemisphere and the world in the 1970s. By contrast, the security issue is a "reality" only to the extent that the United States (with a little help from its Brazilian friends) insists that it is. Of course, since U.S. foreign policy has been oriented to problems of sovereignty, investment, trade, aid, and international organizations *in a certain way,* it follows almost inescapably that an immense "security" issue would result, creating its own dynamics, institutions, and vested interests. But however paramount the security issue appears to be to certain U.S. elites, it is clearly derivative of the positions taken on other issues. It derives from decades of attempting to control and channel social, political, and economic change in certain ways in circumstances where the status quo no longer serves. But since the list assembled above concerns issues that "a realistic U.S. foreign policy for Latin America would *have* to confront," security does not merit inclusion. Though it is the natural consequence of a certain orientation toward other problems, it should not be confused with the problems themselves.

Listing issues in this fashion provides a framework in which the coherence of U.S. foreign policy in Latin America, from Eisenhower to the present, becomes easier to grasp. What is dramatic is that in almost every case where an issue can be conceptualized along a dimension opposing the status quo with innovation, the official U.S. policy has been "no change"–whether its instrumental expression has been through the White House, the Congress, the State Department, USAID, or the CIA. Of course, since the substance of issues changes, policies and practices change. It was an "innovation" to exclude Cuba from the OAS (that particular way of forcing ideological-political homogeneity had never before been tried). It was an "innovation" to create and fund the Overseas Private Investment Corporation (that particular way of ensuring continued U.S. corporate activity in Latin America had never before been tried). But the obvious intent of such "innovations" is to return to or reinforce the status quo. It is this coherence in the expression of anti-innovative activity and opposition to change that forms the common core of U.S. policy in the hemisphere and the common denominator of Latin American opposition to that policy.

The minimal requirement of anything we may legitimately call a *change* in U.S. Latin American policy thus becomes evident: it must associate itself with the *innovative* side of one or more of the policy issues listed above. To truly change its Latin American policy, the United States must, through concrete actions, favor the future of Latin America rather than the past. And it requires no great imagination to identify such concrete actions. Like the issues to which they are related, suggestions abound in public dialogue, both north and south of the Rio Bravo. For purposes of illustration and discussion, I have listed a dozen such concrete policy steps that could be considered innovative with respect to existing U.S. policy–that is, policies implying change:[3]

---

[3]With the exception of general mention of the Cuban and Chilean situations, the list is not country- or problem-specific. Nor is it in any way exhaustive; it does not touch on the substance of disputes such as those involving fishing rights, the Panama Canal, the Andean investment code, and so on and on.

1. Termination of all military and police aid and missions.

2. Dissociation of investors' claims for compensation from all official U.S. actions overseas, leaving nationalized corporations to seek resolution of differences through direct negotiation with the governments concerned.

3. Liquidation of the Overseas Private Investment Corporation, leaving capitalistic enterprises to run the risks that supposedly entitle them to profits.

4. Negotiations with Cuba toward normalization of relations, to be conducted bilaterally or in conjunction with the OAS, whichever proves most feasible.

5. Cessation of all governmentally orchestrated political and economic pressures directed against Chile.

6. Removal of all special barriers to travel by Latin Americans to and within the United States, whatever their political histories and expressed beliefs (generalizable to all travelers).

7. Active pursuit of the reorganization and relocation of the OAS.

8. Renunciation of functional veto power in the IBD and the World Bank.

9. Granting of limited trade preferences to developing countries (not alone those in Latin America) on the pattern already adopted by Western Europe and Japan.

10. Initiatives in debt rescheduling.

11. Active efforts to transform as much developmental assistance as possible into fully untied grants, as opposed to partially tied loans.

12. Acceptance of the UN goal of 1 percent of GNP as the developed-country norm for assistance to the third world.

At first glance this would seem to be an extremely modest and even noncontroversial list. It is little more than a "liberal," somewhat technocratic array of modifications and changes that taken together would begin to define a more enlightened foreign policy in Latin America and— by implication and extension—in the third world generally. There are no calls for support or encouragement of revolutionary regimes or socialist experiments, no advocacy of the 200-mile limit or Panamanian sovereignty over the Canal, not even any suggestion that Guantánamo ("that obsolete coaling station") be given back to the Cubans.

But the list is deceptive. In the context of the United States of the 1970s it is more "radical" than it would seem. In fact, much of it would probably be considered somewhat heretical by "responsible" bureaucrats and politicians of a variety of stripes and colors. And although one or two of these suggestions, such as terminating the OPIC, might become official policy at any time in the interest of cutting losses and lowering costs, most would be difficult to implement even under a new national administration.[4] We may well ask why this should be the case.

Detailed analyses of impediments to the implementation of even a modestly progressive policy in Latin America exceed the scope of this commentary, but a number of myths should be deflated and a number of other factors emphasized:

1. The often used explanation that "Congress wouldn't buy it" is inadequate and misleading. Given the immense power concentrated in the modern U.S. Executive, many innovations involve the Congress only marginally if at all. Of course certain trade and aid issues must necessarily pass through the legislative branch, but much else that is central to foreign policy need not. Negotiations with Cuba are an example. The blockade, the invasion, the exclusion from the OAS, in fact the entire aggression against the Revolution was orchestrated in the Executive branch and conducted from the White House (sometimes with cheers from Congress). It could all be undone with a few Presidential signatures and a slightly larger number of telephone calls, *if* a President so wished. And if reminders of executive independence and power are called for, we might remember that a White House and Justice Department as committed to prosecuting ITT for violations of national and international law as they were to prosecuting various anti-war activists for their supposed "crimes" could *in theory* act as independently of the Congress in the first case as in the second. If such things don't happen, explanations must be sought elsewhere.

2. Related, but more nebulous, claims about bureaucratic inertia, intra-governmental opposition, and public disinterest are even more misleading. Any national government that can mount a multibillion-dollar war in Southeast Asia, mobilize the financial and human resources necessary to do so, and convince the majority of Americans that wholesale murder of civilians and the wastage of a subcontinent are necessary components of global policy, by definition has extant the power necessary to remove bureaucratic and public-opinion stumbling blocks to innovation in Latin American foreign policy. The quite spectacular rearrangements in U.S. relations with China and the less dramatic developments with the Soviet Union stand as testimony to the vast fields for maneuver that the U.S. Government enjoys *under certain circumstances.*

3. If this room for maneuver in an *innovative* direction seems so limited in the case of policy toward Latin America, explanations must be

[4]If the list included more truly radical suggestions, implying active support of revolutionary experiments in Latin America, it would be nonviable to the point of total fantasy. In this regard, however, it would be useful for comparative purposes to speculate on the geopolitical, historical, and economic factors that have led a country as Western, bourgeois, and capitalistic as Sweden to concentrate its entire Latin American aid budget in Cuba (after Castro) and Chile (after the Unidad Popular came to power).

sought outside the substance of intra-governmental relations and public disinterest. Einaudi gives us a clue about where to look when he advocates, if indirectly, "a broader sense of the national interest." But what can this possibly mean? Even a tentative answer must begin with an attempt to characterize the ongoing, operative definition of the national interest as it guides the formulation of Latin American policy today, and as it has done so for at least the past 25 (some would say 200) years.

Minimally, I would suggest that the national interest of the United States in Latin America has *in practice* been defined as *the preservation and extension of North American political, economic, and cultural influence and domination in the hemisphere, at the lowest possible cost.*[5] If this definition indeed approaches reality, what is then striking about the dozen policy prescriptions listed above is the manner in which the majority clashes with it. Put bluntly, it is "not in the national interest" to carry most of the prescriptions out, for their implementation would imply the *reduction* of North American political, economic, and cultural influence and domination in the hemisphere. An innovative foreign policy, as defined here, even if at first glance only *appearing* "liberal," is thus difficult to convert to practice, since it requires *as a precondition* not just a "broader sense of the national interest" but a fundamental redefinition. And any policy having fundamental preconditions for its implementation is itself by definition radical.

4. If a fundamental redefinition of the national interest is required for profound innovation in U.S. Latin American foreign policy, it becomes easier to place the "inadequate and misleading explanations" mentioned above in perspective. What is really implied by most statements of the sort "no Secretary of State could possibly do that" (e.g. suggest the relocation of the OAS), or "the Congress would never vote for that" (e.g. trade preferences for LDCs) or "the Treasury Department would never advocate that" (renunciation of the functional veto in the IDB and the World Bank) is nothing less than recognition that the policy-making process is under the control of "interests" that will not countenance innovations tending (or intended) to reduce American hegemony in the hemisphere. Hegemony *can* be eroded by circumstances and Latin American initiatives; and in the face of such events, a least-cost criterion of national interest or a simple inability to respond will frequently dictate

---

[5]The phrase "at the lowest possible cost" is crucial. Sharp contradictions in actual policy derive from the struggle over differing definitions and estimates of costs and benefits, and also from the impossibility of agreeing upon relative utilities (and interests) across political, economic, and cultural spheres of action. As is emphasized by O'Donnell (this volume), these are the chief reasons why U.S. foreign policy so often seems contradictory, confused, and changing when examined in detail, despite its overall coherence and continuity.

recognition and acceptance of a *fait accompli*. *But the initiatives that really count cannot come from the North.*[6]

Seen from this perspective, the stumbling blocks to an innovative foreign policy in Latin America can be incorporated into a more inclusive vision of American society. On both historical and logical grounds, it would seem that the political economy of American capitalism, as expressed through an alternately active and inactive state apparatus, is such that an innovative Latin American policy is *structurally* difficult if not impossible. Who speaks effectively for a nonhostile posture toward socialist experiments? Who with any economic or political clout argues for trade preferences, investment codes with teeth, an end to military and police aid, a change of international institutional arrangements? The White House? The Congress? The Treasury Department? The State Department? The Defense Department? The CIA? The multinational corporations? Texas oil magnates? California agribusiness? Labor unions? Farmers? The mass media? An occasional voice crying out in the wilderness perhaps, but nowhere in the institutionalized structure of power in the United States is there a faction or sector whose political and economic interests would be served by an innovative redefinition of U.S. Latin American policy. On the contrary, each of the institutions, factions, or sectors mentioned has substantial vested interests in "the preservation or extension of North American political, economic, and cultural influence and domination in the hemisphere," and it is in defense of their separate (and sometimes conflicting) interests that the operative national interest in Latin America achieves definition. A radical redefinition of the latter thus implies at least a partial readjustment of the former—hardly a short-term assignment, given the institutional stability of American capitalism.

The argument I have sketched out is not one likely to offer hope to North Americans committed to a more progressive U.S. foreign policy toward Latin America. If a radical redefinition of the national interest is a precondition for profound changes in policy, if current operational definitions of the national interest are so deeply rooted in the political economy of American capitalism, and if the latter is not likely to change in the short run, what is to be done? As the last six (if not 60) years have demonstrated, there are no easy answers to the question, and certainly

---

[6]Note that the generalized model implied here cannot be rejected by citing such events as the U.S.-Chinese rapprochement. No redefinition of the national interest was required, and no reduction of U.S. political, economic, and cultural influence was entailed. In any event, the Latin American situation has sufficient historical specificity to warrant consideration apart—or at most in a third-world context. Big-power politics are played by a somewhat different set of rules.

none that can be developed in a few pages. I do, however–in the spirit of Einaudi's urging that academics and intellectuals inject themselves into policy debates–feel obliged to comment briefly.

The critical questions, of course, turn around different understandings of "injection into policy debates." As recent antiwar activities in the United States have demonstrated, there are all sorts of ways of "injecting," from burning draft-board records, to marching on the Pentagon, to writing Congressmen. In the case at hand, however, I would emphasize two responsibilities.[7]

First, given the immense political, economic, and cultural power of the United States, and the historic misuse of that power, there is a clear responsibility to participate in what might be called "documented denunciation"–essentially muckraking and informational activity, often less than scholarly by conventional definitions, but absolutely vital if the worst excesses of the exercise of North American power, whether perpetrated by the Marines or by the multinationals, are to be held in check. It is an activity for which North Americans with academic and intellectual pretensions are particularly well suited and well situated. It is also an activity that–as all recent national administrations have reminded us–can get one branded as a "disloyal citizen."

The second responsibility is, in its own way, more complex, more far-reaching, and more conventionally scholarly. It might be called "the structured exploration of the possible." It implies prying into every corner and crevice of the policy-making process and the configurations of power to clarify what kinds of change *are* possible given existing or foreseeable short-run realities in the United States. It has already been argued, for example, that executive autonomy is sufficient to permit relatively rapid termination of the economic and political blockade of Cuba should the "will" to do so exist. The existence of such a "will" is quite imaginable within a conventional, liberal administration of the sort that might follow Nixon. What other kinds of change could be reform-mongered through by an executive branch with somewhat progressive tendencies in a post-Watergate and post-Vietnam world? Could travel restrictions be raised? Could the OPIC be quashed? Could military and police aid and missions be terminated? What non-executive-centered strategies could be developed for what kinds of other issues? Well-argued answers to such questions are not readily at hand, although off-the-cuff speculations abound.

---

[7] In no way are these emphases meant to suggest that other responsibilities are unimportant. On the contrary, Einaudi's call for the creation and promulgation of a "new vision" of U.S.-Latin American relations (see his closing sentence) is probably the most important academic-intellectual-political responsibility of all. But what is equally clear is that the creation and promulgation of an *anti-imperialist* "new vision" in the United States (1) is not what Einaudi had in mind, and (2) involves a long-term, multifaceted range of activities of which the two mentioned in the text form only a part.

It is important to note that pursuing this exploratory, reform-mongering, future-oriented kind of research does not involve abandoning a model of the United States in which structural change in existing political-economic arrangements is seen as a precondition to a truly innovative and extensive about-face in policy toward Latin America in particular and the third world generally. On the contrary, what is being urged is that an empirically based attempt be made to discover what is *fundamental* (i.e. structurally determined) in the Latin American foreign policy of American capitalism in the 1970s and what is *secondary* (i.e. subject to manipulation and change when contexts, administrations, and persons change). We have only the dimmest outlines of where the boundaries lie. The earlier list of a dozen proposals is itself ambiguous and unexamined in this regard. Taxonomic and theoretical formulations specific enough to guide explorations into the limits of foreign-policy reform in the Latin American case are lacking. And simplistic extensions of past and current political styles are also inadequate. The crackpot realism of Democratic cold warriors and the nineteenth-century robber-baronism of Republican free enterprisers are both genuine products of postwar America. But neither by itself suggests what the possibilities for the 1970s may be.

In closing, let me emphasize that to concentrate on the discovery of what are by definition "secondary" elements of American foreign policy is not to do work of secondary importance. These elements have real meaning in Latin America itself. Implementing only four or five of the dozen "modest proposals" above would palpably encourage the progressive forces in Latin America even while it opened new possibilities for moving ahead in the United States. The domestic-international interactions attending such moves are dynamic, complex, and themselves poorly understood. In short, the contradictions and possibilities in the U.S. policy-making process are quite large enough to permit this kind of progress (if not now, then in a short-run future), and academics and intellectuals should be in the forefront of those ferreting them out and systematizing their implications. Only from this kind of theoretical-empirical platform can viable attacks on current policy be launched. And, at least for those who live the daily consequences of the exercise of North American power, these "possible" changes would have substantial importance.

Part Three
Brazil, Mexico, and the United States

Brazil and the United States from the 1960s to the 1970s

CARLOS ESTEVAM MARTINS

The subject of this paper is Brazilian-U.S. relations during the decade 1961–71. My aim is to clarify the evolution of these relations by examining them from Brazil's point of view. That is, I shall limit my treatment of the subject to the key factors in the Brazilian Government's changing policy toward the United States.

The Anti-imperialist Years

My point of departure is the period when anti-imperialism, with Quadros and Goulart, reached its apogee in Brazilian political life. Previously, during the second Vargas government, another important anti-imperialist campaign had been undertaken. Its impetus, however, was severed at the root—first with the coup resulting in the President's suicide, and later with the Kubitschek policy of intimate collaboration with foreign capital and the U.S. Government. Indeed, there seems to be no doubt that the first four years of the 1960s were in most ways a resumption of the first four years of the previous decade, separated by an interval characterized by the so-called developmentalist alliance led by Kubitschek; this phenomenon must be taken into account in order to grasp what followed.

At the outset of the 1950s, under Vargas, the dominant coalition—led by the state and the industrial, commercial, and financial bourgeoisie—included *latifundista* sectors producing for the domestic market, new strata of the middle class, and urban lower-class sectors incorporated into the industrialization process. In contrast, the agro-exporting sectors, the interests tied to foreign capital, and the most traditional sectors of the middle class were relatively marginalized; and the urban masses not tied to industry or to the state apparatus, as well as the totality of the rural working population, were excluded.

Two conclusions can be drawn from an analysis of the early-1950s

Carlos Estevam Martins is a member of the Brazilian Center for Analysis and Planning (CEBRAP), São Paulo.

power structure. The first is that such a structure tended to generate nationalism, but nationalism of a moderate brand: since the principal antagonism that arose among the economically dominant classes was the pitting of sectors linked to the domestic market against those oriented toward foreign markets, nationalism was provoked. However, nationalism with these origins tends to be limited in scope and intensity to the extent that the anti-national forces are drawn from social groups remaining domestic despite their foreign interests. Within this framework, the principal conflict tends to be over the appropriation and reallocation of the resources received from exportation—resources that by definition have long been subject to national control. Furthermore, since during this period the prices obtained in foreign markets were favorable, the resulting situation presented, not "foreigners," but rather domestic interests tied to foreign interests as the adversary confronting the dominant coalition. Such an adversary provoked a nationalistic reaction of only moderate degree and scope.

The second conclusion that can be deduced from an analysis of this power structure is that it generated populism—but populism, again, of a moderate sort. The structure was based on a power coalition in which the economically dominant classes, instead of forming a bloc, found themselves stripped of an important component (the agro-exporting sector). With this class ally thrown into the opposition, its structural weight would have been sufficient to upset the balance of power had its loss not been compensated for by the dominant alliance's downward expansion—an expansion that sought to co-opt new political allies among the dominated classes. At the same time, however, the populism implied in this expansion needed to go neither very far nor very deep in terms of social structure: a populism of moderate proportions more than sufficed, for the simple reason that the dominant coalition included almost the entire industrial bourgeoisie and almost the entire nonexporting latifundista sector.

By the beginning of the 1960s, however, this picture had been profoundly altered by the period of the developmentalist alliance. Neither nationalism nor populism could remain unaffected—either in content or in intensity. It could in fact be said that what caused their downfall in 1964 was probably their inability to attain the depth the new power structure required, a depth that represented the threshold beyond which the two would have been transformed into a revolutionary socialist movement.

Aside from the exhaustion of the import-substitution process, the fundamental difference between the early 1950s and the early 1960s was the flow of foreign capital that entered the country from 1955 on in the form of direct investments in the most dynamic sectors of the industrial system. The developmentalist alliance, supported by the policy of capitalization through foreign resources, at first offered certain advantages over its national-populist predecessor. First, to the extent that an alternative source was opened for the financing of the industrialization process, a certain relief from pressures on the exporting sector was provided—relief that was all the more appreciated as foreign prices became less favorable. Second, besides permitting the inflationary process to be contained in the short run, the alliance created the conditions needed to meet the modern urban sector's salary demands. Finally, the alliance helped strengthen industrial groups, both those linked to foreign capital and those that remained autonomous.

Commenting on this point, Cardoso and Faletto stress the creation of

... a transitory coincidence between political and economic interests that permits a reconciliation among protectionist aims, pressure from the masses, and foreign investments. In fact, so long as the development process increases import substitution, the penetration of foreign capital is not perceived as an essential problem. . . . Since the substitution process produces a snowball effect, domestic industrial sectors acquire new fields for investment. . . . At the same time, the impetus foreign investment gives to this process accelerates the selective incorporation of certain workers and other technical-professional sectors into the industrial economy—all of which helps maintain the developmentalist alliance.[1]

The developmentalist project—with its broad national support and infusion of foreign capital—reached its limit with substitutive industry's loss of dynamism, which, since complementary investments were made in durable and production goods, exhausted market reserves. According to M. C. Tavares and J. Serra, "The economic system's growth possibilities were limited by the lack of resources to finance new investments and the lack of demand to make new investments profitable. . . . Thus, the solution consisted in changing the composition of demand—redistributing income upward to favor the middle and upper classes, while at the same time increasing the profit-salary ratio through squeezing, even in absolute terms, the wages paid to less skilled workers."[2]

From 1961 on, this situation was reflected clearly in the political sphere: if such a plan of action were necessary to save the economy, it was apparent also that in form and style it would collide head-on with the interests represented by the national-populist alliance. These forces chose to reverse the trends of the developmentalist period and to install,

[1] F. H. Cardoso and E. Faletto, *Dependência e Desenvolvimento na América Latina* (Rio de Janeiro, Zahar: 1970).
[2] Maria Conceição de Tavares and J. Serra, "Más allá del estancamiento," *Revista Latinoamericana de Ciencias Sociales,* June-December 1971.

in their stead, a development model based on the nation's potential for independent action, as reflected both in production and consumption and in action in the international sphere.

Actually, the independent-action development plan was adopted chiefly because of the interdependence between the political and economic interests of the national-populist alliance's leading sectors. From a purely economic standpoint, the model of exclusive-partner development seemed to offer an attractive future to many sectors of the bourgeoisie, the middle class, and the bureaucracy. Politically, however, the option appeared to be suicidal; in effect, at the outset of the 1960s, the groups and class factions that led the national-populist alliance had little access to governmental power. Control over the decision-making process by these groups and factions depended less on their role in the economic process than on their ability to win an electoral majority. Their political fate being linked simultaneously to the maintenance of the liberal-democratic regime and the electoral support of the masses, it was inevitable that these sectors would choose an independent-action development plan based on the nation's internal strengths, despite the fact that the success of such a plan required foreign savings, upward income redistribution, and a salary squeeze on less skilled labor.

Once this strategy was defined, the national-populist tactic would be elaborated in the context of the legacy left by the Kubitschek period. This involved the creation of a power structure involving increases not only in participation but also in the degree of internal solidarity of the forces with foreign ties—forces divorced from the masses and hurt by the existence of a representative government. More emphatically than in the early 1950s, national-populism had now to confront the foreign interests having investments in Brazil, as well as their respective governments. This required an increased dose of both political and economic nationalism, domestically as well as internationally. At the same time, with the Kubitschek period's having divorced substantial sectors of the middle class from the power structure—sectors drawn into partnership with foreign capital and into technical and administrative posts related to the dynamic of "associated" development—the new power structure demanded also that the alliance intensify its populist tenor. Moreover, the longer the national process took to revert to the logic of independent-action development, the greater the dose of populism it needed to compensate for the loss of allies brought on by political radicalization and by the contrary dictates of the associated economy and the national-populist economic policy. Finally, the successive attempts to restore political equilibrium by increasing the participation of the lower classes were to reach their limit with the Goulart government's efforts to open up the system, efforts that far exceeded not just the populist plans of Vargas or Janio Quadros, but the original intentions of the Goulart government itself. These efforts included the mobilization of the rural masses and of the lower echelons of the Armed Forces, and they unleashed a series of consequences fatal for the alliance's survival: the alienation of rural property owners and of the constitutionalist military; a horizontal split in the party system; a stalemate between executive and legislature; and, finally, the rejection of the regime by the very forces that owed it, if not their life, then at least the political importance they had come to enjoy.

The foreign policy developed by the Brazilian Government in the years 1961–64 becomes more understandable, then, if we examine it in the light of the following hypotheses:

1. First, the survival of the national-populist alliance, within the framework of the power structure inherited from the Kubitschek period, depended on the steady intensification of both nationalism and populism.

2. This intensification, in its turn, tended to consolidate these two alternative policies in a single bloc. To be sure, there was no inherent reason why nationalism should have united with populism. Were it not for the existence of a national bourgeoisie that was relatively divorced from other sectors of the dominant classes—a national bourgeoisie increasingly marginalized owing to the context of the import-substitution process, and desperately in need of a development model that would ensure it a dominant role in the future course of history—we would not likely have witnessed such a close relationship as came to be established between nationalism and populism. Whoever engaged in the defense of the nation's economic and political emancipation, confronting foreign interests in general and North American interests in particular, would sooner or later almost inevitably have become involved in opening up the system to the participation of the masses.

3. As is generally agreed, the content and scope of nationalist ideology is determined essentially by the structural characteristics of the class or class sector whose private interests manage to be universalized as the nation's general interests. In Brazil during this period, the independent domestic bourgeoisie occupied this position. And the national-populist alliance depended on it in more than one sense. Most important, the bourgeoisie's presence as a dominant element was an indispensable condition for the legitimization of the alliance itself, in the eyes not just of society in general but also of key allies such as the latifundistas and the constitutionalist military. Without the bourgeoisie, the alliance would settle into a coalition of primarily subversive forces, and the intra-bourgeoisie dispute would become an open class struggle. So much importance was attributed to the national-bourgeois element that its effective participation

in the coalition was significantly inflated by the rhetoric of political leaders—who themselves privately questioned the very existence of such a bourgeoisie. The participation, real or fictitious, of the domestic bourgeoisie had the critical consequence for the national-populist alliance of according it the class parameters that determined the conception and implementation of the nationalist effort. That is to say, the limits and the goals of the nationalist movement were set by the bourgeoisie's class perspective.

4. More specifically, given that the national bourgeoisie—represented as it was precisely by the most backward and least monopolistic strata—played a key role in an alliance that included sectors of the lower classes, it was to be expected that the resulting brand of nationalism would carry the imprint of its origin. Among other signs of its origin were the intensity of the conflict between foreign and private domestic capital, the urgency attributed to the anti-imperialist struggle, the notable absence of an imperialist perspective of its own, and a conceptualization of the conflict with the dominant countries that adhered far more to the model of a dispute between boss and employee than to a competition between one entrepreneur and another. Apart from this, as Octavio Ianni points out,[3] ". . . the experience of several populist governments demonstrates that they antagonize imperialism much more as a technique for reformulating the conditions of dependency and dividing up the economic surplus, than as an instrument for the destruction of imperialism. All populist governments break off their anti-imperialist struggle short of its becoming an open class struggle, and therefore a struggle against the capitalist mode of production itself." It was the class interests and the economic and political perspectives of the Brazilian bourgeoisie of the period that gave meaning to these and other characteristics of the nationalist ideology. For example, the emphasis on the harmful effects of foreign capital and on the urgent need to curb these effects would probably not have been so great had it not been for the fact that foreign capital penetrated the private sector of the economy, where it seized the most lucrative profit opportunities. In other words, the same process seen from the perspective of another class or of other sectors of the dominant class would probably not seem so incurably "denationalizing," nor so undesirable in the short or medium run.

The Sub-imperialist Years

In the power structure that arose after the defeat of national-populism, the dominant positions were occupied by international capital (basically

[3]Octavio Ianni, *Estados Unidos e América Latina* (São Paulo, CEBRAP: 1972), mimeographed.

North American), the bourgeoisie directly or indirectly linked to foreign investments, the most modern sectors of the urban middle class, the U.S. Government, and the civilian and military bureaucratic elites who controlled Brazil's state apparatus. On the fringes of this dominant coalition were agro-exporting interests and the traditional agrarian oligarchy. Industrial and mercantile sectors not involved in the "internationalization of the market" were shorn of power and prestige. And in an extremely marginal position were the largest sectors of the rural and urban lower classes, as well as the less conservative sectors of the middle class.

In general, the dominant characteristic of the post-1964 period was the adoption of the development model that some authors have come to call "sub-imperialism."[4] Given the lack of consensus regarding the meaning of this term, I shall use it here in the none-too-rigorous sense of a development process involving a division of functions (economic, political, military, and ideological) between the United States and its favored allies in the context of the inter-American system. Imperfect as it is, this conceptualization nevertheless has two advantages: it makes possible a relatively satisfactory differentiation between the Castelo Branco government and those that followed it; and it helps clarify the significance of the political conflict characterizing the present power struggle.

Basically, the sub-imperialist model involves the restructuring of the international system (in this case the inter-American subsystem) toward the end of alleviating problems caused by the tightened integration attendant upon the transfer of capital from the center to the periphery. Such problems are manifested chiefly in two areas: (a) the restricted size of the recipient country's market with respect to the scale of production characteristic of the new imported technology; and (b) the pressure on the balance of payments exerted by payments on foreign capital and on the importation of the complementary goods and services required by the model of "associated" development. Sub-imperialism is a way of resolving these problems. First, the central country, withdrawing partially from the region, expands the market accessible to the recipient country, thus offering the latter a partnership in the imperialistic exploitation of the periphery (not in the sense that the recipient nation manages this exploitation unaided; on the contrary, it remains the object and not the originator of imperialist actions, though reaping a share of the expanded international trade). Second, at least in principle, the conventional imperialist model is modified by the central country's increased receptivity to the exports of the recipient country.

During the Castelo Branco period, the principal requisites for this sub-imperialist international division of functions were in fact fulfilled. As

[4] Rui Mauro Marini, "Brazilian Subimperialism," *Monthly Review,* February 1972.

the power structure's new hegemonic axis became identified with the dynamic base of the productive system, represented by public and private enterprises integrated into the process of international capitalism, a close complementary relationship evolved between the objectives sought by the dominant coalition's internal forces and the interests of the U.S. Government's hemispheric policy. At the same time, from the moment the premises of dependent development in the economic sphere and of unquestioned U.S. hegemony in the political sphere were accepted, it became possible to assemble a set of measures to implement the sub-imperialist model.

But to do so, the Brazilian Government had to adopt an economic policy capable of creating a safe and healthy climate for the expansion of North American investment into the economy. At the same time, the United States had to reduce its direct presence in Latin America, both politically and economically, allowing Brazil—along with other powers—to fill the vacuum left by the North American withdrawal. On the one hand, Brazil would benefit from the transfer of resources and modern technology; and on the other, she would be given the means to handle the balance-of-payments and scale-of-production problems, because—in addition to opening Latin American markets to Brazil—the United States would grant its southern ally a more substantial share in its own market. In short, since the countries involved saw no major problems in the roles assigned to each, the plan in question presupposed a maximum of solidarity and a minimum of conflict in the development of Brazilian-U.S. relations.

It cannot be said that the Brazilian Government, during the Castelo Branco period, neglected to cater to these expectations. In 1967, when the economy was still in full recession, President Johnson justified the preference for Brazil in the allocation of funds to Latin America by stating that it ". . . showed more dynamism than in any other period of its history: inflation has been reduced, . . . the balance of payments is well under control. . . . The economic situation is better than the most hopeful predictions made three years ago."[5] A few days earlier, Johnson had recalled other achievements of the Brazilian Government: "I can't forget," he said, "that you were the first to support us in coming to the aid of the Dominican people in resisting totalitarianism."[6]

In the overall balance of relations between the two countries, it was apparent that the United States' political debt to Brazil grew substantially. During its first months, the Castelo Branco government passed a new Profit Remittance Law that did away with existing restrictions on the movement of foreign capital. At the same time, diplomatic relations were

[5] *Jornal da Tarde,* February 10, 1967.
[6] *Fôlha de São Paulo,* January 28, 1967.

broken with Cuba and negotiations were authorized for the purchase of American Foreign Power's subsidiary firms at a price of $135 million, the bulk of which was to be reinvested in the country or redirected through loans to Electrobras. Early in 1965, an agreement was signed conceding special guarantees to North American investments in Brazil. Fighting to block the agreement's signing, the parliamentary opposition sought to emphasize its negative aspects, among which were the fact that it would be valid for 20 years from the date of its passage, and that it prohibited the Brazilian Government from adopting its own criteria for sanctioning abuses of economic power. In response to these criticisms, the Ministry of Foreign Relations retorted that

Brazil has already surpassed the cycle of relatively easy industrialization and abundant attractions for the foreign private investor. . . . Our development now demands investments of much greater technical complexity and capital intensity. In the absence of large markets and substantial external economies, the private investor will be less attracted unless there are specific incentives such as the system of guarantees under discussion. Instead of threatening the national businessman, this movement of capital ought to provide him with new opportunities, such as eventual partnerships and an increase in consumers of intermediate products. . . .[7]

In general, a series of measures was adopted that modified the rules of the game in favor of foreign capital, despite the protests formulated by members of the national business community. In mid-1965, for example, the Center for Industries in the State of São Paulo declared that the Government's financial policy would end up ". . . ruining national business. The thesis that the Government should stop financing inefficiency is wrong, for this would be to deny support and stimulus to the organizations of a country that has only recently begun its march toward development."[8] In the name of the same principles, the Parliamentary Investigating Commission's report on the economy's denationalization process stated that SUMOC's Ruling 289 created ". . . a means by which foreign firms began to avail themselves of credit privileges, and, more importantly, of extremely low interest rates."[9]

The principle of national sovereignty shared the fate of the national bourgeoisie's interests. Neither were now regarded as legitimate in themselves; they became redefined as simply parts of a broader totality, to whose functioning and expansion they must adjust. As President Castelo Branco stated in a speech given in Itamaratí as early as September 1964,

. . . the political expression of independence has been disfigured and has lost its descriptive utility. . . . The concept of independence is operational only under certain practical conditions. . . . In the economic sphere, the recognition of interdependence

[7]*Revista Brasileira de Política Internacional*, 1966, pp. 33–34.
[8]*Correio da Manhã*, May 14, 1965.
[9]R. Medina, *Desnacionalização* (São Paulo, Saga: 1970).

is inevitable, not just in trade, but especially in matters of investment. . . . Brazilian foreign policy has frequently reflected irresolution as the result of the doubtful nature of certain dilemmas: nationalism vs. interdependence; unilateral vs. multilateral negotiation; socialism vs. free enterprise. . . . More recently, nationalism was distorted so as to appear favorable to socialist systems, whose possibilities for trade with us and capacity for investment in Latin America were overestimated. . . . Brazil seeks to follow a policy of free enterprise and of orderly receipt of foreign capital.[10]

A year later, the Minister of Foreign Relations summarized these same ideas in the following manner: "From the operational standpoint of foreign policy, independence and nationalism must give way to international interdependence, be it in the military, the political, the economic, or the cultural spheres. Political isolation and economic autarkies have been buried in the graveyard of history."[11]

The new international division of functions, which the official ideology presented as if it were a plan rooted in transnational vision, required the sacrifice of the classic principles of self-determination and nonintervention. The cold war, exploited by the Quadros government as a backdrop conducive to national self-assertion, now justified a break with the past. Since the conflict between capitalism and communism was the principal determining factor in the world situation, and in light of the internal manifestations of foreign aggression, the strict application of either one of these principles could result in the virtual annulment of the other. In order for the country to integrate itself effectively into the new framework of inter-American relations, it was necessary to give priority to collective security. In contrast to noninterventionism and self-determinism, this view was inherently compatible with the other elements of the subimperialist strategy. As Minister of Foreign Relations Juracy Magalhães stated, the significance of the growing solidarity among the continent's economic systems is equally as important as the strengthening of collective security, since the one, in the economic sphere, is the legitimate counterpart of the other, in the military-political sphere.[12]

In 1964, this same line of thought was to guide Minister Leitão da Cunha's statement on ". . . the resituating of Brazil within a framework of priority relations with the Western World." "This means," said the Minister, ". . . defending the security of the continent against subversion and oppression, from without or within, and the consolidation of all kinds of ties with the United States, our great neighbor and friend from the North."[13]

As stated in a newspaper editorial, the 1964 revolution, "having dealt

[10] *O Estado de São Paulo,* August 1, 1964.
[11] *Visão,* October 1965.
[12] Speech delivered at the OAS, September 15, 1966.
[13] *O Estado de São Paulo,* July 4, 1964.

a serious blow to the international communist movement, . . . altered the cold war balance of power." Previously, "it was up to the United States alone to maintain the Western democratic system. With the 1964 movement, this system won a new and strong ally, Brazil."[14] "In the eyes of the world, [Brazil] assumes its proper role as the undisputed leader of the cause of democracy and liberty in Latin America."[15] These ideas, fitting neatly into the framework of the new division of functions that was the basis of reciprocal cooperation between the hegemonic power and its most favored ally, were manifested on several occasions.

In 1965, when President Frei presented his plan to create a Latin American common market, he was faced, as was expected, with the Brazilian Government's firm opposition. This position, coinciding with that of the United States, would accept continental integration only if the United States were to be included and if integration were accompanied by the creation of other inter-American institutions. Emphasized among the latter, of course, was a permanent military organization for maintaining order in the region. In the spirit of broadened cooperation, similar claims were made to sub-leadership the moment the Dominican crisis was identified by Washington as a serious threat to the inter-American system. Justifying the deployment of Brazilian troops in the Inter-American Peace Force, President Castelo Branco explained that the decision adopted was based on widening the concept of Brazil's defense perimeter—extending the perimeter all the way to the Caribbean.[16]

Although Brazil's interests now encompassed the entire region, they typically did not extend beyond the continent except in special cases. In highly coherent fashion, "castelismo" corrected the country's former foreign policy by opening it up to and over the Americas. "This correction," asserted Minister Vasco Leitão, "consists in the establishment of a perspective of widening concentric circles, the most important and immediate being naturally that of a River Plate policy, followed by a South American policy, then by a hemispheric policy, and finally by a policy toward the West."[17] In his speech on taking office, Minister Juracy Magalhães expressed the same view, although during the negotiations in which he took part throughout the region the view was subsequently modified. Though he recognized the United States as ". . . the leader of the Free World and the principal guardian of our civilization's fundamental values," he stated that Latin America was ". . . our natural sphere for trade. It is here that our history unfolds and our future is forged. To

[14]*O Estado de São Paulo,* editorial, August 15, 1964.
[15]Ibid., April 10, 1964.
[16]*Fôlha de São Paulo,* May 22, 1965.
[17]*O Estado de São Paulo,* April 30, 1964.

integrate ourselves in the world through and with Latin America is one of our foreign policy's primary objectives."[18]

At the same time, Brazil's Asian and African policies were predominantly timid. Commenting on the scope of the Friendship and Consultation Treaty signed with Portugal, Deputy Daniel Faraco insisted that the agreement ought to include more than sentimental considerations, that it should move into the field of defense in order to guarantee the security of the entire South Atlantic and African coasts. If unwilling to face problems and to accept international responsibilities, Brazil could not aspire to a future as a great nation conscious of the importance of foreign markets for its products and the expansion of its investments.[19]

Another effort to increase Brazil's coincidence with the global objectives of the United States was the Brazilian Government's official position on the demographic problem. As a U.S. House Subcommittee on Appropriations report revealed, the Brazilian Government took the initiative in this matter, requesting help in undertaking demographic studies that might lead to a birth-control program.[20] It should be noted that the Canadian ideal of "less people living better" goes hand-in-glove with a subordinate role in the international political scene. The introduction of birth control was thus indispensable to the achievement of harmony within the sub-imperialist framework.

For quite some time, General Golbery do Couto e Silva, one of the most prominent figures of the Castelo Branco period, had been supporting the thesis that in order to survive Brazil must accept "Washington's wise counsel"—namely that ". . . everything a nation receives as a favor will be repaid later with part of its independence."[21] Considering the nature of the policies put into practice under Castelo Branco, it would therefore be reasonable to expect that, having given so much of herself, Brazil deserved something in return. Although "castelismo" had taken a route opposite that of the Quadros government, when it came time to savor the returns expected from the United States, the former found itself on the same footing as the latter—hoping it had done enough to warrant preferential treatment. "The Brazilian Government," said the Minister of Foreign Relations, "asks its North American friends . . . *to consider Brazil's new perspective.* You are Brazil's best client in the international market. . . . We are quite concerned about the prices of our raw materials, and for this reason we are seeking here in your country . . . better

---

[18]Juracy Magalhães, *Minha experiência diplomática.*
[19]*Jornal do Brasil,* September 1, 1966.
[20]*Jornal do Brasil,* August 4, 1966.
[21]General Golbery do Couto e Silva, *Geopolítica do Brasil* (Rio de Janeiro, José Olympio, 1966).

international trade terms, better and more stable prices for our primary products" [emphasis in the original].[22]

It was thought that the dignity of giving would be reciprocated by material expressions of gratitude from the other party. According to information supplied to the press by aides of the Minister of Planning, "All previous measures taken by the Brazilian Government were directed officially at the removal of problem areas." From the mineral policy to the Investment Guarantee Agreement, these measures were classified as "first-phase." The second phase, meaning the North American counterpart of the new international division of functions, would include concessions of various sorts. One of these, discussed in Washington by the Minister of Planning, was the establishment of a guaranteed market in the United States for Brazilian exports. The Minister's aides regarded this measure as "the definitive step in finalizing Brazil's foreign economic and financial policy."[23]

But sub-imperialism's global strategy could not form a coherent whole without the reestablishment, at the national level, of the liberal-democratic institutions previously corrupted by populist degeneracy. This facet of castelismo, often underestimated, is essential in understanding the subsequent evolution of Brazilian-U.S. relations. Without question, the Castelo Branco government's basic plan had a liberal stamp, both politically and economically. This orientation, however, was strongly inhibited by the circumstances surrounding both its rise to power and its rule during the years 1964–67.

Basically, the new governing circles were faced with the necessity of dismantling the structures, organizations, and mechanisms that might facilitate the return of opposition forces. This required the use of the repressive instruments then in existence—or those newly created for the purpose—at least until the new regime achieved a reasonably reliable degree of institutionalization. The resulting political hardening did not subsequently ease, but was only aggravated, both by the economic crisis and by measures taken to stimulate development that were based on the exclusion of both the popular masses and the most backward sectors of the bourgeoisie. Thus it was not really the existence of the dictatorship, but rather the persistence of the attempt to tone it down, that requires explanation.

To understand this phenomenon, it would be best to begin by giving it a name. For lack of a better term, "liberal-imperialism" will do. With respect to its social base, liberal-imperialism differs from national-populism,

---

[22]Speech by Vasco Leitão da Cunha, read by Juracy Magalhães in New York, November 16, 1964, *Revista Brasileira de Política Internacional,* March 1965, pp. 137–42.

[23]*Fôlha de São Paulo,* April 7, 1965.

on the one hand, and from national-authoritarianism, on the other. It is the specific ideology of the internationalized bourgeoisie. The preeminent allies of this sector of the bourgeoisie are: (1) foreign capital interested in Brazil's domestic market (as amplified in Latin America through sub-imperialism); and (2) the U.S. Government, inasmuch as it is interested in maintaining the pattern of vertical association that subdivides the center-periphery system and guarantees the U.S. position as the main gravitational pole among the American nations.[24]

Liberal-imperialism is the whole of which sub-imperialism is a part. As a bourgeois ideology, it is inherently opposed to the authoritarian state, to the excessive centralization of the instruments of power in the hands of the bureaucracy, and in particular, to the unlimited growth of the public sector of the economy. By definition, its basic characteristic is the promotion of progress through increasing integration into the world capitalist system. Actually, it is precisely because liberal-imperialism proposes the opening up of the economy to the outside world that it requires the opening up of the state internally. Quite rightly, the second policy is viewed as a guarantee of the first. Indeed, the rule of law, more than any other form of political organization (when kept within the bounds of the liberal conception), is extremely susceptible to manipulation by the interests that dominate the private sector of the economy. Since in a country that chose dependent development these dominant interests controlling the dynamic poles of the economic system are precisely the interests of the internationalized bourgeoisie, nothing could be more understandable than liberal-imperialism's resistance both to populist tendencies, which displace power toward the dominated classes, and to authoritarian tendencies, strictly speaking, which retain power within the state apparatus. Representative democracy of a liberal cast thus develops as the formula that maximizes the political power of the internationalized bourgeoisie within a context in which the other available alternative would maximize the power of the state bureaucracy.

If this argument is not persuasive, there are others leading to the same conclusions. These become clearer if we separate foreign capital into two sectors according to its market interests: production for internal consumption (as broadened through LAFTA) and production for foreign consumption (for the rest of the periphery and/or metropolitan markets). It is the interests of the first sector, not the second, that constitute the heart of liberal-imperialist policy. In other words, it is with one eye on the expansion of its power and another on the expansion of its market that this sector of the internationalized bourgeoisie supports its ideal of the liberal-democratic method of resolving conflicts of values. In fact, by

[24] Aníbal Pinto and Jan Kñakal, *Notas alrededor del sistema centroperiferia* (ECLA: 1971), mimeographed.

permitting the other classes and sectors of society to exercise a certain degree of influence on the decision-making process, a more "natural" equilibrium (one less artificially created through state intervention) may be established between the planning of production and the possibilities of consumption.

As the principal spokesman for liberal-imperialism indicated, "The best political option for us is a participatory democracy with a strong executive. The appropriate model is that of reconciliation."[25] This model would include the following elements: (1) the creation of an open class society through the increase of channels and incentives for social mobility; (2) the strengthening of private enterprise and of the market economy, with a reasonable degree of state control; (3) the revitalizing of the system of party representation as an instrument of executive control and a means of access (to power) by bourgeoisie sectors linked to different parties; (4) the restoration of civil and political rights, as synthesized in freedom of the press, to promote more effective ideological indoctrination, formation of public opinion, and defense of society from the abuses of state power; (5) the institutionalization of mechanisms of "popular reconciliation," both to improve communication between the elites and the masses and to replace coercion with persuasion; and (6) the avoidance of the extremes of both "distributional populism" and "exacerbated nationalism" by means of an economic and political pluralism in which—in an ever more "interdependent" world—others interested in exchange and dialogue also participate.

In short, liberal-imperialism has come to be the ideology of a sector of the internationalized bourgeoisie that, having chosen dependent development tied to foreign capital, is incorporated as an unconditional ally into the global strategic policy of an imperialist power that in response relegates to it a specific subregion of the center-periphery system. Subimperialism, it should be added, is no more than the means by which this sector of the internationalized bourgeoisie realizes its relations with the central country and the various sectors of the outside world.

Liberal-imperialism's rise to power with Castelo Branco was the main feature of Brazil's relations with the United States during the period 1964–67. This development has since been greatly obscured by the emphasis placed on such concurrent events as the establishment of a military dictatorship and the setting up of an economic-recovery program. Given the urgent and exceptional character of the political and economic situation during that period, it was understandable that the bourgeoisie should reach an accord with the state, abdicating—for a time and to a certain point—its capacity to determine and control the functioning of

---

[25] Roberto de Oliveira Campos, *O Estado de São Paulo,* June 17, 1970.

the state's executive branch. In so doing, it granted to the state the decision-making independence and freedom of movement necessary to accelerate the restructuring of political and economic relationships. That this agreement was conceived of as having limited reach and duration was made clear by the Government's treatment of the organs through which liberal opinion was expressed—Congress, political parties, elections, and the press. These institutions were treated as temporarily marginalized elements, definitely part of the regime. Freedom of the press was respected; and strong efforts were made both to maintain the electoral calendar established before 1964, and to defend the investiture of candidates elected by the opposition.

But it was not just a combination of circumstances that restrained the liberal-imperialist project. Other obstacles, with structural roots, also had to be overcome. In short, the power struggle had not ended in 1964; on the contrary, it had still to pursue an eminently intra-bourgeois stage before liberal-imperialism could legitimize the institutionalization of sub-imperialist policies within a rule-of-law framework capable of guaranteeing both the nation's internal political stability and the occupation of the nation's decision-making centers by the direct or indirect representatives of the internationalized bourgeoisie. Referring to the obstacles facing the Castelista attempt at "institutionalizing the revolution," F. H. Cardoso recalls that "within the Army there were groups—the hard line—who sought to radicalize the process even more, that is, to extend the anti-communist and anti-corruption struggles, for which strict military control over the decision-making system would be necessary. These groups probably had both nationalist and moralist tendencies. The two currents fed each other, to the right of the Government, and unleashed actions sufficiently vigorous to tie the Government's hands in moments of crisis."[26]

In other words, through castelismo, liberal-imperialism was in power but not in command. Worse still, when attacked by the forces backing the Costa e Silva candidacy, it was forced to surrender to its adversaries most of the positions of authority it had controlled up to that point. This defeat, reducing liberal-imperialism to an opposition force (though a force still active domestically), was the first step in a process that was to culminate in the attempt, now under way, to reformulate the relations between Brazil and the United States.

The "Pre" Years and National-Authoritarianism

Given space limitations, I shall not deal at length with the Costa e Silva period. For our purposes it suffices to note that this government constituted a moment of transition during which alternative leadership

[26] F. H. Cardoso, "El modelo político brasileño," *Desarrollo Económico* (Buenos Aires), nos. 42–44, March 1972, p. 241.

patterns took shape, groups in conflict achieved definition, and the methods of action used today were perfected. Basically, the Costa e Silva period was characterized by the use of trial and error on the part of the various groups and sectors in the political system. Each current of opinion experimented with its own formulas for gaining power only to discover that its calculations had been wrong. One of the most illustrative examples of this process was the effort made by nationalist sectors led by General Albuquerque Lima and Admiral Silvio Heck to marshal supporting forces and to seize power. Their efforts succeeded only in showing them they had made at least two serious mistakes: (1) in assuming that the national bourgeoisie could still be accepted as representative of the national interest; and (2) in believing that power could be monopolized by an ideologically homogeneous and politically radical group. The flaws in this reasoning were soon revealed by the overwhelming reaction of forces that had not been taken into account. The same can be said with regard to President Costa e Silva's tentative attempts to open up the political system and to encourage national unity with mass participation. Agreement on the rules of the game and on who would take a legitimate part in constituting the new regime was finally arrived at with Institutional Act Number 5 and the adoption of a system for selecting the new president.

What were the basic elements and relationships in this newly constituted framework? The answer should probably be sought at three levels of analysis: (1) that of the power structure's social bases; (2) that of the groups or factions that contended for power; and (3) that of the governing circle itself. Each will be examined in turn.

Social bases of the power structure. The basic lines of the existing power structure are the same as those that came into being in 1964. Its main elements are still foreign enterprise, associated national capital, and the state. What has changed since then is that relations among these elements have tended to shift. As was to be expected, developments exacerbated the contradictions inherent in a system that brings the state and foreign enterprise together as central agents of the development process.

As M. C. Tavares and J. Serra have pointed out,[27] the relations between these two protagonists can be analyzed on two levels: on the subjective level—that is, with respect to the decision-making process—these relations may take the form of submission, antagonism, negotiation, or mutual tolerance; on the objective level, the alternatives are organic solidarity, pure and simple disjunction, or a clear division of areas. On the objective level there is no doubt that, during the years 1964–71, the model of organic solidarity was chosen both deliberately and systematically. Of

[27]Tavares & Serra, p. 17.

course, "the increased participation in the economy of the dynamic sectors controlled by the state and international capital constituted an integrated nucleus for expansion, giving rise to a growing solidarity between the two in investment and production in the so-called strategic sectors: petrochemicals, mining, steel, electrical energy, transportation, and communication."[28] On the subjective level, by contrast, mutual dependence led to a series of unexpected consequences, many of which did not reflect the intentions of the principal parties responsible for the original choices.

The first contradiction inherent in the organic-solidarity model lies in the fact that the model required a sustained expansion of state structures throughout society. Because of this objective—in contrast to that sought by liberal-imperialism—it was impossible to restrain the process (initiated by the revolution of 1930) by which the state was increasingly able to intervene, not only as a planning and regulatory agency capable of exerting decisive influence on the allocation of resources by manipulating instruments of economic policy, but also as a direct economic agent that could save, lend, invest, produce, and consume. For various reasons, political and economic relations with foreign capital contributed to the strengthening rather than the weakening of the state's position with regard to the different sectors of society.

The breaking of commitments made before 1964, for example, disposed of the need to respond to the national bourgeoisie's largely parasitic demands, and made even less relevant the pressures of the lower classes for distributive measures. The freeing of resources and the elimination of political and ideological obstacles made possible a notable reorienting effort—an effort reflected in the modernization of public activities, in increased rationality and efficiency in the administrative machinery, and in the growing importance accorded the state's entrepreneurial role. As a result of these transformations, resources available to the Government registered a substantial increase. Between 1963 and 1968, for example, the tax load rose from 18 percent of the GNP to 26.7 percent.[29] More important, the instruments through which it became increasingly possible to subjugate economic forces to the conditions imposed by the state were multiplied and perfected. This process of concentrating and centralizing power in the hands of the bureaucracy controlling the state apparatus took a variety of forms: Institutional Act Number 5 eliminated resistance deriving from the free functioning of institutions such as the Congress, the press, political parties, the unions, state governments,

[28] Ibid., pp. 18–19.
[29] F. A. Rezende da Silva, "A Evolução das Funções do Govêrno e a Expansão do Setor Público," *Pesquisa e Planejamento,* December 1971, p. 252.

business associations, religious organizations, regional interest groups, and associations linked to the educational system. At the same time, mechanisms were perfected that allowed the Government to expand its influence in various spheres of economic policy—from currency and credit to foreign trade. A series of administrative reforms created new agencies and revitalized old ones (a newspaper associated with liberal-imperialism recently observed, "Just think of the powers concentrated in the following agencies: The Rediscount Office of the Central Bank, The Commission on Customs Policy, and the Interministerial Price Council"[30]). In summary, it could be said that although these transformations were introduced for the purpose of facilitating the expansion of foreign capital, the state unquestionably used them to further its own ends.

A second contradiction inherent in the scheme of organic solidarity between the state and foreign capital lies in the fact, again, that the division of productive tasks between the two strengthens, rather than weakens, the bargaining powers of the state. Partly, this is so because this association requires a continued expansion of the public sector, to the detriment of the private sector of the economy. Partly, it is so because in this division of tasks the state must provide the strategic inputs used by private enterprise. Consequently, the greater the degree of organic solidarity, the more international capital stimulates the growth of state capital, and the more it may be affected by changes in the state's behavior as entrepreneur. For this reason, it becomes particularly important for foreign enterprise to establish reliable criteria for the filling of leadership posts in the state apparatus; if it failed to do so, there would be no guarantee against the eventual surfacing of the contradictions implicit in its relations with the state.

Third, this development model is based on the assumption that the inflow of foreign capital should be compensated for by a proportionate increase of commodity exports. To the extent that the state, in dealing with its balance-of-payments problems, is dependent on the willingness of foreign enterprise to export the goods it produces, it is apparent that the interests of the one do not necessarily coincide with those of the other. Depending on the kind of international strategy that gives rise to foreign investment, the interests of foreign capital—as we noted when discussing the sub-imperialist model—may not extend beyond the limits of the Brazilian market or, at the most, beyond those of the LAFTA area.

Finally, to maintain political stability in the face of adverse conditions, which to a large extent resulted from the need to adjust the economy to the penetration of foreign capital, the armed forces found themselves obliged to place the state apparatus under their direct control. This move

[30] *O Estado de São Paulo*, September 24, 1972, p. 3.

resulted in the redefinition of their relationships to civilian administrative agencies and the broadening of the powers of such institutions as the National Security Council, the General Staff, the "Casa Militar" of the Presidency of the Republic, the War College, and the Military Courts. It also meant the creation of new channels of information and control, such as the National Information Service and the Special Public Relations Advisory Board, and an increase in direct participation by members of the armed forces in crucial posts at all levels—including the public sector of the economy. Ultimately, identifying themselves corporatively with the basic objectives of governmental plans, the armed forces began to deal with security and development as two sides of the same coin.

These and other potentially contradictory aspects of the objective relationship of organic solidarity between the state and international capital may or may not result in—on the above-mentioned subjective level—the replacement of the pattern of state subordination to foreign enterprise by a pattern of negotiation, or even by one of antagonism. Everything depends on knowing how these contradictions might affect the conflicts among the groups competing for power. In other words, to identify the effects of these contradictions on the decision-making process, it is necessary to move away from a level of analysis in which the social bases of the power structure are considered, and move toward the second, subjective level mentioned above. At this level, politically active groups operate—groups motivated by specific objectives, intoxicated by their own ideological illusions, and guided by strategic and tactical considerations based on an imperfect knowledge of reality.

Groups or factions contending for power. Under the existing institutional model, the role of parties as centers of political struggle has been taken over by other kinds of political groupings. From the structural bases representing the state bureaucracy and the international enterprises, groups or factions come together that are not political parties as such, but which in various ways act as if they were: they produce and diffuse ideological and programatic concepts, they seek leadership posts in the state apparatus, and they vie for the favor of an electorate that, although restricted in number and internally stratified in terms of power, does possess the basic rights of vote and veto. In short, to the extent that they mediate between the social bases of power and the policies actually implemented by the governing circles, these intermediary structures serve as filters for the real interests in conflict in society.

With regard to these groupings, Fernando Henrique Cardoso has observed that it is necessary to think of the Brazilian political system "in terms of rings that cut horizontally through the two basic bureaucratic structures, the public and the private. In this way, parts of the public-enterprise bureaucracy can be captured by the system of interests of the multinational corporations. The same process can ensue with other sectors of the state (ministries, executive groups, etc.). Conversely, parts of the sector controlled by private enterprise (including its class organizations, such as unions, federations, etc.) can ally themselves with segments of the state bureaucracy to form a pressure ring."[31]

Using this analysis, we could say that as far as its "legitimate" organization is concerned, the Brazilian political game takes place within a tripartite system consisting of the following coalitions or rings:

1. The liberal-imperialist coalition, described above as the ideological and political project pursued by a sector of the internationalized bourgeoisie in alliance with military sectors, the civilian bureaucracy, and the technobureaucracy.

2. A smaller grouping with no real potential for taking power, linked to the essentially negative ideologies of anti-communism and anti-progressivism in general. Its members are recruited, on the one hand, from agencies or posts at the fringes of the state (the Air Force or the Navy, less vocal units of the Army, marginalized elements of the public sector of the economy, agencies of the repressive apparatus, and second-rank ministries—such as the Ministry of Justice—whose importance is a function of crisis situations). They are recruited, on the other hand, from secondary spheres of the economy and the society (traditional agrarian and mercantile interests, conservative sectors of the Church, and retrograde segments of the educational and cultural system). On the whole, this reactionary-opportunist coalition is a relatively inactive force so long as the system is able to guarantee a minimal level of social order and economic prosperity.

3. The national-authoritarian grouping, which, though it should not be confused with the governing circle, is the current that has been on the rise since the fall of Castelo Branco and—more dramatically—after President Medici took office. Since the next presidential succession, and thus the Government's future foreign policy, will most likely not be decided by a confrontation between liberal-imperialism and national-authoritarianism, it would be wise to examine in some detail the nature and aims of this grouping's vision of national emancipation.

The governing circle itself. Before doing so, however, it is necessary to clarify the distinction between the cited groupings or rings and the third level of analysis undertaken here. In effect, the governing circle itself is the level on which both the factors originating in the power structure and the influences exerted by the pressure rings are converted into concrete political measures.

---

[31] F. H. Cardoso, *Estado e Sociedade* (São Paulo, CEBRAP: 1972), p. 20.

First of all, the policies of the governing circle reflect the material interests that ultimately guide the decision-making process. All three of the so-called "governments of the revolution" remained faithful to the basic requisites of a capital-accumulation process favoring big business, both domestic and foreign.

Second, in the event that the dominated classes, alone or in alliance with dominant sectors, continue to be incapable of modifying the regime's operational rules, the governing circle's behavior will remain a function of the relative political power of the three groupings or "rings" mentioned above. In reality, the governing circle comprises the delegates that these groupings manage to place in key positions within the decision-making system. Naturally, the proportion of delegates from one grouping or another varies in relation to the political circumstances of the moment, but the fact that the governing circle is a product of clashes among underlying forces does not prevent it from enjoying a certain degree of autonomy.

Finally, governmental circles must emphasize strongly the value of unity, cohesion, hierarchy, and discipline. In so doing, the Government not only strengthens itself, but also helps obscure the contradictions among clashing interests at its base. In other words, contrary to what occurs in liberal democracies, the present regime is characterized by the impossibility of accepting as legitimate the rule of one governing party. Given that only the nation has the right to govern the nation, the private interest represented by each group runs the risk of being eliminated (as happened to the "albuquerquista" group) if it should present itself purely in group terms. This explains the pathological preeminence acquired by the word "pragmatism" in the Brazilian political vocabulary. From Ministers of State to messenger boys, everyone who calls himself an authority defines himself as "pragmatic," proudly claiming that he is incapable of judging reality from a private point of view. (This is essentially the phenomenon that Bolivar Lamounier identified as "the ideology of the state" in Brazil.[32])

These considerations weaken—but in no way invalidate—the assertion that national-authoritarianism rose to power during the Medici period. With regard to the central thesis of this paper, this means that Brazil's foreign policy, to the extent that it reflects national-authoritarianism's participation in governmental circles, embarked on a collision course with the interests of the U.S. Government and the liberal-imperialist sectors linked to it. If this is indeed the case, one should ask, if only in a perfunctory manner, how and why this occurred.

To do this, national-authoritarianism in itself should be examined,

---

[32]Bolivar Lamournier, *O Que É e o Que Vale* (São Paulo, CEBRAP: 1972), mimeographed.

apart from its role in the Government. Essentially, it is the expression of the interests of one class sector, the state bureaucracy, insofar as it is the administrator of the public sector of the economy and responsible for directing the country's development process. With respect to the above-mentioned contradictions between the state and international enterprise, national-authoritarianism is on the side of the state, in the sense that national-authoritarianism sets itself up as spokesman for the interests favored by bureaucratic domination. Thus we find ourselves confronted by a truly new phenomenon, for national-authoritarianism is strictly dependent on the implementation of a development model based on the joint expansion and centralization of the state and foreign capital.

National-authoritarianism's originality becomes apparent when it is compared to its predecessor, national-populism. The differences between the two are many and pronounced. Economically, both are tied to domestic capital, but each in its own way. National-authoritarianism is distinguished by having its socioeconomic roots in the public sector of the economy and in the national treasury, rather than in the interests of the domestic bourgeoisie. For this same reason, it has been able since 1964 to expand and consolidate its strength, while national-populism has been in decline. Ideologically, both are nationalistic, but in ways so different that the nationalism of one is incompatible with that of the other. National-authoritarianism is not necessarily opposed to the opening-up of the economy to foreign investment. Indeed, the "denationalization" involved in capitalization by means of foreign resources changes its meaning according to the observer's viewpoint. From the domestic bourgeoisie's standpoint, it implies, directly and automatically, the transfer of control over production decisions: the territory immediately invaded by foreign capital is that occupied by the private sector. The state must therefore act as mediator. To the state bureaucracy, which opted for capitalist development, the speed of the accumulation process is more important than the particular national or foreign private interest to which it must adjust. It seems that what is crucial for the state bureaucracy is to determine which of the two, national or foreign interests, offers it better prospects for profit at each stage of the process. It is this independent point of view that permits the state bureaucracy to adopt a "pragmatic" position in the decisions it takes with regard to the problem of the "denationalization" of an economy in which capital formation by the public sector maintains a steady advance. As noted above, the nationalism of national-populism gave a sense of urgency to the anti-imperialist struggle. But for the reasons given above, the nationalism of national-authoritarianism underestimates this problem: it thinks less in terms of short-run self-defense and more in terms of long-run self-expansion. This is precisely why it was articulated in a pre-imperialist policy—whose anti-imperialist content was localized and specific—rather than in a policy with widespread and generalized anti-imperialist content.

Before pursuing this line of argument, however, I must emphasize another point. National-authoritarianism sharply separates what national-populism closely unites: nationalism in foreign policy was separated from populism in domestic policy. Domestic authoritarianism, the closing of the system that populism had opened, began to be regarded—both politically and economically—as a precondition for the outward projection of national power. To be nationalist, in the contemporary sense of the term, no longer implies favoring mass participation in political and economic life. On the contrary, it requires the suppression of popular movements and demands that these movements be replaced by organizational forms, political leadership, living conditions, and ideological content preferentially planned and carefully granted from the top down through the channels of the repressive and propaganda-information apparatuses. Given the characteristics of the political situation, this means that unless the lower classes adopt a fully revolutionary position, the defense of their interests presupposes the formation of a coalition in which the popular forces march alongside liberal-imperialism.

In short, there is an evident convergence among all those interested in broadening the internal market. Both the capital that was attracted to this market's potential, and the most integrated sectors of the popular classes whose income level would be raised by a policy of internal expansion, tended to view national-authoritarianism as their common enemy. This coincidence in the economic sphere is repeated in the political sphere. For reasons already indicated, both stood to benefit from the opening-up of the system to democratic processes. By contrast, national-authoritarianism's chance for survival lies in the opposite direction.

There are many reasons why national-authoritarianism adopts a strategy of concentrating power and cutting back drastically on the political participation of various sectors of society. First, its chances for holding power are good only when political discussions and recruitment remain closely confined to bureaucratic circles; any expansion of these limits that would increase the number of extrabureaucratic alternatives introduces outside competitors and interests into the arena of "public power." Second, the central objective of the national-authoritarian project, symbolized by the ideal of Brazil as a great power, would be unthinkable without the accumulation of an extraordinarily concentrated mass of power that permits the unilateral imposition of the means considered necessary for the desired ends.

An official version of this position was presented in 1970 in a document entitled *Goals and Bases of Government Action.* Among the basic norms promulgated in this document were the following: "Avoid promises and the creation of excessive expectations"; formulate domestic and foreign policy "without resorting to extreme solutions or discriminating against outside collaboration"; "with respect to foreign collaboration, consolidate authentic sovereignty in economic and technical cooperation and in the transfer of technology"; increase "Brazil's ability to maneuver in determining the volume, form, and occasions for that collaboration."[33] The principal objective is defined as "Brazil's entrance into the developed world, before the end of the century, [which entails] the construction of an effectively developed, democratic, and sovereign society ensuring Brazil's economic, social, and political viability as a great power." After recognizing that this goal presupposes "the capacity to make important decisions in selecting the sectors and projects of greatest priority," the document explains that "the national effort involves three perspectives": the medium-range perspective (Medici period), the perspective of the 1970–80 decade, and that of "a generation lasting until the year 2000." Between 1969 and 1973, increases of the following sort were expected: GNP (41 percent); gross investment (58% percent); industrial production (51 percent); exports (46 percent). As for general economic growth, the document stipulates that at a minimum this should remain between 7 percent and 9 percent annually and eventually approach a rate of 10 percent.[34] Obviously, the length and magnitude of this program do not allow for the slightest compromising of the principles of political stability, administrative continuity, and unity of command. Consequently, the reestablishment of liberal democracy is seen only as the crowning, in the year 2000, of an arduous striving toward a future as a great international power. Until then, accumulation and its corresponding prerequisites will presumably continue to be accorded first priority.

More specifically, national-authoritarianism must at all costs avoid political pluralism. It must thus separate nationalism from populism, because not only the continuity but also the simple plausibility of the nationalism it professes depend crucially on the success of its export policy—that is, the uninterrupted increase of exports. Moreover, it is not enough simply for exports to grow; they must do so at a rate higher than the GNP, since the latter, in its turn, must be indefinitely maintained at increasingly "miraculous" levels. To meet these expectations, three conditions are necessary: (1) the ability to hold down salary levels in order to prevent rising internal costs from reducing the competitive advantage of Brazilian exports; (2) the capacity to force major sectors of foreign capital

[33]*Metas e Bases para a Ação do Govêrno,* 1970, p. 9.
[34]Ibid., pp. 15–16.

to redefine their international strategies and to channel an increasing part of their Brazilian production into the foreign markets they control; (3) the capacity to oblige the United States to accept the "excessive" expansion of Brazil's interests, inside as well as outside the inter-American system—an expansion implying a pre-imperialist movement that plans to establish, in alliance with powers outside the Pan-American orbit, growing control over access to new foreign markets.

The first of these conditions cuts the tie with the lower classes; the second, along with reinforcing the need to close the political system, leads to conflict with liberal-imperialism's social bases; the third not only extends this conflict to the international sphere, but also incorporates pre-imperialist policies into the global strategy of national-authoritarianism. The three obviously presuppose a high degree of monopolization of power by the state elite.

There is no need to dwell further on the first point. As for the second, two examples of recent conflicts are worth mentioning, for they illustrate the Government's effort to reorient the behavior of foreign investments opposed to exporting. One case involved the law restricting importation of parts by automobile companies to a third of the total net foreign-exchange earnings from exportation, while also maintaining the level of national participation at 95 percent (in value) for those who "do not present export programs or do not carry them out."[35] The second is Decree 1,236, which permits the importation of complete industrial factories as long as their production is aimed *"essentially"* at exportation." Commenting on the scope of this measure, one of the technobureaucrats responsible for drawing it up stressed the probability that the nonexportable surpluses from these plants would create a "healthy breeze of competition" in the domestic market. And he added, "Today, the productive classes already understand that the Government makes decisions in the interests of the nation, interests that are obviously of a higher order than the interests of firms. Not all firms can bring their interests into line with those of the nation, and it is natural that there should be a certain degree of conflict."[36] Euphemisms aside, this is a typical example of the conflicts national-authoritarianism tends to generate.

Also associated with point (2) above is the concomitant conflict with Washington's interests, which I shall take up further below, and which makes perfectly clear why liberal-imperialism is developing a growing virulence that does not preclude even the possibility of a coup within the coup. Indeed, a few days before being officially forbidden to express his political opinions in the press, Castelo Branco's ex-minister Roberto Campos stated,

[35]*O Estado de São Paulo*, August 25, 1972.   [36]*Visão*, September 11, 1972, p. 59.

It is rumored that plans exist to guarantee the continuity of the revolutionary mission until the year 2000. . . . Since 1964, Brazil has been governed by an alliance between the military and the technocrats. Social tasks are not immutable through time, however: this alliance has proved itself to be extraordinarily efficient in the development phase in which the accumulation process has priority; it will be less effective when the GNP has reached a certain level and we have been forced to reorient our priorities in the direction of redistribution. The growth of production is a technical problem; redistribution is a political problem. . . . In Argentina and Peru, the armed forces took on undue responsibilities, since there they practically destroyed the political class and the institutions that here Castelo Branco merely sought to reeducate and to reform. . . . The military-technocratic co-government should not entertain notions of indefinitely replacing political parties. . . . Nothing can replace the political party in its triple function of uniting aspirations, forming loyalties to the system, and disciplining protest and regularizing the transfer of leadership.[37]

Point (3) remains to be dealt with. In general terms it can be said that the internal consistency of the national-authoritarian position requires a pre-imperialist foreign policy, just as sub-imperialism is inherent in the liberal-imperialist position.

The principal objective of a pre-imperialist foreign policy (which makes it more aggressive than independent) is not a frontal attack on imperialist domination, but on the contrary the gradual improvement of the country's relative position within an international order characterized by the omnipresence of imperialist relations. Essentially this means cultivating opportunism (or "pragmatism") in coexistence with other nations, avoiding situations of sharp conflict, and exploiting opportunities for international mobility—all of this with a view toward creating the preconditions for the future exercise of the national will from positions of advantage that, in time, will gain tactical legitimacy and acquire aspects of irreversibility. Basically, it is a matter of making the most of divisions, frictions, and anomalies that arise by chance in the center-periphery system—a process in which the gains, small as they may be, are more important than most of the concessions made. In a sense, such a policy could well be defined as the practice of Bonapartism on the international level.

The premises guiding this policy coincide in large part with the elements stressed in recent analyses of the international system:[38] (1) the internal diversification of the system's central nucleus as the result of the emergence of other centers (Western Europe, socialist Europe, Japan); (2) a decline in the U.S. hegemonic presence and weight; (3) the emerging potential for the intermediate powers (China, India) to act as subcenters, to the extent that their own bargaining power increases with the multiplication of "alternative sources of support" that they use to back

[37] *O Estado de São Paulo*, August 1972.
[38] Aníbal Pinto and Jan Kñakal, *El sistema centroperiferia 20 años después* (ECLA: November 1971).

up their demands; (4) the greater freedom of movement won by the countries able to separate themselves from the mechanism of domination—a mechanism that by means of "vertical association" links the periphery's subgroups to a regionally hegemonic center.

The exploitation of these and other peculiarities of the current international order has permitted an expansionism that develops gradually in many directions. A significant example of this policy was the decision to extend the limits of territorial waters to 200 miles. In reality, this decision was typical of the so-called "national interest diplomacy," and could even be regarded as the true archetype of a new style of foreign policy. It was conceived in bureaucratic circles and implemented with no popular support; it fell outside the realm in which Washington's self-defense reactions are automatically triggered; its motivation was more political and diplomatic than economic; it neither went so far as to demand international "recognition" nor was so timid as to appear to lack "respect" for national sovereignty; it set a localized Brazilian interest against diffuse North American interests; it resorted to neither emotional nor ideological arguments in treating imperialism or colonialism; and it frustrated in advance all possible reprisals by using every means to avoid behavior that could be termed illegitimate or subversive in the present international order.

This same style was to be found in other policies that play both sides of the street—such as those having to do with Portugal and Portuguese Africa, for example. There, Brazil postulated a "mulatto solution" to the African problem, in contrast to North American interests (the "black solution") and European interests (the "white solution"). At the same time, however, nothing could be more legitimate than Brazil's desire to establish "fraternal bonds" with Portuguese-speaking peoples. If there is room for an alliance with the sectors of Portuguese society that want to save the "race" even at the expense of the "nation," if the right to receive the foreign-exchange earnings from Brazilian exports to the region requires that the Brazilian Government take an interest in the price paid in hard currency for the exports of the "overseas provinces," and if this interest leads to a relationship with these provinces that tends to convert them into parts of a Luso-Brazilian federation, then nothing authorizes the central powers to attack as illegitimate Brazil's claim to be helping things along on their "natural course." In reality, the final objective of broadening the economic and geopolitical basis of national power is no more than an attempt to alter the correlation of forces within the structural framework of the status quo; this is a matter not of a colony that seeks independence, but rather of a dispute between powers with conflicting interests in a colonial region.

Equally innocuous, but the product of the same logic of pre-imperialist realignment, is the policy of increasing closeness to Japan. This move is an attempt to increase Brazil's negotiating power with the United States not by means of an "illegitimate" association with neutral countries, but by winning an alternative source of support in a maneuver that does not require any modification of the rules of the game. The move is simply a matter of increasing ties with a power that, on the one hand, lies outside the inter-American system and, on the other hand, occupies a central position within the world capitalist system. Once again, it is difficult to label behavior that injects such a small dose of heterodoxy into orthodoxy as disloyal or intolerable. In terms of international trade, for example, the fact that from 1964–67 to 1968–71 the U.S. share in Brazil's total exports declined from an average of 33 percent to 26 percent, whereas that of Japan rose from 2 percent to 5 percent, does not constitute a decisive change. Gradualism, and not radicalism, is the distinctive characteristic of "national-interest diplomacy." Behind the scenes there is talk of a new alliance with a Japan that presumably will dominate the world some day. But in fact, if such a plan for an alliance does exist, it cannot be detected at the level of concrete decisions.

With respect to Latin America, the differences that distinguish national-authoritarian pre-imperialism from its anti- and sub-imperialist predecessors are no less visible. On the one hand, unlike the period before 1964, pre-imperialism is not a matter of mobilizing the Latin American nations in a united front of the weak against the strong. Apparently, the slogan "Unity makes for strength" was replaced by another more compatible with the bureaucracy's hierarchic spirit: "The subordination of the inferior makes for the strength of the superior." In general, the aim seems to be to revise, on a narrower scale and with more "pragmatically" conceived hegemonic ends, Perón's attempt to lead a "justicialista" bloc composed of the countries most vulnerable to Argentine influence. Certainly, there are those who see in the present Brazilian strategy simply a manifestation of sub-imperialism. In reality, however, its special characteristics provide a good illustration of the difference between sub- and pre-imperialism.

As we have noted, the sub-imperialist scheme presupposes a division *reached by common accord* between the United States and each of its "favored allies," on the one hand, and *among* the various "favored allies," on the other. Naturally, the agreement ultimately remains within the bounds of U.S. interests. In other words, the scheme does not permit any of the favored allies to entertain hegemonic designs in the region, nor does it allow the development among these nations of conflicts regarding the areas under the jurisdiction of each. In fact, any excess by any party touches on North American interests, and consequently goes beyond strictly sub-imperialist behavior. Strictly speaking, this "going beyond" is the difference between sub- and pre-imperialism.

From the U.S. standpoint, the excessive expansion of one of its allies means an equally excessive reduction of the sub-imperialist opportunities reserved to the other allies. The latter, in turn, seeing their own sub-imperialist perspectives restricted, will tend to demand compensations that of course can no longer be granted within the terms of the scheme made inoperable by the "out of bounds" country. To avoid such situations, the only choice for the United States is to try to check and contain within tolerable limits the expansionist activities of the most aggressive junior powers. In so doing, however, the United States, and not its rival, is forced—in the name of a diffuse and questionable interest—to violate the norm of the maintenance of friendly relations among allies. Although Washington might be willing to go this far, there is no doubt that it would be much safer to substitute national-authoritarianism for liberal-imperialism.

The new shape of Brazil's foreign policy was recently defined relatively precisely by Ambassador Araújo Castro in a text published by (and thus in a certain sense backed by) the War College.[39] The Ambassador begins by distinguishing between Brazil's *foreign* policy and Brazil's *international* policy. The first would deal with the defense of general principles, such as the sovereign equality of nations and the peaceful solution of international disputes. Significantly, the continuation of friendly relations with the United States is one of the principles of Brazil's foreign policy. Brazil's international policy, however, is another matter. Under this heading are drawn together the guidelines governing Brazil's conduct with respect to the problems of the contemporary world. From this standpoint, Brazilian-U.S. relations cease to be considered in a vacuum; on the contrary, "they become defined in light of the events and realities of the world in which we must live."[40]

For Brazilian diplomacy, the fundamental characteristic of the present world order is the existence of a "firm and undisguised tendency toward the stabilization of existing patterns of world power."[41] And this tendency, in turn, is held to be a typical product of the growing rapprochement, observed since 1962, between the United States and the Soviet Union. It should be noted that, in formulating the world situation in these terms, the Brazilian Foreign Ministry stresses the identification, rather than opposition, between the interests of the United States and those of the Soviet Union. Seen this way, Brazil's international policy seems to be an attempt at self-defense in response to the tightening of a superpower coalition.

[39] Escola Superior de Guerra, *Segurança e Desenvolvimento*, vol. 145, 1971.
[40] Ibid., p. 65.   [41] Ibid., p. 66.

In other words, the expression "Brazil's international policy" signifies a change of perspective bearing three important implications. First, the cold war is no longer the key element or concept for thinking about the world situation: the axis around which international relations turn involves more of a North-South or bisegmented conflict than an East-West or bipolar conflict. Second, the reduction of U.S. solidarity with Brazil— as a consequence of commitments made with the West's archenemy— implies a proportionate increase of Brazil's mobility in the international arena. Finally, the need to take autonomous initiatives tends to become imperative to the extent that the U.S.-USSR rapprochement encourages and strengthens the policy of stabilization of the world power structure, an event considered directly contrary to Brazil's strategic interests. In the words of Ambassador Araújo Castro, "Brazil should continue to oppose firmly any attempt at containment, especially since it is clear that among all the nations of the world—more than India, Mexico, Argentina, and the United Arab Republic, for example—Brazil would be the most hurt by a policy of stabilizing world power."[42]

To be consistent in these terms, Brazilian diplomacy must resist every concrete manifestation of the containment policy advocated by the two superpowers. According to the Ambassador's report, this is exactly what has been happening.

1. The effort to make the political-strategic framework immobile and static is seen, for example, in the intransigent defense of the United Nations Charter. In contrast to the superpowers, "Brazil has steadfastly set forth the problem of the Charter's revision, arguing that we cannot live forever in the year 1945."[43] "Basically," explains the Ambassador, "it is a matter of deciding whether the states in the UN will accept a collective responsibility in the field of economic development. . . . In the realm of bilateral assistance, the great powers' positions generally coincide in firm resistance to the developing nations' demands," when in reality this assistance should be understood "as just and equitable conditions for international commerce."[44]

2. Another basic instrument of the stabilization of world power is the Nuclear Nonproliferation Treaty, which "institutionalizes the inequality among nations and seems to accept the premise that the strong nations will become increasingly stronger."[45] By contrast, in the Geneva Disarmament Conference, jointly presided over by the U.S. and the USSR, the superpowers have favored conventional and regional disarmament: "To disarm the countries now armed seems to be the slogan and the program of the Conference."[46] "No UN delegation has been as active and forceful

[42]Ibid., p. 71.   [43]Ibid., p. 68.
[44]Ibid., p. 69.   [45]Ibid., p. 66.
[46]Ibid., p. 67.

as Brazil's in identifying and denouncing these attempts to establish a Directorate or Co-Chairmanship that would be responsible for a reordering of the world system."⁴⁷

3. Stabilization of the world power structure is also sought through policies of population control and the fight against pollution. Brazil's international policy leans in the opposite direction: "Instead of stressing the increase of the dividend, that is, the GNP, this policy (of the superpowers) stresses the immobilization of the divisor, the population."⁴⁸ At the same time, the Foreign Ministry rejects attempts to preserve an environment that "has not yet had the chance to be contaminated."⁴⁹

4. "The technical consideration of political matters is one of the elements of the policy of stabilization of world power; it is well known that developing nations are much less prepared for discussion in this area." ⁵⁰ For this reason, "the great powers seem interested in depoliticizing the UN" through the setting up of committees composed of experts selected for "their knowledge, put at the service of defending the interests of the highly industrialized countries." The Brazilian Government's position, favoring greater politicization of the international arena, is a significant example of the apparently contradictory character of national-authoritarianism: domestically, the technocratization of decision-making is offered as a way of favoring the interests of all the classes and sectors of the population; in the international setting, it is denounced as a weapon used by the rich and powerful countries against the poor and oppressed.

5. In order to bring about a better international order, "the great powers seem now to favor a concept of interdependence that would involve a considerable weakening of the concept and the practice of national sovereignty."⁵¹ In other words, the concept of interdependence, which in the Castelo Branco period characterized the official position of the Brazilian Government, began to be identified as the ideology of the superpowers, contrary to the true interests of the Brazilian state: "We maintain that interdependence presupposes the independence, the economic emancipation, and the sovereign equality of states. First, let us be independent. Then we can be interdependent."⁵²

6. "The same tendency [to stabilize the present power structure] prevails in matters concerning maritime rights. The great powers are firmly opposed to setting [new] limits to territorial waters.... It is argued that national sovereignty should give way before supranational norms."⁵³ However, with regard to what affects the "right to exploitation of marine resources, the great powers, who have a monopoly over technology in this

⁴⁷Ibid., p. 67.   ⁴⁸Ibid., p. 69.
⁴⁹Ibid., p. 69.   ⁵⁰Ibid., p. 70.
⁵¹Ibid., p. 71.   ⁵²Ibid., p. 71.
⁵³Ibid., p. 70.

field, persistently cling to the traditional right of sovereignty."[54] In opposing this policy, "at the Brazilian delegation's initiative the 24th UN General Assembly adopted a resolution by which a moratorium was established on the exploitation of seabeds."[55]

Finally, the recognition of these points of conflict, and of others that do not depend on the convergence of U.S. and Soviet objectives, is accompanied by the idea that in a number of specific fields Brazil and the United States complement one another. The development of relations between the two countries is guided by the goal of active reconciliation of interests. However, the discrepancy between the two perspectives is again an obstacle to defining adequate means for reaching that goal. From the Brazilian standpoint, "It seems indispensable to us that Brazilian-U.S. relations be carried out on a Government-to-Government basis—that is, that a previous political definition shape the countries' bilateral relations."[56] Underlining its status as U.S. ally, Brazil exerts pressure to accentuate the political dimension of the relationship and to induce the United States to give priority to its global national interests, which would be promoted rather than hurt by the compensatory economic concessions it would be required to make. In other words, Brazil's international policy tends to exploit the contradiction between U.S. strategic objectives and the private ambitions of economic groups centered in the United States. The former would have nothing to gain from "nationalistic protectionism that hinders the entrance of some Brazilian manufactured and semi-manufactured products."[57] For economic relations between the two countries to fit into a pattern of long-range cooperation, the United States will have to recognize that "A country with Brazil's capacity and potential must negotiate directly with the U.S. Government and not with the lobbies and special-interest groups that operate within it."[58]

In general, these are the main aspects of Brazilian-U.S. relations at the outset of the 1970s.

[54]Ibid., p. 71.　　　　　　　[55]Ibid., p. 70.
[56]Ibid., p. 74.　　　　　　　[57]Ibid., p. 74.
[58]Ibid., p. 75.

Commentary on C. E. Martins

MARIA CONCEIÇÃO TAVARES

The paper by Carlos Estevam Martins has two chief virtues that I wish to stress before undertaking a critique of certain of its aspects that are more closely related to my own field, political economy. The first of these virtues is its courage in posing some problems still pending in the interpretation of Brazil's international relations, and in posing them strictly from Brazil's viewpoint, without relying on the usual interpretations found in dependence theory or in orthodox versions of imperialism. Obviously this approach would not simplify the theoretical task if his purposes were all-encompassing, but it does permit him to accomplish what he set out to do: to analyze the decisive factors in the policy-making of the Brazilian Government with a greater freedom of focus and with a wealth of information that would be difficult to fit into conventional "theoretical" molds.

The paper's second virtue, in my opinion, lies in the fact that the analysis is not developed on a strictly political level; it uses a structural approach to clarify certain aspects of the Brazilian political process, seeking answers to certain questions that arise at the interface of politics and economics. Herein lies the novelty of the essay; and although it is open to the inevitable criticism of "specialists" in Brazilian economics, it does succeed in basing its political analysis on economic processes without falling into the easy temptation of economism.

As an economist I recognize the twofold difficulty confronting Brazilian social scientists today. One difficulty lies in the opacity of the political process, a struggle rooted in the ambivalence of the Brazilian state and in its special development: on the one hand, this opacity severely hampers a definition of the very nature of this state; on the other, it explains the superficiality and the abstract nature of attempts to define the new political model. The second—and fortunately circumstantial—difficulty

Maria Conceição Tavares is a member of the faculty of economics at the University of Campinas, Campinas, Brazil.

is the limited and fragmentary nature of the economic studies of the decade, studies that serve as the basis for attempts at analysis.

Given these virtues and difficulties, however, the "sin" I find in certain sections of the three parts of his paper is that of "ideologism." Specifically I would refer to his attempts to characterize "liberal-imperialism" and "national-authoritarianism" as something more than ideologies or political-ideological currents of thought. He portrays them almost as historically concrete (and different) forms of the organization of power. In this respect, I think he stretches the notion of the "ideological" in interpreting the "intentions" or the rationalizations of certain governmental figures as political facts that led or are leading to changes in the organization of power. Moreover, although his methodological point of departure is correct—separating (for the transition from the "sub" years to the "pre" years) three levels of analysis: (1) the social bases of the power structure; (2) the groups or factions contending for power; (3) the governing circles as such—his discussion of these three levels is not sufficiently integrated and developed to clarify the problem of power in the present stage of capitalist development in Brazil.

Once again, I should make clear that this lack of integration is due neither to weaknesses of analysis nor to the author's practice of sidestepping certain critical questions. It is my firm view that the opacity of the political process in Brazil is not something deriving from unintelligible analysis; rather, it is a structural fact rooted in the ambivalent character of the Brazilian state. No doubt one could go a good deal further in elucidating the nature of the Brazilian state and society, but it is also evident— in light of the few relevant essays known to me—that the ambivalences and, even more, the "contradictions" that animate and move our society (even on an infrastructural level) are not yet clear. On the level of political *practice,* the system is so thoroughly closed that there is little reason to hope for more than a relatively plausible speculation about the upper echelons of the power structure.

It seems to me that a good way to proceed is still to invoke the tradition of political economy, in order that we might rescue some meaning for state action apart from the infrastructural level. Thus, instead of pursuing merely a systematic critique of Martins's essay, I shall attempt to present some parallel hypotheses that, I hope, will complement his ideas. I shall concentrate my comments almost exclusively on his third section, since it is there that some problems tying the economic to the political become important and of current interest. Moreover, it is in that context that I can pose some questions the answers to which are not sufficiently clear—either to me, to the author, or, probably, to the majority of the Brazilian analysts concerned with these matters.

My basic differences with Martins lie with what he calls contradictions in the subjective and objective levels of the pattern of organic solidarity between state and foreign capital, and in particular with the way in which he contrasts the Castelo Branco period with the present. We agree on the fundamental lines of the power structure, but not on the development of contradictions on the level of "the groups or factions contending for power"; and we attribute different meanings to the relatively hidden and apparently ideological disputes at the level of "the Government circles as such."

In order to clarify this last point I should stress that in my judgment the conflicts within the bureaucratic-military apparatus comprising the upper echelon of the Government do not and cannot evoke today a clear response at infrastructural levels. These conflicts are in-house quarrels over "power *per se*," quarrels typical of any authoritarian regime in which access to the top level of political power is restricted and in which the system of replacement is not clearly defined. The conflicts' ideological expression (liberal-imperialism vs. national-authoritarianism) varies, exhibiting alternatives and combinations that do not constitute even a clear ideological pattern. This is even more the case when one of these ideological currents has an opportunity to assume "power." This is in fact one of the primary superstructural reasons for the murkiness of the Brazilian political pseudo-model. There are also, however, profound reasons why intergroup conflicts, inside and outside the state apparatus, cannot be characterized as contradictions clearly reflected in the infrastructural base of Brazilian society. As a suggestion, with no claim to originality, I shall cite just two types of structural problems that substantially complicate the understanding of the nature of the state and of its possible identification with the interests of bourgeois subsectors, whether national or international.

First, there are the successive strata of emerging local bourgeoisie, whose dynamic of accumulation and of relations with the state apparatus is not well known. It should be possible to identify the rise of at least three new strata of industrial bourgeoisie of some importance in the postwar period. The first was that which, having risen with Getúlio Vargas, established itself economically primarily during the Korean War under the protective wing of the foreign-exchange benefits granted by CEXIM and of the internal credits extended by the Banco do Brasil. The second stratum, belonging to Juscelino Kubitschek's period (1956–61), took advantage of (though protesting "nationalistically") certain subsidies available under Ruling 113. This ruling, although generally favoring foreign subsidiaries, also served "national" businessmen—above all those in the metallurgical and metal fabricating field—who could offer substantial possibilities for expansion by substituting imports. Furthermore, this is the period in which the large construction combines were formed and the new São Paulo financial groups were consolidated and expanded. Finally, the third stratum of the bourgeoisie comprises the new financial and rural groups that established themselves in the post-1968 "boom" and, without actually liquidating it, replaced the old oligarchy economically. In addition to these grand bourgeois groups there is a set of small and medium-sized industrial and financial firms, which grew out of the dynamic of economic expansion, that is important in softening inter-capitalist competition. Also in the public sector there has been an expansion of large public firms and of a developmentalist (desarrollista) state apparatus that, although created under nationalistic inspiration, in practice supports the expansion of foreign capital, despite the ideological position of a great part of the state technocracy that continues to be antagonistic toward the "favors" granted foreign subsidiaries to ease their entry into new areas.

Structurally, therefore, by the end of 1962 conditions were such that once the crisis of the "developmentalist alliance" had passed (and the political alliance with the popular sectors had been broken), opening up a new cycle of expansion, organic solidarity was established in the pattern of accumulation among the various "advanced" sectors of the local bourgeoisie, the international subsidiaries, and the public firms. Obviously this did not take place painlessly, even for the dominant classes. The price was the economic and political liquidation from 1964 to 1967 of wide sectors of those rural and urban bourgeoisie that were the weakest or the worst located in the new framework of "association." This situation, furthermore, was not easy to stabilize, given the emergence of new urban and rural groups—above all financial (national as well as foreign)—that began to compete furiously for the new investment and expansion opportunities in a process of accumulation unprecedented in Brazil's recent economic history.

The second problem in the new system of relationships is found in the increasing mixture of imperialist groups with different interests. Without taking into account the many points of contact and fusion among the different groups, we must stress clearly the fundamentally different situations characterizing, on the one hand, the installation of international groups during the 1957–62 period, and, on the other, Brazil today. During Kubitschek's presidency, the flow of foreign capital into Brazil consisted primarily of direct investment, representing the *internationalization of the internal market*. Competition among foreign groups was relatively slight, and there was a reasonably explicit division of economic terrain between national businessmen and state-owned firms. The pattern of accumulation was complementary and did not yet involve the dilemma of structural solidarity vs. sporadic, aggressive competition. From 1968 on, the flow of private capital into Brazil took place within the framework of sharp inter-imperialist competition. Financial capital, particularly speculative capital, was dominant. The characteristic mode of these new ties of dependence today is not direct investment in clearly defined sectors, but rather the circulation of capital within the larger framework of increased growth, on both a national and an international scale.

It is within this new framework of the internationalization of sharp inter-imperialist competition that an effort must be made to interpret the new patterns of association and the resulting possibilities for "conflicts." This historically unique situation requires a redefinition not just of the role of the state, but also of the "foreign" policy of the subsidiaries of large international corporations. In strategic decisions concerning the international division of labor among subsidiaries, Brazil increasingly tends to become the center of the process of accumulation (on a worldwide scale) for the Latin American region. This process of international accumulation transcends to a great extent the concept of "sub-imperialism"—understood as the utilization of Brazil as a bridgehead for Latin American integration under the hegemony of U.S. capital. Even though this concern might form a part of the strategy of certain international subsidiaries in Brazil, it involves only a "micro-economic" problem of locating subsidiaries, and at the most leads to a regional redivision of inter-subsidiary responsibilities. What I intend to deal with here is the possibility that Brazil is becoming a "new frontier" for the expansion of a world capitalism in search of new investment opportunities, given the extremely novel combination of a peripheral nation with highly developed productive forces, extensive natural resources, and a strong, business-oriented state. This combination of extremely favorable conditions for accumulation is what explains international capitalism's enormous interest in Brazil, and not simply the cheap labor costs and the authoritarian nature of the regime, characteristics shared by dozens of peripheral countries.

Only by taking these basic structural traits into account can the possibility of conflict or antagonism among the different groups sustaining the power structure in Brazil be made fully evident. None of these groups, however, seems able to exercise hegemony to the point of "identifying" itself with the interests of the nation and in this way taking command of the state apparatus. Thus the "need" Martins mentions as an important aspect of the regime:

governmental circles must emphasize strongly the value of unity, cohesion, hierarchy, and discipline. In so doing, the Government not only strengthens itself, but also helps obscure the contradictions among clashing interests at its base. In other words, contrary to what occurs in liberal democracies, the present regime is characterized by the impossibility of accepting as legitimate the rule of one governing party. Given that only the nation has the right to govern the nation, the private interest represented by each group runs the risk of being eliminated (as happened to the "albuquerquista" group) if it should present itself purely in group terms. This explains the pathological preeminence acquired by the word "pragmatism" in the Brazilian political vocabulary.

Paradoxically, Martins later asserts "that these considerations weaken, but do not invalidate the claim that national-authoritarianism rose to power during the Medici period." Note that he does not say that it became the dominant ideology, but rather that it is an alternative to liberal-imperialism, a form of power that—once asserted—will tend to clash with the interests of the U.S. Government.

How came Martins by this idea of an antagonistic tendency between the "national-authoritarian" state (Brazil) and the leading imperialist power (the United States)? He drew upon two interpretations of pre-analytic schemes, one to which I contributed, the other of which I am innocent. What I am in part responsible for is not having better clarified the pattern of organic solidarity among the state, foreign capital, and associated national capital. This is no easy task for economists, and in the essay "Beyond Stagnation," written by José Serra and myself, which I used to develop my own hypotheses a bit, it was in fact proposed as an argument to be developed by other social scientists.[1] The author's other supporting hypothesis, which I consider incorrect, concerns a possible division of the bourgeois imperialist sectors and the associated nationals into two groups with contradictory interests involving either the expansion of the internal market or the expansion of exports. Further on I shall offer some suggestions regarding this latter point.

Finally, it seems to me erroneous to use the term "pre-imperialism" to characterize the present stage of Brazil's international relations, not just because this is a "preconception" or a "pre-analytic" intuition (I firmly support the use of exploratory categories in attempts to analyze novel situations), but because I think the term obscures Brazil's real situation. "Pre-imperialism" suggests that the country is on its way to becoming a great national-imperialist power, a view that seems to me absolutely untenable within the historical limits of what is analytically foreseeable. Actually (and here I run the risk of being labeled a "dependientista"), I prefer the ambivalence of the dependent-national-state category. It seems to me that this construct serves better to capture the situation of ambiguity in which the Brazilian state finds itself, owing to its international ties.[2]

---

[1] "Más allá del estancamiento: una discusión sobre el estilo de desarrollo reciente en Brazil," *Revista Latinoamericana de Ciencias Sociales,* nos. 1–2, June–December 1971, pp. 2–38.

[2] In the introduction to my book, *Da Substituição de Importações ao Capitalismo Financeiro*

Now that these "clarificatory" comments have been presented, I shall
turn to my "critical comments," beginning with a brief discussion of various points raised by Martins in his analysis of the two most recent periods.
In the first place, it does not seem to me that the Castelo Branco period is well characterized by the term "liberal-imperialism"; the same
term, with different connotations, could be applied to the present period.
The first post-1964 period was not liberal, either politically or economically, and its actual integration with imperialism was weaker and less well
defined than that of the present regime. If one does not confuse the concrete facts of power with intentions or ideological rationalizations, one
must recognize that during the Castelo-Campos period the structural
weight of the public sector of the economy increased sharply. This did
not happen as a mistake or in apparent contradiction with "intentions,"
but rather as a strategic decision to increase and to centralize the state's
power. Former Minister Roberto Campos, like the current minister, was
never a liberal in the orthodox sense of the term. He was more a liberal
in the modern sense, aiding private accumulation—through state action—
to reach its maximum capacity, whatever the price. In this respect, the
expansion of the public sector does not occur "to the detriment of the
private sector of the economy," but to its advantage. Obviously, the price
involved in the first stage was economically more costly, not just for the
popular strata but also for some "straggling" sectors of the bourgeoisie.
Yet it was less painful politically than in the subsequent period—after Institutional Act Number 5.

Both tendencies, economic hardship and "relative" political softness,
are perfectly comprehensible given the situation of economic slowdown
and the degree of apparent "legitimacy" of the era's "restoration" ideology. Therefore, the increased "economic liberalism" of Minister Delfim
Netto, in the wake of a cycle of capitalist expansion, is also structurally
intelligible to me, as is the political authoritarianism of the regime, once
attempts had failed to legitimize and institutionalize—within a "democratic framework"—a state centralism so notably exclusive both economically and politically.

The discussion of the more or less "national" character of both periods
remains open. This is a much more complicated problem than the former,
and I do not in any way claim I can clarify it in a few lines. However, I
would again like to emphasize the apparent contradiction between what
is ideological and what is real. Owing to the prevailing historic context,
the Castelo-Campos doctrine of interdependence did not lead to greater
integration or internationalization of the Brazilian economy than that

---

(Rio de Janeiro: Zahar, 1972), I try, without much success, to point out the ambivalence in the
dependent national character of a modern peripheral state such as Brazil, and to indicate the
complexity of the analytic requirements needed to fully understand this situation.

which existed previously. On the contrary, in spite of the ideology of the national state and the real strength of the state as "apparatus" and as entrepreneur, at the present time the Brazilian economy is experiencing a much more organic integration with foreign capital in all possible respects. And precisely here lies one of the intrinsic ambivalences of the Brazilian state's structural ambiguity with respect to its national dependent character.

As for the potentially contradictory nature of the objective relation of organic solidarity between the state and foreign capital, as Martins sees it, it seems to me that when this relation becomes established, the pattern of the state's subordination to the foreign firm is no longer valid; the general pattern becomes one of negotiation. Possible antagonisms develop with some specific business groups, not with the foreign firm in the abstract, nor even with North Americans. At any moment the national state can exercise its rights and force any national or international group to behave in accordance with the rules of the game of "organic solidarity." It cannot, however, break these same rules, since they are the very source of its survival. That is, it cannot be *anti-imperialistic.* The existence of this type of rhetoric or of some local conflict in no way alters this fundamental fact.

Consequently, neither does it seem to me correct to assert that "the future foreign policy of the Government will be decided in terms of the confrontation between liberal-imperialism and national-authoritarianism." Regarding foreign policy, and above all diplomacy at the level of the Foreign Ministry, I do not think Brazil will venture far from its traditional patterns; I do not foresee its managing to develop a "national" strategy of international relations. The statements of Ambassador Araújo Castro in the United Nations, attempting to separate foreign policy from international policy and to assert Brazil's role in both areas, are not sufficient to accomplish this. As a "sovereign nation" Brazil can define, in ideological terms, the foreign policy that suits it internally. However, as a "dependent nation" it has not the slightest possibility of autonomously determining its international relations. With respect to the former, Brazil follows an old, established tradition of maintaining, and even of leading, certain trends of "independence" in Latin American foreign policy.

To refer only to the most recent period, from "operation-Americana" of 1958 to the 200-mile limit and the denuclearization agreements, with the brief interregnum of the famous interdependence thesis (Castelo-Campos and Juracy Magalhães), the Ministry of Foreign Relations has almost always maintained a tradition of "independent" diplomacy. What must also be recognized is its inability to carry this out in practice—for example, to develop a viable policy of international economic relations. This inability derives not only from the fact that the focal point of this policy has almost always been in the Ministry of Finance, the Ministry of Planning, the Central Bank, or wherever the economic policy of the Government decides it should be, but also from the fact that the actual implementation of the relevant negotiations always occurred under the shadow of the major economic and financial groups operating through internationally associated bureaucrats and technocrats. In these negotiations the Brazilian Government always adopted a markedly "pragmatic" approach, of which everyone boasted, from Minister Osvaldo Aranha, to Santiago Dantas and Roberto Campos, to the present Minister of Finance (to cite but the most famous of Brazil's "negotiators").

Once more, the ambivalence of the situation is due not to the lack of a strong national state, but to the minimal economic and political importance of a national bourgeoisie that acts both as support and as counterweight in the negotiations with the international bourgeoisie. If Brazil can be classified as an "independent nation," it is still, and increasingly so, a "subsidiary nation" with respect to its economic organization. Here is where its ambition to become a great power is frustrated, and consequently where any claims that it is in a pre-imperialist "transition" are exhausted. In order to make use of its economic presence in international relations and to wield its full weight as a capitalist nation, it is obliged to recognize the increasing predominance of the subsidiaries of large corporations and the mediation of a technocracy associated with the state apparatus. The present economic policy team is perfectly aware of this situation, just as its predecessors were, although the latter expressed this with less honesty. The recent statement of a finance advisor, regarding the need to give foreign subsidiaries an important role in the "trading companies" being formed for the Government's new export strategy, is a splendid complement to Minister Araújo Castro's statements, and it succinctly illustrates the ambivalence we are trying to emphasize.

All of this should not be crudely understood as evidence that the state is subordinated to the interests of "American imperialism"[3] or to those of any other imperialist nation, as if we were dealing with a "semi-colonial" country. Depending on the internal and international situation, Brazil has sufficient structural strength and complexity to be able to differ ideologically and politically with the United States, within the "limits of the policy of alliance," as well as to avoid routinely favoring American groups in the internationalization of its economy. And at the same time, in not having (unlike some Latin American nations) mining enclaves of U.S. origin, in the present stage of the "nationalist" struggle of the region,

---

[2] It is of course necessary to make clear which are the concrete interests of American imperialism in Brazil or in Latin America and what its strategy is, if this exists. At the seminar in Lima it seemed evident that there was absolute confusion on the matter.

Brazil does not run much risk of conflict with the United States so long as it maintains a regime that functions satisfactorily in the framework of the general interests of world capitalism.

Obviously, there are conflicts or contradictions between the different imperialist groups and the local associated bourgeoisie, even between the latter and the authentic local bourgeoisie—just as there are also conflicts over deciding the rules of the game of the division of tasks or the linkages with state-owned firms. It is therefore clear, as Martins puts it, that "it is particularly important for foreign firms to set up reliable criteria for filling directive posts in the state apparatus." The problem arising at this level—a problem whose repercussions have been developing in Brazil since 1968, and which in light of the growing strength of the state is politically uncontrollable by any specific sector of the bourgeoisie—is that the guarantees offered by the Government to the private sector in particular but also to foreign firms necessarily tend to be "general" and to be presented ideologically as in the interests of the nation. This is one of the best structural leads Martins follows, and it seems to be the most reasonably meaningful in explaining the marked "national-authoritarianism" of the ideology of the current regime. But neither the "nationalism" nor the authoritarianism of the Brazilian state constitutes, in my judgment, a serious threat to foreign firms or a possibility of conflict with the United States. This possibility does not arise when there are no real tendencies (not even an expressed ideology) toward radically anti-imperialistic state capitalism.

As for the possible contradictions between foreign and national associated groups with privileges in the internal market and those with export privileges, or between the foreign groups and the state identified with either of the two ideological currents, Martins seems to me quite mistaken. His mistake, in my view, derives as much from the lack of adequate information about the behavior of subsidiaries and international groups in Brazil as it does from the near nonexistence of relevant interpretive economic studies. Even taking one of the few good existing studies, that of Fernando Fajnzylber, as a starting point, not much can be said that would support this kind of political analysis.[4] It seems apparent that the macro-economic importance of exporting is unanimously accepted, as much by the state as by the group of foreign subsidiaries (which have their own balance of payments and in the long run cannot pay off if they continue developing in the internal market alone). This does not mean, however, that there are no problems in the division of the national, regional, and international markets, problems that imply specialization and an increase of inter-firm competition. The most dynamic American firms

---

[4] See Fernando Fajnzylber, *Estrategía Industrial y Empresas Internacionales* (Rio de Janeiro: Edición IPEA/INPES, 1971).

(e.g. IBM, Ford) have complementary interests in the two markets, the internal and the external, and others (e.g. Volkswagen) can be "forced," according to the rules of the game—and with tremendous subsidies—to redivide their regional markets or to invest the profit from their industrial activity in the new primary line of exports.

The macro-economic stage of the division of interests between the internal market and exportation is a thing of the past. Today, Brazil's new condition of dependent integration requires a merging of these two complementary movements around two export efforts: a new primary line of diverse natural resources and raw materials, and an attempt to export industrialized products.

I have sought, briefly, to clarify some of Martins's interpretations that to me seem excessively influenced by the political-ideological differences manifested or half-hidden among some intellectuals and in some sectors of the Brazilian technocracy. That these ideological fluctuations obscure rather than reveal the true differences existing in the highest Government circles, or among groups that support the power structure, seems to me an unfortunate but unavoidable situation. The opacity of these quarrels is in turn due to the near impossibility of fitting them into a structural context as complex and novel as that which exists in Brazil today. To a large extent this complexity reduces the possibility of constructing a "political model," a trap into which I have no intention of falling.

To conclude with a challenge, I would dare to predict almost the opposite of that which Martins foresees, regarding one final point. I refer to his claim that national-authoritarianism might drastically separate that which national-populism closely united: nationalism in foreign policy and populism in domestic policy. Appearances seem to support him, but, again, it would be easier to document the growth of populist tendencies (which depend as much on the inner pattern of accumulation that will develop hereafter as they do on the degree of manipulation and control exerted on the salaried population) than to imagine nationalism as a state ideology being converted into a truly anti-imperialist nationalism.

The strength of structural trends seems to be greater than that of ideologies, no matter how reasonable the latter seem to be, and it would be interesting to explore the "middle range" hypothesis of "national-authoritarian populism." As for anti-imperialist nationalism, it has ideological and practical strength only when linked either to a break with past dependence or to a critical stage in the transition to a new dependent relationship. Brazil has already had its great crisis and has continued successfully on toward a new model that is at this moment being consolidated. Thus its "nationalism" in foreign policy seems to be primarily a doctrine for internal use by an authoritarian state, i.e. an ideology of domination.

And since, on this ground, there appear to be no differences between the author and his critic, I can thus peacefully conclude the confrontation begun in Lima.

Mexico in the 1970s and Its Relations with the United States

OLGA PELLICER DE BRODY

Mexico was for a number of years the only Latin American country in which the developmentalist policy of import substitution seemed to have taken hold. The undeniable advance of the industrialization process, the country's political and monetary stability, and the maintenance of a growth rate higher than that of most underdeveloped nations made it possible to believe in the existence of exceptional circumstances under which a veritable economic miracle could be produced.

The political events in Mexico at the close of the 1960s, the drop in the growth rate in 1971, and more precise knowledge of the extent of the country's indebtedness and of the circumstances of marginal groups put an end to confidence in the Mexican miracle. Consequently, certain ideas concerning the search for ways to overcome existing bottlenecks in the Mexican economy have taken hold among the country's political leaders. These ideas, most of which have been discussed at CEPAL and UNCTAD conferences over the course of several years, stress the necessity that Mexican exports have a greater share in international trade. Increasing exports has a dual purpose: decreasing the country's foreign debt and increasing industrial production, which is now limited by the size of the internal market. If in theory the validity of these ideas seems undeniable, in practice their feasibility depends to a large extent on the nature of Mexico's international relations, and in particular its relations with the U.S. Government and investors.

The subject of Mexican-U.S. relations in recent years has not been dealt with in the many studies on contemporary Mexico, the bulk of which have been done by North Americans. The peculiar and certainly fascinating aspects of the Mexican political system, and the almost mysterious success of the industrialization process, often tended to focus attention on what occurred within national borders. It did not seem necessary to

Olga Pellicer de Brody is with El Colegio de México, Mexico City.

relate internal developments to what was happening in the United States. It seemed even less necessary to speculate about the extent to which a reorientation of the economic-development pattern in Mexico would require, in its turn, a modification of the complex network of relations being established between the two nations.

This paper is an effort of the latter sort. Its first section provides a general panorama of relations between the two countries as they have been taking shape since 1945. The second section offers a summary of the Mexican economy's principal problems at the beginning of the 1960s, along with the policies proposed to solve them. Finally, I shall undertake a more detailed commentary on Mexican-U.S. relations in the spheres of trade and foreign investment, for the purpose of examining the manner in which these relations shape the possibility of establishing a mechanism for reorienting the Mexican economy. The conclusions reached emphasize the narrowness of the framework in which the Mexican state moves in attempting to introduce reforms in the existing economic system. At the same time, they suggest that if these reforms were successful, they would give a new cast to the country's structural dependence without changing its basic character.

The Mexican View of Relations with the United States since 1945

Mexico's policy toward the United States from the postwar period until the close of the 1960s was characterized by an interest in maintaining an independent stance with respect to the United States in the realm of hemispheric relations. It was also characterized by the search for a "special relationship" between the two countries, a relationship based as much on geographic proximity as on the advantages that Mexico's growth model offered U.S. political and economic interests.

Mexico's relative independence in inter-American relations has its origin in the country's historic experiences. Particularly important were memories of the post-revolutionary period when the United States exerted strong pressures on the Mexican Government in an effort to block the implementation of some of the objectives of the 1917 Constitution.[1] In the wake of these experiences, Mexico, in the Pan-American confer-

---

[1] The United States was concerned with preventing the application of the clauses in Article 27 that reestablished the nation's ownership of subsoil wealth, which, in accordance with certain rulings passed during the Porfirio Díaz regime, had been granted to private parties—principally foreign investors. The literature on this subject is extensive and includes: David E. Cronin, *Josephus Daniels in Mexico* (Madison, Wis.: 1960); Robert Freeman Smith, *The United States and Revolutionary Nationalism in Mexico, 1926–32* (Chicago: 1972); Manuel González Ramírez, *Los llamados tratados de Bucareli* (Mexico: S.P.I., 1939); Lorenzo Meyer, *México y los Estados Unidos en el conflicto petrolero* (Mexico: El Colegio de México, 1968); Aarón Sáenz, *La política internacional de la Revolución* (Mexico: Fondo de Cultura Económica, 1961).

ences held throughout the 1930s, became the primary defender of such principles as nonintervention and sovereignty over natural resources.[2]

At the time, the defense of those principles was an accurate reflection of the nationalistic spirit dominant among Mexican leaders during the formative period of the national movement for independent development. But nationalism gradually faded in the following years. At the outset of the 1940s, war conditions and the needs of Mexico's industrialization process had already underscored the dependence of Mexico's economy on the international capitalist system, and in particular on the North American economy.[3] Nevertheless, this turning point in the country's historical development had the paradoxical effect of fitting well with the ruling circle's taste for the traditions established in the realm of inter-American relations, traditions that included the possibility of preserving some of the values sustaining the legitimacy of the Mexican political system.[4] Thus, the main elements of Mexican policy in the Organization of American States were maintained for nearly 25 years. Mexico's mistrustful attitude regarding proposals to create a powerful regional organism equipped to intervene automatically and effectively in the problems arising in the hemisphere was the most persistent of all. Consequently, there was continuing Mexican opposition to an inter-American military organization, to the granting of substantial political powers to the OAS Council, and to agreements implying a broad interpretation of the concept of aggression in the hemisphere.[5] Frequently these points of view came into conflict with the hemispheric policy of the United States. Evidences of this are the discussions about the Caracas Declaration, the Eighth Consultative Meeting of the OAS, and the creation of the Inter-American Peace Force.[6] This opposition has been presented to the Mexican public

[2] A summary of the Mexican position in these conferences may be found in Gordon Connell-Smith, *The Inter-American System* (New York: 1966).

[3] Interest in Mexico's economic dependence, as it has been taking shape since 1940, developed recently as a result of the influence of theories of dependency, such as those articulated by Osvaldo Sunkel, Fernando H. Cardoso, and Enzo Faletto, among others. See, for example, *El perfil de México en 1980*, vol. 3 (Mexico City: Siglo XXI Editores, 1972), especially, Ricardo Cinta, "Burguesía nacional y desarrollo"; Julio Labastida, "Los grupos dominantes frente a las alternativas de cambio"; Manuel Villa, "Las bases del Estado mexicano y su problemática actual."

[4] On the bases of the legitimacy of the Mexican political system, see Vincent Padgett, *The Mexican Political System* (Boston: 1966).

[5] On Mexico's opposition to military aspects of inter-Americanism, see Edwin Lieuwen, *Arms and Politics in Latin America* (New York: 1960), and Lloyd Mecham, *The U.S. and the Inter-American System* (Austin, Texas: 1962); on the other two subjects, see Connell-Smith, *Inter-American System.*

[6] At the Caracas Conference in 1954, Mexico presented several amendments to the proposal on international communism made by the United States. These amendments attempted to prevent collective actions against member states of the OAS in the event of the development of a situation that was difficult to characterize and that fell under the internal jurisdiction of the state: specifically, the domination or control of a state's institutions by communism. The Mexi-

as supreme proof of its leaders' efforts to defend national sovereignty, to oppose imperialism, and, in short, to follow the traditions of a government having roots in a nationalistic revolution.[7]

While the autonomous positions within the OAS were strengthened, a less explicit but no less important trend in Mexican foreign policy took shape respecting the establishment of a "special relationship" between Mexico and the United States. The social and economic ties born of the border situation, and the importance of a sound understanding between the two countries as a "touchstone" for defining U.S. relations with the rest of Latin America, were seen by Mexican leaders as important motives for justifying this relationship.

"It is the responsibility of all of us," stated President Alemán during his visit to the U.S. Congress in 1948, "to add to the Good Neighbor policy a Good Neighbor economy. Whatever Mexico and the United States achieve will serve Mexico and the United States, but it will also serve all of America, for the border of our republics is a connecting point, a touchstone for guiding the future manifestations of hemispheric contacts."[8]

Over the years, the elements that in the opinion of the Mexican Government should constitute the U.S. Good Neighbor policy toward its southern neighbor became more defined. On the one hand, cooperation was sought in order to better confront border problems, such as the use of the waters of international rivers,[9] or the status of Mexican braceros

---

can amendments were rejected by a vote of 17 against and only three in favor (Argentina, Guatemala, and Mexico). In 1962, Mexico and Cuba were the only countries that voted against the convocation of the Eighth Inter-American Consultative Meeting, in which Cuba's expulsion from the OAS was to be decided. A few years later, at the Consultative Meeting held as a result of the crisis in the Dominican Republic, Mexico protested, together with Chile, Ecuador, Peru, and Uruguay, against the dispatching of the Inter-American Peace Force, which lent a collective character to the United States' unilateral intervention.

[7] The use of these ideas may be observed in the *Informes Presidenciales* presented annually to the Congress of the Union. For a general analysis of the utilization of Mexico's foreign policy for purposes of domestic policy, see Olga Pellicer de Brody, *México y la revolución cubana* (Mexico City: El Colegio de México, 1972).

[8] The Secretariat of Foreign Relations, *Memoria 1948-49* (Mexico City: SRE, 1949).

[9] The problems related to the international rivers running through the United States and Mexico have had diverse origins. They were caused, on the one hand, by the capricious changes in the riverbed of the Rio Grande, the border between the two countries, and, on the other, by the use made by North Americans of the waters of the Rio Grande and Colorado rivers, both of which reached Mexico notably reduced or contaminated. The latter problems were partially resolved in the *Tratado de Aguas de 1944* [Water Treaty of 1944], published by the Secretariat of Foreign Relations (Mexico City: 1945). However, even when this treaty was being signed, observers saw that it did not solve the problem of the salinity of the Colorado River waters, caused, as it was, by the use of the river to irrigate North American farms. The problem grew more serious in the following years, causing the destruction of the Mexicali Valley in Mexico. At the present time, this is one of the thorniest conflicts between the two countries. On this subject, see Luis G. Zorilla, *Historia de las relaciones entre México y los Estados Unidos, 1800-1958* (Mexico City: Editorial Porrúa, 1965), pp. 511-29.

doing seasonal work in the United States.[10] On the other hand, preferential treatment was sought for Mexican exports as well as a complete lifting of restrictions on the entry and spending of North American tourists in Mexico. Finally, a sustained flow of capital was expected from the United States in the form of Government loans or direct investment—a flow that should obey the "rules of the game" imposed by the Mexican Government. As we shall see, these rules tended to preserve national control over strategic sectors of the economy[11] and to fend off loans openly accompanied by strong political conditions.

The Mexican view of the "special relationship" with the United States was well defined during Rockefeller's visit to Mexico in the spring of 1969:

"Our Government considers," stated the then Secretary of Industry and Commerce, "that the sharing of a border and the consequences of this on the economy are elements that should be taken into account in the U.S. Government's decisions on trade and credit policy, international air traffic control, restrictions on its citizens who visit Mexico, and other related matters. In short, Mexico hopes that the United States will recognize our nation's right, in various economic areas, to be given the treatment of a border nation."[12]

Interest in obtaining this treatment perhaps explains the concentration of Mexico's foreign policy activity on bilateral contacts with the United States and its indifference toward the diversification of its international relations. Thus, an observer of Mexico's foreign policy pointed out in 1960:

Until quite recently, past administrations did not make an effort even to establish Mexico's true political and cultural presence in Latin America, or even in Central America. . . . Mexico's relations with the numerous African and Asian states that have become independent have been minimal, in spite of their increasing importance in international life. . . .[13]

---

[10]"Braceros" are Mexican workers who immigrate temporarily to the United States to satisfy the need for farm labor that arises during harvest time. Their history goes back to the war years, when at the request of the United States the first international agreement was signed between the two countries to establish the criteria that should govern the status of these workers. At the end of the war, negotiations were begun for a new agreement, which was signed in 1951 and lasted until 1964. In that year, under pressure from some North American unions, the agreement was annulled. This has not prevented Mexican workers from continuing to cross the border, legally or illegally, in search of work. On this subject, see Robert G. Jones, *Mexican War Workers in the U.S.* (Washington: Pan American Union, 1945). Also, see Mario Ojeda Gómez, "Estudio de un caso de decisión política: el programa norteamericano de importación de braceros," in *Extremos de México* (Mexico City: El Colegio de México, 1972), pp. 385–410.

[11]See Wolfgang Konig, *La política mexicana sobre inversiones extranjeras* (Mexico City: El Colegio de México, Colección Jornadas, 1968).

[12]Statements reproduced in *Comercio Exterior* (Mexico City), 1969, p. 334.

[13]Jorge Castañeda, "México y el exterior," in *México, cincuenta años de revolución,* vol. III (Politics) (Mexico City: Fondo de Cultura Económica, 1960).

This situation tended to change during the 1960s, when for essentially economic reasons Mexico began to draw closer to other geographic regions.[14] Nonetheless, a cautious position was maintained regarding the underdeveloped world's joint efforts to exert pressure on the industrialized nations through speeches or denunciations in world organizations. In Mexico's reluctance to unite with these efforts we can perceive, as a Mexican official pointed out on one occasion, the confidence that "Mexico is able to resolve its foreign economic problems through bilateral agreements with the directly concerned parties."[15]

In general, the U.S. Government responded positively to Mexico's aim of maintaining a margin of independence in hemispheric relations. It suffices, for example, to recall how, after Mexico's opposition to the holding of the Consultative Meeting in Punta del Este, President Kennedy visited Mexico and was given one of the most cordial receptions any visiting foreign dignitary had ever received. And when Mexico decided to vote against the (OAS) resolutions on breaking relations with Cuba, a representative of the U.S. Government stated that Mexico was the best friend the United States had.[16]

However, the understanding and the good will present in U.S. policy toward Mexico in the realm of inter-American relations has been less evident in the case of bilateral relations. It is true that U.S. capital from both public and private sources has come to Mexico, quite intensively, since 1950; but this is the extent of the "Good Neighbor" policy—a policy conceived in a far broader fashion by Mexican leaders. Problems such as the salinity of the waters of the Colorado River, restrictions on Mexican

---

[14]For the changes that took place in foreign policy during the López Mateos period, see Mario Ojeda Gómez, "México y el exterior," *Foro Internacional* (Mexico City), nos. 22-23, 1966.

[15]Speech given by Plácido García Reynoso, chief of the Mexican delegation at the 1968 UNCTAD conference; reproduced in Secretariat of the Presidency, *Chile, Serie de Estudios Núm. 3* (Mexico City: 1972).

[16]There are various ways of explaining this acceptance by the United States of the Mexican Government's inter-American policy. In the first place, Mexican governing circles have not attempted to influence the policies of other Latin American nations; Mexico's positions in the OAS have been essentially solitary ones. This stance may be the result of a correct appraisal of the possibilities of finding a response in other Latin American nations, or perhaps of the conviction that an attempt at assuming leadership would jeopardize the United States' friendly disposition toward Mexico's relative independence. In the second place, Mexico has not carried its positions in the OAS to the point of challenging interests vital to the United States. During the Cuban missile crisis, Mexico supported the blockade, and for a long time its relations with Cuba did not lead to an increase in commercial relations capable of lightening the effect of the economic blockade against the island. Finally, the importance of Mexico's foreign policy as a factor in internal stability might be a reason why that policy would be accepted by the United States—which is a country clearly interested in avoiding, south of its border, the problems of coups, terrorism, or guerrilla activity that have permeated the political life of other Latin American nations. On this, see de Brody, *México,* and Mario Ojeda Gómez, "El perfil internacional de México en 1980," in *El perfil de México* (see note 3), pp. 289-324.

exports to the United States, or the treatment of Mexican workers in the United States have frequently darkened the two countries' relations. These problems tend to be minimized by Government spokesmen, however, especially by the North Americans. It is as if U.S. respect for Mexico's independence in the OAS, U.S. investors' attraction to Mexico's internal market, and the maintenance of a substantial growth rate in Mexico were reasons enough to lend credence to the idea of an almost perfect relationship between the two countries. Thus, it is not until quite recently that the sharpening of some problems in the Mexican economy has led to a questioning, if indirect, of the healthiness of the ties established between Mexico and the United States.

The Problems of the Mexican Economy

From a strictly quantitative point of view, Mexico's economic growth until early 1970 was one of the most rapid in the underdeveloped world. Mexico's GNP increased at an average rate of 6.5 percent annually, which, despite a substantial demographic growth, permitted a per-capita growth of approximately 3.5 percent. But the advance of the industrialization process, based on consumption and technological patterns of foreign origin, has not solved, and on the contrary tends to aggravate, the unjust distribution of income, underemployment and unemployment, and the ever more acute crisis in the external sector of the economy.[17]

The problems in the country's international economic relations have become serious since the late 1950s as a result of the drop in prices of traditional Mexican export products and the increase of imports required by the country's industrialization process. Thus industrialization, aimed at freeing the country from dependence on imports, had the paradoxical effect of creating increased and more complex dependence. Although Mexico has cut back its imports of consumer goods as much as possible, it has at the same time come to import raw materials and the intermediate goods and replacement parts needed to maintain and expand established industries. This situation is evident in the fact that between 1960 and 1966 the proportion of the internal demand for capital goods met through imports was always over 50 percent, fluctuating from a high of 59.8 percent in 1965 to a low of 52 percent in 1961.[18]

[17] For an examination of the problems and perspectives of the Mexican economy in the 1970s, see CEPAL, *México: notas para el estudio económico de América Latina, 1971* (Mexico City: CEPAL, March 13, 1972); OAS, CIAP, *El esfuerzo interno y las necesidades de financiamiento externo para el desarrollo de México* (OAS, Ser. H/XIV, CIAP/562, July 19, 1972); David Ibarra, "Mercados, desarrollo y política económica; perspectivas de la economía de México," in *El perfil de México* (see note 3), vol. I, 1970; Miguel Wionczek, ed., *¿Crecimiento o desarrollo económico?* (Mexico City: Colección SEP 70, 1972).

[18] See Jorge Eduardo Navarrete, "Desequilibrio y dependencia en las relaciones internacionales de México," in Wionczek, ed., *¿Crecimiento?* p. 155.

While this was occurring, the growth of Mexican exports was relatively weak. In the second half of the 1960s Mexico's traditional exports, principally agricultural products (which constitute three-fourths of total exports), grew at a quite moderate rate—3.2 percent annually. The overall growth of exports therefore depended on an eventual increase of sales abroad of manufactured and semi-manufactured products—which amounted to only slightly over one-fourth of total exports.[19]

Confidence in the possibility of financing part of the balance-of-trade deficit with the income obtained through tourism, border transactions, etc., was fading. These earnings did not grow at the hoped-for rate. This discouraging performance, together with the outflow of capital from tourism abroad, remittances on foreign investments, and interests on Government loans, in 1969 gave rise for the first time to a deficit in the financial balance—which in turn had to be added to the trade deficit.[20]

Thus, in the 1960s, an equilibrium in the country's international accounts was only possible thanks to the sustained flow of direct foreign investments and loans to the public sector. This situation alarmed Mexican Government officials when the payments on interest and amortization of the debt rose to 25.3 percent of the income of the current account. It then became apparent that recourse to foreign credit was becoming a mechanism for multiplying imbalances in the balance of payments, as the servicing of the debt grew more rapidly than the income in current accounts.[21]

The latter situation led some sectors of the public bureaucracy to become aware of the threat of a crisis in the external sector of the economy that could paralyze imports vital to the functioning of Mexican industry. Mexican leaders then insisted on the need to find new strategies for the country's economic development. It was proposed, in particular, to promote a policy of employment, of increasing the income of the public sector, and of steering away from import substitution to concentrate more effort on the creation of export industry.[22]

[19] Navarrete, in "Desequilibrio," points out that Mexican industries export their products only when they have surpluses with respect to the national market. In addition, many exports simply reflect the taking advantage of a transitory favorable condition in the external market, rather than the obtaining of an internationally competitive position (pp. 158ff).

[20] Ibid., pp. 168ff.

[21] Ibarra, "Mercados," pp. 136–37.

[22] An editorial that appeared in the magazine *Comercio Exterior* (Mexico City) said, "In general it is thought that, as the decade changes, the Mexican economy is arriving at a point at which it is necessary to redirect the course of its development. . . . At the end of the 1960s the conclusions of an economic analysis are that it is necessary to strengthen the internal market through employment, salary, and income redistribution. Also necessary are the allocation of greater resources to the public sector for direct productive and social investment, through greater tax revenues, and a confronting of the balance-of-payments restrictions through increasing current foreign-exchange earnings." (1970, p. 3.)

The validity of these ideas was confirmed when statistics were published on the external sector of the economy in 1970. In that year there was an unusual increase in imports, tourism abroad, and remittances on foreign investments. In addition, Mexican agricultural problems during the 1969–70 season resulted in a decrease in exports (-1.2 percent). Thus, the deficit in the current account rose to $900 million in 1970, doubling that of the previous years.[23] The gravity of this situation clearly explains the publicity given to export activity in Mexico, exports being the keynote of the economic policy of the Government taking office in 1970. According to official statements, the best perspectives for exports lay in Mexico's growing participation in the Latin American Free Trade Association (LAFTA), and in the rise in sales of manufactured products throughout the 1960s. These declarations obscure the fact that Mexico continues to be, fundamentally, an exporter of agricultural products, and despite efforts at diversification, the country's foreign trade is concentrated in the United States.[24] It therefore seems that at least in the short run the future of Mexican exports will be strongly influenced by economic relations with the United States; these thus deserve a more detailed analysis.

Mexican-U.S. Trade Relations

The preponderant role that the United States was to assume in Mexico's foreign economic relations was underscored during the war years, when— with the closing of the European markets, principally those of Germany and Great Britain—86 percent of Mexico's exports were directed to the United States. Although at the close of the war Mexican leaders expressed their concern about this situation, they did not or could not take the measures necessary for developing an export capacity capable of regaining the old markets. Thus, at the close of the 1950s, more than 70 percent of Mexican sales abroad went to the United States, a very high percentage when compared with the exports of other Latin American countries as different as Argentina, Brazil, Colombia, or Peru.[25] The situation began to change in the 1960s, with the increase in exports to LAFTA, the European Common Market, and Japan, which to some extent reduced the concentration of exports to the United States. In 1964 the United States received 64 percent of Mexico's total exports. However, this trend again

[23] Banco de México, *Informe Anual* (1970).

[24] In 1971, 61 percent of all the purchases made by Mexico abroad, which totaled $2,411 million, came from the United States, and 71 percent of Mexico's exports, amounting to $1,433 million, went to the U.S. market.

[25] According to figures presented by Ojeda Gómez, "El perfil," in 1966 Argentina sold 7 percent of its exports to the United States, Brazil 33 percent, Colombia 43 percent, and Peru 42 percent (p. 304).

shifted in later years, and by 1970 sales to the United States once more accounted for 70 percent of Mexico's total exports.[26]

In spite of Mexico's industrial development over the past thirty years, agricultural products continue to be the predominant export to the United States (65 percent). The significant change in the structure of exports took place in the 1940s, with a drop in the percentage of mineral sales (formerly two-thirds of total exports) and a marked rise in sales of agricultural products.[27] At first glance, the diversity of the export capacity developed in Mexico under the stimulus of the war (including coffee, cotton, sugar, henequen, etc.) was an encouraging sign with respect to the reduction of the Mexican economy's dependence. If these signs had some validity, however, it is no less true that a high percentage of the new products were developed with the sole aim of supplying the U.S. market. Thus, agricultural exporters who had been strengthened in Mexico at the beginning of the 1940s—owing to a national and international situation in which, in the name of productivity and earning foreign exchange, they were allowed to sacrifice some of the agricultural policies of the Cárdenas period—were now weaving a more subtle and complex network of dependence.[28] Responding exclusively to U.S. stimuli, they did not develop the techniques of transport or of winning markets that would allow their products to travel farther than the U.S. border. Such efforts seemed secondary, given the extent to which the proximity of the United States guaranteed a privileged place for export development in Mexico. This optimistic view has not, however, been confirmed by the trade relations between the two nations over the past thirty years.

One of the principal aims of the Mexican rulers' economic policy from 1940 on was to assign to the agricultural sector the role of earner of the foreign exchange required for the country's industrialization. This policy

[26] Banco Nacional de Comercio Exterior, *Informe Anual* (1970).

[27] A review of the evolution of Mexico's foreign trade from 1935 to 1955 can be found in Banco Nacional de Comercio Exterior, *Comercio exterior de México* (Mexico City: BNCE, 1956), pp. 5–28. It is pointed out there that during the prewar years 30.4 percent of Mexico's foreign trade was with the European continent; during the war this trade was only 3.5 percent of Mexico's total.

[28] No study has been made to date of the influence that foreign demand for some Mexican farm products had on the course of Mexican agrarian reform since 1940. Some figures suggest that, given the possibility of acquiring foreign-exchange earnings, there was no hesitation in putting a halt to policies favoring cooperative farmers (ejidatarios)—policies that may have implied a short-term drop in productivity. The case of henequen is one example. From 1942 to 1945, the American Defense Supply Corporation bought nearly the total henequen production of the State of Yucatán. Under these circumstances, the Government decided to return the fiber-processing machinery—which had been given to cooperative farmers—to its former owners. The economic upsurge created by foreign demand at that time prevented this action from eliciting a negative reaction from the campesinos. From Blanca Torres, *The Mexican PAN, a Case Study of the Party in Yucatán,* thesis for the Ph.B. Degree, Oxford University, 1971.

justified, for example, the growth of new latifundios in the north of the country in which export agriculture, principally cotton, was to be developed. Nevertheless, the increase in Mexican exports to the United States came to a halt in 1955. In subsequent years, the value of Mexican exports suffered a substantial drop, such that by 1959 the total was just 80 percent of what it had been in 1955.[29] Only the development of tourism, favored by geographic proximity and the country's natural and archaeological beauties, saved the Mexican economy from a crisis similar to those suffered by other Latin American nations as a consequence of the collapse in export prices.

Mexican sales to the United States made a recovery in the early 1960s, but fell off again in 1963. Since then, exports to the United States have risen at a steady but moderate rate[30] that does not counterbalance the growing increase of imports of machinery and equipment from the United States.[31]

It would be unfair to attribute to U.S. trade policy the principal responsibility for the scant growth in Mexican exports. Quite diverse factors, both national and international in nature, have been involved in this poor performance: on the one hand are the world market conditions for the exports of underdeveloped nations, given the high agricultural productivity of some industrialized nations and the appearance of synthetic materials that frequently replace raw materials; on the other hand are the indifference and passivity of Mexican producers, the absence of an adequate policy to stimulate exports, and the internal consumption of crops that could be exported (this being profitable because of official price-support policies).[32] However, these factors do not override the fact that U.S. trade policy has been fundamental in weakening or stimulating the Mexican export economy.

[29] An overview of the situation of Mexican exports in this period can be found in Banco Nacional de Comercio Exterior, *Comercio Exterior de México, 1959* (Mexico City: BNCE, 1960).

[30] From 1965 to 1970, exports to the United States grew at an average rate of 5.6 percent at current prices; at real prices the percentage would be considerably lower.

[31] The balance of trade between Mexico and the United States has shown an increasing deficit since the end of the war. Whereas in 1960 this disequilibrium amounted to 5,004 million pesos, in 1970 it reached 9,144 million pesos. The principal products imported by Mexico from the United States are electrical and mechanical machines and apparatuses, spare parts for automobiles, iron and steel products, parts for public-transport vehicles assembled in Mexico, synthetic materials, measuring and precision instruments, butane gas, garments, and weaving materials. Source: Secretaría de Industria y Comercio, *Anuarios de Comercio* (Mexico City).

[32] The subject of the international market and exports to underdeveloped countries has been broadly discussed in various UNCTAD and CEPAL reports. See, for example, CEPAL, *El comercio internacional y el desarrollo de América Latina* (Mexico City: Fondo de Cultura Económica, 1964). On Mexico's policy of international trade, see Bela Balassa, "La industrialización y el comercio exterior; análisis y proposiciones," in Wionczek, *¿Crecimiento?* (see note 17), pp. 45–83.

As in the majority of industrialized countries in the capitalist world, the foreign economic policy of the United States has had a twofold aim: first, to protect its citizens, especially its farmers, from the competition of products from countries where cheap labor provides a comparative advantage; second, to channel the activities of underdeveloped nations toward the exploitation of their natural resources, creating obstacles, sometimes insurmountable, to their exporting of processed or semi-processed products.[33] The furthering of the first objective has perhaps been the most frequent source of friction between the United States and Mexico, an understandable situation in light of the fact that some of Mexico's principal exports are also produced in the United States.[34] Under these circumstances, when the U.S. Government seeks to check the growth of some imports or to abruptly stem purchases being made, it relies on a complex system of voluntary quotas, seasonal tariffs, "anti-dumping" laws, etc.[35] All of this is facilitated by the powers that the U.S. Congress gives to the Secretary of Agriculture to take measures when there are indications that the internal market is being endangered.

During the second half of the 1950s, problems relating to cotton purchases caused quite severe conflicts between the two countries; the drastic reduction of Mexico's sales of this fiber threatened the stability of the Mexican peso in 1958.[36] More recently, the most serious conflicts have been caused by the sale of tomatoes, which in the past few years has become one of the most dynamic lines of Mexican exports. Thus, at the beginning of 1969, the U.S. Government's restriction on purchases of Mexican tomatoes resulted in a $300 million loss to tomato producers in the north of the country, some of them U.S. investors. According to statements that appeared in the press, this in turn caused the layoff of

[33] The following example is illustrative: In the case of tomatoes, one of Mexico's principal export products, U.S. import tariffs run from 1.5 to 2.1 cents per pound for fresh tomatoes to 13.6 percent ad valorem for canned tomatoes. A general examination of the United States' foreign-trade policy and its consequences for underdeveloped countries may be found in Henry Magdoff, *The Age of Imperialism* (New York: 1968).

[34] The principal products exported by Mexico to the United States (which together represent 41 percent of the value of all Mexican sales to the United States) are sugar, coffee, frozen shrimp, beef cattle, tomatoes, ungalvanized sheets of iron or steel, parts for machinery used in agriculture and industry, and apparatuses used in the installation of electrical conductors.

[35] Voluntary quotas are restrictions that the exporting country imposes on itself in agreement with U.S. authorities who, in the absence of such quotas, would set explicit quotas for a volume less than what is being exported. These quotas, together with the interpretations the U.S. Government occasionally gives to the anti-dumping law, constitute perhaps the most serious barrier to the growth of Mexican exports to the United States. As an example of the latter, see recent discussions on the sale of Mexican sulphur to the United States, which, according to U.S. authorities, is taking place under conditions of "dumping." *Comercio Exterior* (Mexico City), 1972, p. 728.

[36] Zorrilla, *Historia,* p. 559.

15,000 farmworkers who subsequently swelled the ranks of Mexico's rural army of the unemployed.[37] Others were perhaps able to cross the U.S. border, legally or illegally, to become a part of the Mexican minority so often discriminated against by U.S. employers.[38]

The sale of manufactured products has not had much better luck. Throughout the 1960s, the United States' protectionist policy against these imports became increasingly rigid. In 1962 only seven categories of manufactured imports were subject to quantitative restrictions, but by 1970 these restrictions covered 67 categories. At the same time, a system of rising tariffs on imported products, based on their degree of industrial processing, was being perfected: primary products are practically free of import duties, intermediate goods are taxed at an average rate of 18 percent ad valorem, and finished goods are taxed at an average of 16 percent ad valorem. The situation is aggravated by a system of sliding tariffs that establishes various quota levels. At each higher level the tax rises progressively until it becomes nearly prohibitive, as is the case for steel products from Mexico.[39]

The events of 1971, which reached a climax in August with the U.S. Government's decision to impose a special 10-percent tariff surcharge on imports,[40] do not suggest that a weakening in U.S. protectionist tendencies is likely. On the contrary, what can be expected is a veritable war of trade restrictions among advanced countries, whose first victims will be the underdeveloped nations. This situation explains why the effort to increase Mexican exports is focused on manufactured goods, and is principally directed toward the conquest of less developed markets such as the Central American or the LAFTA countries. An additional problem comes into play here: that of the influence of international, and especially North American, corporations in Mexico's manufacturing industry, a problem that ought to be examined within the general framework of foreign investment in Mexico.

Foreign Investment and Exports

Mexico's policy toward foreign investment undoubtedly constituted a key aspect of the restructuring of relations between Mexico and the

---

[37]*Comercio Exterior* (Mexico City), 1969, pp. 277, 430.

[38]A good analysis of the situation of Mexican workers in the United States is found in Ernesto Galarza, *Merchants of Labor, Mexican Bracero History* (Charlotte, N.C., and Santa Barbara, Cal.: 1964).

[39]Beyond a certain quota, taxes on steel products from Mexico become 106 percent ad valorem.

[40]On this occasion the Mexican Government—perhaps confident in its "special relationship"—attempted bilateral negotiations with the United States for the purposes of obtaining preferential treatment for Mexican exports. The U.S. response gave no grounds for hoping this preferen-

United States after 1940. Mexican leaders firmly believed in the rightness of stimulating these investments, but they imposed conditions on them that, in the light of other Latin American nations' policies, seemed highly restrictive. It was a question, first, of preventing investments in areas considered to be strategic; second, of subjecting investments to a juridical system that prevented the repetition of the widely known international pressures that had conditioned Mexico's foreign relations up until 1938; and, finally, of giving the national bourgeoisie a share in its benefits through a policy favoring investments linked with national capital.[41]

From 1950 on, foreign investors seemed to accept these rules of the game with no major conflicts. Between 1950 and 1960, foreign investment nearly doubled, jumping from $566 million to $1,081 million; from 1960 to 1968 it again doubled, rising to $2,300 million, one of the highest figures for any Latin American country. Concurrently, the predominance of U.S. capital became more marked. In 1940, U.S. capital constituted 61 percent of the total foreign investment in Mexico; by 1950, it was 68 percent; and from 1960 to the present, it has risen to approximately 83 percent.[42]

For a number of years, Mexican Government spokesmen stressed the secondary and complementary character of this investment. The almost total lack of data on the real role of foreign capital in the country permitted the survival of the notion of national control over the industrialization process. The first studies of the matter that have appeared in the past years, however, tend to demonstrate just the opposite.[43] They make

---

tial treatment might be received. On the effect this experience had on recent changes in Mexico's foreign policy, see Olga Pellicer de Brody, "Cambios recientes en la política exterior mexicana," *Foro Internacional* (Mexico City), no. 50, 1972.

[41] The course of foreign investment in Mexico is determined not only by the fragmentary legislation relating to it, but also by ad hoc rulings. From these sources it can be seen that the so-called basic sectors of the economy—oil, petrochemicals, electrical energy, communications, and railroads—are reserved for the state. Agricultural activity as well as the financial sector and some other industrial and commercial activities of relatively less importance are reserved exclusively for Mexican nationals. In other sectors of manufacturing, as well as in mining, majority control must be Mexican when the industry is in a field related to a list of basic activities (the latest additions to this list included the steel, cement, glass, and aluminum industries). Finally, if foreign capital does not accept these terms, it cannot claim the fiscal privileges given in the Law of New and Necessary Industries. See Konig, *La política mexicana,* and Lorenzo Meyer, "Cambio político y dependencia; México en el siglo XX," in *Foro Internacional* (Mexico City), no. 50, 1973.

[42] Miguel Wionczek, "La inversión privada en México; problemas y perspectivas," in *Comercio Exterior* (Mexico City), 1970.

[43] Although these studies are still infrequent, they already provide an idea concerning the role played by foreign investment in Mexico. See, for example, Flavio Derossi, "The Mexican Entrepreneur: Preliminary Report" (Paris: O.E.C.D., Development Center, August 1970), mimeographed; Ricardo Cinta, "Clases sociales y desarrollo en México" (Santiago: Latin American Seminar on Development, November 1970), mimeographed; Wionczek, "La inversión privada"; Meyer, *México* (see note 1).

evident the fact that foreign investment is concentrated in the sectors that grew most rapidly during the past two decades, and, moreover, that foreign investment has gained controlling interests in firms that produce capital goods, thus obtaining a strategic place in the Mexican economy.[44] This predominance becomes more significant in light of the fact that, because they are multinational, many of these firms are part of a much broader complex. According to Harvard University figures, the 187 most important North American multinational corporations control 70 percent of direct U.S. foreign investment in the field of manufacturing. In 1967, 179 of the 187 were operating in Mexico. As a result of mergers and sales, by the end of 1967 only 162 were still operating. These corporations had 412 subsidiaries, 225 of which were in the manufacturing sector (including assembly), 31 in commercial activities, 14 in extractive industries, and the remaining 112 in unidentified activities.[45]

The apparent complacency with which Mexico's governing circles and the national bourgeoisie witnessed this predominance of foreign investment in the country's industry was perhaps justified by the supposed contribution of this investment to the solution of the balance-of-payments difficulties, and to the investment's positive effect on the levels of welfare and technology of developing economies. Though no studies exist that verify the latter effects, there certainly are enough data to definitively refute the notion of a favorable influence on the balance of payments. The most recent studies on the Mexican economy indicate that one of the most troublesome aspects of the current account of the balance of payments in the next years will be the increase of the profit remittances made by foreign investors.

According to some predictions (see Table 1), these remittances will increase from approximately $418 million in 1972 to $615 million in 1976; following these in importance will be interest payments on the foreign debt, which are projected to rise from $337 million in 1972 to $517 million in 1976 (even though the new debt is contracted at a 6-percent interest rate with an average amortization period of 15 years).

---

[44]Using statistics from the 1965 Industrial Census, and including only industrial plants with a total gross production of over 20 million pesos (64 percent of the total gross industrial production in 1965–1,117 plants controlled by 938 firms), we find that among the 50 largest enterprises, 48 percent of their gross production is in firms under foreign control, 30 percent is in private national firms, and 22 percent is in state-owned firms. Examining the composition of the 116 largest firms producing capital goods, we find that 53 percent are under foreign control. Of the 88 most important firms producing intermediate basic goods, 11.9 percent are foreign. The proportion of foreign control continues to drop as firms producing nonbasic intermediate and consumer goods are examined. This emphasizes the fact that foreign capital is concentrated in the industrial capital-goods sector. Furthermore, even though the statistics on the matter are not complete, there are indications that foreign capital controls the most dynamic sectors of tourism and trade. Figures are cited from Meyer, "Cambio político."

[45]Wionczek, "La inversión privada."

TABLE 1
Balance-of-Payments Projections for Mexico
Maintaining Historical Trends[a]
(Millions of U.S. dollars)

Transfer category	1972	1973	1974	1975	1976
Exports of goods and services					
(Excluding factor payments)	3,424	3,691	3,979	4,287	4,616
Merchandise	1,528	1,634	1,748	1,870	2,001
Agricultural	832	882	936	993	1,055
Mining	240	250	260	271	283
Manufactured	314	349	387	428	472
Other	142	153	164	177	190
Tourism	677	747	822	902	987
Border transactions	1,020	1,100	1,184	1,275	1,372
Gold and silver	49	51	54	56	58
Other services and transfers	149	159	171	184	198
Imports of goods and services					
(Excluding factor payments)	3,605	3,900	4,227	4,589	4,982
Merchandise	2,603	2,833	3,091	3,376	3,689
Raw materials	875	947	1,026	1,113	1,207
Capital goods	1,158	1,266	1,391	1,529	1,684
Consumer goods	570	620	674	734	798
Tourism	200	218	237	259	281
Border transactions	643	688	736	789	845
Other services and transfers	159	161	163	165	167
Balance of goods and services					
(Excluding factor payments)	181	209	248	302	366
Others	-100	-110	-120	-130	-140
Profit remittances	418	461	507	559	615
Interest on deficit in current account before "additional effort" and without considering effect of increased interest of a larger deficit	836	934	1,051	1,195	1,358
Net "additional effort" of export of goods and services to maintain deficit of resources at the 1972 level	1	19	48	92	146
Deficit in the current account after the "additional effort"	835	915	1,003	1,103	1,212

Source: OAS Secretariat.

[a] Under the supposition that the new debt will be contracted at a 6-percent interest rate and with a 15-year amortization period.

To counteract this situation it was necessary to encourage the foreign firms in Mexico to export more of their production. This became even more urgent when, on initiating a serious effort in this direction, the Mexican Government came face to face with some of the most severe problems in the nation's industrial structure. On the one hand, the industrial structure is oriented almost exclusively toward satisfying internal demand; on the other, the development of Mexican industry has taken place under excessively protective conditions, which have given rise to a large number of relatively uncompetitive firms that would only in rare instances have access to international markets. Thus, export possibilities are to be found among the more productive firms—precisely those most often dominated by U.S. capital. For example, official statements on export possibilities in Central America indicate opportunities there for manufactured products from Mexico, such as canned foods, machinery and transport equipment, medicines, etc. All of these lines are controlled by the subsidiaries of the large international corporations.

Until now these firms have not shown great interest in exporting, owing in part to the existence of a strongly protected Mexican market that offers the possibility of obtaining very high profits, even with underutilization of plant capacity. Also important are the restrictions placed by international corporations on their foreign subsidiaries, such as the prohibiting or limiting of exports when the latter involve competition within the firm itself. Thus, a recent UNCTAD study of the export restrictions found in some contracts for the transfer of technology to Mexico indicates that of the 109 agreements examined, 104 contained clauses that to a greater or lesser extent limited exports.[46]

Under these circumstances, the Echeverría Government confirmed the country's traditional sympathy toward foreign investment when it took office, but it immediately began to take action aimed at obtaining the fullest possible cooperation of these investors in the export effort. In early 1971, *Business International* reported that the Government had warned that importation permits on the materials necessary for the automobile industry would be stopped if by 1977 it was not possible to export as much as was imported. At the same time, the magazine reported indications that the Government might reconsider the requisite of "Mexicanization" for firms that used Mexico as a base for exports.[47]

This policy of discreet pressures on foreign investors was suddenly abandoned near the end of 1972, when, apparently responding to internal pressures, the Government began a nationalistic campaign against the control of key sectors of the Mexican economy by foreign capital. This

[46]Cited in *Comercio Exterior* (Mexico City), 1971, pp. 383–85.
[47]"Business International, Mexican Roundtable; Briefing Paper," *Business International* (Mexico City), 1971.

campaign culminated in November of that year with the approval of a Law on the Transfer of Technology and the formulation of a Bill for the Control of Foreign Investment.[48] In appearance, both documents go further than the initial aim of obtaining an increase in the exports of foreign firms. As concerns the former, the registration of all technology-transfer contracts signed in the country was made a legal requirement; moreover, guidelines were set for turning down such registrations. Among these guidelines, one of the most important is the prohibition of or limitation on exports made by firms that buy technology; another concerns the failure to acquire technology that is already in the country. The second bill carries the notion of "Mexicanization" to its ultimate consequences by stipulating, as a general rule, that foreign investors in Mexico ought to control only 49 percent of the stock of a firm. Nevertheless, both documents leave the door open to a flexible policy by placing in the hands of special commissions the right to decide, in any particular case, the applicability of the general rules.

In spite of these conciliatory aspects, the formulation of these laws immediately gave rise to concerned statements by the U.S. Ambassador in Mexico. According to comments that appeared in one of Mexico's most influential dailies, his declarations were "closer to those of the manager of a U.S. company or of a U.S. Chamber of Commerce official than to those of a politician, much less to those of a diplomat." At the same time, the statements made by owners' associations in Mexico revealed that the country's most powerful economic sectors, the majority of them tied in one way or another to U.S. capital, were not ready to lend unrestricted support to Government action along these lines.[49]

In light of the latter circumstance, as well as the difficulties of the Mexican balance of payments, the new laws seem principally to be a way to increase the power of the Mexican state in its negotiations with foreign investors. But these are not negotiations that would be aimed at imposing a real check on the influence of such investment in the Mexican economy; they would, on the contrary, seek to make the foreign firm a key part of the export program that has been given such importance within the Government's policy in recent years.

Conclusions

Mexican-U.S. relations from the end of the Second World War to the present have responded to the Mexican Government's desire to maintain

---

[48]The former was approved by the Mexican Congress in November 1972; the text is reproduced in *Comercio Exterior* (Mexico City), November 1972, pp. 1009–11. The latter is being discussed as this paper is being revised; see the proposal in *Excélsior* (Mexico City), December 27, 1972.

[49]*Excélsior* (Mexico City), October 12, 1972.

a margin of independence in inter-American relations; but it has not been entirely possible to establish a "special relationship" that was, among other things, aimed at eliminating conflictive border situations, reducing the vulnerability of Mexican exports, and assuring that the influx of U.S. investments in Mexico would be "complementary" to national capital. Thus, the ties actually established between Mexico and the United States differ little from those characterizing relations between the more industrialized countries of the capitalist periphery and a hegemonic nation: the most dynamic sectors of the Mexican manufacturing industry tend to be in the hands of foreign investors, principally North Americans; the profits of these industries are remitted in large measure to home offices; and a sector that exports agricultural products and is subject to strong pressures and fluctuations in the U.S. market still exists.

These relations were not at issue while the Mexican economic and political system was able to maintain a growth rate and level of political stability that served the interests of the dominant national and foreign groups. As the first signs of the weakening of this system began to appear, however, the necessity arose—until now felt principally in Mexican Government circles—to make some modifications that would prevent a violent crisis in the system. The most important modification, for the purposes of Mexican-U.S. relations, is the relative increase of Mexican exports. To bring this about, it was necessary to insist that the United States accord preferential treatment to imports from Mexico, but the internal conditions of the United States are such as to impede this type of solution. The most viable course, under political conditions prohibiting profound changes in the Mexican "status quo," is that of a reformulation of the "rules of the game" existing between the Mexican Government and foreign investment. This investment now may have to find some way of defending the interests of its home offices while at the same time increasing its participation in the sales of Mexican manufactured goods abroad.

If international corporations perceive the situation thus, Mexico could specialize in the exportation of manufactured products in which cheap labor, ensured by rural unemployment and control over workers, would give it a comparative advantage. We would then find ourselves at the beginning of a new stage of the "international division of labor," which would confirm the dependence of the Mexican economy, perhaps opening the door to a new era of industrialization in Mexico that would gradually incorporate some newly privileged sectors into the modernization process. The path toward this new understanding between the Mexican state and foreign investment can, as recent events indicate, place stumbling blocks in the way of Mexican-U.S. relations. These problems might become even more pronounced, for to increase its negotiating power the current Government is accentuating nationalistic policies that have traditionally been expressed in its hemispheric relations and that are now also reflected in organizations such as UNCTAD.[50]

There are, however, several reasons for thinking that these problems will be dealt with rather easily. Whatever response U.S. capital gives to the aims of economic development put forth by the Mexican Government, the fact is that the attitude of economically powerful groups in Mexico renders unlikely a serious confrontation with U.S. interests. So long as the strength of these groups does not lessen, we can predict that there will be an accommodation in Mexican-U.S. relations, an accommodation posing no threat to the ties that have developed between the two countries over the past thirty years.

[50] See de Brody, "Cambios recientes."

Commentary on Pellicer de Brody

EDELBERTO TORRES RIVAS

International relations have come to form a specific focus for study and to define a problem area that has pretensions to theoretical and conceptual autonomy. The generally accepted assumption is that nations are the subjects of social relations in the same way individuals are, but on a different level. "National" status would thus explain the nature of international relations—and not the other way around—just as the individual's position in the social structure is the most important factor in explaining his conduct.

In general, this theoretical view is backed up by an investigative strategy. Opinions and attitudes—as the external manifestation of an internal rationality that is basically permanent, recognizable, and recoverable on the level of empirical experience—constitute the data to be analyzed. In analogous fashion, official declarations, diplomatic propositions, official conduct in international assemblies and meetings, etc., can be thought of as the "attitudes" of the nation-actor. Such "attitudes" may be converted into data for analysis (content, frequency, etc.) to establish reciprocal patterns of conduct that on this level make up the content of the science of international relations.

However, this traditional view—according to which international relations are carried out by political units thought of as personalities—corresponds only to the superficial level of what is a more complex matter. The interior structure of the political unit is decisive because it too is contradictory. It is not true that foreign policy begins only where domestic policy ends. Even less is this the case for the great powers, for their important goals of domestic policy can only be achieved in connection with foreign-policy goals, and it is thus difficult to separate the one from the other.

For the lesser countries of the international system, however, the

Edelberto Torres Rivas is a member of the Central American Program for the Development of the Social Sciences, San José, Costa Rica.

situation is different. Until a certain moment of the twentieth century, European politics was practically synonymous with international politics. In other words, European national interests determined international politics.

In Latin America, countries in the immediate geopolitical sphere of the United States were forced to accept North American hegemony, and thus developed no foreign policy of their own. Mexico, for example, has been subject to aggressive, annexionist international relations, like coastal nations before her at whose expense the large, "despotic, mercantile, salvationist" empires were formed.[1] In other words, the internal structures of the lesser political units appeared not to generate any capacity for active international relations, below a certain point in international development. In the opinion of Henry Kissinger, whom the news media now portray as representing the will of the United States, the postwar period marks the beginning of an era of truly global foreign policy.[2] That is, foreign policy became global following the appearance or consolidation of numerous states with the capacity to make an impact in any part of the world through direct use of their power or instantaneous transmission of their ideologies, thereby producing enormously significant results, whether symbolic or real.

It is important to ask, in the context of the work on which we are commenting, whether Mexico is able to generate those foreign policies that will convert her to an equally important nation-actor in international relations. It is, however, equally useful to analyze whether the "uniqueness" of Mexico's position as the United States' neighbor gives rise to internal structures that allow for the formulation of independent foreign-policy goals.

As Pellicer's paper points out, the feasibility of a certain kind of national development depends on the character of international relations. From another point of view, the nature of relations with the United States conditions the ultimate character of national development. On this level, international relations are asymmetrical relations between societies at different stages of development, resulting in reciprocally conditioned situations of subordination and supra-ordination. Moreover, since sub/supra-ordinate relations establish only the general conditions for national development, different internal conditions have their own effects on national history.

Thus Pellicer concludes that in general the Mexican state—today as always—is forced to move within very narrow limits when it comes to

---

[1] Darcy Ribeiro, *El proceso civilizatorio, etapas de la evolución sociocultural* (Caracas: ECV, 1970), Book II.

[2] Henry Kissinger, *Política exterior norteamericana* (Barcelona: Plaza y Janes S.A., Editores, 1971), p. 15.

economic reform. On balance, the situation is bitter, since even if the reforms now considered necessary were successfully carried out, they would not really change the structural bases of the dependency that Mexico suffers. Such are the dynamics and the content of Mexican international relations, especially with her nearest and most important neighbor, the United States.

Certain decisive historical events highlight Mexican foreign relations in this century. On the one hand, Mexico has been subject to recurring foreign aggression, from independence until the period following the Great Depression. At that time, foreign threats gave way to a coexistence full of diplomatic pressures, and an economic offensive that again produced considerable dividends for the United States. On the other hand, the overthrow of the pro-foreign, oligarchic Porfirio Díaz government unleashed a broad politico-military movement that marked the collapse of an important sector of the ruling class—precisely that sector that collaborated with foreign influence and capital for control of the nation's principal sources of wealth: public services (i.e. railways), export agriculture (i.e. sugar, coffee, and fruit), and the mines.

Both the multiple aggressions of the powerful neighbor and the anti-oligarchic revolution have contributed to the profound nationalism of Mexico's domestic politics. They have made possible the identification of the will of the ruling groups—who arose from the armed conflict—with the interests of the nation. They now manipulate all of this without challenge, such that the Revolution and the nation have come to be two sides of the same coin. The nation's internal unity, in the face of counterrevolutionary danger, and its external unity in the face of foreign threat, have thus nourished Mexican nationalism and given rise to certain national-development and domestic-policy goals that have inevitably affected foreign relations.

The above-mentioned events constitute the antecedents of the "special relationship" that both nations have attempted to construct. But has it really been a mutual effort? To what extent can a dominated nation really participate in the elaboration of this kind of relationship?

We should first emphasize the uniqueness of the ties between Mexico and the United States, accepting on principle, and only as a preliminary step, the possibility of an analysis in terms of nation-states or political units. This uniqueness is part of the attempt to formulate a "special relationship" between the two countries, based on the following facts:

Defensive nationalism—part of the process of the rise and consolidation of an industrial and financial bourgeoisie backed by the state—served as a means of uniting state policies and institutions with ruling-class interests. That is, the state and the ruling class are one and the same, but the former does not appear as the direct expression of the latter. Instead, the state appears not only as an arbitrator among the Mexican people, but also as representing them in the face of their traditional enemies. The uniqueness of the Mexican case is based to a great extent on this situation of relative autonomy, the result of profound structural changes and readjustments within the ruling class of a dependent state, in the framework of an international system characterized by market forces and domination.

A "natural" factor, geographical proximity, is also important. In addition to more than 2,000 kilometers of border, Mexico and the United States share hydraulic and ocean resources. A kind of common destiny (imposed by the virtually recolonizing U.S. expansion in the nineteenth century) contributes to a situation that facilitates or reinforces the taking of realistic, objective positions. In effect, in recognizing and accepting U.S. superiority, Mexico's foreign policy toward her northern neighbor has always been realistic—particularly so since 1945, a date the Pellicer study rightly takes as a point of departure.

A brief digression will facilitate our understanding of the above analysis. The "invisibility" of North American imperialism is in sharp contrast to European territorial colonialism. On the basis of that difference there arose an official history according to which the United States never systematically carried out a policy of territorial expansion. Nevertheless, a number of years ago, some historians unaffected by conventional patriotism, while studying the westward movement of the frontier during the nineteenth century, showed how territorial expansion had been a constant factor in North American history from the very beginning. Certainly the nonterritorial aspects of the United States' economic and political development have been most important, once the process of geographical consolidation was over. But does not the "occupation" of extensive territory in the West and Northwest—partly empty, but largely subordinate to another sovereign power (first Spain, then Mexico)—have the virtues (and defects) of colonialism?[3]

The search for a "special relationship" thus grows out of a long period of crises and readjustments, and makes sense only in a particular moment of domestic development giving rise to related foreign-policy needs. Did the Mexican growth model offer foreign interests special advantages? Or, inversely, is this model of national development a consequence of the presence and operations of those foreign interests?

---

[3]"A Kentuckian boasted in 1810, for example, 'that his countrymen were full of enterprise,' and 'although not poor, are greedy after plunder as ever the old Romans were. Mexico glitters in our eyes—the world is all we wait for.'" As originally quoted in William Appleman Williams, *The Contours of American History.* Cited in Gareth Stedman Jones, "The Specificity of U.S. Imperialism," *New Left Review,* no. 60, March-April 1970, p. 66.

In other words, we have also to ask what is "special" in the relationship between the United States and, for example, Brazil or Argentina. Is it enough to say that a common border is the one distinctive, irreproducible root of the relationship? On that basis, the relation between the USSR and Finland is also "special."

The search for special treatment had a good opportunity to prove itself during the 1971 monetary upheaval, especially following the establishment of a 10-percent surcharge on world imports. The Mexican Government, along with all other Latin American governments, foresaw the catastrophical consequences of the measure, but refused to participate in a hemispheric bloc in defense of monetary parity and international trade rights. While Chile and Peru attempted to organize a regional defense, Mexico sought a direct solution by way of special treatment—which was denied.[4] Was this merely evidence that "specialness" fades or disappears when the dependent, not the dominant, country takes the initiative and presents demands? The documentation and economic data, together with statistical evidence from other sources, present Mexico as a typical victim of imperialist relations—i.e., political sovereignty, insofar as it survives, is secondary to other dimensions of those relations.

In effect, political sovereignty manifests itself only where it does not affect vital interests, claiming a wider margin of action, for example, in certain international forums. There, Mexico's position is important, and takes on shades of independence, even though it is a lone voice seeking no leadership position (and is tolerated for that reason). It would take a detailed study either to establish the long-range coherence of such a policy or to conclude that the wayward positions are manifested only in isolated situations, or where the Mexican tradition will not allow ambiguity. In any case, accustomed to a new "realpolitik," we should not be surprised that in the same decade Mexico—without conflict—has maintained diplomatic relations with "outlaw" Cuba while nearly doubling North American industrial capital investments.

It is clear that the development of modern industrial capitalism becomes a mode of economic and political domination with respect to nations where the system is weaker or less developed. The exercise of political sovereignty however, in its formal, juridical dimension has not played a central part in international domination. The various solutions to such a contradiction—forms of economic domination that recognize or accept the dominated nation's political sovereignty—form the substance of international relations. That is, international relations are imperialist relations,

----

[4] A delegation headed by Ministers Torres, Manzo, and Margaín met with high-ranking North American officials at the time; but the talks were conducted in such extreme secrecy that we do not know the extent of the Mexican failure.

the nature of which is historically determined according to different periods and countries.

Mexico's uniqueness also lies in the fact that she was the first Latin American country to receive a heavy flow of direct foreign investment. Foreign capital, second in amount only to that received by Venezuela, was directed to manufacturing because of the high growth rate of the emerging national market. To this ought to be added an additional economic factor of extraordinary psychological and cultural significance: international tourism. Tourism is really an investment in consciousness or customs in order to create the impression of communicability, imitation (often false), and mutual influence. The tourist "industry," the country's most productive sector, is often mentioned as the financial operation that saves Mexico's annual balance of payments. Additionally, there is the growing border trade, which has begun to have special importance because Mexican factories assemble imported U.S. component parts for reshipment to the United States. In summary, certain aspects of Mexican-U.S. relations served as an example of what future U.S. ties with the rest of Latin America would be like, while other aspects suggest how geographic proximity makes the Mexican experience unique.

Part of the President of Mexico's Annual Report to Congress is eloquent by way of example here. Mr. Echeverría declared in 1972:

We have always defended the right to forge our future. The repeated experience of foreign interference has made us intransigent defenders of the principles of nonintervention and the free self-determination of peoples. For years we have acted firmly, yet with caution. In defense of our international principles, we are now taking more direct action. In the future, Mexico will assume a more important role in the assembly of nations.[5]

But as has begun to be pointed out in recent analyses—breaking through the entanglement of official rhetoric that has hidden the truth for so long—relations between the United States and Mexico show how the Good Neighbor policy of the former got transformed into bad business for the latter.

Mexico is the number-one market for U.S. goods; in 1971 alone, U.S. products were 61.4 percent (totalling $1,479 million) of Mexico's total imports. During the postwar period, moreover, the basically agricultural character of Mexican collaboration has been reinforced, thus increasing dependency on one market. Modern agricultural expansion and relative diversification, as well as the substitution of agricultural products for minerals, is a response to North American demand. This total dependency on

---

[5]"Aspectos económicos del Informe Presidencial," *Comercio Exterior* (Mexico City), September 1972, p. 802.

external stimuli and the internal ad hoc responses are the economic substance of the international domination underlying international relations.
With respect to the foregoing, another matter should be mentioned at
this point. Until now we have respected the structure of reasoning implicit throughout Pellicer's paper, a structure assuming that on the level
of international relations it is the nations that act, benefit, or suffer as
internally monolithic blocs. It is clear, of course, that they do not act as
equals, that there are moments of (external) subordination, domination
of sovereignty, and limits to the exercise of autonomy.

Relationships of dependency, however, even though they seem to involve nations, always reflect class relations. The U.S.-Mexican relationship, like any relationship between unequally developed countries, is an
imperialist relationship between dominant classes in different, but not
necessarily contradictory, positions in the international system. Contrary
to traditional views of the problem, international relations are not based
simply on the inevitable links between states, nor on mere economic relationships in the world market; rather, they arise from the correspondence
of interests between national social agents or dominant economic groups.
Though their correspondence of interests seems to take place on an international level, it is in fact the result of the interdependence of two asymmetrical and complementary markets.

The different kinds of correspondence or conflict of interests between
the peripheral society's ruling groups and those of the hegemonic nation
are thus the basis of international relations. In examining a situation of
subordination, the critical task is to show how those interests are determined, and how different international positions affect class relationships
within the nations.

The foregoing means that the Mexican bourgeoisie, while economically
and politically dominant at home, is actually subordinate to the North
American bourgeoisie—whose power no one doubts. Economic dependency is expressed in a relatively broad coincidence of interests between
these groups, a coincidence that only intensifies in moments of growth or
danger. For example, the search for a "special" relationship is an attempt
to take full advantage of a period of high correspondence of interests.

Generally, such an "arrangement" is established through the state at
the level of political representation. Today, political sovereignty serves
as the filter through which economic agreements that eventually affect
the entire society must pass. It is quite obvious that different social classes
derive quite unequal benefits from these arrangements. For example, during the nineteenth century, a correspondence of interests between the
national and foreign bourgeoisies was produced by the extractive-export
trade. Sometimes, both national producers and foreign buyers benefited;

but often, as in the case of the mining and agricultural enclaves, there were no national producers, and the almost vertical economic integration *increased* the underdeveloped nation's dependency. The international disputes that inevitably accompany trade relations (prices, quotas, duties, etc.) were often resolved according to the dominant capitalist country's laws. The dependent society's bourgeoisie was inevitably the loser, and thus functioned simultaneously as both a dominant and a subordinate class. Today, these conflicts are solved through the nation's political representatives, through state institutions that assume the defense of private interests.

In the complexity of today's financial and industrial relations, not to mention the traditional trade relations of the prior period, interests between central and peripheral dominant economic groups become more completely and organically complementary, and the "partnership" with the native industrial bourgeoisie becomes more lopsided. Under these circumstances, the state assumes the role of the nation's representative, and becomes the national bourgeoisie's principal instrument of control and influence. The disputes of this period are different from those of the past, for they seem to arise in the internal market of the subordinate nation rather than in the foreign sphere. The coincidences and conflicts of interests between the respective dominant groups often take the form of diplomatic disputes or open conflicts between the imperialist bourgeoisie and the dependent state.

This is particularly true of Mexico, where the nationalist-revolutionary tradition—as both the dominant ideology and a set of political-economic practices—leads to an image of the Mexican nation as a unified front without internal factions, as a single will, where contradictory, irreconcilable class interests have no place. Thus in the international sphere the state appears to represent the entire subordinate nation, when it is really acting in defense of the dominant/subordinate bourgeoisie's private interests.

Mexican development from 1940 on has above all been directed toward strengthening an industrial and financial bourgeoisie whose rise and growth cannot be explained apart from the role played by political power, by its capacity to control the state. The national unity that developed during the Revolution and was thereafter maintained as a mobilizing myth, has been used to strengthen a class whose national interests are not in contradiction with those of the international (in this case, North American) bourgeoisie. Is this class dominant because it represents the interests of that international class? Certainly the interests of the dominant economic groups in Mexico coincide with those of the international (capitalist) system; they run in the same direction, and they adapt themselves to the course of capitalist economic progress.

Mexican relations with the United States, however, express only a relative coincidence of interests between the countries' respective bourgeoisies. For example, as shown in Pellicer's paper, the national power groups have seen fit to admit foreign investment under conditions different from those traditionally found in the rest of Latin America. Mexican law prohibits direct foreign investment in the strategic sectors of production reserved for the state—petroleum, petrochemicals, and public services such as railways, electricity, communications, etc. Similarly, no private bank loans are allowed to go directly from foreign institutions into the national private sector. Everything must pass through Nacional Financiera, which thus has the opportunity to set policies for protecting the internal market. There are also sectors of mining and manufacturing activity where national participation must predominate.

The economic consequences for Mexico of relations with the United States include an enormous foreign debt, an export trade based on agriculture and food (which in volume is similar to that of the early 1900s), increasing foreign control of manufacturing, and dependency on tourism and border transactions—all of which have weakened Mexico's position. Despite all of this, Mexico has still been able to maintain a relatively independent international policy.

Inroads of foreign capital in manufacturing inevitably weaken the native bourgeoisie as a national class, since it is thereby associated with, and must cede ground to, foreign interests. But the weakening of its national bases—that is, the relative loss of areas of economic power—serves only to increase the native bourgeoisie's political power. Thus the groups most closely associated with international investors today form the nucleus of the ruling class, because of the breadth of their organization, their influence in national politics, and the interpenetration of their interests with those of the political-bureaucratic groups governing the state. In addition, their interests and those of their principal associates are in tune with contemporary capitalist development, the internationalizing of national markets, and the increasing cosmopolitanism of economic elites.

The foregoing argument would seem to be contradictory in the sense that the bourgeoisie's national economic power base weakens as its international power base grows stronger. In the rapid development of this situation, the state always appears as the ultimate representative of the nation—at least as long as the dynamics of the international system require the fiction of political sovereignty. It is by now clear that the Hobbesian concept of a sovereign state exercising unlimited power in foreign relations is not applicable to the dependency our countries have suffered from the very beginning. Dependency is by no means simply economic and political; it is a condition that affects all of society and its historical processes.

It is difficult to predict how much longer the nation-state, the liberal concept of sovereignty, and the associated form of international relations will be able to sustain themselves. The whole context is increasingly penetrated by enterprises that are to some extent autonomous from the dominant economy, and there are pressures toward the internationalization of capital and markets. The concept of ruling class makes sense only within the framework of the nation, and it exercises its control from that base. It is unclear, then, what will happen to the dominant/subordinate class in the future.

Will strengthening the techno-bureaucratic apparatus prepare the state to confront the growing hegemony of multinational corporations in the international arena? In other words, can those sectors that are themselves dependent on the state apparatus act independently of the interests of the system they serve and thus alter the path of national development? There are many possible replies, but suffice it to say for now that several Latin American leaders are conscious of the danger. Some of President Echeverría's speeches, for example, give fleeting glimpses of a consciousness divided between an awareness of the danger facing the nation and the impossibility of avoiding it. It is the dilemma of having to saw off the limb on which one sits.

What will happen in the 1970s should be a part of this commentary, but I have no taste for prophesy. As Hannah Arendt has said, the dreams of the futurologist will only come true in a world where nothing ever happens.[6] Predictions, even when based on facts, are nothing more than current situations projected into a future where, by definition, nothing unexpected occurs. And in my opinion, the people of Latin America have not yet said the last word.

[6] Hannah Arendt, *Sobre la violencia* (Mexico City: Cuadernos de Joaquín Mortiz, 1969), p. 12.

Part Four
Armed Forces and Multinational Corporations in Hemispheric Relations

From Counterinsurgency to Counterintelligence

JOHN SAXE-FERNÁNDEZ

There is no contemporary topic demanding our attention with more urgency than the use and abuse of power. Since C. Wright Mills, no rigorous and focused work has examined the nature of those structures that support political irresponsibility in individuals and in the dominant institutions of our time. Furthermore, if we reflect on the predicament of our epoch, we must conclude that it is equally imperative to address ourselves to the problem of the use and abuse of knowledge.

In this paper, I shall describe how the two questions are intimately related, and appear to be growing more so. The first—abuse of power—increases immeasurably with the aid of technology. The second—an immoderate and tyrannical use of knowledge—emanates from the institutional capacity of the military establishment and intelligence services to utilize knowledge and, thus, to increase their power: the abuse becomes more brutal and senseless to the degree that the centralized military establishment grows and is unrestricted in determining the options of others.

In regard to the first point, Mills argued—against the prevailing conventional wisdom of sociology—that a distinguishing feature of the North American power structure is the particular importance it attributes to military predominance. The subsequent consolidation of the U.S. national-security establishment—characterized by its reckless policies and arbitrary expenditures—has confirmed Mills's penetrating observations.

Considering the events making up our historical experience, from the crematoriums of Auschwitz and the tragedy of Nagasaki and Hiroshima to the genocide and ethnocide that the Pax Americana has brought to the Third World, it is legitimate to draw a conclusion: though it is true that we must inquire into the roots and origin of the national-security establishment (and the analysis of Mills, followed by those of Melman,[1]

John Saxe-Fernández is on the Faculty of Political and Social Science, National University of Mexico, Mexico City.

[1] Seymour Melman, *Pentagon Capitalism: The Political Economy of War* (New York: 1970).

Barnet,[2] Klare,[3] and others, has raised the level of investigation and understanding of its impact both within the United States–Watergate–and abroad), it is equally true that examining the second problem I have mentioned–the abuse of knowledge–may well lead to further clarifications and illuminate other perspectives on North American foreign policy.

It would be difficult to find a better example of this abuse of knowledge than the utilization of social science for counterintelligence. This typifies the increased militarization of social science in general, and, in particular, of the plans, studies, and ideologies that have grown up to justify informational support to the initiation and promotion of U.S. policy in underdeveloped areas.

It should not be inferred from the preceding sketch that I intend to set up a dichotomous paradigm between the two problems in order to consider the exercise of power. To proceed in that manner would violate the empirical integrity of the problem. Realistically, who could doubt that associations between the advisory groups, which channel the flow of information and analysis, and the decision-making circles are intricate, and at the same time diffuse? Studies of complex organizations and, more specifically, the studies and documents that examine the ties existing between the intelligence services (particularly, the military intelligence services) and those who implement foreign policy have proved this to be the case. The casual and sporadic mode of the relationship–together with the interference of irrational factors, such as temperamental proclivities and the narrow political interests of groups and key figures–increase the complexity of the phenomenon immeasurably. This is one of the most important lessons of the Pentagon Papers. Bureaucratic distortion, favoritism, the desire to increase and maintain spheres of institutional control, sordid conspiracies and counter-conspiracies, systematic distortions of reality, personal timidity, affectation, special favors, and general contemptuousness (the arrogance of power) all enter into the formation of North American foreign policy. But can this be taken to mean that there is no bridge between the essays and empirical studies of social science and the structuring of international policies and programs?

This paper has been conceived, precisely, from the supposition that there is such a bridge. I propose, in fact, that sociological analysis and investigation provide such faithful indicators and manifestations of the type of thinking prevailing in the strategic community (military and intelligence services) that their careful examination furnishes a necessary guide to the disentanglement and explanation of the pivotal factors on which U.S. foreign policy is based.

[2] Richard Barnet, *Roots of War* (New York: 1972).
[3] Michael Klare, *War Without End: American Planning for the Next Vietnams* (New York: 1972).

These observations do not suggest that scrutinizing the context of counterintelligence allows us to obtain immediate, definitive, and entirely satisfactory answers to the problems that preoccupy our generation. Particularly, they do not explain the barbarity with which the national-security establishment north of the Rio Bravo employs its technological efficiency and politico-military power: peasant massacres of the My lai type; military-industrial complexes that support the continued stockpiling of biological, chemical, and atomic arsenals while monopolizing vast economic and political resources; saturation bombing of technologically underdeveloped populations; increased interference in the internal affairs of other nations; the virtual dismantling and destruction of the Jeffersonian and Jacksonian institutions that characterized the Republic; vicious attacks on the Vietnamese rice fields; extension of military espionage to the political and academic sectors in North America that repudiate and resist a national-security establishment which has taken over the political life of the country; the involvement of the Military Assistance Program (MAP) and the "Public Safety" program (AID) in the gestation and support of authoritarian regimes in Latin America; the implicit admission of torture; systematic counterrevolutionary subversion through para-police and para-military tactics of the "open" regimes that still exist in this hemisphere; and, finally, military insubordination and usurpation in the hemisphere as a whole. Many studies have exhaustively verified that these are not accidents or exceptions, but are rather the typical expression of a political and economic system that has erupted vigorously in the post-war period. We can assume that the utilization of social science for espionage and police-military control is simply one more indication of this historical and structural development.

The point to be clarified, then, is the nature of this use. As a first approximation, it can be symbolized by various facts. It reflects a set of epistemological and axiomatic assumptions prevailing in contemporary sociology: an emphasis on value-free neutrality and the "strict" separation between "science" and "politics" have facilitated a cross-fertilization between the strategic and social-science communities. Moreover, the importance of the military has grown in the decision-making process—a development that coincides with the increased political and military interventionism of the United States and the vigorous expansion of its post-war economy. The militarization of social science provides the institutional and economic base for this type of operation. The use of social science in counterintelligence is just one aspect of a general merging of sociology with the military and intelligence apparatus. This merger took place as much because of the theoretical premises and research priorities of social science as it did because of the need for institutional and economic support: its present content makes it the internal and external projection of the North American national-security establishment.

Those familiar with the literature on such topics as psychological warfare, ideological offensives for the cold war, social science and national security, or military sociology, among others, will probably be surprised to find that this paper examines, in preliminary fashion, the use of the social sciences as "instruments" of intervention. I have taken such a course because of my conviction that a whole generation of Latin American thinkers, and even large and critical North American publics, are unaware that the role of social science goes beyond "analyzing" or "criticizing" interventionism. It is true that the Camelot incident stirred up interest beyond the academic community—and the mysterious aura that surrounded the topic was a sign of the importance of this supra-national phenomenon. But ironically, in Latin America, one of the areas most affected by this type of operation, no one has attempted a plausible explanation according the topic the significance it deserves. I believe a framework should be presented that provides a path beyond incidental commentary.

The question immediately arises, why this unusual and inexplicable disregard? I believe, at least in part, that for a long time analysts have employed categories with basically *economic* empirical referents to assess North American imperial expansion in Latin America. Only occasionally have they ventured to study the political dimension—and even then, only when it served some very immediate purpose in the discussion. With an almost Biblical fervor, it is implicitly assumed that the economic perspective exhausts interpretive possibilities. The results emerge in empirically exhausted and stereotyped studies. In keeping the discussion tied to traditional concepts of imperialism, much effort is wasted, at best, on linguistic variants of the same theoretical framework and, at worst, on puerile imitations of the existing theoretical and empirical impasse.

But what is clear is that all varieties of explanatory efforts should be combined to create viable, theoretical models that can clarify a phenomenon as complex and vast as the present North American transnational system. This, I say categorically, has been made evident both by the Pentagon Papers and the recent experience of Chile with the International Telegraph and Telephone Company (ITT).

In addition, no analysis of imperialism can be complete if it does not take into account the degree of "applicability" of contemporary social science to interventionist practice. This means, among other things, reassigning the political dimension to the prominent place it properly holds in studying the imperial problem, and in addition, making explicit the urgent need to begin theoretical and research projects on the politico-military dimension of imperialism. Consequently, the detailed study of counterintelligence is a path that—even though it does not assure doctrinal purity, precise methodology, statistical quantification, or continual lionization of the deities of nineteenth- and early-twentieth-century social-political thought—is of great importance in efforts aimed at arriving at an intelligible view of the Pax Americana. This is true because, though the intervention of one state in the internal affairs of another is a phenomenon as old as international relations, the twentieth century has witnessed some substantial modifications in the practice of intervention. It may be useful to note first that, in the course of their operations, the international actors cannot restrict themselves to manipulating purely economic variables, tactics, and motivations—or even politico-military ones. The elements making up the international system are so numerous and interdependent that exclusive concentration by the intervening power on studying and gathering facts about economic vulnerabilities, to be used in strategy formation, would considerably raise their probabilities of failure. Intra-state conditions, and inter-state or inter-imperial relations, currently involve a complex of factors forming a continuing, interdependent set that at the same time is technological and military, political and social, and even anthropological and psychological.

The RAND Corporation, one of the institutes traditionally assigned to implement many of the goals noted above, has thus explicitly recognized the need to develop interdisciplinary research. In addition, it offers an organizational framework that encourages an interdisciplinary mode of work in its academic personnel: after all, the phenomenon around which it works *is* interdisciplinary. As stated in an annual report:

Because the physical problems of national security cannot be understood apart from their causes and consequences, work was initiated early in the social sciences. . . .

The inclusion of experts in the social sciences on RAND's staff served to broaden its interdisciplinary approach to research, and resulted in studies that contributed basic understanding of economics, foreign aid, arms control, organization theory and decision making, communications, game theory and conflict resolution, mental health, education and training, linguistics, social welfare, and many other facets of social behavior—*all within the broad definition of national-security research.*[4]

Consequently, disciplinary exclusiveness would be strategically unacceptable whenever a unidimensional stance toward a reality that tends increasingly to intensify its levels of *complexity* and *interdependence* would translate itself into a real loss of power. In addition, maximizing the chances of failure would be offensive to the sensibility and professional capabilities both of those who practice the art of intelligence and of those who administer national security.

[4]*RAND Corporation Annual Report* (Santa Monica, Calif.: The RAND Corporation, 1968), p. 7, emphasis added.

In view of all this, it is not difficult to understand why social science was transformed into a vital element in developing counterrevolutionary administration and planning on a wide scale. It is not by chance that the new closeness in the relation between social science and the military establishment began in the 1950s and that these relations took on a more stable and closely fitted character as North American politico-military activity expanded in the Third World. Activities like counterinsurgency, unconventional warfare, military "assistance" programs, civic action, and the implantation of supra-national military systems all require wide knowledge of the sociopolitical environments in which they are to be carried out. In other words, because the fundamental variables in these types of situations are anthropological and social, the result was an interest in bettering the social-science informational capacity of the strategic community. The North American experience during the Second World War—in the Pacific theater, particularly—had clearly shown analysts the need for adequate knowledge of enemy nations and also of "potential" enemies—even allies—on all levels. From that period on, one finds the intensive use of sociological and psychological knowledge, both in formulating strategic plans and in implementing "unconventional" warfare— that is, types of "offensive" actions intended to influence the attitudes and behavior of certain groups of other nations, designated as "targets." The purpose of conducting exhaustive analyses is subsequently to "direct" attitudes and behavior in a way that benefits preestablished politico-military objectives.

One of the objectives in creating the Yale University Human Relations Area Files (HRAF) in 1956 was, precisely, to provide the informational infrastructure for psychological warfare. The U.S. Army also established the Special Operations Research Office at American University. Since 1958, SORO has developed a whole series of *Area Handbooks,* and afterwards, was in charge of the aforementioned Project Camelot. Latin American audiences should be informed of the contents of these manuals:

> Planning for psychological operations and unconventional warfare requires an understanding of the likes, dislikes, attitudes, and human strengths and weaknesses of target groups. This *Area Handbook* presents sociological, economic, political, and military background information essential to such understanding.
>
> The information presented has been selected to assist in identifying target areas, estimating their probable reactions to given situations, developing applicable techniques of persuasion, and avoiding inappropriate actions.[5]

[5]*Special Warfare Area Handbook for Guinea,* prepared by the Foreign Areas Studies Division, Special Operations Research Office, operating under contract with the Department of the Army, December 1961. Quote from the Foreword.

Another SORO project attempted to study the informal communications networks of certain countries and, in particular, to identify those persons and/or groups who actually or potentially provide adequate means to communicate certain types of information through personal contact. That is, besides studying and utilizing mass communications to affect attitudes, or to "feed in" certain types of information when suitable, the North American military establishment also pays considerable attention to the effect of so-called "word of mouth" communicators, or what are known in our countries as "effective gossips" (*chismosos efectivos*).

The foregoing has suggested the importance of social science to the practice of intervention; but it would be useful to add to our discussion more concrete examples of how social science acts in this domain. At the beginning of the 1960s, there was a widespread acceleration in mobilizing economic and academic resources to oppose, efficiently and cheaply, internal conflicts and limited war—that is to say, guerrilla warfare and other small-scale conflicts.

Project Camelot and the large number of similar undertakings that followed it sprung from the evaluations and recommendations of various working groups that included distinguished members of the social-science community and specialists in systems analysis and cybernetic simulation. Detailed studies of social research, conducted by the Defense Department, revealed serious deficiencies. In the first place, the studies revealed incomplete knowledge and a lack of basic understanding of the cultural, economic, and internal political conditions that generate conflicts and confrontations among national groups in the underdeveloped countries. There was an evident need for the stimulation of empirical research on these topics by civilian and military organizations. "There is slight prospect of substantial improvement in this situation," the specialists warned, "until a significant increase in the overall level of research is achieved."[6] Among the methodological errors pointed out were the following: (1) lack of quantification of information and of statistical analysis in many areas where these methods would be appropriate; (2) errors in designing the studies—which made it impossible to draw adequate conclusions from the results; (3) lack of organization in multidisciplinary programs and in using techniques such as operations research.

The intricate nature of the international system is implicit both in what is currently understood by "intelligence" and in the efforts to develop analytic schemes that facilitate the manipulation and operational opti-

---

[6]Seymour Deitchman, in U.S. House of Representatives, Committee on Foreign Affairs, "Behavioral Sciences and the National Security," Hearings, 89th Congress, 1st Session, December 6, 1965, p. 72.

mization of the growing available data base. In its present state, the tasks of "intelligence" comprise a complex of operations designed to gather, classify, and methodically interpret information on the environment in which a particular government operates.[7] In preparing a suitable intelligence "picture," it is necessary to include and utilize information and studies on the multitude of variables that outline weaknesses or strengths, at least in the areas mentioned. Conceptual and methodological advances in the social sciences have had a strong impact on these operations; and, conversely, the intensification of intelligence operations has profoundly affected the professional definition of the social sciences.

Among these advances should be emphasized the use of techniques to generate and store data that, with the advent of the electronic computer, have been intensified and improved. For example, in the area of mathematical and statistical analysis, methods have been formulated that increase the ease with which a considerable number of variables can be manipulated simultaneously in order to break down complex groups of interrelationships. This facilitates the evaluation of available qualitative data. Consider, for example, how multiple-regression analysis allows researchers to elaborate optimum models to predict statistically the behavior of international actors; or how factor analysis helps to determine the patterns of interrelation that exist in the relations between countries or among the internal attributes of those countries; or how multidimensional scaling or dimensional analysis help to determine standards of similarity in the relations between countries. The availability of these analytic tools, even with all their limitations, plus the intensified effort to discover and untangle the sociopolitical dynamics of underdeveloped areas give a peculiar and uncomfortable character to the social science of our times; the distinction between academic work and intelligence work tends, virtually, to disappear. This line of reasoning lends support to the assertions of Klauss Knorr, of the Center of International Studies at Princeton, that "social science has influenced intelligence production very considerably; indeed, as now practiced, intelligence is inconceivable without the social sciences."[8] Speaking both from his activities and inquiries abroad and the analyses that he has made, Knorr says,

---

[7] A "standard" definition of intelligence would run along the lines of the following: "The intelligence process is traditionally described as various procedural "steps" in a cycle. . . . First comes collection, the procuring of all data believed to be pertinent to the requirements previously set. . . . Second is evaluation and production, sorting and assessing the reliability of the information, drawing inferences from its analysis, and the interpretation of such inferences with reference to questions posed by planners, policy-makers, and operators. Finally comes the communication of findings in the most suitable form to appropriate consumers." David L. Sills, ed., *International Encyclopedia of the Social Sciences* (New York: 1968), vol. 7, p. 418.

[8] Klauss Knorr, *Foreign Intelligence and the Social Sciences,* Research Monograph no. 17, Princeton University, June 1964, p. 7.

There are academic economists who study the rates of Soviet economic growth and political scientists who study the pattern of political life in Indonesia or Nigeria or some other country; and there are intelligence specialists who are concerned with the same information and presumably keep track—at least to some extent—of the relevant academic output.[9]

Or, as Ray Cline, subdirector of the Central Intelligence Agency, said, "The real invention of modern intelligence organization is the awareness that it takes scholarship—that more is required than chasing firetrucks. I'm not a cloak-and-dagger twirler; I want to explore relevance in social-science terms."[10]

As I have mentioned, the accelerated merging of the social sciences with the activities of the national-security apparatus has shown itself in the latter's efforts to incorporate effectively the work of social scientists into its own operation. The result of this symbiosis—expressed in formal contracts—has been the perceptible loss of academic autonomy and the gradual incorporation of the academy into the administrative and ideological structure of the state. The relative ease with which this process has taken place bears witness to the drastic changes in the structure of the social-science profession and, more generally, in the value system of a community that one would suppose to be a center of scientific objectivity and moral worth. In the course of these years, this same academic community has shown that, indeed, the social sciences have something to offer national security—both by developing their capacities to organize and interpret the copious information from diverse work groups scattered in various countries, and by offering professional and technical services to gather data, deduce certain conclusions from available reports, and help establish the validity of the conclusions. Among the benefits offered the state were not just statistical analysis, techniques of content analysis, surveys, interviews, and simulation, but also the prestige generally accorded to academic activity that in turn facilitates North American access to information, study centers, and foreign specialists.

The second fact about the international political context that should be indicated in our analysis affects long-range interventionist practice. This is the notorious fluidity with which "hostile" nations are transformed into "friendly" ones, allies into "potential hostiles," and so on. For the United States, Japan was an enemy during the Second World War; now she is a friend. The Soviet Union was at one time a friend, then a bitter enemy, now once again something of a friend. Germany, the arch-enemy, is now part friend and still part enemy. Outside of Europe, the situation is even more complex and changeable.

[9] Ibid., p. 11.
[10] As quoted in *Newsweek* (New York), November 10, 1969, p. 40.

These rapid fluctuations in the perception of hostile political entities and friends in the international panorama generate, both in the general population and in the high councils of power, a *sui generis* attitude of national security: "Anyone might be my enemy at any moment." Consequently, recent historical experience shows the convenience and necessity of planning defensive and offensive contingencies toward "enemy" nations, "potential hostiles," and even "allies or friends."

The Camelot incident demonstrated that the expansion and intensification of intelligence activities directed at "potential hostiles" or "friends," such as France or Chile, inevitably provokes a growing crisis in the credibility of North American intentions toward its allies. Roger Hilsman, ex-director of the State Department's Office of Intelligence and Research, remarked in referring to this problem that, "The need for the United States to engage in clandestine activities will continue and so will the tension between this need and the need to preserve the asset of belief in our intentions and integrity."[11] As a result of the diplomatic embarassment brought about by the Camelot incident—and presumably with the desire to reestablish a level of confidence and integrity proper between "allies"—President Johnson, in a message directed to the Secretary of State on August 2, 1965, said:

Many agencies of the Government are sponsoring social-science research that focuses on foreign areas and peoples and thus relates to the foreign policy of the United States. Some of it involves residence and travel in foreign countries and communication with foreign nationals. As we have recently learned, it can raise problems affecting the conduct of our foreign policy.

For that reason I am determined that no Government sponsorship of foreign-area research should be undertaken that in the judgment of the Secretary of State would adversely affect U.S. foreign relations. Therefore I am asking you to establish effective procedures that will enable you to assure the propriety of Government-sponsored social-science research in the area of foreign policy.[12]

Nonetheless, according to a document issued by the Director of Research and Engineering for the Defense Department, from the date on which the Presidential order was put into effect until the end of fiscal year 1966, the State Department vetoed only 5 of the 141 overseas social-science projects financed and directed by the Defense Department.[13] This must be considered another example of the relative weight of the military in defining priorities, contingencies, and decisions related to the international arena. Or, conversely, it is an example of the relative eclipse of the

---

[11] Roger Hilsman, *To Move a Nation: The Politics of Foreign Policy in the Administration of John F. Kennedy* (New York: 1967), p. 87.

[12] U.S. Senate, Committee on Foreign Relations, "Defense Department Sponsored Foreign Affairs Research," Hearings, 90th Congress, 2nd Session, Part 2, May 28, 1968, p. 20.

[13] Ibid., p. 20.

State Department in the function formally assigned to it—"to conduct foreign policy." "In any case," said Vice-Admiral H. G. Rickover, "already the State Department is, to all intents and purposes, but a junior partner. In its own area of responsibility—foreign affairs—it receives but a tenth as much for research as the DOD."[14]

One cannot ignore that it was in the period just after the Camelot incident when intensified efforts were made to establish methodological and policy bodies that would facilitate maximum operational use of the Defense Department's politico-military activities overseas, especially in the underdeveloped countries. It is true that an element of political and bureaucratic expansionism exists within the military establishment, which leads it to assume for itself more and more responsibilities and spheres of influence. This is responsible, in part, for the expansion of military operations in the Third World. But only partially. The military experience—and failure—in Vietnam played, if not the fundamental role, then at least a dramatic one by showing the usefulness of social science in keeping a situation of internal conflict under some control. In all of this one can clearly see that if social science is important to the intelligence services, it is no less so to the military as a whole. The "death" of Project Camelot did not in any way signify the end of these activities. In the hearings of the Subcommittee on International Organizations and Movements of the House of Representatives' Foreign Affairs Committee, held during the week in which Project Camelot was cancelled, General W. W. Dick, Jr., then Director of Research and Development for the Department of the Army, exclaimed:

First, let me say it was Project Camelot that was cancelled. This does not mean that we have backed off in any way from the objective that Project Camelot was designed to meet. . . .

Camelot is out, finished. The objective of Camelot to try to attain the social-science kind of information that would allow for better response in the future is just as important today as it ever has been.[15]

The use of social science as an essential support element for the Defense Department and intelligence services was recognized, officially sanctioned, and administratively stimulated and financed under the Kennedy Administration. That administration's interest in developing flexible forces for response and attack on a limited level led it to reorganize the Defense Department in order to enable the latter to attract and, directly or indirectly, coordinate academic resources for social research. Seymour J. Deitchman, former Special Assistant for Counterinsurgency

---

[14] Ibid., p. 13.
[15] U.S. House of Representatives, "Behavioral Sciences" (see note 6), pp. 48, 53.

in the Office of the Director of Research and Engineering of the Defense Department, has made it clear that

The Defense Department has therefore recognized that part of its research and development efforts to support counterinsurgency operations must be oriented toward the people, United States and foreign, involved in this type of war; and the DOD has called on the types of scientists–anthropologists, psychologists, sociologists, political scientists, economists–whose professional orientation to human behavior would enable them to make useful contributions in this area.[16]

During the 1960s, as the war in Vietnam grew and its failure became more apparent, the potential contribution of social science became more and more appetizing to military and intelligence administrators. For example, the Defense Department spent approximately $700 million on military, political, and sociological studies to analyze the revolutionary dynamic in Vietnam and develop an "adequate" response.

Pursuing the strategic thinking of General Maxwell Taylor and the tactical-administrative line of ex-Secretary of Defense Robert McNamara, both of whom recognized the material and human impossibility of conducting various conflicts at the intensity reached in Southeast Asia, a continuous search was carried on for cheaper and more effective counter-revolutionary mechanisms to control the forces that threatened North American hegemony in the underdeveloped world. Specifically, the possibility of making extensive and intensive use of social sciences and cybernetic advances to elaborate a *symptomatology for counterrevolution* was outlined–that is to say, a vast informational and analytic infrastructure that would allow the detection of focal points of conflict antagonistic to national security. Combining the abilities of cybernetic simulation with analyses and data from social science, an "early-warning system" for conflicts in less developed regions of the globe was formulated. This early detection (or "targeting") proved indispensable for carrying out rapid and low-cost operations in counterrevolutionary "prevention." The cybernetic-instrumental manipulation of such an enormous data base would make it easier to locate and then contain "incipient" insurgency before it could mature politically and organizationally and thus subsequently require the use of large quantities of economic and military resources for its suppression. This strategic need to sharpen and accelerate the ability to *localize* insurgency in its "incipient" or "potential" stage, in order to *"abort"* it from the womb of history, intensified with the disproportionate investment of resources in Southeast Asia. As Seymour Deitchman explicitly stated, ". . . proper use of 'nonmaterial' tools represented by sound knowledge and actions in the nonmilitary sphere can obviate the need to involve large military forces."[17]

[16] Ibid., p. 5R.   [17] Ibid., p. 72.

The suggestions from social scientists themselves generally refer to these dilemmas while at the same time proposing strategic-theoretical justifications for *preventive counterrevolution* that inevitably imply and justify the budgetary and political expansion of the North American military and intelligence organizations. "It is imperative," says T. H. Tackaberry in a statement to the Defense Department and the academic social-science community,

... to attack the problems of the emerging states before these problems reach crisis level, as happened dramatically in Vietnam. The key is prevention. But how is prevention to be achieved? As U.S. elements have become engaged in the developing areas, they have discovered a gap in their knowledge about the problems of political evolution.[18]

I must explicitly re-insist at this point that the effort to avoid other Vietnams—to contain conflicts, as much as possible, in their "nonmilitary" phase—includes maximizing the collection of information on the internal conditions of various political systems and making that data operational to facilitate intervention in their internal affairs. Particular emphasis is given to data on political institutions that are currently or *potentially* subversive. That is to say, great efforts are spent in pinpointing groups or organizations (including, for example, universities in Latin America) that, in the judgment of the analysts, hold the "potential" of rebellion. Lack of information on the internal conditions of these institutions, according to the RAND Corporation analysts, ". . . make(s) it easier for R [rebellion] to get started, and harder for A [authority] to detect it until it has reached a stage of organizational firmness where the chance of aborting it is lost, and the costs of controlling it have risen."[19]

Characteristically, with the sharpening of these requirements for order and authority, massive "police" assistance programs were initiated and the politico-military and academic community continued to receive exhortations to participate. Max Belof, echoing these sentiments, asserted that the United States

badly needs a coherent theory of intervention, particularly in its relations with the underdeveloped world. . . . [The Wilsonians] believed that simply by ridding themselves of European colonial ties, the new nations would surge up in all their splendor and would obligingly cooperate with the Pax Americana. Just let the North American prince kiss the Sleeping Beauty, and the spell will vanish.[20]

[18]T. A. Tackaberry, "Social Science Research: Aid to Counter Insurgency," *The American Journal of Economics and Sociology,* vol. 27, no. 1, January 1968, p. 4.

[19]Nathan Leites and Charles Wolf, Jr., *Rebellion and Authority: An Analytic Essay on Insurgent Conflicts* (Chicago: 1970), p. 132.

[20]Max Belof, as quoted in John Saxe-Fernández, "Ciencia social y contrarrevolución preventiva en Latinoamérica," *Aportes* (Paris), no. 26, October 1972, p. 105.

Even though the spell wore off several decades ago in Latin America because of the frequent visits and unexpected stays of the Prince, the doctrine and practice of counterintelligence might yet take the Princess Celestina and her footmen by surprise.

Commentary on Saxe-Fernández

ALFRED STEPAN

First, I want to associate myself closely with one of the central themes of this volume, namely that, owing to our different cultural, institutional, and national backgrounds, we inevitably have somewhat different theoretical and political orientations, and we can learn much by exchanging, or at least by being confronted with, alternative perspectives. One of the areas where we are most in need of new theoretical and political perspectives concerns the role of the military in hemispheric politics.

On the question of U.S. support for counterinsurgency the basic facts are now clear but the full implications are much less so. Following the war and at the outset of the cold war, the United States established a virtual monopoly on foreign military missions in Latin America, involving military-arms assistance, technical assistance, and extensive educational programs. Latin American military officers and enlisted men were trained in schools run by the United States in Panama, Fort Leavenworth, and elsewhere, and were heavily exposed to U.S. doctrines at the Inter-American Defense College in Washington. With the rise of Fidel Castro and the start of the Vietnam war, the Kennedy government shifted the rationale of the U.S. Military Assistance Program away from that of hemispheric security and campaigned throughout Latin America for the idea that the Latin American armies should divert their energies toward counterinsurgency and civic action.

The dissemination of the new doctrine was rapid. *The Air University Index to Military Periodicals* does not contain categories for counterinsurgency or civic action in its 1959–61 volume. In the volume covering 1962–64, there are 160 entries for counterinsurgency, 42 more for counterinsurgency study and training, and 33 for civic action.

Alfred Stepan is in the Department of Political Science, Yale University, New Haven, Connecticut. He wishes to make clear that publication deadlines prevented him from seeing the final version of Saxe-Fernández's paper, or the supporting footnotes, which were not part of the original presentation; and that this paper should therefore be read more as a self-contained reflection on the general questions raised at the conference than as a critique of Saxe-Fernández's paper per se.

The militant cold-war tone and proselytizing nature of much of the military writing in the United States is revealed even by a cursory analysis of the contents of the military journals. Some characteristic titles of the early 1960s were as follows: "MATA (Military Assistance Training Advisor) Army Conditioning Course Puts Cold War Warriors on the Spot"; "Counterinsurgent Allied Soldiers—By the Hundreds"; "Counterinsurgency: Global Termite Control"; "The Search for and Development of the Soldier-Statesman."[1] The U.S. counterinsurgency doctrine clearly called for the Latin American military to study, and to become involved with, all areas of society. A faculty member of the U.S. Army War College summed up the policy:

"Counterinsurgency" is by definition geared to military, political, economic, and civic action. . . . The major problem before us is to learn to orchestrate the magnificent counterinsurgency resources we have into a single symphony and to persuade the governments we help to apply their energies and resources against threats that confront them.[2]

Exportation of the "New Professionalism of Internal Security"

The export of the ideology (and the supportive techniques and equipment) for counterinsurgency, civic action, and military "nation-building" has contributed to the emergence of a new model of military professionalism that I have called the "new professionalism of internal security." The *content* and the *consequences* of this model are diametrically opposed to the ideal type of "old professionalism of external warfare" found in the works of Samuel P. Huntington. According to this older theory the specialized skills needed by the military to carry out the mission of external defense are such that the vocation of officership "absorbs all their energies and furnishes them with all their occupational satisfactions."[3] Indeed, the functional specialization needed for external defense meant

---

[1] For an elaboration of this argument, as well as for detailed citations, see Alfred Stepan, *The Military in Politics: Changing Patterns in Brazil* (Princeton, N.J.: 1971), pp. 126–27. A Spanish translation of this book will soon be published by Amorrortu Editores, Buenos Aires.

[2] Cited in Stepan, *The Military in Politics,* p. 127. U.S. policy-makers were explicit about the reasons for the shift to internal security. A guide to their argument can be found in Michael J. Francis, "Military Aid to Latin America in the United States Congress," *Journal of Latin American Studies,* vol. 6 (July 1964), pp. 389–401. For a detailed listing and documentation of U.S. Government aid and military-schooling programs, as well as formal military treaties in Latin America, see William F. Barber and C. Neale Ronning, *Internal Security and Military Power: Counterinsurgency and Civic Action in Latin America* (Columbus, Ohio: 1966). See also, of course, the works of Saxe-Fernández, especially his *Proyecciones hemisféricas de la Pax Americana* (Lima: Campodónico–IEP Ediciones, 1971).

[3] See Samuel P. Huntington, "Civilian Control of the Military: A Theoretical Statement," in Heinz Eulau, S. Eldersveld, and M. Janowitz, eds., *Political Behavior: A Reader in Theory and Research* (New York: 1956), p. 381.

that it was "impossible to be an expert in the management of violence for external defense and at the same time skilled in either politics or state-craft or the use of force for the maintenance of internal order. The func-tions of the officer become distinct from that of the politician and police-man."[4] Thus a major argument of this view is that military professionalism contributes to civilian control precisely because military men are so pre-occupied with the requirements of military specialization that they are apolitical. "Civilian control is thus achieved not because the military groups share in the social values and political ideologies of society, but because they are indifferent to such values and ideologies."[5]

Prima facie, however, it seems to me that the new roles and missions assigned to the military by counterinsurgency doctrine have radically changed the nature of military professionalism. Instead of functional spe-cialization focused on external defense, we now see military profession-alism focusing on an increasingly broad range of subjects designed to ana-lyze, prevent, and combat insurgency abroad and at home. Whereas the traditional theory sees military professionalism as engendering apolitical attitudes, I see the "new professionalism," especially in the poorer na-tions, as being concerned with the relationship between internal security and national development, which tends to mean that the content of mili-tary professionalism gradually encompasses all areas of the polity, thus contributing to a deep politicization of the military and often to an *authoritarian military role-expansion.* The key variables, assumptions, and hypothesis of each model[6] can be presented schematically in the form shown in Table 1.

Though my thinking was still evolving in regard to the full theoretical and political implications of the "new professional" model, this was what I had in mind when I wrote that "U.S. policy urging the Latin American military to become more deeply involved in all stages of society . . . can be considered a contributing factor in the creation of military regimes."[7] For the specific case of Brazil (though I analyzed at length national fac-tors that I considered very important), I said that the evidence clearly pointed to the fact that "U.S. attempts to influence the course of Brazil's development in the 1960s show that on economic, political, and military grounds the United States was supportive of the events that led to the

---

[4] Samuel P. Huntington, *The Soldier and the State: The Theory and Politics of Civil-Military Relations* (New York: 1964), p. 32.

[5] Huntington, "Civilian Control of the Military," p. 381.

[6] This argument is developed at greater length in my "The New Professionalism of Internal Security and Military Role Expansion," presented at a workshop on Brazil held at Yale Univer-sity in April 1971 and published in Alfred Stepan, ed., *Authoritarian Brazil: Origins, Policies and Future* (New Haven, Conn.: 1973), pp. 47–65.

[7] Stepan, *The Military in Politics,* pp. 127–28.

TABLE 1
Contrasting Models: The "Old Professionalism" of External Defense and The "New Professionalism" of Internal Security and National Development

Category of impact	"Old Professionalism"	"New Professionalism"
Function of military	External security	Internal security
Civilian attitudes toward government	Civilians accept legitimacy of government	Segments of society challenge government legitimacy
Military skills required	Highly specialized skills incompatible with political skills	Highly interrelated political and military skills
Scope of military professional action	Restricted	Unrestricted
Impact of professional socialization	Renders the military politically neutral	Politicizes the military
Impact on civil-military relations	Contributes to an apolitical military and civilian control	Contributes to military political managerialism and authoritarian role expansion

overthrow of Goulart and the establishment of the military government in Brazil."[8]

Reimportation of "New Professionalism" into U.S. Politics

Though the new professionalism was "made for export" it clearly has had an impact on U.S. domestic and foreign policy-making patterns, and by the mid- and late 1960s was rapidly being "reimported" back to the United States. In a very real sense the tragedy of U.S. action in Vietnam was partly rooted in the widespread belief among American policy-makers that fundamental political problems were capable of containment and resolution by the new tools of counterinsurgency. In general, the growing concentration on security, rather than on politics or development, in international affairs meant that military mechanisms and officers were increasingly relied upon in all phases of foreign affairs. Military intelligence and policy-making channels were frequently recipients of more support, and were wielders of more power, than the State Department.

In domestic affairs there was in the late 1960s a trend toward involving the military in a new series of nation-building and civic-action activities. "Project 100,000" of the Defense Department, to induct and train

[8]Ibid., p. 131.

many young men who would otherwise be passed over by the draft, brought the armed forces into a new health-and-education role. The same was true for "Project Transition," designed to give useful civilian skills to those about to be discharged from military service.

Of more central political importance was the determination by civilian political officials that the Army begin to use at home the internal security "expertise" it had developed for use abroad. First the National Guard, and then the Regular Army, were deeply engaged in riot control. A number of the best Army combat units spent much of their training time preparing for domestic missions. In 1968 the Army was put under orders to be prepared to send as many as 10,000 men simultaneously to each of 25 cities in the event of major riots.[9] Once the Army had been given this major new function, the internal logic of "new professionalism" came into play; and given the function of maintaining internal order, its next professional task was to inquire into the nature of the "potential enemy." An examination of the curricula at some of the key U.S. military schools shows that by the late 1960s the first courses began to appear on such critical groups as "student activists," "minorities," and "political extremists." This academic inquiry was coupled with the natural "new professional" steps of intelligence-gathering about civilian activities and policy-planning for maintaining internal security. For example, in 1968 an official Army document was widely disseminated to units stationed in the United States. It shows how Army leaders perceived that their service had become profoundly concerned with domestic American policies:

> The current civil-disturbance situation dictates a change in the degree to which the Army must seek advance information concerning potential and probable trouble areas and troublemakers. . . . [It] must know in advance as much as possible about the wellsprings of violence and the heart and nerve causes of chaos.[10]

These events are alarming but not irreversible. With respect to military domestic-surveillance activities, a powerful press and academic reaction and a far-reaching Congressional inquiry by Senator Sam Ervin of North Carolina appear for the moment to have slowed military role-expansion in this vital area. Certain political and intellectual tasks are evidently important: monitoring and documenting all evidence of military role-expansion; analyzing the dangers "new professionalism" may present for national political institutions; continuously evaluating and suggesting alternative solutions; and guarding against abdication of responsibility by civilians.[11]

[9] *New York Times,* December 24, 1970, p. 22:2.
[10] *New York Times,* March 1, 1971, p. 34:2.
[11] These are some of the key themes raised in Bruce Russett and Alfred Stepan, eds., *Military Force in American Society* (New York: 1973).

The Military and Research

Since the Latin American military plays such a powerful and central role in the political systems of Latin America, a number of observers have suggested that any basic research on such issues as their self-images, ideologies, and internal structures can be put to intelligence uses by external forces such as U.S. agencies. Such concerns raise a number of serious and difficult questions. For example, since it is unfortunately true that most research results and publications can be put to a wide variety of uses by a wide variety of persons, should there be a moratorium on research on the Latin American military?

The Latin American military, because of its political centrality, is clearly a high-priority information target for external agencies. Precisely because of its political centrality it is also a key research area for any social scientist attempting to analyze the political dynamics of Latin America. Most particularly, from the viewpoint of political activists on the left, it is obvious that the military meets the key requirements making it a top-priority target for detailed information and informed analysis, namely:

1. The importance of the target.
2. The security threat posed by the target.
3. The relative urgency of the need for information on the target.

In Chile the Allende government urgently needed to make correct assessments on the type of actions (given the self-images, ideology, internal organizations, and social structure of the Chilean military) that would enable it to retain a sufficient amount of military support. In Peru, many younger activists who feel they are on the left are joining such figures as former guerrilla leader Héctor Béjar, ex-Aprista Carlos Delgado, and left-Catholic activist Hélan Jaworski in the military government's new instrument of political mobilization, SINAMOS.[12] Thus some of the most important questions for the left to be researching and analyzing of necessity involve considerations of military attitudes and structures. For example, what are the power relationships between the elected representatives of the sugar cooperatives (many of whom, after the April 1972 elections in the cooperatives, are now former trade union leaders) and the military-commanded SAF–CAP?[13] Or, more generally, what is the military's position on participation? Is its very extensive and complex electoral system for local representation in such functional and geographical units as cooperatives and Pueblos Jóvenes the beginning of real political-economic participation, as many of the young-left activists in the field with SINAMOS

[12] Sistema Nacional de Apoyo a la Movilización Social.
[13] Sistema de Asesoramiento y Fiscalización de las Cooperativas Agrarias de Producción Azucarera.

believe? Or is it the scaffolding of a powerful system of corporatist organization? If these are indeed some of the key questions, research such as
Víctor Villanueva's on the ideology of CAEM, and Julio Cotler's ongoing
work on the ideological and organizational models of military-sponsored
modernization, must be considered basic. From this perspective a moratorium on research and analysis on the military is neither intellectually
nor politically justifiable.

A Brief Comment on the Future

It would be dangerous to underestimate the diverse mechanisms and
factors that contribute to dependency. Nevertheless, in the field of military dependency we might want to consider some new factors that could
work to lessen dependency relationships in the 1970s. In the early 1960s
the cost of U.S. equipment was relatively *low,* owing to an extensive program of grant aid and large military-assistance budgets. This was combined with the relatively *high prestige* that the American military system
enjoyed in the eyes of many Latin American military professionals. The
debacle of Vietnam has reversed these two factors. American military
prestige is clearly *now lower.* But owing to the U.S. foreign-exchange
problems and political pressures against military spending, the cost of
obtaining U.S. equipment is higher, since equipment *sales* rather than
grants now dominate. Despite the 1972 election results, the ideological
climate also shows some signs of change. One of the leading candidates
for the 1976 Presidential election, Senator Kennedy, was recently reported to have advocated the complete withdrawal of U.S. military missions from Latin America, the evacuation of Guantánamo, and the opening of relations with Cuba.

Despite these rays of hope I find the suggestion made by Hélio Jagua-
ribe and others that military regimes have the potential to make a 180-
degree break with dependency by an act of voluntarist will not too compelling. The "military as institution" in a number of Latin American
countries will undoubtedly react against the strong dependency relationships that characterized the 1960s, but "the military as government" will
still find itself enmeshed in a host of inherited structural-dependency
relationships that it will have to attempt to overcome.

The Politics of U.S. Multinational Corporations in Latin America

LUCIANO MARTINS

Let every nation know, whether it wishes us well or ill, that we shall pay any price, bear any burden, meet any hardship, support any friend, oppose any foe, to assure the survival and success of liberty.
John F. Kennedy, Inaugural Address, 1961

Amerca cannot—and will not—conceive all the plans, design all the programs, execute all the decisions, and undertake all the defense of the free nations of the world.
Richard M. Nixon, State of the World Message, 1970

Come home, America!
George S. McGovern, Nomination Speech, 1972

In Lenin's classical analysis, 55 years ago, imperialism was conceived as the "ultimate stage of capitalism." At the risk of invoking irony, it might be said that the formation of a "third economy" controlled by multinational corporations is the most recent ultimate stage of capitalism. This phenomenon, on the one hand, and the reorientation of political behavior on a worldwide scale, on the other, are introducing new and complex patterns of relations between the economic and political orders—at national and international levels.

The most direct insight into the phenomenon can be had by examining it in the context of two apparently contradictory processes. Economically, the trend is toward the "internationalization" of capitalist production and internal markets; politically, the appearance of neo-nationalist ideologies (in both "central" and "peripheral" countries) suggests that nation-oriented behavior is reemerging as a basic political feature. It would be tempting to argue that the second trend is simply a reaction to the first, and that their momentary meeting at the peak of a curve obscures the fact of their ascending and descending trajectories. But things are more complicated than that.

The two processes reached perhaps their most interesting development in the overseas economic expansion of North American corporations, and in the simultaneous tendency of the United States toward worldwide political and military disengagement. Between 1960 and 1970, direct private North American investments abroad jumped from $31.9 billion to $70

Luciano Martins is with the Institute of Advanced Studies on Latin America, University of Paris.

billion;[1] more significantly, whereas U.S. production capacity in manufacturing increased 4.7 percent between 1960 and 1968, in the "third economy" controlled by the multinational corporations it grew at an average annual rate of 11.5 percent during the same period.[2] Now, at the height of the economic expansion of American corporations abroad, the U.S. Government seems to be undertaking a political withdrawal toward its own frontiers, as indicated by the substitution of Kennedy's and Johnson's "new stick" policy by Nixon's "low profile" policy.

In Latin America, private American investments, although growing at a slower rate than in the other regions, rose from $7.9 billion to $13 billion between 1960 and 1968 (in manufacturing they grew at the rate of 12.8 percent per year).[3] At the same time (actually, between 1960 and 1971), some 25 U.S.-owned companies were nationalized, not including those expropriated by Cuba.[4] While Washington watched these nationalizations without adopting stern retaliatory measures, American corporations were left to take their own political initiatives. To understand what underlies these two apparently asynchronic moves is the first concern of this paper.

Although it is common knowledge that Latin America does not figure in Washington's strategic priorities, and represents only 20 percent of U.S. investments abroad, the situations emerging in the area may contribute to a better understanding of the new set of political problems posed by the multinational corporations and by the end of the cold war. The nationalizations, the positions adopted by the Andean Group concerning foreign investments, the decisions by several countries to extend their sovereignty over the continental shelf, and other exercises in dissent (such as the vote of 22 nations favoring the OAS' acceptance of Ecuador's claim, in February 1971, of being a victim of U.S. coercion) are indicators of a new political climate in Latin America. Brazil, Argentina, and Mexico, by contrast—where 74 percent of American capital invested in manufacturing in the area is concentrated—have maintained a very favorable climate for American investment. To understand these different situations is the second concern of this paper.

The dissenting mood in Latin America and Washington's relative passivity regarding it are being received with apprehension by American

---

[1] CEPAL, *Estudio económico de América Latina, 1970* (Estudios Especiales), E/CN.12/868/ Add. 2, p. 10; Stephen Hymer, "Some Empirical Features of U.S. Investment Abroad," Yale University, Economic Growth Center, August 1970, mimeographed, p. 7.

[2] CEPAL, *Estudio económico,* p. 37.

[3] CEPAL, *Estudio económico,* pp. 10–11.

[4] With the exception of three industrial firms in Chile (subsidiaries of, or partially owned by, Ford, DuPont, and General Tyre), and three banks (Bank of London and Bank of America affiliates in Chile; Chase Manhattan affiliate in Peru), all other firms hit had their activities in the primary and tertiary sectors.

investors. David Rockefeller, one of the most conspicuous representatives of the multinational corporations, describes the situation in the following terms: "The breach in our hemispheric alliance, caused in large part by the growing spirit of independence in Latin America, is further widened by . . . a short-sighted reversion to 'Fortress America' sentiment here at home."[5] Underlying this diagnosis is a central question. Two observations, however, are in order before we turn to it. First, the multinational corporation still constitutes, in spite of the emergence of new capitalist giants, a predominantly American phenomenon; it is sufficient to consider, for example, that an estimated 200 American companies had been transformed into multinationals up to the mid-1960s, as against only 30 European companies.[6] Second, if the present rates of growth are maintained, "internationalized" production will account for, in Stephen Hymer's estimate, 50 percent of capitalist production worldwide by the end of the century.[7] The central question, then, is the following: if this rate of growth is to be maintained, can the multinational corporations do without the political-military protection of a police state? But perhaps a more practical approach is to ask first to what extent the United States' present tendency toward political-military disengagement implies an actual loss of such protection. Although these questions far exceed the purposes of this paper, it is important that they be allowed to guide our investigation.

Three complementary hypotheses, then, will guide my analysis: First, diverging economic interests within American society and the U.S. tendency for political-military disengagement are leading the multinational corporations to develop their "own" political capability. Second, this capability is being established on three fronts, simultaneously: the "privatization" of U.S. "foreign aid," the manipulation of international financial institutions, and the creation of joint-venture investment companies. Third, the likelihood of conflict between the multinational corporation and the state in peripheral countries is greater where foreign investments control the primary sector and less where they are concentrated in manufacturing.

Multinational Corporations and National Policy

To focus on what seems to be a new set of problems in the relation between the economic and political orders, two initial clarifications are

[5] David Rockefeller, "An Alliance for Development" in Council of the Americas, *Annual Report,* 1971, p. 14.

[6] Raymond Vernon, "Multinational Enterprise and National Sovereignty," *Harvard Business Review,* vol. 45, no. 2, April 1967, p. 158.

[7] Stephen Hymer, "Some Empirical Features," *Harvard Business Review,* p. 10; Jack E. Behrman, *National Interest and the Multinational Enterprises—Tensions Among the North Atlantic*

essential. The first is that we are confronting a very recent process, one whose outlines are still poorly perceived, and whose fate may be to produce *several* outcomes. In short, we may be dealing only with the visible part of the iceberg. Accordingly, what follows should be understood as a first and tentative approach to the problem. The second clarification deals with the notion of the "third economy," a notion evidently deriving from the association of two pieces of evidence. One is that the value of the multinational corporations' overseas production is exceeded only by the American and Soviet national economies: the value of American subsidiaries' production abroad reached $130,000 million in 1968—four times the value of U.S. exports in the same year.[8] The other fact in evidence is that the multinational corporations tend collectively to form a subsystem whose operational area transcends national frontiers and whose overall thrust is fed and set in motion by a transnational strategy.

The very definition of the multinational corporation is in fact a matter of some dispute, the best course being, in my view, to consider the term "multinational" as distinguishing "world-oriented" companies from those that, although maintaining operations abroad, are "domestically oriented."[9] The concept is of course subject to empirical validation (through, let us say, the study of the decision-making process in a significant number of corporations), and is perhaps more accurate as a description of a tendency than as a definition of an actual development. Its virtue, however, lies in introducing the *market,* and not the nation, as a key political dimension. What I am suggesting, in short, is that the operations of a multinational firm (cost determination, resource allocation, technology adoption, profit interdistribution, etc.) are determined by a policy that has as its target to maximize the *global operations* of the parent corporation—not simply its best interests.

Both the pursuit and the realization of a transnational policy were made possible by the extent to which decisions have become centralized: 187 conglomerates control, through some 10,000 subsidiaries around the world, about 80 percent of all American overseas investments.[10] In other words, an extremely small number of decision-makers, without legitimization of any sort, is in a position to dictate (from a room on Park Avenue, in the Bahamas, or in Luxembourg) production terms, growth rates, export policies, consumption patterns, financial arrangements, etc., that

---

Countries (Englewood Cliffs, N.J.: 1970), p. 10. Behrman estimates that by 1990 nearly half of the GNP of the capitalist countries could be owned by foreign companies.

[8] Osvaldo Sunkel, "Capitalismo transnacional y desintegración nacional en la América Latina," *El Trimestre Económico* (Mexico City), no. 150, April–June 1971.

[9] *Business Week* (New York), April 20, 1963, p. 63.

[10] Raymond Vernon, *Report of the Research Project on the Multinational Corporations,* Harvard Business School, 1970, mimeographed.

can affect substantially the "national" economies and ways of life of a great number of countries. The potential impact of these decisions on local economies should be evident from the fact that in Latin America, subsidiaries of American companies control approximately one-third of the manufacturing industry, and their activities as a whole represent about 14 percent of the gross industrial product of the region; in 1966, 35 percent of all Latin American exports (41 percent for manufactured goods) were produced by American subsidiaries.[11]

It is precisely this capacity to make macro-decisions, i.e. to rival state power, that transforms these corporations into political actors. Thus, much of the relevant literature perceives a contradiction between the multinational corporation and the nation-state. The problem is accepted by the corporations themselves under these terms of reference, and a new ideology is being formulated. According to this ideology, the multinational corporation represents "a modern concept designed to meet the requirements of a modern age," while the nation-state "is a very old-fashioned idea."[12] It is not clear—I quote here from former Undersecretary of State George Ball—if the American nation-state is also "a very old-fashioned idea." But the question has, of course, to be considered. First, however, there is something to be said about certain confusions that the presentation of the problem in these terms may involve.

The multinational corporation, like the nation-state, is not an abstract organization, but a historical reality. Each is shaped by a set of specific social relationships, and each is, as presently constituted, the product of a given structure of domination. Relations are not established between a modern entity and an archaic one, but between *groups of individuals* who control the corporation's and the state's decisions, as well as between these groups and other groups of individuals who are subject to these decisions. Both types of groups have particular and specific interests—which may be contradictory or not—and both interact not only with each other but also with other societal groups and components of the international system. It is this whole complex of socially and politically significant relationships—and the resultant national and international power structures—that tend to be obscured when the problem is presented as a contradiction between the multinational corporation and the nation-state.[13] I prefer, therefore, to approach the problem through the relations between the multinational corporation and the state, both considered as hierarchies resulting from a given structure of domination.

[11] Sunkel, "Capitalismo transnacional."

[12] George Ball, "The Promise of the Multinational Corporation," *Fortune* (New York), vol. 75, no. 6, June 1, 1967, p. 80.

[13] This point has already been raised by Stephen Hymer, "Some Empirical Features," p. 11.

In this connection, what matters is to know, first, whether conflicts exist or not: between multinational corporations and other economic interests predominantly oriented toward the domestic market; between "internationalization" of production and the labor force of the "central" countries; between the production system that multinational corporations are shaping in the "peripheral countries" and other local social structures of these nations; between the local allies of multinational corporations (the affluent elites) and the "desperately poor" masses excluded from the market and condemned to "inhuman deprivation" (to quote a humanist of recent Vietnam-war-fiasco vintage, World Bank President Robert McNamara).[14] What matters second is to know how these conflicts are being projected in a given country's policy.

What David Rockefeller perceives as the neo-isolationist impulse in the United States and the "growing spirit of independence" in Latin America, what he deplores as being responsible for the "breach" in hemispheric relations, constitutes a precise political expression of these conflicts of interests. In the first instance these conflicts are taking two forms: an asymmetry between the multinational corporations' interests and the "low profile" adopted by the U.S. Government; and tensions between some Latin American governments (or political groups) and the multinational corporations. Both developments are by-products of two mutually conditioning variables: the redefinition of internal and external patterns of domination; and the differentiation of national and international economic interests. But in a broader sense, these developments are part of the adaptation process of societies and nations to the post-cold-war world order.

The new political terms established by the détente between the two superpowers (the détente itself being an expression of the contradictions the two were led into during the cold war) had, as a first result, the relaxation of discipline in their respective peripheries and the loosening of bonds of "national loyalty" within their own borders.[15] As a consequence,

[14]*International Herald Tribune*, September 26, 1972, p. 2.

[15] An official U.S. survey shows that of the people involved in the summer riots of 1967, 40 percent (in Detroit) and 52.8 percent (in Newark) stated that the United States "was not worth fighting for in the event of a major world war." *Report of the National Advisory Commission on Civil Disorders* (New York), 1968, p. 138. In Vietnam, U.S. desertions jumped, in one year, from 13,000 to 55,347—the equivalent of three and one-half divisions—according to Pentagon data. *Newsweek* (New York), March 17, 1969, p. 16. Also in Vietnam, between August 1 and October 18, 1970, American soldiers died from an overdose of heroin at the rate of almost one a day; a neologism had to be created (*fragging*) to designate a new pattern of behavior: the act of an (American) soldier throwing a fragmentation grenade at an (American) officer. *Newsweek*, January 11, 1971. Concerning the Soviet Union, as far as we know, surveys are not conducted in psychiatric asylums where dissenters are confined, since they are considered by the Soviet bureaucracy (and by some Latin American governments cheered by U.S. corporations as "modernists") as "internal enemies." Nevertheless, an indirect indicator is the fact that the Soviet Penal

the United States and the Soviet Union are being forced to readjust both the form and the substance of their instruments of political domination, internally as well as externally. Of course, in dealing with these tensions, both powers follow distinct rhythms and modalities, according to the cohesion between, and the instruments at the disposal of, their bureaucracy and dominant classes.

In the case of the United States, the politics of the cold war, during which the great American economic expansion took place, assured the satisfaction of an ample spectrum of economic interests. Galbraith shows, for example, how technological-military competition became a quasi-ideal substitute for the diversified range of goods previously consumed on the battlefields; it was of course very much to the advantage of these interests that, after Korea and until Vietnam, with the American people not engaged as combatants, cold-war politics retained considerable internal support, including that of the working class.[16] Internal political cohesion was also fostered by the existence of a nuclear-armed enemy, and was fed by the myths spun out by what is vulgarly called the "industrial-military complex." One of the better-known of these myths, to whose acceptance the totalitarian nature of the countries in the Soviet orbit undoubtedly contributed, was the overseas defense of "democracy." Until the mid-1960s, the American people's response to cold-war politics was not only conformity but effective consensus. In this respect, the "high profile" adopted by the United States in those years—faithfully expressed by Kennedy's worldwide commitment to the "defense of liberty"—could be considered a truly *national policy.*

Without looking more deeply into economic factors, which would exceed my competence, it will suffice to establish that the diversification of capitalist economies and the irrationalities of cold-war politics—each expressed symbolically in the amazing fact that the nation capable of televising from the moon depends on Japanese industry to watch that transmission[17]—have generated acute economic as well as political contradictions. These contradictions are manifesting themselves both in a cleavage between economic interests and in the political dissension the American society is experiencing. In a word, "pluralism" was converted from an academic category (or ideology) into a political reality. It is not by chance

---

Code was changed, in 1966, in order to include a disposition (art. 190) sentencing anyone to three years for the "oral or written diffusion" of "statements offensive to the regime." *La Russie contestataire, documents de l'opposition soviétique* (Paris: Fayard, 1971).

[16] John K. Galbraith, *The New Industrial State* (London: 1968), p. 330.

[17] Manufactured products accounted for less than 50 percent of all U.S. imports in 1961, and for more than 65 percent by 1971. U.S. imports of radio and TV sets rose from $435 million in 1966 to $1.3 billion in 1971. *Fortune,* July 1972, p. 59.

that two major issues of the 1972 U.S. electoral campaign were the redefinition of "national priorities" and the "new populism." The problem is located precisely, at least while this phase of "social indecision" lasts, in the American state's apparent inability to reconcile the powerful, divergent interests now expressing themselves in American society. This brings us back to the multinational corporations and the differences between their interests and those of "domestically oriented" groups.

The Hartke-Burke Bill, recently submitted to the U.S. Congress, provides us a fresh indication of these controversies over issues and conflicts among interests. Dependent on the AFL-CIO's strong support for its approval, and considered by multinational corporations as a "serious threat" to them,[18] this bill has as its main purpose to defend the domestic market and level of employment. This defense is to be prosecuted through proposed restrictions on movement of American capital and technology to other countries and through trade-protectionist measures—in short, by curbing the multinational corporations' activities, as well as the trend toward the internationalization of internal markets. The restrictions take the form of a higher taxation on firms' and executives' incomes earned abroad (an increase of 50 percent on firms' total tax burden, so say the firms), of an obligation on the firms' part to report as income any gain realized in the transfer of patents and processes to their overseas subsidiaries, and, finally, of imposing higher duties on intermediary goods and parts produced abroad (or re-imported to the United States) by multinational corporations. The protectionist measures proposed consist, basically, of the creation of quantitative restraints on imports of almost all categories of goods, rolling back the U.S. imports to the average level of 1965–69, i.e., a reduction of $17.1 billion (37.3 percent in the estimate of the multinational corporations).[19] Last, but not least, the bill would give the U.S. President new authority to prohibit any direct or indirect transfer or use of U.S. patents overseas where this would contribute to unemployment in the United States. It is to be noted that decisions concerning these measures, as well as the enforcement of the overall policy, are to be left chiefly in the hands of three commissioners: one representing industry, another labor, and the third "the public."[20] It is eloquent testimony that neither industry nor labor may any longer present their particular interests as "the public's." Whatever the fate of this bill in Congress, its content represents something new.

A second indication of controversy and conflict is provided by the reshaping of "foreign aid" policy, which merits our special attention because

---

[18] Council of the Americas, memo to CoA members; from Michael D. Miller, March 6, 1972.
[19] Ibid.
[20] *Foreign Trade and Investment Act of 1972* (S. 2592 H.R. L0914–Hartke/Burke), Title II.

it has always been a good indicator of U.S. federal and private strategies
for what are now called the "less developed" countries. The purpose of
"foreign aid" in Latin America, according to the Senate testimony of a
director of the Agency for International Development, is to promote the
"national interests of the United States."[21] These were defined (in relation
to Brazil) as being, first, the maintenance of "a government or society"
consistent with the security interests of the United States in the hemisphere; and second, the protection and expansion of American economic
interests, trade, and investment.[22] Of course, these have always been the
objectives of "foreign aid." What seem to be new are two other developments: first, the political split between economic and security interests
and, second, the cleavages within the economic interests. Obviously, both
developments make the task of defining current U.S. "national interests"
much more difficult.

A clearer line of demarcation between security and economic programs,
a line admittedly blurred in the past, was one of the recommendations of
a Presidential Task Force commissioned by President Nixon in 1970 to
carry out a thorough study of the Foreign Assistance Program. In this
study, known as the Peterson Report, the new strategy recommended is
to shift "foreign aid" from bilateral programs to multilateral programs,
with the consequent transfer of aid funds from institutions like AID to
those under World Bank jurisdiction.[23] The emphasis on economic objectives rather than on security—more precisely, on the long-range attainment of the latter through the former—is also the more sophisticated
approach advocated by World Bank President McNamara, to whom "in a
modernizing society, security means development."[24] Notwithstanding
the fact that one need not be a genius to arrive at this kind of conclusion—
and it is worth noting that Latin American military elements are building
an ideology on the same theme—the adoption of this approach represents
a significant change in the "foreign aid" concept. The emphasis upon economic objectives has further important implications for the underdeveloped world and the role played in it by multinational corporations. But
we shall examine these implications later. Our concern now is to show
how the reshaping of "foreign aid" policy is arousing conflicts between

---

[21] *United States Policies in Brazil—Hearing Before the Subcommittee on Western Affairs of
the Committee on Foreign Relations, 92d Congress, 1st Session, May 4, 5, and 11, 1971* (Washington: U.S. Government Printing Office, 1971), pp. 164, 165–66. Hereafter cited as *Hearings
on Brazil.*

[22] Ibid., p. 165.

[23] Task Force on International Development, *U.S. Foreign Assistance in the 1970s: A New
Approach* (Washington: U.S. Government Printing Office, 1970). Hereafter cited as *Peterson
Report.*

[24] *New York Times,* May 19, 1966.

multinational corporations and "domestically oriented" groups in the United States.

In 1960, 41 percent of all commodities financed by AID were purchased in the United States, as a result of what is called the "tied-aid" provisions. The noncompetitiveness of U.S. domestically produced goods in the world market–aggravated from the mid-1960s on by Japanese and European expansion and by inflation and labor costs in the United States– increased the dependence of American domestic production on the aid given by "foreign aid." A First National City Bank report stated, for example, that without such "aid," the United States' commercial surplus could vanish.[25] Eximbank funds not being sufficient, in fiscal year 1969 the percent of the "tied-aid" in AID operations jumped to 99 percent, representing about $1 billion.[26] This obligation to buy from domestic American firms, imposed on the recipient countries "regardless of cost," to quote from the Rockefeller Report's criticism,[27] was the object of protest from the 21 Latin American foreign ministers at the Viña del Mar meeting (May 1969). Nixon yielded to these demands and announced that, beginning November 1, 1969, loans to Latin America under AID would be "free to allow purchases" anywhere in Latin America.[28] In other words, the "recipient countries" would be free to purchase from American subsidiaries established in the region. This move in the direction of the multinational corporations' interests met the opposition of the AFL-CIO. The labor unions strongly protested against any measure that could deprive AID of its "vital functions," as well as against "American interests establishing runaway plants in lower wage countries."[29] The Hartke-Burke Bill is probably the unions' response to the untying of "aid."

In short, the pattern seems to be that to defend capitalist domestic production (i.e. wages and jobs), the American working class is going more and more "nationalist," whereas to defend increasing profits and their share of the world market, important segments of American capitalists are going more and more "internationalist"–or "transnationalist." Perhaps we could add–and this is, of course, only my own personal impression after interviewing several corporation executives–that the multinational community is also growing more and more disillusioned with "traditional parliamentary democracy." As one of the interviewed executives

[25] First National City Bank, *Monthly Economic Letter,* April 1970.

[26] Agency for International Development, *Annual Report,* various years.

[27] Nelson A. Rockefeller, *Quality of Life in the Americas–Report of a U.S. Presidential Mission for the Western Hemisphere* (Reprinted by AID), mimeographed, p. 75.

[28] Richard M. Nixon, "Address to Inter-American Press Association," Washington, October 31, 1969 (USIS press release).

[29] AFL-CIO's Executive Council Statement. *Congressional Record,* U.S. Senate, March 23, 1970.

put it, "I am sure you Latin Americans cannot afford democracy. I begin to wonder if we Americans can." The Council of the Americas, the voluntary political association created by David Rockefeller to represent the 200 American corporations with business in Latin America, provides us with further evidence. This organization submitted in a memorandum to its corporate members— with the recommendation that it "might be appropriate for mention in the articles, speeches, house organs, and everyday conversation"—the following slogan of doubtful intelligence: "Consumer democracy is considerably more intelligent than political democracy."[30] In other words: the market—and not the regime or the nation—is the key political reference. What is new is not really the concept (after all, the market has always been the major capitalist point of reference), but the demise of democracy and the nation as justifying ideologies.

All this seems to indicate that the corporations' drive toward "transnationalism," which was motivated primarily by the logic of capital expansion, tends to be *politically* hampered by the conflicting interests set in motion within the United States and in the periphery. Simultaneously, these very situations tend to reinforce in the corporations' view the need for creating new political tools and stronger transnational alliances in order to guarantee continued expansion.

What we are suggesting is that as long as these internal and external cross-pressures are allowed to influence the U.S. decision-making process, restricting the benefits from the well-known ties between government and corporation officials, limiting the corporations' range of domestic alliances, and inhibiting the United States' role as policeman to the world, the multinational corporations will be led to look for new strategies and new patterns of political behavior—domestically, as well as abroad. It is significant, for example, that to fight the Hartke-Burke Bill in the U.S. Congress, the multinational-corporation community decided to mobilize "Latin American governments, business, labor, and media" to reinforce its lobby.[31] Another example is ITT's failure to move the American state machine to prevent the election of, and later to overthrow, Allende's government [this was written prior to the successful coup: ed.]—in spite of a reference, in one of the published memoranda, to Nixon's having given the coup the "green light."[32] These two initiatives express in some way the situation that multinational corporations are facing: to help curb opposing domestic interests they are led to call on Latin Americans; to curb

[30] Council of the Americas, Memo to CoA members; from Henry G. Geyelin (the Council's Executive Vice-President), New York, July 26, 1971.

[31] Council of the Americas, Memo from Miller.

[32] Secretaría General de Gobierno, *Documentos secretos de la ITT. Fotocopia de los originales en inglés y su traducción al castellano* (Santiago: 1972, 1st ed.), p. 40.

Latin Americans they are led to call on the American state—without, apparently, being very successful in either case.

After hearing a senior staff member of the U.S. National Security Council expound the politics of "less U.S. Government intervention" in Latin America, a corporate representative (John F. Gallagher, Senior Vice-Chairman of the Council of the Americas and Vice-President of Sears Roebuck) summarized the situation as follows:

The Executive Branch of the U.S. Government has indicated on numerous occasions that it is pursuing a policy of "low profile" in Latin America, and that this policy limits the capacity of the U.S. Government to involve itself on behalf of U.S. private foreign investments. We know, for example, that practically no sanctions will be invoked by the U.S. Government in cases of expropriation. We also know that leading members of the Congress concerned with Latin America accept this "low profile" posture of the Executive Branch. All this must lead us to the conclusion that, as far as the protection of U.S. private investments in Latin America goes, we in the business community are literally on our own.[33]

How are the multinational corporations actually coping with this situation? What I have suggested, in the foregoing, is that the economic expansion of American corporations overseas can no longer be undertaken, as was the case during the cold-war period, under the full protection of the American state and with the political consensus of the nation. Now I shall approach the problem from a different perspective, namely, the multinational corporations' search for a substitute political capability. They are acquiring it, in my view, through the following complementary activities: (1) the appropriation of direct control of U.S. "foreign aid"; (2) the reinforcement of alliances and the dampening of political opposition through the creation of multinational *joint ventures*.

The Search for a New Political Capability: "Privatization" of Foreign Aid

The financing of the capitalist drive for control over resources and markets on a worldwide scale in this century has, as is well known, taken different forms and followed different political patterns. Private banks and financial houses—it is sufficient to remember Rothschild's exploits around the world—played a major direct role in this drive until the early 1930s. From the depression years onward, the state has been called upon to assume, directly or as mediator, a larger part in the financing of capitalist world enterprise. From the point of view of U.S.-Latin American relations, the creation of Eximbank and the Pan American Conference of Buenos Aires, during the New Deal years, represented two landmarks in the new government-to-government dealings under the form of bilateral

---

[33]Council of the Americas, *Report,* September 1971, vol. 7, no. 3, p. 10.

agreements. The creation of multilateral financial institutions, after the war, gave the American state new instruments for more effective leadership of, and better control over, worldwide capitalist expansion, as we shall see.

The linkage between the economic and military aspects of this expansion was officially established—for reasons beyond the scope of this paper—by the Truman Doctrine, in 1947. In that year, and for the first time, the United States extended the frontiers of its security to wherever internal or external movements sought to impose "totalitarian regimes" upon "free peoples," to use Truman's rhetoric.[34] "Foreign aid," through its economic and security programs, was the main tool of this expansionist policy, a commitment undertaken under the political responsibility of the American state and founded on its nuclear might. Twenty-three years later, Nixon's statement that America cannot undertake "all the defense of the free nations of the world"—a statement followed by the United States' recognition of the Soviet Union and Communist China as *de jure* participants in the balance of power in Europe and in Asia, as well as the announced "less intervention" policy in the hemisphere—seems to inaugurate a new course. How are these changes affecting the U.S. "foreign aid" concept and how are the multinational corporations coping with them?

During the Kennedy years, and following the Bay of Pigs fiasco, almost all of the U.S. bilateral economic and military aid programs around the world were centralized under the authority of the Agency for International Development (AID). According to the Peterson Report, security programs accounted for 52 percent of all foreign-assistance expenditures in fiscal year 1969; development programs, for 42 percent; and "emergency relief programs," for 6 percent.[35] From the same source we know that 26 percent of the appropriation for economic programs was "actually for security purposes."[36] The Vietnamese *aventura* is, of course, in great part responsible for the weight of the security item. Nevertheless, "foreign aid's" worldwide concern over security is clearly documented in the three cases cited in the Peterson Report: "budget support for political purposes" and "temporary help for governments" granted to Indonesia (after Sukarno's overthrow), to the Congo (after Lumumba's fall), and to the Dominican Republic (after the Marines' invasion).[37]

The criticism that this type of bilateral "aid" is now arousing within U.S. political circles is well demonstrated in the Brazilian case. During

[34] Norman A. Graebener, *Cold War Diplomacy, 1945–1960* (New York: 1962). Document No. 4: Truman's Speech to Congress, March 12, 1947.
[35] *Peterson Report*, p. 6.
[36] Ibid., p. 5.   [37] Ibid., p. 12.

the populism crisis in Brazil (1961–64), AID programs totalled around $100 million a year.[38] Former Undersecretary of State Thomas Mann stated in no uncertain terms that it was for political reasons that all U.S. credits were cut off during the closing days of the Goulart regime.[39] During the five years following the military take-over, total U.S. Government bilateral-program expenditure jumped to $2 billion, as explained by an AID official to the U.S. Senate. This provoked Senator Frank Church's thoughtful remark: "So we have pumped in [to Brazil] $2 billion since 1964 to protect a favorable climate of investment that amounts to about $1.6 billion."[40] (The latter figure represents AID's estimate of the book value of total American investment in Brazil up to 1970.)

Senator Church's arithmetic approach is a clear indicator of a new concept: U.S. protection of private investment overseas is too "expensive," even in the case of a country of such decisive importance for U.S. dominance in Latin America as Brazil. Perhaps even more significant is the inclination to dispute the political wisdom of the rationale underlying the "foreign aid" policy inherited from the cold war. This is clearly shown by the following interjection by Senator Church, then Chairman of the U.S. Senate Subcommittee on Western Hemisphere Affairs, during an exchange with an AID director regarding Brazil:

The principal argument made for a foreign aid program, economic assistance, in the Congress, is that this money is an investment against the growth of Communism, and that as economic development occurs there is less tendency in underdeveloped lands to resort to a leftist government, Marxist governments, Communist governments, however we may describe them, and all lumped together as inimical to the interests of the United States. That thesis needs much more searching analysis than it has heretofore been given. . . . So it is this thesis that has been the cornerstone of the aid program and has been repeated over and over again and accepted as gospel that I question. That is why, it seems to me, that when you say the program we have financed in Brazil has promoted the national security interests of the United States, I don't see the evidence that that is necessarily so. . . . if we had to pay that kind of money ($2 billion) for cordial relations all around the world we would soon go broke.[41]

In short, the "low profile" approach, advocated as the best posture for the American state to adopt toward Latin America, seems to be supported by the following reasoning: (1) ICBMs and Polaris submarines have rendered previous geographic concepts of security irrelevant; (2) any serious threat to U.S. political interests around the world will be settled, in the

---

[38]*Hearings on Brazil,* p. 162.
[39]Cited by Alfred Stepan, *The Military in Politics: Changing Patterns in Brazil* (Princeton, N.J.: 1971), p. 125.
[40]*Hearings on Brazil,* p. 165.
[41]*Hearings on Brazil,* pp. 176–78.

last resort, through direct U.S.-USSR negotiations; (3) there is no evidence of positive correlation between poverty and Communist upheavals, and should such upheavals occur, advanced anti-guerrilla technology has proved to be effective; (4) leftist and nationalist regimes, military or not, have been established in countries where large amounts of American investment have been made; (5) solving the major Latin American economic and social problems is beyond the U.S. Government's capability.[42] It is the knowledge of this trend that probably leads corporate executives to feel that, as far as American state protection is concerned, they are "on their own." Let us see to what extent this is so.

The Peterson Report's recommendation for a clear separation between security and economic programs in some way represents an acknowledgment of the need for new lines of demarcation between the state's and the corporation's roles and interests. This approach brought forth two new guidelines: (1) conversion of a political issue into a financial issue by transferring from the state to the taxpayer the cost of protecting private investment abroad; (2) splitting the "foreign aid" economic program between aid to domestic U.S. industry and aid to American investors overseas, and transferring the control of the overseas programs from public administration to direct private control. These orientations, which have already been in part adopted through AID's Office of Private Resources, took new shape with the creation in 1969 of an Overseas Private Investment Corporation. OPIC has as its parents, "or at least as its midwives," the leading U.S. business associations (National Association of Manufacturers, U.S. Chamber of Commerce, etc.) and enjoys representation in AID's Advisory Council.[43] OPIC represents something new.

First, OPIC is a state-chartered corporation (the U.S. Government is its only shareholder) in which private-sector representatives hold, by Congress' decision, the majority of executive seats. This private management of public funds (OPIC is also staffed primarily by private personnel) is justified as being the most adequate to the purpose in view, since such a structure (as opposed to a governmental agency and bureaucracy) will be more "sensitive to the needs and problems of private investors."[44]

Second, OPIC took over, and in certain aspects has the authority to exceed, many of AID's former functions, whether in promoting pre-investment expertise (i.e. forecast of investment climate) in underdeveloped

---

[42] Mark L. Chadwin, "Foreign Policy Report/Nixon Administration debates new position paper on Latin America," in *National Journal*, vol. 4, no. 3, January 15, 1972, pp. 97–107.

[43] *Overseas Private Investment Corporation, Hearings Before Subcommittee on Foreign Economic Policy of the Committee on Foreign Affairs, House of Representatives, 91st Congress, 1st Session, August 5, 6, and 12; September 16 and 18, 1969.* (Washington: U.S. Government Printing Office, 1969), p. 42. Hereafter cited as *Hearings on OPIC.*

[44] *Hearings on OPIC,* pp. 86–90.

countries and making the results available to foreign investors, or coordinating investment in these countries, or, finally, in guaranteeing loans from U.S. private financial institutions (banks, insurance companies, etc.) to borrowers undertaking new business abroad. In short, activities that were traditionally under the jurisdiction of Government authority now shift to the domain of private decisions. Institutionalization of private control over OPIC management made participation in it by the Secretary of State and other Government officials almost a symbolic presence. This was, not incidentally, the aspect that aroused the most opposition during legislative approval of OPIC.

Third, OPIC has the authority to insure investment abroad against commercial risks (up to 75 percent) and political risks (up to 100 percent). The latter encompasses: (1) the inability to convert into dollars—or to transfer from one country to another—earnings on investment or compensation for sale; (2) losses due to expropriation or confiscation of the investment; (3) damage to physical assets provoked by war, revolution, or insurrection. In other words, to lessen internal demands for direct American state intervention (through the application of the Hickenlooper Amendment or through other means), in case of a confrontation between a corporation and a foreign government, the payment for loss or damage inflicted on private property abroad is transferred to the taxpayer. This power used to be under the authority of the Government's Office of Private Resources. It is now transferred to OPIC, which is not accountable to Congress. With an estimated $100 million capitalization for the first five years, OPIC has the authorization to insure up to $7.5 billion—a total that can be doubled. Since its creation, OPIC underwrote insurance at the rate of $1.2 billion a year. More than half of the total guarantees ($6.5 billion) concerned investments in Latin America, as of September 1971.[45] The Chilean nationalizations (all American companies hit were insured) apparently led OPIC into a difficult financial situation; Congress, therefore, will probably be asked for additional appropriations.[46]

Finally, OPIC's insurance coverage may be extended to joint-venture firms even if they are incorporated in a country other than the United States, and even if not wholly owned by U.S. citizens. If it is true that in this last case insurance is theoretically issued only to the extent of the American share of the ownership, it is not difficult to understand that local partners in underdeveloped countries are likely to feel much more confident in OPIC than in their own governments—*with a corresponding shift in loyalties.* This is the implication from the underdeveloped countries' perspective. From OPIC's perspective—and this is what seems to

---

[45] Council of the Americas, *Report,* September 1971 (Statement by OPIC's President), p. 7.
[46] Chadwin, "Foreign Policy Report," p. 107.

underlie OPIC President Bradford Mills's recommendation that 100-per-cent American ownership is "unwise"–these local partners will be encour-aged to play an active political role in their countries to prevent any dam-age to joint-venture interests.[47] A second OPIC anti-risk measure is the involvement of developed-country partners (Japanese and European) in any new investment project. As Mills put it: "Multinationalization can give protection against economic nationalism."[48]

The American business community's views (and hopes) concerning OPIC, at least at the moment of its creation, may be summarized through the following Senate testimonies of two leading corporation representa-tives: the first hailed OPIC for the "flexibility, speed, and absence of inhi-bitions" that only a "nongovernment institution" can have;[49] the second cheered OPIC's creation as being "an institution totally dedicated to (over-seas) private industrial development."[50] These are, indeed, the two most important OPIC features, as a first *solution de rechange* for the multina-tional corporation's political losses resulting from the "low profile" stand. The practical consequences are: (1) the liberation of a substantial part of "foreign aid's" public funds from "government restraints"; (2) the institu-tionalization of private control over an agency that can play a more im-portant role for industrial development abroad than Eximbank played for American domestic industries. A second, and complementary, political-alternative solution is the joint-venture strategy.

The Joint Venture: A "Prismatic Profile"

The joint-venture strategy must be approached through its two com-plementary aspects: multilateralization of "aid" and multinationalization of investments. Both are basic recommendations of the Peterson Report and both became the new common language of Government officials and corporate executives.[51] In short, these two developments mean the spread-ing out among other governments of the costs of American corporations' protection (through U.S. manipulation of international financial institu-tions); and the sharing of the world market and of production among multinational corporations, with the help of local elites in underdevel-oped nations.

To understand the first point, it is necessary to describe briefly the international apparatus created, since the war, to foster capitalist world expansion. Unfortunately, empirical studies concerning the actual func-

[47]Council of the Americas, *Report,* September 1971 (Statement by OPIC's President), p. 7.
[48]Ibid.
[49]*Hearings on OPIC,* pp. 94–95.
[50]Ibid., p. 84.
[51]See the National Association of Manufacturers' Statement Before the House, in *Hearings on OPIC,* pp. 86–90.

tioning of these institutions are, to my knowledge, scarce—or nonexistent.[52] A very rough scenario—and I insist on the word—regarding the division of work among these institutions could be composed as follows:
International Bank for Reconstruction and Development (World Bank).
Created at the Bretton Woods Conference, the World Bank undertook as its main task to finance the basic infrastructure in the underdeveloped world, i.e. the infrastructure needed for the implantation of foreign-owned industries in these countries. Out of a total of $1.8 billion loaned to Latin America between 1965 and 1969, for example, approximately 65 percent was granted for transportation and electric power.[53] Under McNamara's presidency, the World Bank is shifting its concerns to education and to the enlargement of the underdeveloped countries' internal markets. The latter is urged through a constant criticism of income concentration and through incentives to agribusiness (large-scale production of cash crops).[54]

International Finance Corporation. Created in 1956, as an affiliate to the World Bank, IFC has as its main function to assure the takeoff of private companies abroad. Direct loans (without Government guarantee), equity investment, and the underwriting of debenture offers are the procedures adopted. Apparently, IFC was conceived to function as a double mediator: organizing investment joint ventures in developing countries and, later, opening its portfolio to multinational private banks. As of 1969, about one-third of IFC's cumulative commitments had been sold to U.S. and European banks. More than 50 percent of the sales from its portfolio has come from investments in Brazil, Mexico, the Philippines, and Colombia.[55]

International Development Association. The repayment of all this aid (Eximbank alone lent to Latin America more than $3.5 billion for the purchase of U.S. goods and services from 1946 to 1966)[56] creates a heavy burden on these countries' balance of payments. This represents a danger to, among other things, profit remittances. To help solve this problem, and keep the expansion machine working, IDA was created in 1960, also as a World Bank affiliate. Its main purpose is to make "soft loans"—usually 50 years, with a 10 years' grace period and only a 0.75-percent service

[52] As far as we know the only (critical) book on the World Bank is Teresa Hayter's *AID as Imperialism* (Middlesex: 1971). The information used in this paper concerning the international financial institutions relies heavily on Hector Melo's and Israel Yost's report "Funding the Empire: Part 2, The Multinational Strategy," in *NACLA Newsletter*, vol. 4, no. 3, May–June 1970.
[53] IBRD, *Annual Reports*, 1965–69.
[54] McNamara's Address at the Annual Meeting of the International Monetary Fund (*International Herald Tribune*, September 26, 1972), p. 2; IBRD, *Annual Report*, 1970.
[55] James C. Baken, *The International Finance Corporation* (New York: 1968), pp. 78, 191.
[56] House Foreign Affairs Committee, *U.S. Overseas Loans and Grants and Assistance from International Organizations* (Washington: U.S. Government Printing Office, 1966), p. 27.

charge.[57] The debt-servicing problem (Brazil is paying, according to AID data, over 25 percent of all its exchange earnings per year for such service)[58] is now also being approached through incentives to the tourism business.

International Monetary Fund. The IMF was also created at Bretton Woods. Its main function, with respect to Latin America, is to make short-term loans (generally in the form of "standby" loans) needed to meet emergency situations. The counterpart of the loan is a "letter of intent" forwarded by the recipient country accepting the fiscal and monetary policies dictated by the IMF. Eighteen Latin American countries made standby agreements between 1965 and 1969.[59]

Along with the regional organizations (such as the Inter-American Development Bank), these are the main multilateral institutions. Their control is in the hands of developed countries, for they are the major contributors. The lack of studies on how decisions are made in institutions that play a major role in the shaping of the world economic order leaves us in the domain of inferences. Since the U.S. Government holds the majority of votes (in World Bank's case, for example, the United States has 24.7 percent of the votes, all other developed countries 30 percent, and Latin America 8.5 percent), we may suppose that the United States has a strong voice in the decision-making. The projects approved by the U.S.-Brazilian Joint Commission in the early 1950s, for example, had to be accorded a prior *nihil obstat* from the State Department before being approved by the World Bank. But if we consider, at the same time, the interlocking between the World Bank's and the corporations' boards (out of five World Bank presidents, three came from Rockefeller firms and one from Ford),[60] we may infer, perhaps, that corporations also have a voice in these institutions' decisions.

Nevertheless, the international mystique imposes on short-term private interests some respect and some restraint on pressure brought to bear. In spite of the fact that the penetration of American capitalism has always been central to these institutions' overall strategy, the underdeveloped countries' problems have been examined by them in a broader perspective. Moreover, the voting power of the United States and other developed countries was used with moderation. Apparently, decisions were made by consensus; i.e., controversial projects were never submitted to the board.[61]

[57] IBRD, *The World Bank, IDA and IFC: Policies and Operations,* April 1968.
[58] *Hearings on Brazil,* p. 171.
[59] Melo and Yost, "Funding the Empire," p. 4.
[60] Ibid., p. 3.
[61] Chadwin, "Foreign Policy Report," pp. 104–6.

A more overt role in the fostering of multinational corporations' interests is now assigned to these institutions. The weight of the U.S. Government will also be more clearly felt.[62] This stance is part of Washington's new foreign-policy strategy, for two different but convergent reasons. First, there is the (obviously naive) idea that if U.S.-Latin American problems are treated in a multilateral context (and not bilaterally), the U.S. presence will be diffuse, direct risk of confrontation will diminish, and anti-American resentment will decline[63]—in short, an attempt to conceal the "low profile" in a "prismatic" one, a move that is perhaps a by-product of the identity crisis experienced by American society. Second, and more important, there is a recognition by the United States of the "very rapid growth" of other countries' "foreign aid" and overseas investments[64]—in other words, a perception that it is wiser to form, within the financial institutions where the United States has a strong voice, a sort of "international corporate directory" capable of promoting the division, by consensus, of the economic opportunities at hand in the underdeveloped world. A senior staff member of the U.S. President's Council on International Economic Policy (CIEP)[65] was quite explicit about this approach in a talk delivered to American investors with business in Latin America:

The first principle [leading to the reorganization of the foreign-assistance policy] is that increasingly we will rely on the international financial institutions to take a leadership role in assessing performance, in defining aid requirements, and in negotiating with countries about the economic-policy changes that may be necessary and desirable before aid can be used effectively.[66]

[62] *Peterson Report,* p. 22.

[63] The Statement of Robert Hormets (Senior Staff Member, National Security Council) in Council of the Americas, *Report,* September 1971, pp. 9–10.

[64] Ernest Stern's statement in Council of the Americas, *Report,* September 1971, p. 8; also Peter G. Peterson (Executive Director, Council of International Economic Policy), in the same report, pp. 14–15.

[65] A brief incursion into Washington bureaucracy is necessary here. The Council on International Economic Policy is the communication channel (a function carried out before by Dr. Kissinger's staff) between the U.S. President and the National Advisory Council on International Monetary and Financial Policies (NAC). NAC (operating under Executive orders 11.269 and 11.334) has as its purpose to coordinate the attitudes of U.S. representatives in all agencies or international institutions that make or participate in making foreign loans. NAC's Chairman is the Treasury Secretary; other members are the Secretaries of State and Commerce, the Chairman of the Board of the Federal Reserve System, and the President of Eximbank. Very appropriately, an ad hoc Undersecretaries' Committee on Expropriations was also created. Even the State Department made its contribution to Latin American affairs by creating an Interdepartmental Group for Latin America (currently its Chairman is Charles Meyer, ex-Vice-President of Sears Roebuck). In the overall reorganization of the "foreign aid" bureaucratic apparatus, AID is to be replaced by a "development corporation"; a "development institute" is to be created for research in the physical and social sciences (in addition to the Inter-American Social Development Institute, that was created at the same time as OPIC); and, finally, a special agency dealing with all security programs (economic and military) is to come under State Department guidance.

[66] Stern's statement.

Another principle, according to the same source, is manifested in the U.S. administration's move "to a greater reliance on contractors and private intermediaries to implement the aid program."[67] The reference is not to OPIC, which belongs to the domain of bilateral programs, but to private intermediaries of multilateral aid. Three main implications of this policy can be identified. First, the relationship between the underdeveloped countries and the international financial institutions will no longer be (at least overtly) mediated by the U.S. Government; as a consequence, financial arrangements will be settled outside the political context. Second, the international financial institutions' recommendations to these countries, concerning the "economic-policy changes" required for receiving the "aid," will depend on private assessments, since a greater role will be given to "private contractors." Third, the trend is also toward minimizing the role of underdeveloped countries' governments in their dealings with international financial institutions, since the move for greater reliance on "private intermediaries" will permit multinational firms to borrow directly (i.e. without Government mediation) from institutions such as the World Bank. In other words, the planning of economic development will shift from the Government to the private domain, and will be implemented on a worldwide scale according to corporative options. And here the privatization-multilateralization syndrome strikes its target: the multinational joint-venture investment.

A joint venture is, essentially, the sharing of ownership of a local business between two or more investors of different nationalities. Although ownership is the most usual form, control can also be assured by other devices: financial arrangements, management contracts, technological dependence, etc. Joint ventures may assume the following forms: (1) two or more corporations from one or more countries associate themselves to invest in a third country; and (2) foreign investors associate with local partners to invest in the country of the latter. The local partners may be private firms, state-owned firms, or both.

The most complete, most refined example of an extended joint venture, as well as of the new channeling structure for information and financial resources, is to be found in the Atlantic Community Development Group for Latin America (ADELA). Incorporated in the early 1960s in Luxembourg, ADELA associates 235 of the largest banks and industrial firms in the United States, Europe, Japan, and Latin America, representing a total of 23 countries, of which five are Latin American. With an available capital (stock and loan funds) of $187.3 million in 1969, one-third of which was in the hands of U.S. corporations, ADELA par-

[67] Ibid.

ticipates in more than 100 enterprises in Latin American countries.[68]

ADELA combines the multinational and conglomerate approaches; and as a multipurpose enterprise, it provides us with a possible vision of the future already upon us, i.e. a vision of what could be the next development of the "ultimate stage" of capitalism. Three facts support this view. First, its primary function is to generate investment opportunities in Latin America for large multinational corporations and to create, through the help of local partners, a favorable "climate" for them—a role previously played by the international financial institutions and/or the U.S. Government. Second, ADELA's penetration strategy is carried out simultaneously through direct investment, management and technical assistance, marketing analysis, insurance, underwriting, and contracts with the international financial institutions. Third, ADELA-backed projects extend to practically every sector, including agriculture, fishing, and food processing (20 percent of the capital invested), general manufacturing (16.9 percent), pulp and paper (12.4 percent), financial firms (11.2 percent), textiles (7.9 percent), wood products (7.5 percent), and chemicals (6.6 percent); still other sectors are capital goods and machines, service industries, iron and steel, mining, and mineral processing.[69]

As an "open" enterprise (theoretically any private corporation from any country can make an equity investment from $100 thousand to $500 thousand), ADELA succeeded in increasing its available capital at the rate of 100 percent a year in the period 1964–69. Its most important feature, however, is that, since it is backed by the financial strength and technological and managerial know-how of the world's most powerful corporations (Bank of America, Barclay's Bank, Ford, IBM, DuPont, Standard Oil, etc.), it has an effective power far beyond its book-value resources. Furthermore, ADELA plays the role of mediator between the international financial institutions and the underdeveloped countries, a role now ascribed to private corporations. As stated in its 1968 Annual Report:

In addition to the $10 million long-term loan granted by the Inter-American Development Bank to ADELA for the financing of small- and medium-sized projects that are not within IDB's direct reach, IDB has made parallel loans to larger projects in which we have invested. With the International Finance Corporation we have an increasing number of joint projects, including joint sponsorship of very large investments. With both institutions, because continuous contact and free exchange of information is maintained, duplication of effort is avoided in the areas of developing and evaluating investment opportunities.[70]

[68] ADELA Investment Company, S.A., *Annual Report,* 1970; also *Interinvest Guide—Brazil and International Capital* (Rio de Janeiro, 1971), p. 654.
[69] Ibid.
[70] ADELA, *Annual Report,* 1968.

Although a similar corporation was created for Asia (PICA) and one for Africa is under study, ADELA is probably nonetheless an exception. More precisely, it is the first inbred offspring of a new generation of multinational enterprises. However, the joint-venture approach, in its simpler form, is undoubtedly a solid trend. In 1957, 17 percent of U.S. direct investments in underdeveloped countries were joint ventures, and U.S. investors had minority stock in only 5 percent of the total U.S. investment overseas.[71] In 1966 they accounted, respectively, for 30 percent and 12 percent.[72] The trend has been strengthened in manufacturing investment in Latin America. Before 1946, 83 percent of all new U.S. investment in manufacturing was wholly owned by American subsidiaries; from 1958 to 1967 (latest data available, to my knowledge), this figure dropped to 44 percent.[73] Furthermore, the view that joint ventures "ideally provide a highly desirable arrangement" was adopted unanimously by the representatives of the world's most powerful corporations, at the Amsterdam Panel on Foreign Investment, in February 1969.[74] This unanimous view, in the final analysis, is nothing more than the official adoption of the new strategy best satisfying the requirements of monopoly capital in a politically policentric world. As the Chairman of the Pfizer Corporation put it:

We would like nothing better than to sit in New York and manage an export operation. . . . We have not gone the exporting route because we *can't get the business that way.* . . . To obtain, hold, and improve market positions abroad requires an integrated approach in terms of direct investment in local plants, exports, licensing, and so on, operating throughout the world, in both the developed and the developing world [emphasis added].[75]

The political side of this integrated approach is taking shape through the "prismatic profile" in both its forms: the multilateralization of "foreign aid" and the joint-venture investment.

As a preliminary conclusion, we might observe that the internal cleavages within American society, and the low-keyed role the American state was led to adopt, deprived multinational corporations of their traditional political support; nevertheless, alternative political resources are being created to guarantee their continued expansion. How these changing

[71] W. Friedmann and G. Kalmanoff, eds., *Joint International Business Ventures* (New York: 1961), p. 9.

[72] U.S. Department of Commerce, *United States Direct Investments Abroad, 1966* (Washington: U.S. Government Printing Office, 1970).

[73] *Business Latin America,* January 15, 1970, p. 20; cited in NACLA, *Yanqui Dollars,* 1971.

[74] Panel Document No. 6, February 19, 1969, in *Hearings on OPIC,* p. 78.

[75] John J. Powers, "The Impact of U.S. Controls on Foreign Investment," speech delivered at American Management Association meeting on April 10, 1968, in New York; cited in NACLA, *Yanqui Dollars.*

patterns are actually affecting the political behavior of multinational corporations in Latin America, and how conflicts between corporations and the state are developing, will be taken up next.

The Trojan Horse Tactics: The "Corporate Citizen"

The multinational corporations' capacity to make commanding *macro-decisions* transforms them automatically into de facto political actors of consequence. Their importance is felt most fully in the developing countries, where they display the ability—owing to their current position in the productive process and/or their technological, financial, and organizational advantages—to set parameters for economic decisions. For this very reason only the state rivals their power at this level of decision-making. But the foreign corporations—to the extent their identity is evidenced and so long as the nation-state is not unanimously considered an "old-fashioned idea"—cannot have their overpresence in these countries legitimized politically. Thus, in spite of their formidable economic power, they are politically vulnerable in one context: involvement in an overt conflict with the state. A brief historical detour will be instructive here.

Since the state in Latin American countries was traditionally the political expression of the pact celebrated between local oligarchic elites and international economic circles, following the particular patterns of integration of the former in the world market, the presence of foreign investors as political actors was "legitimized" by the elites' consensus. Furthermore, the political pact was guaranteed by the U.S. Government, reinforcing its natural tendency—for geographical considerations, among others—to intervene in the internal affairs of Latin American countries. This guarantee attained its most perfect (i.e. juridical) form under the Platt Amendment in Cuba; but usually the arrangements were not so perfect, as when General Smedler Butler of the U.S. Marines led his troops ashore in the Dominican Republic in 1916 to make that country safe, in his own words, "for the boys of the National City Bank."[76]

Overt conflicts used to occur where the local elites' domination was challenged by other social groups, producing a situation in which the local state was momentarily incapable of enforcing a political pact. In such cases, the American corporations' and/or local elites' traditional method of dealing with the situation was to appeal to the power of the U.S. Government. Following (overt or covert) intervention, the pact was reestablished and the presence of foreign corporations was once again "legitimized." An exception was Mexico, during the Cárdenas regime, among other reasons because the initiative in the conflict was taken by the elite

---

[76] Cited in Tad Szulc, "ITT Case Evokes Memories of Latin Interventions by U.S.," *International Herald Tribune*, March 28, 1972.

itself. During the cold-war period, the fusion of American economic and security interests provided this interventionist pattern with a new political rationale, and the United States was particularly successful in proving the veracity of Mme Roland's last words, as the Guatemalan case shows. If Cuba escaped the rule, it was because the United States was confronted with a counter-elite, enjoying wide revolutionary support, as well as a delicate international situation. The Bay of Pigs fiasco led directly to the replacement of the naked-power approach by a more juridical form of protecting American investment abroad: the "guarantee agreements" signed between governments in the early 1960s.

Beginning in the mid-1960s, both the new role played by multinational corporations and the internal social changes experienced by Latin American societies introduced new variables. Conflictive situations between corporations and the state became more frequent—whatever the immediate causes and issues involved in the conflict—as a consequence both of the obsolescence of the traditional pact and also of the inherent contradiction between the two major actors' different rationalities: corporations are exclusively profit-oriented and states are increasingly social-oriented. The latter trend results from the accumulated social and economic contradictions in the developing countries, and the need for local states to cope with them in order to preserve the basic patterns of domination in their own societies. Overt conflicts have more frequently occurred precisely where corporations maintain exploitative operations and concentrate their investments in those economic sectors (oil, mining, large-scale agriculture, and services) that still reflect the old pact features, i.e. the traditional international division of work. It is worth noting that these conflicts typically occur with U.S. corporations. This happens not so much because of the shadow of the United States—as the corporations like to believe—but rather because of the corporations' overpresence and their old-fashioned forms of imperialistic exploitation in Latin America. After all, U.S. firms are not nationalized in Europe; nor are Unilever, Phillips, or Bayer, for example, in Latin America.

Today, the scenario in which these conflicts must be settled has drastically changed. For one thing, the initiative in the conflict belongs to local elites, who have either tight control over the state (Peru) or substantial social support (Chile) to back their action; moreover, intercapitalist rivalries increase local state bargaining power. For another thing, the political split between U.S. private economic interests and U.S. state security, in conjunction with all the other factors discussed, has undermined the corporations' support "at home" and the interventionist rationale itself. This last aspect is aggravated when the new dissenting elites are products of Washington's War College effort (Peru); or have as their only sin an ideological outlook ("Marxism") that, thanks to the recent

American discovery of the Soviet and Chinese market potential, is no longer considered so sinful.

The important point, however, whatever the political circumstances involved, is that when the political pact is denounced by local elites, on the one hand, and the U.S. Government's action is inhibited, on the other, foreign investors are deprived of their two sources of political legitimization. This is the situation in the early 1970s. Since the political capability the corporations are acquiring, to compensate for the "low profile" stance is not yet sufficiently built up to cope with the situation in the field, American investors are experiencing the situation of being "on their own." And this takes place at a particularly difficult moment, considering the drive of Japanese and European incursions into the developing countries. Between 1964 and 1968, for example, portfolio and direct investment of American firms in these areas increased at an annual rate of 15.4 percent, that of Japan at 32 percent, and that of West Germany at 50 percent.[77] How are U.S. corporations dealing *in the field* to regain some kind of "legitimization" for their overpresence? The question is prospectively important, since as de facto major political actors their behavior may greatly influence the future of Latin American societies.

Although data are relatively scarce, and sources are not always dependable, there is some evidence that U.S. corporations with business in Latin America oscillate between two different attitudes—and probably adopt both wherever possible. The first, conventional attitude is typically oriented toward the maintenance of the status quo. The second, more sophisticated attitude consists of claiming citizen status for the corporation through Trojan Horse tactics. What follows is an attempt to discuss both.

The International Telephone and Telegraph Company (ITT) is the eighth largest corporation in the United States. In 1971, its ventures in 70 other countries, employing 398,000 workers, produced 59 percent of its profits. Revenues and sales from its 331 subsidiaries (which in turn are believed to control 700 others) exceeded $7 billion in 1971. Only 23 percent of its earnings come from the telecommunication field. ITT feeds people (Continental Baking), houses people (Levitt & Sons), lodges people (Sheraton Hotels), rents-a-car to people (Avis), insures people (Hartford Fire Insurance), kills people (Loran, and TPS-25 ground-surveillance radar, used in Vietnam), and tries to overthrow Latin American presidents.[78] Out of all these activities the last seems to have been, until

---

[77]CEPAL, *Estudio Económico 1970,* vol. 2: *Estudios Especiales* (E/CN. 12/868/Add. 2), p. 96. See also the excellent study by Aníbal Pinto and Jan Kñakal, *El sistema centroperiferia 20 años después,* 3a. Versión Ampliada (Santiago: CEPAL, 1971).

[78]*NACLA's Newsletter,* vol. 6, no. 4, April 1972, pp. 2–4; *Fortune,* September 1972.

now, the only frustrating one. Considering ITT's success in the other fields, an examination of its behavior in this particular one may contribute to a better knowledge of the multinational corporations' political problems and promises.

The main facts are the following, according to what was revealed in the published documents. From September to November 1970, ITT acted to prevent the inauguration of a foreign country's President chosen in a democratic election–by conspiring with local political and military elites, by mobilizing the Latin American and European media against the elected President, by using its political power to set in motion the whole U.S. state apparatus (White House, State Department, Department of Commerce, CIA, etc.), and by offering to "contribute" to the operation's expenses with "sums up to seven figures."[79]

Not being successful in these attempts, in part because of U.S. Government hesitation but largely because of the internal integrity of political forces in Chile, ITT submitted to the White House a year later, on October 1, 1971, an 18-point plan designed to assure that President Allende "does not get through the crucial next six months."[80] This plan called "for extensive economic warfare against Chile to be directed by a special White House task force, assisted by the CIA; the subversion of Chilean armed forces; consultation with foreign governments on ways to put pressure on the Allende regime; and diplomatic sabotage."[81] The idea was to promote (1) denial of international credit, (2) a ban on imports of copper and other Chilean products, and (3) the cutting off of vital exports to Chile, all in order to convince the local armed forces to "step in and restore order,"[82] i.e. an order compatible with ITT's interests in Chile. To precipitate the political crisis, the employment of CIA services in the field and a "deliberate interruption of fuel supplies for the Chilean Navy and Air Force" were also suggested–certainly to ease the Army's "step-in."[83] These are the known facts, to which we may add that the proposed "economic squeeze" was later partially executed, under White House orders.[84]

ITT's interests in Chile are represented chiefly by a 70-percent share in the Chilean Telephone Company (CHITELCO), which in ITT's estimate is worth $153 million (the Chilean Government's evaluation, for negotiat-

---

[79]*Documentos secretos de la ITT,* p. 8 (memo to W. R. Merriam from J. D. Neal, September 14, 1970).

[80]The document was obtained by the *New York Times,* which published large extracts of it. Cf. "ITT Document Urged U.S. to Topple Chile's Marxist Regime–'Action Plan' Sent to White House in October," *International Herald Tribune,* July 3, 1972.

[81]Quoted from *New York Times,* article cited.

[82]Ibid.   [83]Ibid.

[84]Ibid.

ing purposes, is $24 million). Even accepting ITT's figure as closer to the mark, what do we have? A multinational corporation feels entitled to conspire to throw a country of 10 million inhabitants into economic chaos and disrupt all of its institutions and political life in order to avoid —"protectively" at first, reactively later on—the nationalization by a foreign state of 1.5 percent of its total assets (at market value), i.e. the equivalent of 2 percent of its annual sales and revenues. It is important to add that *even were CHITELCO totally expropriated, ITT would probably lose no assets at all:* its holdings in Chile were insured by OPIC.

To what extent may this account be considered the norm for multinational corporations' behavior? From a number of references in the published memoranda we know that ITT was unsuccessful in inviting corporate partners to join in a coup d'état venture.[85] If we interpret this fact as reflecting genuine policy on the part of the other corporations, and not simply the result of their better evaluation of the operation's chances, what explains ITT's behavior? The available data are not sufficient to permit a direct answer. Nevertheless, ITT's behavior may be related to the very fact of the existence of multinational corporations and of their particular "political culture."

The fact that ITT's properties in Chile were insured against political risks, considered in the light of the insights the published documents afford into the thinking of ITT's executives, suggests that probably two issues were at stake: a long-term economic interest and a political "principle." First, if one hopes to discover some "rationality" in ITT's behavior, we may explain that behavior not as a defense of insured property, but as a defense of a market position probably important in ITT's long-range penetration strategy. Second, considering the "mentality" revealed by the memoranda, we may conclude that a multinational corporation's political capability was also at stake. It is amazing to note, for example, the lack of conviction of ITT's argument in presenting the Chilean situation to Washington as a "political threat" to the hemisphere. What is interesting here is not so much determining which of these interests—the economic or the political—was felt to be more at stake, as it is reflecting that they are two sides of the same coin: for ITT, Chile is neither a country with a history and a political will, nor a society with a given culture and its own political institutions, but a *market.* And this is a political outlook that is being increasingly developed by the very existence of multinational corporations. In this sense, what appears to be ITT's deviant case may in fact be pioneering behavior—an indicator of a burgeoning new political

---

[85] References are made to the refusal of Ford, General Motors, and other American companies. *Documentos secretos de la ITT,* pp. 21, 32 (Telex, September 29, 1970; Memo, October 9, 1970).

sub- (or supra-) culture, with its own references and its own "code of honor."

It is not difficult to understand the ideology underlying both the tendency to reduce political entities to markets and the tendency to consider (as does a well-known Sicilian organization that is *also* the generator of a subculture) such a "market" as a *cosa nostra.* Since the nation-state is considered a "very old-fashioned idea," there is no reason why the political references historically born with it should not also be considered "very old-fashioned"; and since the multinational corporation is touted as the new concept designed to meet the requirements of the coming brave new age, it is up to the multinational corporation to beget new references. These can only derive from a projection of the prevailing concerns in the exclusively profit-oriented and bureaucratic universe of the corporation. The "principle" that was at stake in Chile was precisely the supremacy of the multinational corporation over a "market." As corporation ideologist Peter F. Drucker says, "Latin America is not underdeveloped, it is just *undermanaged.*"[86] ITT's is certainly one approach to overmanaging it.

But there is a more creative, more astute approach, suitably introduced by the following words of a corporation representative testifying before the U.S. Senate:

Quite honestly, the way to get rid of this small area of trouble (anti-Americanism in Latin America) is not to hold back U.S. investments, but to foment so much that those people will start having a chicken in every pot and two cars in every garage.... [For that] the American corporation, being a guest in the country, has to be a proper industrial citizen, and purer than Caesar's wife, and is, believe you me.[87]

To making sure Latin Americans believe it, too, the Council of the Americas, as a representative of the 200 American corporations with business in Latin America, devotes its best efforts and its official budget of almost $1 million a year.[88] The Council operates in three main roles: (1) as a pressure group in Latin America; (2) as an *entremetteur* for Latin American elites in the United States, and (3) as a think-tank session organizer. In short, it is a kind of private State Department whose main objective is to coordinate Latin American governments and individuals (business, political, intellectual, technocratic, student, and labor elites) as corporate partners in a political joint venture, through which multinational corporations can seek the status of "corporate citizens" in the countries where they operate.

The first of these functions is carried out through the classical means

---

[86] Cited by Enno Habbing (Staff Director, Council of the Americas), in "Gerencialismo: An Ideology for Development?" unpublished article.

[87] *Hearings on OPIC,* pp. 48, 49–50.

[88] The exact amount is $841,450.59. Council of the Americas, *Annual Report, 1971.*

of influencing public opinion and local leaders. Some examples: (1) distribution of 530,000 copies of informative literature throughout Latin America; (2) promotion of TV and radio programs in Argentina (a $200 thousand budget in 1969 to reach an audience of 4 million) to explain the positive role played by private enterprise; (3) the same explanations promulgated through advertisements in 35 periodicals with an impact on an estimated 15 million people; (4) the insertion of *political* articles in Latin American press and radio, articles written at the rate of five per week by the Council's Script Service (during the first five months of 1971: 1,306 column-inches in Colombian newspapers alone).[89] These articles may be signed by local journalists as their own—a practice that would make Caesar's wife, if not the journalists, blush.

The contacts with local leaders (which also include training and orientation programs for students and workers) are normally undertaken by the four permanent Council "representatives in the field," located in Argentina, Brazil, Peru, and Central America. Nevertheless, special envoys and missions, sometimes headed by the Council's President, a Cuban-born Westinghouse executive, are sent for particular purposes. A Council economist, Herbert K. May (an ex-State Department official), was dispatched to Argentina, for example, in order to "assist the entire private sector of the country in trying to make the proposed law to regulate foreign investment an effective instrument for Argentina's development."[90] A mission was sent to Venezuela in early 1971 with the same purpose. The Andean Code is a permanent source of anguish for the Council, which sent special missions to Bolivia, Colombia, Ecuador, and Peru. According to the Council's report, the Peruvian officials "gave interesting indications of flexibility in their thinking [about] the mining, petroleum and industrial sectors."[91] All these visits were made, according to the Council, following invitations received from local governments and business associations.

In exchange for this local help—and this is its second function—the Council explained to key U.S. Congressmen the interests of Colombian coffee planters concerning the international Coffee Agreement; and provided hospitality and contacts in New York for Latin American diplomats and leaders (including a delegation of 40 officers from Peru's CAEM).[92] Further, the Council "and its member companies have been combating the campaign criticizing Brazil, waged by radical elements in the U.S.,

[89]Council for Latin America (later renamed Council of the Americas), *Report,* vol. 6, no. 2, January 1970, p. 5; Council of the Americas, *Report,* vol. 7, no. 1, June 1971.
[90]Ibid.
[91]Council of the Americas, *Annual Report,* 1971, p. 3.
[92]Ibid., p. 10.

Brazil, and other parts of the world."[93] All this is "in line with the Council thesis that it is probably Latin America's best constituency in the United States."[94] A practical demonstration of this thesis is the Council's establishment in its office in Washington of an "extensive press list" that was used, in June 1971, to "express Council support for a larger Latin American share of the U.S. imported-sugar market."[95] In other words, contacts between Latin American officials and Washington political circles and the press are mediated—i.e. privatized—by the Council.

The actions of the Council of the Americas—whatever their actual effectiveness—are in keeping with the new corporations' strategy of multidimensional penetration in Latin America. This strategy, in David Rockefeller's words, "should embrace political development, economic development, and social development."[96] The guidelines for this strategy were widely discussed during one of the Council's think-tank sessions (convoking these sessions is the Council's third major function). According to these views, the fate of corporations in Latin America is linked to the outcome of a conflict between two local tendencies. The first of these tendencies—the "modernist outlook"—is defined as an "option for maximum international cooperation," the only option, supposedly, leading to an accelerated rate of development; the second—the "traditionalist outlook"—is viewed as the option for "the autarchic route to development," which would cost Latin America "decades in terms of economic progress." The triumph of the first (whose exponents are seen as "promising and increasingly influential allies") was considered "crucial" for the fate of private enterprise in Latin America, although the influx "of more foreign influences" could admittedly cause "serious emotional and political anguish" among "the traditionalists."[97] This was the analysis of the thinkers convoked by the Council in 1969, when the military nationalizations in Peru left corporation executives wondering what to think.

Without intending to play with words—and those above are a bit misleading—we might argue that the new situations created in Latin America in the late 1960s provoked a "traditionalist" and a "modernist" response from the U.S. business community. The first is typified by ITT's massive retaliation; the second, by the flexible response counseled by the Rockefeller family. The latter approach calls for the comprehension and acceptance of the "new rising nationalism" in Latin America, with "patience

[93]Council of the Americas, *Report,* vol. 7, no. 1, June 1971.
[94]Council of the Americas, *Annual Report,* 1971, p. 9.
[95]Ibid.
[96]Ibid., p. 15.
[97]Council for Latin America, *The Investment Climate in Latin America,* Special Report, vol. 5, no. 3, September 1969.

and insight."[98] Rodman Rockefeller, in a closed session at the Council on Foreign Relations (whose confidential digest was revealed), went so far as to state that corporations investing multinationally "must renounce their claim to U.S. legal protection"; and admitted that since "self-realization is a requirement for advancement, so the national feeling in Peru is a positive phenomenon."[99] In other words—and here we have the "insight" Rockefeller spoke of—if the Latin American "traditionalist outlook" is wisely co-opted it may be transformed into a "modernist" one.

Underlying the new approach are the following assumptions: (1) Washington's "low profile" may be compensated for, and conveniently so, by a systematic political mobilization of local allies in the countries where multinational corporations operate; (2) this local support must not be limited to governments, but extended to a wide range of social groups, including opposing or dissenting groups (intellectuals, technocrats, students, and labor leaders are commonly cited);[100] (3) to represent politically this "social joint venture," joint associations must be created; (4) through the latter, the multinational corporations may assume full status as local political actors, as "corporate citizens." As an example of this approach we may cite the creation, following the visit of Governor Rockefeller in 1969, of the Brazil-U.S. Businessmen's Council, which became "the chief spokesman of the entire private sector, domestic and foreign, in Brazil," according to the Council of the Americas.[101] Now, let us turn to the possible implications of this approach.

There is some evidence that this strategy is more easily enacted in countries where the *internalization* of foreign investments in industry has created a local social fabric (i.e. an exclusive but complete stratification pyramid) constituting a potential political basis of support for multinational corporations. The state in these countries not only represents the social fabric but tends to establish alliances with multinational corporations at the production level—as demonstrated by the joint venture of foreign investors, national entrepreneurs, and the state in the Brazilian petrochemicals case. By contrast, in countries where as an inheritance of enclave situations control over the primary and tertiary sectors is still predominantly foreign—hampering the drive for development and not

[98] Quoted from David Rockefeller, Speech at the Council of the Americas, *Annual Report, 1971,* cited on p. 14.

[99] Council on Foreign Relations, "Discussion Meeting Report: The United States and Latin America, Fifth Meeting: May 12, 1971, Digest of Discussion." As reproduced in *NACLA's Newsletter,* vol. 5, no. 7, November 1971, p. 29.

[100] References are constantly made in the *Hearings on OPIC,* and in the Council of the Americas reports. The Council, for example, created a "student-business dialogue program." *Report,* June 1971.

[101] Council of the Americas, *Report,* June 1971.

creating a wider social basis of support—conflictive situations tend to occur more readily between the state and multinational corporations.

The new strategy, sponsored by the more intellectually articulate representatives of the U.S. business community, seems to be an acknowledgment of the distinct situations created by the changing patterns of dependence; the increase in the degree of heterogeneity in these "markets"—the condition for the breeding of a wide range of local allies—requires a diversified internalization of investments in the strategic modern sectors of local economies. These are the sectors that may provide the needed allies to open the doors "from the inside." This is certainly an improvement on the tactics the Greeks employed some centuries ago in Troy, tactics the Europeans were the first to apply after the war in their ex-colonies—probably because they are more acquainted with history than their American counterparts.

Conclusions

The U.S. economic expansion abroad, which in the years just after the war followed the classic imperialist pattern, was led to take different forms later, for mutually conditioned political and economic reasons. Beginning in the late 1950s, two complementary factors seem to have accelerated the overseas expansion of U.S. firms and, simultaneously, to have given birth to new forms of dominance. First, the rate of growth of the American economy in the 1950s, as compared to the economic growth of its capitalist competitors, was low;[102] second, the U.S. corporations were forced to maintain their position in international trade through penetration of regional common markets or through bypassing underdeveloped countries' protectionist tariffs. The campaign was of course very rewarding, for U.S. corporations were able to profit from the lower wages and the appropriation of local financial resources. As a 1970 U.S. Tariff Commission report showed, even if a Mexican worker takes 58 percent more man-hours to produce the same amount of apparel, the unit labor cost in Mexican plants is still less than one-third of U.S. costs—owing to the fact that the U.S. worker earns nearly five times as much as his fellow American.[103] But at the same time, UN statistics show that 83 percent of the resources financing American manufacturing firms abroad derive from the countries in which they operate.[104] This is seen as an ad-

---

[102] Between 1953 and 1960 the growth of the American economy (GNP) was inferior to those of France, West Germany, Italy, Great Britain, and Japan. Between 1953 and 1968 the rate of growth of these countries' economies was: 3.7 percent (U.S.), 5.1 percent (France), 6.1 percent (West Germany), 5.4 percent (Italy), 2.8 percent (Great Britain), and 9.9 percent (Japan). See CEPAL's excellent *Estudio Económico 1970*, vol. 2, p. 88; also Chap. 4.

[103] "How to Tell Where the U.S. is Competitive," *Fortune*, July 1972, vol. 86, no. 1, p. 56.

[104] CEPAL, *Estudio Económico 1970*, vol. 2, p. 45.

vantage by the U.S. multinational firms, but no longer necessarily by the U.S. economy. The AFL-CIO, for example, suddenly became concerned with the low wages of its fellow workers abroad; the corporations, in their turn—and we must consider that between 1965 and 1970 unit labor cost in the United States rose by 22 percent, whereas in much-feared Japan it rose by only 3 percent[105]—began to wonder about the meaning of the "democracy" in whose name their investments were committed abroad. These differences between multinationally and domestically oriented groups made it more difficult for the corporations to present their particular interests as if they were the general interests of American society—especially when America's external enemies, namely the Russians and the Chinese, became very civilized. All of these factors combined to make the full use of the U.S. state apparatus by corporations more difficult. Their solution was to build up an alternative political capability to guarantee their overseas expansion. And because of the allocation of resources involved, the move was accompanied by a split between economic and security interests.

This split was made possible, both for the corporations and for the U.S. Government, by the new patterns of dependence created during their previous synchronic expansions. In Latin America, for example, difficulties seem only to be created by countries in which U.S. investment still follows "traditionalist" forms of economic dominance. Because these countries are in the minority (or have a relatively low strategic importance), President Nixon could announce in 1970 that the United States "cannot—and will not—conceive all the plans, design all the programs, [and make] all the decisions." Within the countries where the U.S. economic penetration was more complete, there are now native elites who can conceive, design, and decide, no longer as puppet oligarchies but rather as "modernist" elites acting on behalf of their dynamic joint-venture interests—interests whose parameters are established by multinational corporations. The latter thus enjoy their "own" political capability. As for the deviant cases, things may be conceived, designed, and decided *hic et nunc,* pragmatically, which seems to correspond to what Secretary of Defense Laird called "realistic deterrence."[106]

The corporations' overseas economic expansion and U.S. political interventionism abroad were so mutually conditioned during the cold war that the two appeared as a paradigm of a linear relationship between the economic and political orders. The continued expansion of the multinational corporations and the U.S. Government's world disengagement may

[105] "How to Tell," *Fortune,* p. 57.
[106] *International Herald Tribune,* March 10, 1971, p. 1; see also *The Rockefeller Report,* pp. 50–52, 54.

seem paradoxical in view of the situation formerly obtaining; but considering the new forms of economic dominance, they are not necessarily contradictory.

If this reasoning is correct, the U.S. policy of "less intervention" in Latin America does not necessarily mean a reduction in the political dominance of U.S. multinational corporations in the region. Nevertheless, the policy might produce a change in the political pacts between corporations and local elites: first, because to implement their new strategy U.S. corporations will be led to diversify their investments and to develop their bases of support and operation, through, for example, the enlargement of local internal markets; second, because intercapitalist competition will provide the "modernist" elites with new bargaining power. To the extent that uneven development is a by-product of monopoly capitalism, the new pact, whatever its forms, will not integrate these countries economically and socially in the foreseeable future—but it may broaden the social fabric engendered by this particular mode of production.[107] In short, the new pact may give birth to an international "corporatism" in which a somewhat enlarged structure of income and consumption will tend to parallel the structure of status—though not necessarily the structure of authority. These changes suppose, of course, an approach slightly more sophisticated than ITT's, or than that suggested by the Council of the Americas' literature on the benefits of foreign enterprise.[108]

[107]For a broader discussion of this point, see, for example, Stephen Hymer, "The Multinational Corporation and the Law of Uneven Development," in J. N. Bhagwati, ed., *Economics and World Order* (New York: World Law Fund, 1970); Sunkel, "Capitalismo transnacional"; Celso Furtado, "La concentración del poder económico en los Estados Unidos y sus proyecciones en América Latina" in *Estudios Internacionales* (Santiago), vol. 1, no. 3–4, 1968.

[108]Between 1957 and 1959, 67 percent of total investments of U.S. subsidiaries in Latin America was financed with resources obtained in Latin America; between 1963 and 1965, the use of local resources jumped to 91 percent; i.e., only 9 percent of all U.S. investments in Latin America was financed with nonlocal resources. On the other hand, between 1960 and 1968, Latin America became an "exporter of capital" to the United States, since the difference between total U.S. direct investments and the total profit remittance was negative ($6.7 billion) for Latin America. (Cf. Pinto and Kñakal, pp. 42–45.) This evidence contrasts sharply with the multinational corporation's propaganda on the benefits of foreign capital. Some of the slogans recommended by the Council of the Americas as "appropriate for mention in the articles, speeches, house organs, and everyday conversation," of the 200 U.S. corporations with business in Latin America are: (1) "More than any other institution, the international corporation is concerned with man himself"; (2) "The corporation promotes the pursuit of excellence, which is so much sought and extolled today"; (3) "The corporation allows man a great deal more personal liberty than most other institutions"; (4) "The international corporation is the principal instrument for taking the world out of the traditional culture of poverty into the culture of plenty." Council of the Americas, Memo to CoA Members; from (Vice-President) Henry R. Geyelin, July 26, 1971.

Commentary on L. Martins

THEODORE H. MORAN

Professor Martins's provocative paper touches some of the most crucial issues concerning the role of multinational corporations in "the political relations between the United States and Latin America" over the next decade. There is a profound contradiction, as Professor Martins has pointed out, between the "benign neglect" of Latin America in formal U.S. diplomacy and the continuing and pervasive economic penetration of U.S. corporations into the domestic politics of Latin American countries. As Abraham Lowenthal has put it, "When all is said and done, the Colossus of the North casts its shadow southward no matter what direction we choose to face."[1] "Benign neglect" in principle may turn into "malign neglect" in practice.

I also share with Martins his concern that multinational corporations will increasingly experiment at devising their own private diplomacy, through the construction of transnational alliances—especially alliances involving international finance. I have tried to show in a recent study how natural-resource companies can render operational their desire for security in the face of increasing vulnerability.[2] Such companies are developing various strategies to raise the cost of nationalization by spreading risk among institutions in Western Europe, Japan, and North America (including Canada) that will automatically respond with retaliation against any nationalistic threat. Clearly, as Martins suggests, more research is needed in this area. Finally, the alliances between domestic economic groups and foreign investors within the host countries constitute a crucial focus for our attention. We have at this point very little more than impressionistic evidence to analyze the behavior of "the colonial bour-

---

Theodore H. Moran is with The Brookings Institution, Washington, D.C.

[1] Abraham Lowenthal, letter to *Foreign Policy,* summer 1972, p. 105.

[2] "Transnational Strategies of Protection and Defense by Multinational Corporations: Spreading the Risk and Raising the Cost for Nationalization in Natural Resources," Vanderbilt University: Graduate Center for Latin American Studies, October 1972.

geoisie," "the national bourgeoisie," or the "autonomous" state agencies.

By way of commenting on Martins's paper, I would like to offer some additional data to document the strength of U.S. corporate expansion in manufacturing in Latin America. Then I would like to sketch a model of the dynamics of such expansion and of the reaction to it within Latin America. Finally, I would like to offer an alternative vision of what *dependencia* may look like in future years.

I would like to argue, for purposes of discussion, that Martins has not been Hegelian enough in his presentation, that there is in fact a dialectical process taking place, in the sense that the forces generating the expansion of foreign investment are now creating the means for an equally powerful reaction to it.

First, then, let us look at the dynamics of the expansion of U.S. industry into Latin America. Martins is correct in underlining the shift of U.S. investment away from solely extractive industries and into the manufacturing sector. The strength of U.S. industrial investment in Latin America is not widely enough appreciated. Data from the Harvard Business School study of 187 multinational corporations show that the book value of U.S. investments in manufacturing in Latin America grew from $231 million in 1929 to $4,347 million in 1969, and that the number of foreign manufacturing subsidiaries grew from 56 in 1929 to 950 in 1967 (see Table 1). Moreover, the growth of book value by $3 billion and of the number of subsidiaries by almost 400 during the 1960s represented a penetration of Latin America as strong as the much more publicized "invasion" of Western Europe. If we calculate ratios, by year, of number of U.S. subsidiaries in Latin America vs. number of U.S. foreign subsidiaries worldwide, U.S. investments in manufacturing in Latin America remained, at the close of the 1960s, within 4 percent of the proportion they represented at the outset of the 1960s. If we make the same calculations for ratios of book value, the variation is only 1 percent during the same period. "El desafío norteamericano" in Latin America, then, represented a thrust just as powerful as "le défi américain" in Western Europe. But in relation to the size of the host-country economies, U.S. economic penetration was much more of a challenge in Latin America.

To suggest how the relations between multinational corporations and Latin American countries may evolve in the future, we must begin with some notion of the dynamics of international expansion and the reaction to it. I have found that the most satisfactory model of foreign economic expansion explains international corporate growth as a result of the struggle to enlarge and defend the capacity to exact oligopoly rents. This model has been developed from recent studies of the product cycle and the growth of U.S. manufacturing firms' operations under conditions

TABLE 1
Statistics on U.S. Investment in Foreign Manufacturing

Book value of foreign direct investment of U.S. enterprises in
  manufacturing subsidiaries (millions of dollars):

	1929	1940	1950	1957	1969
Latin America	$231	$210	$781	$1,280	$4,347
Total	1,813	1,926	3,831	8,009	29,450
Ratio	13%	11%	20%	16%	15%

Number of foreign manufacturing subsidiaries of
  187 U.S.-controlled multinational enterprises:

	1919	1929	1939	1950	1959	1967
Latin America	20	56	114	259	572	950
Total	180	467	715	988	1,891	3,646
Ratio	11%	12%	16%	26%	30%	26%

Number of new product lines introduced by foreign manufacturing
  subsidiaries of 187 U.S.-controlled multinational enterprises:

	1901–19	1920–29	1930–39	1940–49	1950–59	1960–67
Latin America	29	43	91	195	435	675
Total	200	365	438	473	1,345	2,921
Ratio	15%	11%	21%	41%	32%	23%

Sources: James W. Vaupel and Joan P. Curhan, *The Making of Multinational Enterprise* (Boston:
1971), Chap. 3; Raymond Vernon, *Sovereignty at Bay: The Multinational Spread of U.S. Enterprises* (New York: 1971), tables 3–3 and 3–4; U.S. Department of Commerce, *U.S. Business Investments in Foreign Countries* and *Survey of Current Business,* various issues.

of unstable imperfect competition. The assumptions of the classical theory of the firm and the neoclassical theory of foreign trade and investment included free availability of information, stable production functions, and no significant returns to scale. Marginal return on investment
was the determinant of foreign investment as well as of domestic investment. Beginning with Hymer's theory of foreign investment and extending through Vernon and Well's studies of the product cycle, the assumptions have been that technology and information are tightly controlled,
that production processes are characterized by large economies of scale,
and that products undergo predictable changes in assembly and marketing over time. With these assumptions, foreign investment is explained as

the strategy of corporations to expand or defend barriers to entry that are repeatedly challenged and eroded.[3]

Most U.S. manufacturing corporations, according to this model, began in each product line with some quasi-monopolistic advantage (differential access to technology, capital, or managerial expertise) that enabled them to supply goods for their home market from behind barriers to the entry of competition. With the passage of time, with the reduction of uncertainty, and with the expansion of the market, however, the initial monopolistic advantage becomes eroded—technology is diffused, production becomes standardized, and marketing strategies are duplicated. Imitation brings new competition and a weakening oligopolic hold over the ability to exact rents for each successive product line.

In the late nineteenth century and the first third of the twentieth century, exports became the first method by which U.S. manufacturing corporations could extend their power to exact economic rents. But the same process of imitation, duplication, and competition that had occured in the home country gradually was repeated in the countries to which the products were exported. Local entrepreneurs or local government agencies found that, sometimes with protection and sometimes without, they could produce locally the goods that had formerly been imported. In Western Europe the response was almost immediate. In Latin America the First World War and the Depression were the great catalysts that first stimulated the process of import-substituting industrialization. In other regions of the periphery the process of replacing foreign exports with domestic production could not take place until nationalistic governments replaced colonial administrations after the Second World War.

The "discovery" of local capabilities and the development of domestic expertise have represented a kind of crisis for U.S. corporations. They began to face all over the world the choice of either setting up local production units to try to extend their hold over the ability to exact rents as long as possible, or losing that ability to local competition. The Harvard 187-Multinational Corporation data show that from 1929 to 1959

---

[3] I have elaborated this model in examining the basis for U.S. direct private investment in manufacturing in my paper "Foreign Expansion as an 'Institutional Necessity' for U.S. Corporate Capitalism: The Search for a 'Radical' Model," *World Politics,* April 1973. For the development of this model, one should consult: Stephen Hymer, "The International Operations of National Firms: A Study of Direct Foreign Investment," unpublished doctoral dissertation, Massachusetts Institute of Technology, 1960; Raymond Vernon, "International Investment and International Trade in the Product Cycle," *Quarterly Journal of Economics,* vol. 80, May 1966, and *Sovereignty at Bay* (New York: 1971); Louis T. Wells, Jr., "Test of a Product Cycle Model of International Trade," *Quarterly Journal of Economics,* vol. 83, February 1969, and *The Product Life Cycle and International Trade* (Cambridge, Mass.: 1972); Richard Caves, "International Corporations: The Industrial Economics of Foreign Investment," *Económica,* February 1971.

the rate of introduction of new product lines manufactured in Latin America increased tenfold (from 43 per decade in the 1920s to 435 per decade in the 1950s) and that the ratio of new product lines introduced in Latin America to new product lines introduced worldwide increased from 11 percent in the 1920s to over 40 percent after the Second World War (see Table 1). A recent study by the U.S. Department of Commerce of companies from nine industries that account for over 90 percent of U.S. direct foreign investment in manufacturing shows that in each case exports preceded direct foreign investment, and that direct foreign investment took place as a defensive reaction stimulated by the threat of local competition.[4]

This dynamic—the desire to chase oligopoly profits in the face of constant challenges to oligopoly power—has provided the stimulus for direct foreign investment in manufacturing. I have argued elsewhere that the corporate calculation combining the desire for gain with the fear of loss is a more powerful predictor of capitalist expansion than either the neoclassical "marginal return on investment" or the neo-Marxist "surplus of capital."[5] This corporate calculation allows for the fact that large corporations are risk-avoiders, not risk-takers. It explains why U.S. investors initially set up only assembly or packaging plants in Latin America—despite the demonstrably lower labor costs and the generous access to local finance—until they were forced by nationalistic governments to go further along the road toward real domestic production.

Host governments in Latin America have profited from this process of oligopolistic diffusion, imitation, and competition in two ways. First, as

[4]Robert B. Stobaugh, Jr., Project Director, "U.S. Multinational Enterprise and the U.S. Economy: A Research Study of the Major Industries That Account for 90 Percent of U.S. Foreign Direct Investment in Manufacturing" (Washington: U.S. Department of Commerce, Bureau of International Commerce, January 1972). The nine industries are: food products (Standard Industrial Classification 20), paper and allied products (SIC 26), chemicals and allied products (SIC 28), petroleum (SIC 29), rubber products (SIC 30), primary and fabricated metals (SIC 33 and 34), nonelectrical machinery (SIC 35), electrical machinery (SIC 36), and transportation equipment (SIC 37).

Stobaugh also found that in the petrochemical industry the lag between the introduction of a product through imports and the beginning of domestic competition decreased in each decade of this century. This was true for both developed and underdeveloped countries, although the lagtime was longer in underdeveloped countries. (Robert B. Stobaugh, Jr., "The Product Life Cycle, U.S. Exports, and International Investment," unpublished doctoral thesis, Harvard Business School, 1968.) G. C. Hufbauer has argued along similar lines in a study of the production of synthetic materials. Leading countries have an initial competitive advantage which they lose after a time-lag to national producers who have filled the "technological gap." (G. C. Hufbauer, *Synthetic Materials and the Theory of International Trade* [London: 1965].) Werner Baer and José Almeida should produce important data on choice and availability of technology in their project of studying "The Transfer of Technology and Labor Absorption in Brazil."

[5]"Foreign Expansion"; for the assumptions about sector-specific investment alternatives, see the Appendix discussing the model.

Martins has rightly pointed out, the spread of technology, of managerial expertise, and of marketing skills has meant that host governments have increased their bargaining power vis-à-vis foreign investors and have enabled the governments to play rival foreign investors off against each other. Second, the host governments have been able to choose domestic producers for favored treatment over foreigners at a decreasing economic cost to themselves.[6] The result has been that the perception of the value of the contribution of any one foreign investor has declined, and the perception of the benefit from squeezing him or taking him over has risen. First in textiles and final consumer goods, then in intermediate industrial goods and some basic heavy industry, and finally in more technologically sophisticated durable goods and in large-scale extractive industries, domestic entrepreneurs and domestic state agencies in Latin America have discovered that the foreigner can be replaced with large gain and small loss. Broadly speaking, I am arguing that the perception of the cost of mobilizing groups through the appeal of economic nationalism has been in a cumulative process of decline and that the perception of the gain from mobilizing groups through the appeal of economic nationalism has been in a cumulative process of ascent.

I agree with Martins (and with Stephen Hymer) that, as the "multinationalization" of corporate production continues, the pace of introducing new products into Latin America (either by exports or by direct production) will probably rise—because information costs and setting-up expenses will decline with scale. And those foreigners that undertake direct investment will doubtless seek domestic allies through joint ventures. But I am hypothesizing that the process of diffusion and duplication and innovation in Latin America will continue, and that this will provide an ongoing basis for economic nationalism.

Therefore, for purposes of argument, let me predict what the structure of *dependencia* will look like in the future. The most technologically advanced and probably the most rapidly growing sectors of Latin American economies will continue to be held under foreign control—or else held under domestic control only at great economic cost. But increasingly large areas of domestic production (and eventually production for export) will be controlled by domestic companies and/or national state agencies.

It is lamentably easy to envision scenarios of treachery and upheaval when ITT-like investors and their domestic allies try to undermine or

---

[6]This, incidentally, need not be construed as an argument in favor of the "national bourgeoisie" because the accumulation of domestic expertise in Latin America has taken place within government agencies and state bureaucracies, as well as within the private sector—paving the way for many kinds of state participation in the economy.

stave off nationalistic challenges to their position. But it is also possible to envision an increasingly rational process of investment and negotiated divestment in which host countries *continually* balance the current contributions of foreign investors against the changing domestic costs of replacing those investors. That is why I have always argued that the Andean Code on investment and systematic divestment was a great step in the right direction—not because it would be an immediate success or because no exceptions would have to be granted, but because the dialectic of foreign expansion and domestic reaction requires some regular, flexible means of adjusting the treatment given foreign investors as the welcome for those investors inevitably declines.

Index